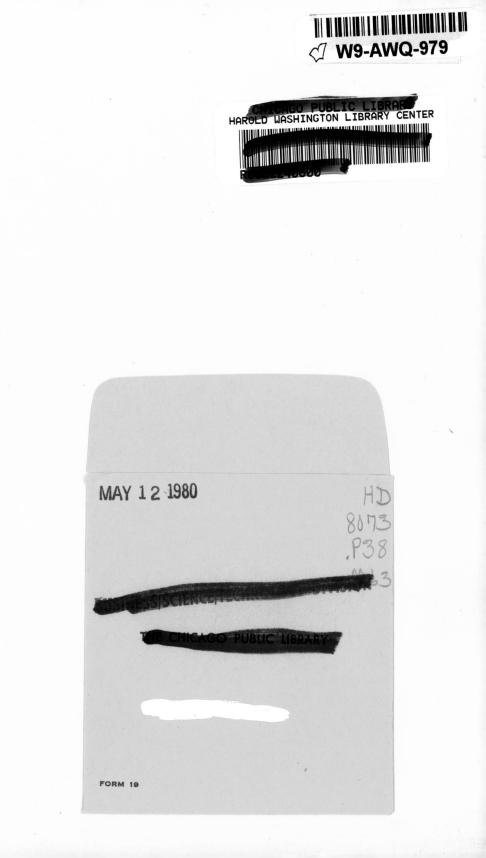

Frances Perkins

"That Woman in FDR's Cabinet!"

FRANCES PERKINS
Secretary of Labor, 1933 - 1945
(Official portrait of the first woman member of the President's Cabinet)

Frances Perkins

"That Woman in FDR's Cabinet!"

by

Lillian Holmen Mohr

N

NORTH RIVER PRESS

ISBN 0-88427-019-X

Library of Congress Cataloging in Publication Data

Mohr, Lillian Holmen, 1926-
    Frances Perkins, that woman in FDR's cabinet!

    Bibliography: p.
    Includes index.
    1.   Perkins, Frances, 1882-1965.   2. Women in
politics — United States — Biography. 3. Labor
policy — United States — History. I.   Title.
HD8073.P38M63   973.917'092'4 [B]   78-23597
ISBN 0-88427-019-X

Picture Credits

Frontispiece photograph by permission of the Department of Labor, Washington, D.C.
The photographs on pages 104, 156, 180, and 233 are by permission of the Franklin D. Roosevelt Library, Hyde Park, N.Y.
The photographs on pages 108, 124, 137, 261, 273, and 275 are United Press International photos.
The photograph on page 210 is from Wide World Photos.
The photographs on pages 225 and 226 are by permission of the International Labour Office, Geneva, Switzerland.
The cartoon on page 202 is reprinted by permission of the New Orleans *Times-Picayune*.
The cartoons on pages 244 and 267 are reprinted by permission of the *Richmond Times-Dispatch*.

Manufactured in the United States of America

Contents

Dedicated to God and Country
— as was her life

Preface

In the graphic words of Ayn Rand, this is the story of a woman who lived with "a sense of enormous expectation, the sense that one's life is important, that great achievements are within one's capacity, and that great things lie ahead." As in Ayn Rand's *The Fountainhead*, the purpose of the story is not philosophical enlightenment. This biography simply protrays Frances Perkins as a person who lived her own life in the best way she knew how. Often her own words are used to tell that story — and to repeat the stories she told. The thoughts attributed to her in this book come from her own statements as to what she thought at a particular time. Some attention is given to the historical detail that impinged on her life and colored her particular environments.

Consistency and accuracy posed special problems because of the large variety of resources consulted and the many discrepancies in them. The author apologizes for any inadvertent errors in fact and for inevitable omissions; every means possible was used to achieve a measure of preciseness. Frances Perkins's life was so full, not everything could be recorded, nor was everything kept in record form. Insignificant incidents are included because they do constitute a part of life that everyone lives on a day-to-day basis, although the daily repetitiousness is perforce excluded.

An author is indebted to many people, directly and indirectly. To Dr. Sidney Sufrin of Syracuse University's Maxwell School of Citizenship and Public Affairs, who not only struggled through the author's doctoral dissertation, but who criticized an early paper on Frances Perkins because of its minimum personal analysis, apologies for writing a book that leaves it to the reader to pass judgment. Special thanks to him and to Dr. Jesse Burkhead for their faith, and to Chancellor Mel Eggers and Dr. Jerry Miner for their lack of it (which also serves as a spur to action). To the late Dean Bernice Wright of the College of Human Development at Syracuse University, special praise for her unqualified support, and to her and Syracuse University for a year's sabbatical for research.

Appreciation to Professor Woodrow Sayre for the first introduction to Frances Perkins; to William L. Clayton, Jr., of the New York *News* for preliminary editing, and to Dr. George Yost, Clara Beyer, and Jonathan Grossman for review of later drafts; to Charles Cavagnaro of the United States Office of Consumer Affairs for an introduction to Lawrence Oxley; to Dr. Raymond A. Mohl for the Alice Barrows manuscript materials, and to David Clancy for transporting library books.

Personal interviews were graciously granted by Clara Beyer, Margaret Bricket, Alice Cook, James Dodson, James Farley, Jonathan Grossman, Averell Harriman, Cora R. Holland, C.W. Jenks, Herman Kahn, John Leslie, Isador Lubin, Maurice F. Neufeld, Lawrence A. Oxley, Evelynn Richards, J. Woodrow Sayre, and Boris Shiskin, and briefly by Gwen Bymers, Mary Dublin Keyserling, and Arch Troelstrup. Also helpful were telephone interviews with Adolph A. Berle, Anna Roosevelt

Halsted, Margaret Janeway, Alice Paul, Howard Taubman, and Charles Edward Wyzanski.

Especially useful correspondence came from Lynn McCree, Curator, Jane Addams' Hull-House, University of Illinois at Chicago Circle; Mrs. Robert Shenton of the Arthur and Elizabeth Schlesinger Library on the History of Women in America, Radcliffe College; Harry Bridges, President, International Longshoreman's and Warehousemen's Union; John W. Leslie, Director, Office of Information, United States Department of Labor; Bernice B. Nichols, Curator, Swarthmore College Peace Collection; Herman Kahn, Director, Franklin D. Roosevelt Library; Hazelle Van Gorder, Administrative Services Officer, University of California–Los Angeles; Celia O. Goodale, Alumnae Secretary, Mount Holyoke College Alumnae Association; Frances Perkins's daughter, Susanna Coggeshall, Newcastle, Maine; and from Cecil Clark Wolman (Mrs. Leo Wolman), Lewis Lorwin, Senator Everett McKinley Dirkson, and Robert Moses.

Libraries and librarians can never praised adequately. My gratitude goes to librarians in the Franklin D. Roosevelt Library, Hyde Park, New York; the Williston Memorial Library, Mount Holyoke College, South Hadley, Massachusetts; the Arthur and Elizabeth Schlesinger Library on the History of Women in America, Radcliffe College, Cambridge, Massachusetts; the Connecticut College Library, New London, Connecticut; Collection of Regional History and University Archives, Olin Research Library, Cornell University, Ithaca, New York; Oral History Research, Special Collections, Butler Library, Columbia University, New York, New York; Harry S Truman Library, Independence, Missouri; Library of the United States Department of Labor, Washington, D.C.; Library of the International Labour Office, Geneva Switzerland; Manuscript Division, the Research Libraries of the New York Public Library, New York, New York; Manuscripts Division, Library of Congress, Washington, D.C.; National Archives, Washington, D.C.; Syracuse Public Library; Library of the New York *News*; and Strozier Library, Florida State University. Although not visited by the author, the librarians of the University of Wisconsin, Goucher College, and the Herbert H. Lehman Foundation, and V. A. Stenberg, Director of Research, Encyclopedia Britannica, were most helpful.

And finally, appreciation for the support of my parents, Erling J. Holmen and the late Christine Eriksen Holmen; my husband, William A. Mohr, and my children, Kristine, Elizabeth, Bill Martin-Erling, and Amelia. Others who figure significantly because of their fine counsel are Louis Russek of Health-Tex Children's Wear; Dr. Joseph Gold of the Syracuse Cancer Research Institute; Raymond Hughes; Dr. James Keller; and David Schoenfeld, who provided the introduction to the publisher, William Cowan, and his discerning editor, Lois Lasater.

Although the author's interest in the life of Frances Perkins dates back to March, 1933, research began in 1960. Other volumes have since been published dealing with this remarkable woman, but more still needs to be said about Frances Perkins. This biography is intended as a step toward a definitive work on the life of one of America's great stateswomen.

I

There Had Never Been One Before

St. John's Episcopal Church in Washington, D.C., looking as though it was plucked out of a pristine Nèw England village, sits primly on a corner across Lafayette Square from the White House. At 10 A.M. on Saturday, March 4, 1933, the tiny "Church of the Presidents" opened its doors for a precedent-setting private preinaugural service. At Franklin D. Roosevelt's invitation, members of the cabinet and their families joined the Roosevelts in prayers for the welfare of the nation and the guidance of its new administration.

Upon her arrival in Washington the night before, Frances Perkins had learned of her expected attendance at the church. The short notice mattered little. An early riser by habit, she was accustomed to attending 7 A.M. matins in her own church, also Episcopalian.

Following the twenty-minute service, chauffeured limousines lined up in front of St. John's to transport the official party the short distance across the square. The drawn-out procedure taxed Frances Perkins's patience, and onlookers were shocked to see the dignified matron duck under the ropes and stride across the square. How should a woman cabinet member act in public? Who could know? There had never been one before.

Perhaps as Frances Perkins walked briskly toward the White House she recalled that the year before on that very date she had wired Franklin D. Roosevelt, "This day next year should be interesting." He had wired back, "I approve your faith." During the frenetic months of campaigning, she never doubted that Roosevelt would occupy the White House, but she entertained no illusions of joining him in a position of national eminence. Her work centered on New York State; her family life and social activities tied her to New York City. Because of friendship with the Roosevelts, she had expected an invitation to view the inaugural ceremonies as one of countless spectators—but hardly as a member of his official family.

Little more than a week had passed since Roosevelt persuaded Frances Perkins to serve as his secretary of labor. Her well-founded reluctance to accept had been genuine. She later admitted, however, "At bottom I knew I had to accept the appointment simply because no other woman had ever been asked to do it before." She merely hoped that she had brains enough to assess the situation.

A robust, energetic woman in her early fifties, Frances Perkins had thirty years of experience to qualify her for the work she would be doing as the head of the Department of Labor. It was still a major feat to get ready for her new role in a matter of days. The better part of those days went to settling her affairs as New York State industrial commissioner and to planning and conferring on her national responsibilities. Unable or unwilling to give up time for personal shopping, she left it to her sixteen-year-old daughter, Susanna Wilson, to buy her inaugural ensemble.

Pretty, party-oriented Susanna Wilson paid little attention to her mother's career and concerns, but she knew her mother's taste. Together with a friend, she selected a long-sleeved black satin tunic dress with a soft chiffon collar. The fine fabric and workmanship gave the simple garment elegance. Her mother's favorite strand of pearls would set it off.

"The effect was precisely as ordered," Frances Perkins later recalled, "Rock of Gibraltar, rather, with a dash of style, and a discreet touch of feminine appeal."

Frances Perkins personally ordered a hat from her regular milliner, Rayna's, on 38th Street in New York City. It cost five dollars, the most she believed in spending on a hat. Its color matched her brown hair rather than her black outfit, a daring combination in 1933. Equally unusual, a definite tricorn brim distinguished the hat from the standard, fashionable cloche.

While watching the inaugural parade from the tightly-packed grandstand on Pennsylvania Avenue, she caught sight of her friend and mentor, former-Governor Al Smith, heading the Tammany delegation of New York. She smiled as Al Smith saluted the president and Roosevelt wig-wagged back in one of their last friendly gestures to each other.

At six o'clock that evening, Frances Perkins, with her daughter and

Molly Dewson as her "family," was summoned to the Oval Study for the formal swearing in of the cabinet. Franklin D. Roosevelt called for the unprecedented evening ceremonies so that the cabinet members' families could view the occasion. The regal Benjamin Nathan Cardozo, justice of the Supreme Court, administered the oath of office. Frances Perkins was the last to say "I do" and to shake the president's hand.

Early the next morning, Sunday, the secretary of labor arrived at the White House and puzzled over the appropriate entrance to use. She joined a line of people, only to learn that they were tradesmen waiting to fill orders for White House provisions.

At that first meeting, members of the cabinet shared a sense of nervous excitement as they took their places as "the board of directors of the nation." More than half of the men were over sixty years of age. The youngest member was a fellow New Yorker, forty-five-year-old James Farley, the postmaster general. Ironically, Frances Perkins sat across from Daniel C. Roper, the sixty-six-year-old secretary of commerce from South Carolina, who was already on record with his reservations about "the premature recognition" of women.

An additional chair placed at the end of the huge cabinet table provided for another of the president's innovations. Vice-president John Nance Garner, invited by Roosevelt to attend the cabinet meetings, seated himself next to Frances Perkins and periodically regarded her with an obviously condescending expression.

Frances Perkins usually impressed people with her air of self-assurance as she strode into a room or joined a group. Her bearing seemed to proclaim that she was right with God and little else mattered. But at that first cabinet meeting she felt decidedly uneasy about the impression she would make on her male colleagues. She resolved to remain silent and merely observe.

The president had other ideas, and when she failed to enter into discussions voluntarily, he called on her to speak. She did so, briefly, touching on her scheduled conference with labor leaders to discuss fighting unemployment through a public works program. On her department rested the most crucial economic problem of the depression—unemployment.

When the meeting ended, Vice-president Garner slapped her on the back and exclaimed, "You're all right; you've got something on your mind. You said it and then you stopped." She sensed approval and acceptance from the others. She enjoyed an auspicious beginning of her term as a member of the president's cabinet.

II

The Tricorn of the Revolutionists

"Success? What is success but a sequel to experience." With this, the new secretary of labor, the first woman in American history to be appointed to a presidential cabinet, put her singular achievement into perspective.

Frances Perkins opened the drawers of her desk that first Monday morning, March 6, 1933, to find cockroaches scooting to the corners—bigger cockroaches than most, she thought, and not totally unexpected in the grimy old Labor Department building sandwiched between a rooming house and a garage on F Street.

The secretary of labor had seen roaches before in Chicago, Philadelphia, and New York City. They were something more than poor housekeeping to her; they represented the humbler of the two worlds she had invaded many years before.

Unflinchingly, the woman in the highest position of any in the country squashed the insects that symbolized poverty, squalor, and filth. She called for cloths to clean off her chair and the large flat-top desk. A war against poverty was like this. She had learned to be practical about such matters as had countless "missionaries" before her—Frances Perkins frequently compared social workers to missionaries, who invariably combined material assistance with moral instruction. Because of her zeal to help others, she was often labeled a "revolutionist," and her tricorn hats served as a trademark and symbolic conversation piece that obviously identified her with the Revolutionary period in American history. She liked to tell reporters that her parents, Frederick W. and Susan Bean Perkins, gave her a three-cornered hat on her tenth birthday. This served as a ploy to provide a story based on her family history rather than on her own private life.

Her most famous ancestor, she related, was James Otis from whom her paternal grandmother, Cynthia Otis Perkins, was directly descended. Otis, a descendant of the family that settled Scituate, Massachusetts, in 1620, was the king's advocate general in Boston when the British government, needing revenue as a result of the Seven Years' War in Europe, sought to enforce the Navigation Act. The royal customs collectors called on Otis to provide writs of assistance allowing them to enter and search for goods on which duty had not been paid. Otis refused, resigned, and became the attorney for the very merchants who were threatened.

A "trumpeter of sedition," Otis was given to powerful oratory and a vitriolic pen. His articles for the *Boston Gazette* inflamed the British rulers as well as the colonial patriots.

James Otis's arguments on the constitutional rights of individuals were quoted in the 1931 Wickersham Report on immigration, which Frances Perkins would later cite as her bible in the handling of the Immigration Bureau in the Department of Labor, little realizing that she would one day face impeachment proceedings because of her stand on this issue.

Another famous ancestor was Mrs. Mercy Warren, James Otis's sister. In 1775 John Adams asked Mrs. Warren, the "penwoman of the Revolution," to write a poem commemorating the Boston Tea Party. Entitled "The Squabble of the Sea Nymphs; or The Sacrifice of the Tuscararoes," it was highly allegorical. Her history of the Revolution, published in 1805, antagonized John Adams because she implied that his stand for a strong central government showed leanings toward monarchy.

Frances Perkins enjoyed telling stories of other, somewhat eccentric ancestors such as Abigail Taylor, her paternal grandaunt. The "Tugboat Annie" of her day, she sailed with her husband across the seven seas until her death of yellow fever in Havana. Her body was shipped home in a keg of rum.

Frequently Frances Perkins used references to her forebears to illustrate a point. One story, told repeatedly to illustrate that statistics must be translated into human terms, dealt with her great-grandfather, who at age ninety-nine marched down the hill to the town's bootmaker to order a pair of boots. He insisted that the boots, which went up to the knees and were pulled on with a jack, be made with the finest top-grain uppers and cross-grain leather soles. The old gentleman fussed until the exasperated bootmaker exclaimed, "You're an old man. You don't expect to live to wear out these boots!"

With a scornful look, the peppery nonagenarian shot back, "Statistics show that very few men die after age ninety-nine!" Such was the spirit that Frances Perkins inherited and frequently exhibited in her own approach to her work.

*****

On April 10, 1880, a child named Fannie Coralie Perkins was born to Fred W. and Susie E. Perkins in Boston, according to a certified copy of the birth certificate from the city registrar of Boston.

Years later Fannie Coralie would become Frances and her birth date listed in *Who's Who,* encyclopedias, F.B.I. records—and her own correspondence—as April 10, 1882. Actually, in terms of vitality and vivacity, she easily could have subtracted more than two years from her age.

The fact that she was a New Englander mattered the most. She identified throughout her life with Maine and Massachusetts and let no one forget it. Reporters would be sharply reprimanded when they tried to pry into other aspects of her life. "Is that important?" she'd ask. "We New Englanders like to keep ourselves to ourselves." Only occasionally was she prodded into reminiscing about her childhood, her self-indulgent mother, and more often, her father.

Frederick W. Perkins outwardly fit the stereotype of a stiff-collared, sternly precise, Victorian patriarch; he was also a self-taught scholar, humanist, and humanitarian. Born in Newcastle, Maine, on August 24, 1844, to Edmund and Cynthia (Otis) Perkins, he descended from colonists and Revolutionists and of many of the original pioneers of Massachusetts, of which Maine was once a part. Along with his two brothers, Frederick received a "common school education," which included a thorough grounding in Greek. One of his brothers succeeded in becoming a lawyer with a practice in Boston. At age twenty-one, Frederick decided to join his brother, a major venture because Boston was 165 miles of hoof-beaten dirt road away from his Newcastle home. He took a job at Jordan Marsh and Company, a large-scale retail establishment. However, this held little promise for him, so he joined the ranks of Yankee entrepreneurs by operating a stationery store and circulating library. He did well as a "periodical dealer" and finally ventured into marriage on September 20, 1877. His wife, Susan Ella

Bean of Bethel, Maine, gave birth to their first child two and a half years later.

When Fannie Coralie was two, her father moved his small family to nearby Worcester, where in October, 1882, he opened a store at 546 Main Street. His first employee, a boy from Cambridge, Vermont, George S. Butler, eighteen years later became a partner in the by then prosperous firm of Perkins & Butler. The Perkinses moved about as their financial situation changed; from 1905 on, her parents resided at 50 Queen Street, the permanent address their oldest daughter would give during her peregrinations.

Over the years Mr. Perkins transmitted his affection for his birthplace to his daughter. One of his most important club affiliations was the Natives of Maine Association, organized the year he arrived in Worcester, and the summer visits to his old homestead near Damaris-cotta-Newcastle, were known to be his chief source of pleasure. The family belonged to the Plymouth Congregational Church, and Mr. Perkins was a resolute Republican.

In later years, Frances Perkins described her mother, Susan Ella (Wight) Bean, as a late sleeper who allowed a grandmother to run the household. Frances had a sister, born on December 15, 1884, Ethel Cynthia—but with almost five years' difference in age, they were not particularly close.

Fannie Coralie and her younger sister grew up in a rapidly-changing industrialized city, but the dates and events of the city's proud history impressed them more than the social revolution they were witnessing.

Like so many old American communities, it seemed that the town transmitted the seeds of bigotry from generation to generation. In colonial days it was not unusual to "warn out" strangers. Recipients of the notice from the town constable were either not of the Congregational faith, or the town's selectmen feared that they might become public charges.

During Fannie Coralie's young years, Swedes and French Canadian immigrants were followed by large numbers of Italians, Poles, Lithuanians, and Greeks, attracted to the employment opportunities of the city's industries. By the time Mr. Perkins chose this growing city as a place to settle his family, the population was well over 25,000. By 1900 the population numbered 120,000. The quadrupling of the population during just two decades produced conflict, and the social cleavage between factory workers in this antiunion stronghold and professional townspeople was pronounced.

When Fannie Coralie was thirteen years old, adverse economic conditions brought about serious unemployment. The townspeople organized a Citizens' Relief Committee that cared for 821 families. Also indicative of the community's social concerns, the Insane Asylum on Summer Street had pioneered in work with mental diseases since 1830. Worcester's almshouse or workhouse provided an alternative to abject destitution, as it enabled the indigent who otherwise would have starved, to survive.

Frances Perkins's life spanned the years from the period of the stagecoach to the jet age. The railroads built between 1830 and 1840 rendered regular stagecoach lines obsolete, but a number of stage-coaches transported passengers from the Worcester railroad station to neighboring isolated villages during her childhood. Her father had occupied his shop on Main Street barely a year when electric lights replaced the old gas lamps.

A number of spontaneous statements made in her adult years suggest that, as a child, Fannie Coralie's equanimity and her sense of security were disturbed by the noise and commotion of technological advances. At times she showed a simplistic Rousseau-like nostalgia for "the good old days" of which she'd barely had a glimpse, and she resented the industrial abuses, human suffering, and devastation of the countryside that resulted from the new technology.

Yet Fannie Perkins was given to change. She herself would eventually change her birth date, her name, her career—and even her religious affiliation. She virtually grew up in the Plymouth Congregational Church on Pearl and Chestnut Street, and taught Sunday school classes there during her senior year of high school and again after she graduated from college.

In a way, the temperament of her home town paralleled her own temperament. Like the town, she showed a somewhat conservative, principled, straight-laced exterior, but was given to exuberant, hell-raising joy at opportune times—Independence Day, the Fourth of July, was such an occasion. The noisemaking would start the night before the Fourth with firecrackers and toy pistols. Early the next morning "the studlefunk procession," a traditional "antique, or horrible parade" dating back to 1850, delighted the children of the town. A military display followed, then the merchants' procession, athletic tournaments, and a ball game.

The Fourth of July had special meaning to the townspeople. Its citizens boasted that the Declaration of Independence had its first public reading in Worcester. On July 14, 1776, a messenger rushing to Boston with the declaration was intercepted by the townspeople. Isaiah Thomas, editor of the *Spy,* one of the colony's earliest newspapers, proceeded to read the declaration to a few people hurriedly assembled in front of the west porch of the Old South Church. The Fourth of July celebration of this historic event eventually got out of hand, with accidents from the use of gunpowder so serious that by 1911 the town had to legislate on behalf of a "safe and sane" celebration of the holiday.

Worcester natives' pride in their heritage and their culture, provided by several established colleges in the community, impinged on the consciousness of a sensitive child. Little Fannie Coralie, described by friends and neighbors as a thoughtful child, apparently both resented and envied the upper socioeconomic class hubris. In her classic book, *The Roosevelt I Knew,* Frances Perkins wrote somewhat enviously of the families who "had the sense of pride and continuity which accumulates around people whose great-grandparents are buried in the town in which they live." The Perkinses were, of course, newcomers to the city, and in spite of their heritage, newcomers to a New England community achieve full acceptance only after they outlive the old-timers. And while the immigrants to the city regarded the Perkinses as middle class because of their "comfortable circumstances," the family was not in the same class as those with inherited wealth and prestige.

A reporter, interviewing Frances Perkins for a "woman's success story" on her appointment to Governor Al Smith's New York State Industrial Commission, chanced to ask, "And were you born in New York?"

"Gracious no!"

"Why?" asked the reporter.

"Why wasn't I born in New York?" she replied with tongue in cheek.

"I mean," the reporter said, "that I wondered why you spoke so decidedly against New York as a birthplace."

"Oh," she laughed, "one never works in one's home town. There is something about it—you know, one can't! That's all there is to it. No one in the town thinks you can, and so you go somewhere else."

Eventually identified as a New Yorker, Frances Perkins's appointment to the president's cabinet was objected to because Roosevelt also named two other New Yorkers to serve in his cabinet. Although her career took her to Chicago and Philadelphia with a long stint in New

York City and Washington, D.C., her strongest emotional ties were to Newcastle, Maine. Like her father, she enjoyed visiting their family's ancestral home outside of the quaint twin villages of Damariscotta-Newcastle.

One did not have to play the young lady here in the country. Fannie liked fun, the fun of running in and out and about the barn playing the games of hide-and-seek that barns seem to be made for. Of course, accidents happened. On one occasion Fannie tumbled out of the loft and fell on her back. She agonized with pain for what seemed to her an unendurably long time, and then, as is the way with children, mended. Almost a half century later, when she took the medical examination required for all federal employees—as a result of her new status as a member of the cabinet—the doctors determined that she had sustained a broken back.

Her family homestead in the "Pine Tree State" provided Fannie with unhampered recreation as a child. As an adult, this is where she "re-created" herself on brief holidays; she confessed, "It's the only place where I can hide."

*****

Not all of the socialization process imposed on Fannie Coralie Perkins as a child was assimilated as readily as her pride in her American heritage. Growing up in a period when children were regarded as miniature adults, she was expected to act like a lady when her natural predilections were to be a tomboy who climbed trees.

Fannie tried to please her parents but seemed doomed to failure. She loved to talk, to babble on about everything and anything. Throughout her life she reminded herself of her father's stern admonition, "Don't waste people's time with vaporings. If you have anything to say, say it definitely and stop."

Yet for all of her tendency to babble, she was painfully shy. Thanks to her father, at an early age she learned to enjoy the companionship of books, yet when she went to the public library, she found herself tongue-tied in front of the librarian. Only her overwhelming concern for the welfare of others enabled her to later overcome, outwardly at any rate, her innate self-consciousness.

Years later, the old friends and acquaintances who remembered her as an "offish" child, serious and set in her ideas, recalled, "She was always an original girl, quite creative and very resourceful. She particularly shone in her diversion and her play rather than in the classroom." Some students develop skill in conforming to an educational system based on scoring well on examinations. Fannie internalized the information that seemed pertinent or challenging to her life. At the Oxford Street Grammar School, a class for sacred study particularly impressed her.

One day we were told to read over the four gospels and pick out some text that attracted us, that seemed interesting or personal to us. I remember I discovered such a text in the Gospel of St. Matthew in the fifth chapter, the forty-fifth verse. The text goes like this:

God maketh the sun to shine upon the good and the evil, And He poureth forth the light upon the just and the unjust.

It made a great appeal to me immediately. It was just wonderful. . . . Even if you are unjust, you will have the rain fall on you and the sun shine on you. I thought, how humane, how desirable, what a good thing that is. That really brings out the goodness of the nature of God.

Although Frances Perkins felt that her upbringing was "pretty sketchy," her grandmother contributed greatly, mostly by precept, during her impressionable middle years. She recalled that her grandmother "would say it to you; she would say it emphatically and she would repeat it over and over again at different times in the course of a week or a month, and it made an impression on me."

The grandmother had authority over her several grandchildren. She would tell them, "To deal fairly, to do justly, to think nobly, to respect your fellow men and to listen patiently, this is the duty of those who have authority over others." When there were quarrels among the children, the grandmother listened patiently before passing judgment; "we all felt that she was doing justly, primarily because she had listened."

Over her lifetime Frances Perkins would repeat, no doubt as often as her grandmother, other aphorisms, such as, "You must be prepared for surprises in your life." With emphasis on the word "prepared," this commonplace statement held prognostic significance to the wondering child, particularly when followed by the advice, "When anyone opens a door for you, my dear, and if you have made no effort to have it opened for you, if you haven't intervened, you walk in and do the best you can." The old lady, who lived to be 101, told the youngsters to take lessons from failure and added, "After all, the most important thing in life is that a man should know himself."

And so Fannie went through a self-searching childhood, and in retrospect, she decided that young people *should* be dissatisfied with themselves. As a child she had "a private life within the mind," but she did not begin to know herself, by her own admission, until she was between forty and forty-five years old.

As proud as Frances Perkins was of her American heritage—reinforced on her tenth birthday with her parents' gift of a tricorn hat—she looked upon her country's shortcomings as an incredible contradiction. The less-than-perfect assimilation of various ethnic groups in Worcester seemed natural enough to her, particularly in the light of the "equalitarian manners" impressed on her by her father—probably the reason why she maintained her dignity more rigidly with the socially disadvantaged than with her peers. She recalled her father instructing her on the proper manners for people who live in a democracy: "How you must never overlook anyone, the least of these, because they are our brothers, and more than that, our fellow citizens; and how you must have a way, an approach to people with whom you talk, while not subservient, not arrogant. I know no better word for it than equalitarian manners. That does not mean rough manners; they are good manners, manners of dignity."

On one occasion when visiting Boston as a child, quite by chance she witnessed a brawl in the streets in which some Irish boys were the victims. The stones thrown at them merely accentuated the taunts, "Paddys! Paddys!" Violence, bad manners—prejudice against immigrants and their children, Catholics and the Irish, and prejudice based on race—these, too, were part of America and a less-than-perfect democracy.

From the Oxford Street Grammar School, Fannie went on to the Worcester Classical High School. Her high school principal, Edward R. Goodwin, encouraged his pupils to go on to institutions of higher learning. Inadvertently, he provided an otherwise bashful, introspective child with the training she needed to overcome her shyness. He strongly supported debating societies, which provided weekly sessions in public speaking. Under his virtual mandate, Fannie joined the Aletheiai Debating Society. An "A" student in science, English, and elocution, she did only average work in most of her other subjects. As for elocution, she naturally acquired a proper New England accent, which meant that she would say "Frawnces" for Frances, "laboh" for labor, "mawses" for masses, and "cleah" for clear. Her precise "high hat" accent would sound affected to Washingtonians until the presidency of an Irish Catholic from her home state, John F. Kennedy, almost thirty years after she first held office.

On high school graduation day, June 20, 1898, Fannie Coralie Perkins took no part in the program, nor did her name appear on the honor list. Her mother considered a suitable marriage as the next step in her daughter's life, and had various beaux lined up, but her father thought she might make a satisfactory school teacher. Earlier in the year, however, her parents had allowed her to apply for admission to Mount Holyoke College, even though higher education still ranked as a "daring departure" from society's norms for a girl from a middle-class family.

* * * * *

Fannie Coralie Perkins considered herself tall for a girl—five foot five, possibly including shoes and a wealth of wavy brown hair amassed on the top of her head. At a time when poke bonnets and parasols protected Victorian ladies' alabaster white complexions from the sun, she had a healthy olive complexion, untouched by make-up. Large brown eyes set off her oval face with its slightly arched nose and thin, well-defined lips. She possessed the beauty of youth, which changed over time to the animated attractiveness of a warm, vital personality, qualities that photographs rarely capture. People invariably noticed and remembered her dark eyes; they communicated as effectively as her speech, their piercing look not readily averted.

For Fannie, going away to Mount Holyoke College meant freedom from the restrictions imposed on her at home. She fully anticipated a happy, carefree time.

The *Herald Tribune* in the fall of 1898 reported that Mount Holyoke College started its sixty-second year with crowded houses and students boarding in the village. Hundreds of applications had been declined since April of that year when the lists were full. Mount Holyoke was the only college in the United States old enough to have students with grandmothers and great-grandmothers who were graduates. Founded in 1837 by Mary Lyon, a pioneer in the education of women of moderate means, it developed from a female seminary with Christian studies to a highly-regarded liberal arts college.

The standards of scholarship set by Mount Holyoke College

conflicted with the preconceptions of one of its freshmen. Fannie Perkins did not think of herself as "having a mind," despite the fact that she had gotten by in her high school courses quite effortlessly. She planned to follow the same system in college. However, she soon found herself a rather bewildered freshman in a required chemistry course given by Dr. Nellie Esther Goldthwaite.

Fannie writhed under the influence of what she described as "Dr. Goldthwaite's hounding personality, the pounding impact of her intelligence, which first aroused in me the consciousness of intellectual life. I discovered for the first time, under the stimulus of that course and of that teacher, that I had a mind. My intellectual pride was aroused and the grim determination awakened in me to get the most I could out of college."

Her resolve faltered frequently, but her Latin teacher also made a strong impression on her during her freshman year and literally reduced her to tears. She later described Miss Esther Van Dieman as a curiously emotional personality of fine intellect who lashed out at "a somewhat lazy student's acceptance of 'well enough' rather than the 'best possible' as a standard." Miss Van Dieman blazed at her for slipping along in a casual way when she might have done a first-class job of translation. She made it clear that Latin prose was something that the girl had to master whether she liked it or not—it was a matter of character.

A course that Fannie especially liked was taught by Miss Annah May Soule, professor of American colonial history. An eye-opener for her, the course added new dimensions to her already considerable knowledge of colonial history. Professor Soule, a progressive teacher, introduced economic and sociological concepts to the subject of history. In addition, she brought them to life by sending students to the factories and homes in the area for information on economic and social problems. For the first time Fannie Perkins understood the social revolution she had witnessed in Worcester, "the other world" of the laboring classes, and history became more than dates and events.

One of her classmates, Alice Little, confirmed the fact that Fannie rated rather poorly with members of the faculty, but she more than made up for this in her popularity with her fellow students. Affectionately dubbed "Fannie the Perk" and "Perky," she fit in with the practical joking to which the class of 1902 seemed particularly prone. She was pleasant to everybody, extremely goodnatured, vivacious, and imaginative. When the junior class found itself without funds, she organized a "junior lunch," a profitable mid-morning sale of sandwiches.

Possibly because of restraints placed on them in their childhood, the young women engaged in activities usually associated with little boys' play. With pell-mell merriment, they raced across campus flying kites—and were chastened by a stern reminder from a Mrs. Mead that they were "the hope of the College." Their penchant for frivolity manifested itself next in spinning tops. They practiced for days before appearing at 6:30 A.M. on May 1, 1901, for a competition in top spinning. They also gorged on spreads of food consumed after the lights-out curfew.

The students belonged to the Young Women's Christian Association, and Fannie served on the Prayer Meeting Committee. She led the Day of Prayer for Colleges in January of her senior year and in June led the class prayer meeting with the theme "Be ye steadfast," I Cor. XV:58, the class motto which appeared in the yearbook as "Beop Stapolfaste."

Years later Fannie excused her far from straight "A" record on the grounds that, "at the time the undergraduate was utterly unprotected against the ravages of student life." She felt that Dr. Goldthwaite and Miss Van Dieman pressured her into the election, not of the easiest, but of the hardest course of study at the college. She majored in chemistry, with physics and biology as her minors. She was almost the only student who took advanced physics, together with the supporting mathematical work. All this despite the fact that she really was "emotionally interested in the humanities."

Actually her appetite for her new-found popularity and her friendships was insatiable, and she resented the schedule of difficult courses that prevented her from enjoying the less strenuous pleasures of collegiate life. She was prone to lament, "I had little time to spare for my friends, even less for walks and recreation." To lighten her load in her last semester, she decided to take a three-hour snap course. The result: "I shall never forget the indignation, the pained surprise of Dr. Goldthwaite, my faculty adviser, as she scanned my tentative schedule. I succumbed and took a course in physical chemistry."

Not one to let anything go, she merely expanded her hours of activity. In February of her senior year she played Brutus in a wild musical burlesque, *The Lamentable Tragedy of Julius Caesar*. On May 27 and June 17 she performed as the courtier, Gaucelme, in Robert Browning's *Colombe's Birthday*. In a women's college, someone had to take the male roles.

Fannie belonged to the Senior Society Sophocles Authors Club, the Athletics Association, and the Golf Club, and she served on the executive committee of the Students' League and as toastmistress for Mountain Day, June 11, 1902. Elected class vice-president in her junior year, and class president in her senior year, she ably demonstrated executive ability by "delegating work, seeing that it was carried out, and keeping everybody in good humor in the meantime." Years later a classmate, Louise Gilman Rounds, described her as "an individual who refused to conform to customs and traditions of college life, always ready to stand for her convictions and take the consequences of her opinions." Because of, or despite this, she ended up honored as "The Girl who has done most for the Class," and the permanent president of the class of 1902.

Fannie spent part of the summer after graduation on the family farm in Maine "as usual," and then she visited a school friend in Pennsylvania, another in Newark, New Jersey, and two in Portland, Maine. At the same time she searched for a position.

"Well, nothing seemed to turn up for me," she wrote in a letter to her former classmates, "and I made up my mind that it was my mission to stay at home and make my family miserable." She returned to Worcester on September 10, intending to care for her father until the rest of the family returned from Maine.

"I had scrubbed vigorously for three days, nearly killed my poor father with my cooking and on the whole was getting quite devoted to my occupation, when one morning I received a telegram asking if I would go to Colchester, Connecticut, at once, as a substitute teacher for one who was ill." Her letter also explained that her father was out of town and thus unable to help her make a decision. She tossed a penny and decided to go, with only two hours until train time. Unnerved as she arrived late in the evening, her misgivings were dispelled when she discovered a friend in Colchester. Two and a half weeks later the sick teacher recovered from her illness, and Fannie took a trip back to Mount Holyoke.

On her return from the Mount Holyoke visit, she received word that the teacher she had replaced was ill again. This time Fannie stayed at Colchester Academy until Thanksgiving and reported to her classmates that she certainly had experiences. "About half of my school were Jews and of the remainder, a third were Irish, so you see there was room for fun. There is a Baron Hirsch colony of Russian Jews in Colchester and the Jews were the brightest and most interesting people in school."

With typical just-out-of-college enthusiasm, she described her situation:

> I certainly had a variety of subjects to teach—Algebra and Geometry, (think of that for this child), Physics, Zoology, Physical Geography, and Geology (bluff) and college English. These came every day. It took harder grinding than I ever did in college. Of course it fell to my lot to take up Julius Caesar with my college English class, and truly, I nearly died over it. It sometimes seemed as though I would have to sing "Portia Dear" or some of those other parodies of 1902 fame. I used to chew my lips all through that class for such funny memories would keep coming up to me.

After Thanksgiving, Fannie returned home for the winter and a year of social gaieties, parties, and beaux—none of whom interested her. She also became involved with a church-sponsored Girls' Club made up of fourteen- to sixteen-year-olds who were working in factories and stores. One night a week she had the girls doing gymnastics and gym games. A second night each week she planned a variety of educational activities intended to improve them, searching for imaginative ways to present material: "It has to be like a sugar-coated pill, for they are very much afraid of being improved. They want fun." The girls enjoyed singing, and she had them rehearsing for a program to be presented around New Year's to raise money to buy a basketball.

One of her young protegees had her hand cut off in a candy dipper. In a day when child labor laws and universal workmen's compensation were still in the imaginations of visionaries, Fannie set about, with the help of a friendly clergyman, to get some funds for the poor girl. The employer finally gave the girl one hundred dollars, little compensation for a missing hand, but better than she would have done without help.

With Fannie's father now quite prosperous, her own lack of financial concerns contrasted sharply with that of the Girls' Club membership. Influenced by the teachings of Professor Annah May Soule and her natural curiosity, Frances tried to understand their plight, for obviously the alcoholism or laziness to which her parents attributed poverty did not apply to her hard-working girls. She discovered the phenomena of low wages:

> ...I myself saw pay envelopes of two dollars a week for cash girls in department stores in major American cities, little girls who were thirteen, fourteen, or fifteen years old. This was the period, of course, when full-grown and experienced women in the same stores earned five dollars a week.

Although, of course, one dollar bought more in those days than it does today, a pair of shoes still cost two dollars and fifty cents, the cheapest coat of any warmth at all eighteen to twenty dollars, so that the purchasing power represented by these wages still spelled poverty of the kind that results in underfeeding, neglect of health, and housing in dark, unventilated, and cold rooms.

Women and low wages equalled poverty, a simple formula that begged more questions than it answered. Was this the land of opportunity—for men only? It seemed so, as she worked with another group of destitute women on Saturdays.

Barely a step ahead of her pupils in the art of sewing a placket or buttonholes, Fannie taught sewing in the church-affiliated mission school every Saturday. In addition to her Sunday-school work, and renewing old acquaintances, she kept physically occupied and mentally preoccupied—though hardly satisfied. She knew she had a mission, a calling, but what could it be?

She received one job offer as an analytical chemist in a canning factory—an occupation related to her education. However, her parents regarded this as unseemly for a proper young lady and worried over her prospects for marriage. She longed to do something actively involved with the world outside of the classroom. Unfortunately, the options for educated women were extremely limited, and she ended up teaching science, mathematics and English at Monson Academy, another private school.

She changed the spelling of her name from Fannie to Fanny, then decided that was inadequate. Who would hire someone with the ridiculous name of Fanny Coralie? Hoping to change her fortune, she adopted the name Frances—with no middle name or initial—because it sounded dignified and better suited to her gradually crystallizing career aspirations. Fanny and Perky became nicknames used jokingly only by her very few intimates. Her former classmates obligingly relearned her name, one she refused to change, even after marriage.

Despite her yearning for something more challenging, in the fall of 1904 Frances Perkins accepted a teaching position at an exclusive boarding school, Ferry Hall, in Lake Forest, Illinois. She taught physics and biology, and handled laboratory work and chaperoning. However, she made this an enjoyable experience, as her description, written in 1906, makes evident: "I have charge of the manners and morals of my corridor, too. Last year this was quite exciting, for I had a set of young imps, and they kept me chasing up and down fire escapes after them half the time."

With her next crop of pupils she formulated a philosophy she dared not put into practice: "This year," she wrote, "I have some perfect angels, the kind that wouldn't turn over in bed without my permission; and the result is that I'm blissfully ignorant of their existence, and the moral of that is if you want to be famous you must be bad, since few of us can be good enough to attract any one's attention."

III

The Discovery of Poverty

"College is for learning afterwards." In making this declaration, Frances Perkins voiced a complaint of generations of students who failed to see the relevancy of their classroom instruction, particularly in nonvocational and highly abstract studies, until they were out of school. Reflecting further, Frances cited as the greatest advantage of the trained and educated mind, "that it can learn not only by its own experience but by the recorded experience of others, and learn to associate these two phases of developing information into one pattern."

Part of her postcollege education derived from voracious, critical reading enhanced by exposure to new ideas—first seeded by her church-related "Lady Bountiful" work in Worcester, then nourished by her "literary discovery" of poverty. Not unnaturally, her exposure to the working poor of Worcester induced intellectual dissonance as her stereotyped notions about poverty changed with exposure to contradictory evidence. It had so long appeared evident that the competent man could readily make his way in the New England states—her father's success proved this; that the poor were the product of slothfulness, drink, or inferior endowment; that women were employed largely because of family misfortune, frequently the physical or economic death of the male breadwinner.

Frances read Hartley's *Mrs. Wiggs of the Cabbage Patch,* a best-seller of the period, and O. Henry's *Unfinished Story,* which she described as a most "gripping piece of preaching." She agonized over Jacob Riis's *How the Other Half Lives,* with its vignettes of poverty based on his experiences trudging through the streets and alleys of New York's Hell's Kitchen, Poverty Gap, the Mulberry Street Bend, Henry Street, and the

Fourth Ward. But she claimed that Theodore Roosevelt's inaugural address of 1905 persuaded her that "the pursuit of social justice" would be her vocation. Theodore Roosevelt had warned: "There is nothing attractive in [social work] save for those who are entirely earnest and disinterested. There is no reputation, there is not even any notoriety to be gained from it." But in keeping with her perennially youthful personality, Frances Perkins added a postscript: "It was *fun* to put 'corruption,' as Theodore Roosevelt called it, to rout."

She particularly recalled reading Charles Booth's *Pauperism and the Endowment of Old Age* and solipsistically judged that Booth's study of the causes of poverty in London made a "startling impact" on her generation: "It was such a piling up of case records that no one could be at ease after the reading." Much of her reaction at this time was emotional, but she would later record:

> Early in this century we in America became conscious of two things which linked us to the London which Charles Booth had showed—two things which had not been problems for our grandfathers. One of these was a vast population—in our case largely foreign born—whose standards of living were not the old standards. The other was the existence of slums. . . .

The slums—tenement houses with cold-water flats, coal soot on window sills, the smell of too much humanity crowded into too little space—were tucked away in parts of cities that most people avoided or critically observed from a comfortable distance. During her visits to Chicago, Frances viewed, as an outsider, life styles that in no way resembled her own white-picket-fence, neatly-trimmed-clapboard-house-and-garden standard. Her curiosity extended beyond the "How can people live like that?" rhetorical query. What was it like; what was it all about? She wanted to know.

A fellow teacher at Ferry Hall boasted of an acquaintance with Dr. Graham Taylor. Dr. Taylor headed Chicago Commons, one of a hundred or so settlement houses in the United States modeled after Toynbee Hall in Whitehall Chapel, England. When in 1893 Dr. Taylor developed a department of instruction at the Chicago Theological Seminary that related religion to human beings and social conditions, he stipulated as a condition of his employment that he "should have liberty to live with the masses,—in simple natural neighborly human relations"—after the pattern established by Jane Addams of Hull House.

The objective of these settlement houses was to bring together people of different backgrounds and material means in order to develop mutual understanding and sympathy. While no particular mission was prescribed or duties assigned, those residents who could help others in need, simply did so. Some people viewed the settlement house as a "sociological laboratory," a label to which Jane Addams objected "because Settlements should be something more human and spontaneous than such a phrase connotes. . . ." She saw settlements as serving to make people aware of the needs of distressed neighborhoods and believed that this local consciousness of problems would help municipalities to solve them.

Arrangements were made for Frances Perkins to meet Dr. Taylor. Filled with more questions than answers, she took advantage of the Christmas break in 1905 to live at Chicago Commons. She later wrote to her friends, "I never got so many ideas in my life as I did in those three weeks. I'm more interested than ever in settlement work; and I do hope to be able to do it for a year very soon." Dr. Taylor also introduced her to the meaning of trade unionism, about which she would learn much more.

She recalled that the Klondike millionaire Raymond Robins and Charles Hallinan, another gentleman concerned with social justice, visited Chicago Commons and that they discussed Bernard Shaw's *Man and Superman* and Vida Scudder's *A Listener in Babel.* She met Jane Addams and others who shared with her their exuberant confidence that poverty could be abolished in their time.

Her meetings with articulate, involved activists concerned with poverty, coupled with her receptivity to their pronouncements on social injustice, helped surface the fact that she had "thrown a hate on teaching as a profession." She was, however, obligated to complete the academic year at Ferry Hall. It was small wonder she found her classes filled with lackluster students.

The year before, she had planned to take a trip to Europe during the summer of 1906. She resigned from Ferry Hall, but did not get to Europe. Possibly, this is when she became a temporary resident of Chicago Commons or of Hull House. Although all of her biographical records show that she worked at Hull House, official Hull House records do not include her as a permanent resident—one who has gone through a probationary period and been "accepted." Other evidence clearly indicates, however, that she received "an education" from Jane Addams that continued with Jane Addams's colleagues, particularly Florence Kelley and Margaret Drier Robins.

Despite the fact that a school teacher's wages were incredibly low, Frances managed frequent visits to Chicago during the school year and came back to Worcester and South Hadley in the summer, in addition to contemplating a trip to Europe on her "hard-earned savings." All this suggests that she received subsidization from her parents. Frances may well have used a fictitious name for the Hull House registry because of her own trepidations over being associated with a purportedly radical movement. More than likely, she kept her new associations a secret from her conservative parents. Settlement houses and social work were still touchy subjects. Her parents undoubtedly shared the popular resentment against social workers who earned a living by doling out what remained after their salaries for relief of the poor, and they would certainly object to her walking the streets of slum neighborhoods.

Already a large-scale enterprise, Hull House covered a city block on South Halsted Street. A few years before Frances Perkins came to Hull House, a third story had been added to the original, remodeled former Hull mansion, and a children's building had been added to the complex, together with a charming old English coffee house with a theater just above it. The Hull House apartments as well as the men's and the women's clubs were only two or three years old. The complex contrasted sharply with the surrounding two-story wooden tenement buildings inhabited largely by European immigrants.

Hull House earned a reputation for radicalism through heated vilifications of the system by members of the Working People's Social Science Club. Although these fiery orators were not residents of the house, newspaper reporters rarely made the distinction and consequently, neither did the reading public.

Dr. Alice Hamilton, the first woman specialist in industrial medicine, claimed that her Hull House residency produced "a deep suspicion and fear of the police and a hostility toward newspaper reporters" that took her years to overcome. Evidently any mishap at the house became a feature story, and simple statements, indiscriminately distorted, projected a warped image of the house's residents. In addition, having a newspaper story retracted merely reinforced the unfavorable publicity.

A *modus operandi* developed so that reporters got their story and only the principals involved knew the true facts. Jane Addams illustrated the strategy with an anecdote that appeared with the title "To Discount the Headlines" in *Survey,* the social workers' journal:

There was a Scotch dame who put the household savings in her stocking and fed her husband sparingly. One day he was working in the garden when he heard her call loudly, "Come in, come in, Sandy. The scones and kippered herring are waitin'." He dropped his hoe and ran toward the house. When he reached the door his faith failed him. Could he trust his ears? "You'd not be fulin' me, Sally?" he cried. "Sure Sandy, I'd not be fulin' ye," was the answer. "I'd only be fulin' the neighbors."

It may have been during her own brief period at Hull House that Frances Perkins caught the same antijournalist virus. Some of the "personal information" that she doled out to reporters suggests that she, too, made a practice of "fulin'"—or confounding them—a wee bit, as well.

To Frances Perkins, Miss Addams symbolized "that period in our national life when we passed from a highly individualistic to a brotherly service conception of human relations in a democracy." Not surprisingly, one day educator John Dewey would describe Frances's career as being of the same "American humanitarian tradition" as Jane Addams. It is unlikely, however, that their personalities meshed. Jane Addams had a rather sad and serious mien; Frances always retained her "Fannie the Perk" sense of humor. In addition, Frances could not readily temper her sentiments, unlike Jane Addams, who never sentimentalized the poor, or labor, or the young radicals who came to her door. According to Dr. Hamilton, "she could never be disillusioned or disappointed," whereas Frances's sensitivities subjected her to both emotions.

In a castigating profile of the two women, journalist Benjamin Stolberg charged, on the basis of his own residency at Hull House, that Miss Addams misled members of her particular ethical-religious cult by imbuing them with the ideal that good will could solve all social ills. Certainly Frances Perkins internalized this concept above all others, as is illustrated by her credit to Jane Addams in a book written some thirty years later:

It was she who taught us to take all elements of the community into conference for the solution of any human problem—the grasping landlord, the corner saloon-keeper, the policeman on the beat, the president of the university, the head of the railroad, the labor leader—all cooperating through that latent desire for association which is characteristic of the American genius.

And her passion for personal anonymity may have stemmed from Jane Addams's *obiter dictum:* "To pride one's self on the results of personal effort, when the time demands social adjustment, is utterly to fail to comprehend the situation." According to those who had Hull House experiences, Jane Addams's pronouncements had the force of religious doctrine. What Frances Perkins failed to absorb while there would be reinforced by Miss Addams's followers elsewhere.

One in particular, Florence Kelley, left her imprint on Hull House and unwittingly benefited her future employee, Frances Perkins. While in Chicago before the turn of the century, Mrs. Kelley investigated child labor, sweatshop and home-work problems and ended up heading an Illinois legislative committee that recommended the first factory law in the state, which brought about the eight-hour working day, prohibited child labor, and established an inspection department. The governor then appointed her chief factory inspector. Frances Perkins found that Mrs. Kelley's annual reports made good reading:

Written brilliantly, they stirred the conscience and recommended improvements as well as reported upon findings. Her first report showed that sixty-eight hundred children in Chicago were working, many of them in the stockyards and in glass factories. Mrs. Kelley took these facts directly to the Board of Education and demanded enforcement of the compulsory education law. The report also showed that there were many accidents to children in these places, some fatal accidents with no compensation because the parents had signed releases.

When she worked at the church in Worcester, Frances had attempted to help a young injured girl obtain redress; in Chicago, Mrs. Kelley made a wider study of the general problem. Frances would learn more about her pattern as one of the coworkers to whom Mrs. Kelley would address questions: "How many? How much damage, distributed or special? How do you propose to correct it? Is that practical? Will it work? How will you get it? How will you enforce it?" Mrs. Kelley believed in legislation to correct society's wrongs; Frances Perkins accepted this, though later she decided: ". . . progress toward social justice does not rest on law alone. It rests on law, plus custom, plus insistence from those who feel the effects of social injustice."

The perennial Hull House subject of social justice for women was influenced by a distant relative of Frances Perkins, namely the feminist author Charlotte Perkins Gilman, who was visited in California by Jane Addams, and who in turn visited Hull House. Her classic *Women in*

Economics, which has gone through countless printings to this day, presaged Simone de Beauvoir, Margaret Mead, and Ashley Montagu. She was one of the first to unabashedly expose the uncomfortable fact that "woman's economic profit comes through the power of sex-attraction," and that "in no other animal species is the sex-relation for sale."

Charlotte Perkins Gilman, before the turn of the century, advocated that the professional woman retain her own name after marriage, noting that "there exists no law whatever against this, but only a convention." She objected to "the convention of the owner of a human being giving that being his own name. As in slave days."

Mrs. Gilman initially kept the name of her first husband, Charles Walter Stetson, who gained notoriety by filing a divorce suit against her in 1892. She had a daughter by him and an established reputation as an author using the Stetson name. Her publishers felt the change of name after her second marriage in 1900 to her cousin, G.H. Gilman, was a decided handicap. She ended up lamenting, "It would have saved trouble had I remained Perkins from the first, this changing of women's names is a nuisance we are now happily outgrowing."

Although Frances Perkins did not attribute to her kinswoman her own immutable stand on retaining her maiden name, she discovered that society had unhappily *not* outgrown a virtual insistence, through the forces of custom, that a woman assume her husband's name. When in later years, Charlotte Perkins Gilman was asked for an evaluation, she described Frances Perkins as "more human than female," a complimentary reference to the man-woman mind in which either may predominate at a particular time.

Frances was swayed by other influences during this period in Chicago. The Congregational church, with its emphasis on the free and accountable individual, fell short of some great spiritual need she felt. Although a Congregational church attended by Jane Addams, among others, neighbored on Hull House, she found what may be described as "intellectual security" in Episcopalianism. She may well have developed her affinity for the Episcopal church through Dr. Graham Taylor's expositions on the church's affiliation with the labor movement, through its Church Association for the Advancement of the Interests of Labor and the monumental *Encyclopedia of Social Reform.*

Although Frances never proselytized openly on behalf of Episcopalianism, once she achieved this conversion—not undertaken lightly—she exemplified the devout Episcopalian for the rest of her life, and on appropriate occasions, such as commemoration of the end of the war with Japan, she intoned from memory the magnificent passages from the *Book of Common Prayer*. One writer speculated that if she had been in England, she would most likely have become an Anglo-Catholic. In later years she ardently admired T.S. Eliot, whose conversion to Anglo-Catholicism was memorialized in resplendent verse.

In June, 1907, she went back East to attend the fifth reunion of the class of 1902. For over a year she had been urging her Mount Holyoke classmates to come with their husbands and babies as well. "Just think how nice it will be to renew our youth," she wrote. The twenty-seven-year-old "spinster" impressed her cohorts not with her advanced age, but rather with her advanced ideas. Everything Frances—the new name took getting used to—said, between reminiscences on end, sounded new and wildly radical to her former classmates; they were both shocked and astonished by her "modern ideas, fads and fancies." As a number of them were teachers or librarians, her straightforward denunciation of teaching as a profession ruffled a few feelings. Although she alluded to her determination to enter another field of work, another couple of years passed before she openly announced her decision to "enter the work called by my scornful friends 'professional uplifting,' but by the sympathetic 'social work.' "

Following the reunion, she spent what she described as "a lazy summer in Italy." She rejoiced in the Renaissance art of Italy and the opportunity to observe another culture. She also made some tentative decisions about her future that she had reason to believe would not please either of her parents.

In the fall of 1907 she began her duties as the general secretary of the Philadelphia Research and Protective Association, at a salary of forty dollars a month. In a letter to her classmates, she explained:

> This society chiefly "researches and protects" immigrants, and as the ways in which they need protection are many and devious, I had some strange and thrilling experiences. Ten cent lodging houses, employment agencies, the offices of the Philadelphia political "gang" and the two police courts all became my haunts. It was often delicate work but the sense that weaker people than I needed the aid I could give pulled me over the hard parts.

She did not report to her genteel schoolmates any details on the seamy side of life to which she was exposed in full measure. In a biography of Al Smith, based on Frances Perkins's papers, Matthew and Hannah Josephson describe one of her more harrowing experiences while dealing with the exploitation of European immigrant and southern black girls. Two black men—procurers whose livelihood she threatened—came after her one rainy night. According to the report, "As they began to close in on her, she dodged around a corner, then wheeled around and thrust her umbrella point-blank at one of the men pursuing her, at the same time screaming for help and calling out his name." The men took off.

This is where Frances Perkins began her penchant for systematic study of social problems. For the Intermunicipal Research Bureau, she completed a comprehensive analysis of the conditions under which working women lived in Philadelphia. The lodging houses that charged half-a-week's salary were specific subjects of her attacks.

Her activities reflected the philosophy of her Hull House mentors. The people she served needed protection from the elements with which they contended. Equality of opportunity was not at issue; people obviously unable to cope needed to look to those who were not equal to themselves—to stronger, richer, able people—for assistance and direction.

Then, as today, families headed by women outnumbered every other category living at poverty-deprivation levels. They outnumbered those families headed by the aged and the crippled, and those headed by black men and migrant workers. Then, as today, this problem received attention hardly commensurate with the relative magnitude of the problem. This factor, as well as the influence of her economics professor at the University of Pennsylvania, Simon Nelson Patten, led her to become involved with the women's movement.

Frances regarded women's suffrage as one of her avocations—but, nonetheless, a "serious pastime." The meaning of a statement to her classmates is, however, somewhat obscure. She wrote them that "woman's suffrage is either execrated so heartily or championed so ardently by all of you that it needs only the bare statement of the fact that I'm one of the 'real ones' to explain the situation perfectly." Her convictions were tempered by her respect for private property: "I fear that only a somewhat antiquated reverence for plate glass windows keeps me from being one of the stone throwing kind." She could never see violence and destruction as a means to a satisfactory solution of problems.

Among her closest friends while she was in Philadelphia were George N. Caylor and his brother, Joe. They were active workers in the Socialist party; as a matter of fact, they hardly lived for anything else.

George believed that "from the admiration Frances had for Joe and the fondness with which she spoke of him when we met, I could not help but assume that she would have married him, had he asked her." Laura Tobey, a schoolmate and close friend of Frances's, confided this to George's wife-to-be, Tema. Joe, however, showed a single-minded interest in the labor movement. George claimed that Joe, the intellect of the family, was "actually a confirmed bachelor from his early twenties." Frances, just seven months older than Joe, was close enough to thirty to see herself as an old maid. But she hardly would act on her family's proddings to find a husband just for the sake of achieving the most accepted status in this country—married. She admired Joe's dedication, his complete authority on labor legislation pertinent to his typographers' union, and she respected him. Their friendship, largely through correspondence, lasted over thirty years.

Frances Perkins wrote nothing about her association with the Caylors, and George Caylor's memoirs provide the only record of her romantic attachment to Joe. The impact of the family's fervent socialistic views on her ever-questioning mind was overshadowed by the profound influence of her night-school classes in economic principles, evident in her internalization of the jargon and concepts of the discipline.

Simon Nelson Patten, possibly the most significant single figure contributing to Frances Perkins's intellectual development, was an economics professor at the Wharton School of Finance and Commerce of the University of Pennsylvania. A brilliant scholar, prolific writer, and president of the prestigious American Economics Association, he achieved immortality as few professors have, through his students. One of them was Rexford Guy Tugwell, his biographer, who became one of President Franklin D. Roosevelt's closest advisors, and another was Frances Perkins, who paraphrased his teachings over the next half-century.

She frequently used his phrase "surplus civilization" and explicated that this, as opposed to a "deficit economy," facilitates generosity and social progress. Franklin D. Roosevelt, a "connoisseur of theories," voiced Patten's optimistic view in his March, 1933, inaugural speech: "This great Nation will endure as it has endured, will revive and will prosper . . . the only thing we have to fear is fear itself . . ."

In his *Theory of Dynamic Economics,* Patten anticipated economist John Maynard Keynes by formulating a theory that consumption is basic to value and distribution theories vis-a-vis production costs. His positive approach to economics was based on a vision of gradual, upward growth taking place throughout the United States. He also believed "social welfare depends quite as much on the way wealth is used as on its amount."

Like the radical professors of today, he achieved a high degree of visibility as an activist, disputatious professor. He led women in their suffragist parades and preached that by eliminating artificial restraints separating the sexes, crude passions would be curbed.

His students undoubtedly heard some of his preliminary thinking for his presidential address before the American Economics Association in December, 1908. "Telling contrasts," he explained in that speech, "get an immortality that is denied books, and the more concise the expression the longer the life and the greater the influence." To illustrate his contention, he cited Hobbes's "state of war," Rousseau's "natural man," Ricardo's "cost prices," and Spencer's "survival of the fittest." "The force of socialism," he contended, "lies in three phrases: 'Class Struggle,' 'Exploitation' and 'Surplus Value.' No one who has mastered these concepts need study Marx's diffuse and obscure argumentation." Frances Perkins's contribution of expressions to the language would be three unacademic phrases: "war bridegrooms," for World War I company unions; "Call me madame," when she became secretary of labor; and "Rosie the riveter," to describe women recruited to do traditional men's work during World War II.

Most meaningful to Frances Perkins, still new to the field of social work, was Patten's description of the field as "a new kind of charity . . . not to undermine energy and productive ability or to create a parasitic class, but to distribute the surplus in ways that will promote general welfare and secure better preparation for the future."

In an interview years later, Frances Perkins described her teacher as "the greatest man America has ever produced." And apparently, as a student, she favorably impressed him. In recommending her for a fellowship at the New York School of Philanthropy, he wrote to Professor Samuel McCune Lindsay that she was "a remarkably good executive . . . I believe she will acquire through her energy and brains an important position among social workers. . . ."

About her studies at the University of Pennsylvania, she wrote her former classmates that she had "made the astonishing discovery that my college experience to the contrary, I really had the normal endowment of brains. I was so 'sot up' over this discovery of symptoms of intellect that I immediately became consumed by a passion for knowledge and advanced degrees."

She also wrote that she had never worked as hard before in her life.

The disillusionment of her near-romance may well have been responsible for her view of herself after her two years in Philadelphia: "And best (or worst) of all, I grew old during that time, so that now I am a settled and mature old spinster with an opinion on every topic under heaven." Having gone through a serious period of soul-searching resulting in some alienation from her family, she added, "But if I have acquired the obnoxious traits of old age, I've also acquired its one redeeming grace—a sense of humor—so that I no longer take myself and my doings seriously."

She could even joke about her first—but far from last—personal experience with financial problems, much as she would some fifty years later when she admitted to her secretary, "I always have enough money for luxuries. It's the necessities that I can't afford!" The forty dollars a month that she earned in Philadelphia covered neither luxuries nor necessities, and she came to regard her watch as her best friend. It went in and out of the pawnshop with the regularity that her washing went to and from the laundry.

In that period around 1909 to 1910, she renewed her conviction that life is "mighty well worth while and right good fun." Her closing benediction in a letter to her classmates reflected a simple Victorian philosophy: "May we be wise enough while walking the path called service to the mountain called achievement to gather the wayside flowers of happiness."

IV

The Fire that Reformers Fanned

Frances Perkins "jumped at the chance," as she put it, when the Russell Sage Foundation offered her a graduate fellowship. In return for a small amount of social investigation, the fellowship provided for graduate study in sociology and economics at the New York School of Philanthropy, later known as the New York School of Social Work. Affiliated with Columbia University since its establishment in 1898 by the Charity Organization Society of New York, it had a one-year curriculum that was being expanded into a two-year graduate program.

The body of knowledge related to social work had developed from the rudimentary concept of poverty as insufficiency and destitution as dependence, to the revolutionary "case method" approach of treating each poor family's problems as unique. Frances was able to combine academic theory with the practical experience gained from field work.

In 1909 she still listed her home address as 50 Queen Street, Worcester, but her return address was in Greenwich Village, at 160 Waverly Place, New York City. She informed her friends that since she lived in a settlement, she felt "in the very heart of both the theoretical and practical efforts to socialize the life of the modern city." She probably resided briefly at the University Settlement, originally the Neighborhood Guild when on New York City's East Side. As with Hull House, it was modeled after Toynbee Hall in Whitechapel, England. Ernest Poole, whose book *The Harbor* came out in 1915, numbered among those "educated" at the University Settlement. Frances regarded him and his wife, a classmate of hers at Columbia University, as among her good friends.

Living in Greenwich Village was an experience in itself. The Village in no way resembled the skyscrapered Wall Street section of lower

Manhattan, the bustling shopping and theater districts uptown, or the fashionable residential areas around Central Park or Riverside Drive. Its respectably shabby townhouses, one adjoining the next like those in old Amsterdam after which they were patterned, rented for a modest fifty to seventy-five dollars a month, and for substantially less when subdivided into numerous small apartments. The self-contained community was fringed on one side by walk-up apartment buildings filled with a cacophony of foreign languages, mostly Italian, and, on the other, by the steam-and-dirt-emitting lofts from which flowed a variety of manufactured goods.

The Village centered around lushly green Washington Square, a perambulator-filled community park. Pigeons fluttered over a life-size statue of Garibaldi, and an arch, similar to Paris's Arc de Triomphe, opened out to the Champs Elysee-like Fifth Avenue. Former factory lofts, silhouetted starkly against the east side of the park, housed the classrooms and offices of New York University. A few blocks further north, the plush John Wanamaker department store of Broadway and Eighth Street clung to its Victorian grandiosity. A few blocks west, quaint gas-lit MacDougal Alley seemed oblivious to the commercial enterprises on neighboring Fourth Street. Its northernmost boundary, perpetually littered and mucky Fourteenth Street, featured pipe-rack bargain shops including Kleins and the original Ohrbachs ribbon shop, as well as notorious Tammany Hall, home of corruption-tinged, liberal politicians.

The Village's central location proved to be advantageous. Like most people, Frances Perkins could not afford to own one of the new Ford motorcars seen in increasing numbers on the streets of New York City, but rather relied on elevated trains, subways, and trolley cars that criss-crossed the island for transportation. Most of her work by day took her to Hell's Kitchen, where she conducted a study under Pauline Goldmark, head of the School of Philanthropy. At night she attended classes uptown. Apparently Frances's undergraduate training "took"; as a graduate student, she managed to balance her activities so that she maintained her friendships and also received high grades.

She read, studied, wrote, and when finances permitted amusements, she went to the opera or theater or dined with friends in quaint out-of-the-way cafes. And, she reflected, "always there is the supreme pleasure of talking my head off with some old college friend who has crossed my path." One of these was Maude Aldrich who reported on her meetings with Frances Perkins in a class letter dated February 11, 1910:

Fanny Perkins I have seen twice—so I have been able to get in touch, indirectly, with most of you. I never knew anyone to keep track of people as she does. I wish you could all see her and have a good visit with her. You would be a Socialist before the visit was over, even though you would talk over 1902, past, present and future most of the time.

The Socialist label was appended to anyone who tried to educate outsiders to the significance of social work as a force for human betterment.

Reinforcement for seemingly radical views came from fellow social-work practitioners who habituated the Social Reform Club on Fourth Street, within walking distance of Greenwich Settlement House. Here social workers spent Tuesday evenings debating current issues on the main floor clubroom. Other times they hunched over tables in the informal basement restaurant, sharing experiences and ideas.

Although social workers without family subsidization fared little better, they moaned over the fact that the average wageworker earned $540 a year, working six days a week and ten or more hours a day. Women worked longer for less. Frances Perkins may well have told of the girl on the Eighth Street cross-town car who lost her transfer. When the conductor asked for her fare she replied, "Why, I can't pay another nickel. This is Saturday and I haven't got another cent." A simple budget analysis, Frances explained, showed that the girls earning six dollars a week had only ten cents left after paying for bare necessities.

Other anecdotes became part of her repertoire. One dealt with a son who was the sole support of his mother and two young sisters. When he was arrested for a petty crime, Frances intervened on the grounds that his imprisonment would mean starvation for his family. As she had learned to do in Chicago, where she defended young prostitutes and attempted their rehabilitation, and in Philadelphia, where the aid of district political bosses proved to be invaluable, she sought help from the Tammany leader of Hell's Kitchen. Boss McManus, a state senator from the area, brought about the boy's release, whereas the charity bureau could and would do nothing.

Of little significance at the time, a tea dance she attended at the Gramercy Park home of Mrs. Walston Brown was her introduction to

Franklin D. Roosevelt. In her book *The Roosevelt I Knew,* Frances wrote that she remembered Franklin D. Roosevelt as the tall, slender young man with a pince-nez primarily because, between dancing and tea drinking, she heard him defend his distant relative, Theodore Roosevelt. Like many in her group, she admired the president's progressive ideas.

Frances was still finding her way. She moved into Greenwich House, the settlement headed by Mary Kingsbury Simkhovitch at 28 Jones Street. Of the many distinguished people associated with the settlement, Mrs. E. H. Harriman, mother of the former New York State governor and ambassador Averell Harriman, helped in the acquisition of 16, 18, and 20 Jones Street. Together with Louise Lockwood, her daughter Mary Harriman Rumsey had established the public-service-oriented Junior League. On the board of Greenwich House, Mary Rumsey became a close friend of Frances Perkins, with whom she would share a Georgetown home in Washington, D.C., some decades later. At the Jones Street settlement and another at 46 Barrow Street, Mrs. Simkovitch noted that people were "brought together with different life experiences and outlooks for the first time." Frances met General Electric's Gerard Swope, the president of Greenwich House, and Henry Morgenthau, Jr., publisher of the *American Agriculturist,* at a meeting there that presaged many in the White House dealing with recovery.

From Mrs. Simkhovitch residents learned that work at the settlement house was not for the weak or fainthearted. One young Wellesley graduate caught the measles while taking a neighborhood youngster to the hospital, developed mastoiditis and died. The meningitis, infantile paralysis, and various epidemics they lived with periodically added to the seriousness and danger of their chosen way of life.

* * * * *

More than any other, the Henry Street Settlement House figured most significantly in Frances Perkins's life. Like Hull House in Chicago, the Henry Street Settlement persevered as a stately, tended mansion, an unlikely oasis in the midst of the degenerate ambience of the people-polluting Bowery, East Broadway, and Mott Street. Its view of the nearby ten-year-old Brooklyn Bridge was obscured by ugly, scarred tenement buildings with fire escapes zig-zagging across the bleak facades.

Here, the colognes and lotions of the financially well-off offset the rancid odors of men and women whose grimy hands had not held a coin for some days, whose blank eyes seemed to focus inward because of the pity or disgust they often saw mirrored in the eyes of others. Here the social workers, the philanthropists, and conscience-stricken met to serve the confused, the crippled, the simple and helpless. Here an idealistic, future "brain truster," Adolph Berle, then an insignificant young law clerk, elected to live for a time. His most vivid memory was of seeing Florence Kelley, Lillian Wald, and Frances Perkins come flying into the dining room, their long skirts flapping around their ankles as they found their places, breathless from their nonstop give-and-take discussion.

Here Frances met the people who influenced the direction of her career. She came to know and appreciate Lillian Wald, who had established the Henry Street Settlement as a nursing service in 1893, and who told stories with unparalleled flair. Influential people enjoyed having her as a dinner guest, although it was said that wealthy men complained, "It costs $5,000 to sit next to Lillian Wald at dinner." As a crusader, she was most effective, and not only the rough-and-tumble politicians of Tammany Hall consulted with her but also the idealistic coterie surrounding John Purroy Mitchel, who would soon be the reform mayor of New York City. Anyone associating for a time with Lillian Wald would inevitably get to know the political leaders of the city. It is most likely that Frances Perkins met Paul C. Wilson, brilliant secretary to John Purroy Mitchel, through her. Frances had discovered the power of statistics; he was an outstanding financial statistician.

Statistics served not only as an analytical tool but as a persuasive weapon against the mental blocks of custom, greed, and prejudice, according to Frances Perkins's principal mentor, Florence Kelley. A resident of the Henry Street Settlement House, Florence Kelley had joined with Josephine Shaw Lowell, founder of the Charity Organization of New York, and John Graham Brooks in establishing the National Consumers League in 1899, and for thirty-three years she served as its first executive secretary.

As executive secretary of the National Consumers League, Florence Kelley formed chapters of the league all over the country. She always traveled by the cheapest means, staying at inexpensive lodging houses or homes of ordinary families, in order to speak on the need for better working conditions and the elimination of child labor.

As Frances Perkins explained the league, it pledged its members "to buy from and patronize only those firms that maintained good working conditions as established by a Consumers League Code." The code of standards, radical for that time, included the provision that working women be permitted to sit down occasionally at their work, prohibited them from working after ten o'clock at night (particularly those who began work at six or seven in the morning), and required a minimum of sanitary facilities. It was Florence Kelley's conviction, according to Frances Perkins, "that if the people knew the facts about inhuman working conditions and the neglect of children, they would desire to act morally and responsibly." This meant exercising the consumers' most effective weapon: the right not to buy.

Mary Kingsbury Simkhovitch of Greenwich House was on the executive board. Pauline Goldmark, Jane Addams, Lillian Wald, and many others whom Frances had yet to meet, such as Mary Drier, Mary Dewson, Julia Lathrop, Grace and Edith Abbott, and Eleanor Roosevelt, belonged to the league. Frances did not believe in token membership in any organization; by joining the Consumers League, she made a serious commitment that had her plunging into investigative activities virtually immediately. In a matter of months, her dedication and conscientious efforts were rewarded by her election by the board to the position of executive secretary of the New York chapter. This was a full-time, paid position, an opportunity to use all of her training, and an acknowledgment, by more experienced people in the field, of her ability.

* * * * *

In 1910 it would be hard to imagine that some fifty-five years later, the *New York Times* would write, "There were some who said that the entire New Deal relief program was nothing more than an expanded version of the Consumers League platform." Frances Perkins's assignments hardly ranked as grandiose or glamorous, but with Florence Kelley's comforting admonition ringing in her ears, "Despise not the day of small things," she tackled each job with vigor.

She reported to the New York State Factory Investigating Commission her personal reactions after visiting about one hundred bakeries scattered throughout New York City and analyzing the studies of many more made by volunteer investigators. Fortunately Frances was young and agile, able to navigate the dark cellar stairs, low-ceilinged passageways, and make her way over blankets on the bakery floors where men who worked sixteen to eighteen hours a day napped. Most of the bakeries, located in cellars, were poorly lighted, without ventilation, and extremely filthy. They reeked of foul lard, poor pie fillers and icings, of sweat pouring down the arms of men hand-kneading bread dough, and of families tending their coughing sick on the bakery premises.

This investigation of cellar bakeries resulted in the production of bread under sanitary conditions and the elimination of sweatshop conditions. But according to one political commentator, "it resulted in throwing the manufacture of bread into the hands of a few large corporations." He claimed, "the General Baking Company, the Continental Baking Company and other members of the so-called 'Baking Trust' give Miss Perkins the credit of securing for them a grip on the baking industry of New York City."

The employment of children and pregnant women was equally relevant to what she termed the overall "problem of human conservation." Her sense of Victorian propriety was shocked by the report that women were employed industrially right up to their confinement and that two or three days after, they resumed hard physical labor.

As a practical person, she reflected on employed children: "I think we should be constantly raising the age at which children may be employed, but owing to our inadequate educational facilities that will have to be done gradually. After fourteen years of age, most of the schooling which children receive cannot possibly interest them. We must have a better system of education before we can successfully keep children in school and away from work."

This type of comment, part of her speeches at teachers' conventions, produced an oft-repeated response: "What will we do with all the children?" New York City schools faced a problem of overcrowding that surpassed the post-World War II baby boom crises.

Frances actively sought speaking engagements before teachers. "I would speak about child labor laws. They were so necessary. Something had to be done about these little children. I had to prove it to teachers. These children were working 60 to 72 hours a week in rush seasons in industries full of dust and fumes. The death rate was very high." She felt that teachers had hearts, that they were responsive, and besides, they were politically potent people. Golf was just becoming popular. As her clincher she would recite Sara N. Claghorn's "Little Toilers":

> The golf links lie so near the mill,
> That nearly every day,
> The laboring children can look out
> And see the men at play.

Early in her career she had been indoctrinated to that panacea, the wrong-righting power of the law. She had yet to learn that it takes more than good legislation to bring about the mandated changes. She may well have felt uneasy about her next assignment, her inherent shyness manifesting itself again, when she was told to lobby for the passage of the Jackson-McManus fifty-four-hour bill for women. This meant going to the state capital in Albany by New York Central Railroad or Hudson River steamboat; it meant collaring key legislators and their aides; it meant presenting hard-hitting facts that included data on how the constituents of the various voting districts felt. If nothing else, Florence Kelley knew it would be a great learning experience for Frances. She expounded the virtues of the bill to the legislators, without success.

* * * * *

Settlement house living catered little to a New Englander's penchant for privacy. A single woman, aged thirty, who thought of marriage "to get it out of the way"—but not seriously—Frances acquired her own apartment on Waverly Place. She became an "in" member of the Greenwich Village community, as distinguished from the not uncommon poseurs, entertained her friends, met neighbors, and enjoyed the privacy and freedom that comes from being on one's own.

She had as many male as female friendships, most of which she regarded as platonic. This evaluation was not always mutual, as was the case with the gaunt, red-headed twenty-five-year-old budding author Sinclair Lewis. He rediscovered New York City—Greenwich Village in particular—and determined that "all seemed fermentation, effervescence, insouciance," and he also saw Frances as part of the rebellion of the "the Young Intellectuals" that he viewed as an outsider. Frances later explained:

> As I remember it, he was at that time tasting of everything that came along, but he was always an outsider. I remember that a number of the men whom I knew very well, like Arthur Bullard and Howard Brubaker, regarded him as a pest and a nuisance and never took him seriously. . . . He was . . .

always making an exaggerated statement of any theory that any one of these people might have been interested in—a statement so exaggerated as to make them feel it was ridiculous and, of course, it made them withdraw from any friendship with him.

In late 1910 and early 1911, nothing about "Red" Lewis suggested his future world acclaim as the Nobel-Prize winning author of *Arrowsmith, Babbitt, Elmer Gantry,* and *Ann Vickers.* Tall, scrawny, uncoordinated, to Frances Perkins he had a "peculiar style of ugliness" exaggerated by "the cheap, ready-made suits of dark blue that never fitted him and made him look like a picked chicken."

Frances had a predilection for people of strong convictions and strong character, who were intellectually well-disciplined and aesthetically sensitive—characteristics that formed the puritanical framework of her personal philosophy. She sublimated her "Fannie the Perk" propensity for fun and frolic. But with Sinclair Lewis, the mimic, the cut-up, the humanist aspect of her warm, responsive, laughter-loving nature could surface. She explained to his biographer that she liked Lewis because he was funny and amusing. Her mother-hen sympathies were aroused. "He was also appealing. That is, he appealed to one's parental sense, and one felt like protecting him and not letting him be hurt by other young men whom one knew, and who tended to make fun of him. . . ." He was the underdog in the Bohemian milieu of Greenwich Village, and she was his defender.

To get away from congested, grimy New York City, she and her friends would go to the one relatively uninhabited borough, Staten Island. Completely unlike the other four making up Greater New York—Manhattan, the Bronx, Queens and Brooklyn—its beaches and gently rolling countryside allowed for communion with nature. On occasion "Red" Lewis would join the group for picnics. Other times, the two of them alone would go just for the ferryboat ride to Staten Island.

In this setting, Sinclair Lewis and Frances Perkins undoubtedly discussed socialism (he as a registered member of the Socialist party), poverty, modern art, the articles he had written and the book she would write, the work she was doing and her uncertainties about her future, women's suffrage, love and marriage.

And for respite, they people-watched, which resulted in an adventure Frances related in an interview. Journalist Genevieve Parkhurst retold the story:

One Sunday Frances Perkins, with Sinclair Lewis as her escort, took a ride to Staten Island. Returning they noticed a girl sitting alone on the boat, unsophisticated and quiet. A young man in passing spoke to her and she seemed bewildered. But she returned his smile, and soon he was sitting beside her. Frances Perkins watched them. There was something wistful and unsure about the girl's attitude as the young man became more persistent. Finally his arm was around her. When the boat docked and the two walked off together, hand in hand, they were followed by Frances Perkins and Sinclair Lewis, who trailed them into the subway, out to the Bronx and through a door of an apartment house.

"If you are not going to do something about this," announced Frances Perkins to Sinclair Lewis, "I am. That lovely girl is not going to have her life spoiled. That boy's intentions are none too good, I know."

In no uncertain terms Sinclair Lewis remonstrated with the young man. The girl took up the cudgel. What business was it of his? How dared he, she asked, interfere with a respectable young married couple?

But our young reformers were not so easily put aside. The superintendent was called in. "Sure they're married," said he, "and a fine young couple they are."

Frances apparently told this story with relish, adding by way of conclusion, "There and then I learned my lesson," she laughed, "never to attack a situation without first being sure of my ground." In recounting the anecdote years later to Sinclair Lewis's biographer, she credited Lewis with initiating the action.

This kind of adventure, punctuated by laughter when related to friends, revealed two overly imaginative, world-righting activists and somewhat contradicts Frances's later statement that "he never was a protective or helpful or romantic young man, or if he was romantic, we thought it was make believe." She did not take him seriously when he proposed marriage to her, "at the top of his lungs on a warm summer evening when all the windows in the apartment building where I was living were open."

But then, he proposed marriage to a dozen women during that time and was accepted by one some months after Frances said her own marriage vows. It is not known if Frances was then being courted by Paul C. Wilson; their mutual friend, Mary Heaton Vorse, recorded that "Red" Lewis, Howard Brubaker, and Paul Wilson visited her regularly at Cape Cod for a change of scenery, to sail and swim.

Frances believed that Sinclair Lewis had a single-minded interest: to write a novel some day. "He used to try out a lot of ideas on me and I seemed to have to listen. . . ." Twenty years later, on the publication of his novel *Ann Vickers,* she had reason to believe, as did others, that he had also listened to her, particularly in connection with her journey abroad in 1913.

Like so many of her friendships, this was an intermittent though enduring one. She wrote him congratulations on his Nobel Prize; he rejoiced in her appointment to the president's cabinet. Forty years after their first meeting, a liquor-sotted Sinclair Lewis phoned her when he learned of her presence in Florence, Italy. She could only commiserate, ". . . but he was so ill, so confused, that I realized sadly that he was gone."

* * * * *

Often Frances Perkins was assailed by the press for being a man-hater. On the contrary, she was little given to hating, and the men with whom she associated, both socially and in the course of her work, provided little provocation for hate. Rather, her experiences around this time would long be remembered with gratitude:

> It seems to me a tribute to American men to be able to recall how many there were [around 1910], when the position of women was not so well established as it is today [1929], who were willing to open the door to a young girl who had no knowledge and only "meant well." What a liberal education I was given, free gratis by technical men of tremendous knowledge in their own fields—engineers, architects, chemists, physicists, men who dealt with the very fiber of modern industrial life! They taught me in private lessons, for nothing, what makes a safe factory.

In December, 1910, an engineer and two fire prevention experts assisted her in the investigation of a factory fire in Newark, New Jersey, in which twenty-five young women were killed. They determined that this and other fatal factory fires followed a pattern that begged for correction by the factory owners and managers. In the early months of 1911 she compiled data that would serve as the basis for safety recommendations for textile mills, laundries, and other commercial enterprises where workers were being maimed because of a total disregard for human safety vis-a-vis business profits that hinged as much on employee exploitation as on sales to consumers.

An apt pupil herself, she shared her knowledge and concern with friends such as Mary Heaton Vorse, a writer who was particularly attracted to the infant and child mortality problems in New York City and, following Lillian Wald's pattern, influential citizens who could be provoked to exert pressures that would change the situation.

Because of what happened afterwards, Frances could not later recall exactly where she had been on that bright spring Saturday afternoon of March 25, 1911. Mary Heaton Vorse tried to telephone her because she thought her friend, Bertha Carter, was visiting with Frances. But Frances apparently was drinking tea with another friend on Washington Square, when screams of "Fire! Fire!" sent them scurrying out to the street. Mary Vorse heard them, too, but they did not meet as the streets rapidly filled with people running to Washington Square East and to Greene Street, next to New York University's old law school. What they saw were human torches jumping from the eighth and ninth floor windows of the Asch Building, which housed the Triangle Shirtwaist Factory. Firemen arrived on the scene and spread their nets, too fragile to hold the slight figures of the young girls careening from such a height. Their bodies smashed through the iron gratings or landed on the mound of those who had jumped before them.

One hundred and forty-six lives were lost in that fire, a fire that testimony later showed followed the pattern of those Frances had studied: exit doors locked so that workers could not pass out stolen merchandise and union organizers could not get in, crowded conditions and floors littered with debris, and dilapidated fire alarm systems, if any at all.

The mangled and burned bodies—all but 15 were women and girls between the ages of sixteen and thirty-five—were removed to a makeshift morgue, the Municipal Charities Pier at East Twenty-Sixth Street, where families could attempt to pick out their own from the 146 remains before them.

This was not a night for sleeping. In Frances's memory forever would be the picture of a young girl clinging to a windowsill until her fingers could hold no longer. Sorrow mixed with anger.

The next day her good friend, Mary Drier, as president, called a protest meeting at the Women's Trade Union League headquarters. Rabbi Stephen Wise named a Committee of Twenty-Five "to improve conditions of safety in working places." Frances Perkins was one of the twenty-five. Henry L. Stimson, who would soon become secretary of war, was named chairman; he was succeeded by Henry Morgenthau.

Local 25 of the International Ladies' Garment Workers Union held the funeral for those whose bodies could not be identified. From ten in the morning until four in the afternoon, 120,000 people trudged through the wet city streets in a grim funeral procession.

On May second, the Metropolitan Opera House filled to capacity for a memorial service from which came the impetus for the Factory Investigating Commission. A union organizer, twenty-nine-year-old Rose Schneiderman, who had unsuccessfully tried to unionize the Triangle Factory, spoke softly but movingly, to the audience.

On June 30, 1911, the New York state legislature established the Factory Investigating Commission, Chapter 561 of the Laws of 1911.

"She Retained Her Maiden Name . . ."

It seemed strange to Frances Perkins at the time that Assemblyman Al Smith and State Senators Robert Wagner and Franklin D. Roosevelt were not in the middle of the Triangle Factory fire disputations. Smith as majority leader of the assembly, and Wagner, president pro tem of the senate, were busily at odds with the uppity Dutchess County freshman senator, Franklin D. Roosevelt, over the state legislature's choice of a United States senator from New York. (At that time U.S. senators were not elected by direct public vote). For eleven weeks Roosevelt and fellow Democratic insurgents had deadlocked the selection of Tammany's "Blue-Eyed Billy" Sheehan of Buffalo. The legislature caucussed daily. Finally, a compromise candidate was proposed on March 31, 1911, and the legislators adjourned for two weeks, went home and attended to other matters.

Historical scholars searched Franklin Roosevelt's prolific correspondence from around this time, but it contained no mention of the Triangle Factory fire. Yet decades later, at a White House press conference, he argued that "business thought has very often been diametrically opposed to the corporate expression of that thought through some kind of an organization," and gave the following illustration:

> For example, the first year I went up to Albany there was a very bad fire in New York called the Triangle Fire. ... There was started in the Legislature a committee of inquiry of which Bob Wagner was chairman and there was a very young, not very experienced woman who acted, I think, as secretary of that committee to investigate factory conditions. Her name was Frances Perkins.

He went on to explain how the committee battled the lobbyists of the chamber of commerce and the merchants and manufacturers associations who opposed safety regulations. Roosevelt believed trade association lobbyists actually misrepresented their membership. In 1911 his theory had limited validity.

At the preliminary hearings of the Factory Investigating Commission, the former fire department chief testified that "a great majority of the people who occupy the various establishments would rather take a chance on the loss of life than to spend five or ten dollars to prevent it." The fire chief told of fire escapes that women and children could not descend and those that pulled away from the building or ended in enclosed yards from which escape was impossible. He explained that in the Triangle fire, which started in a pile of trimmings under a cutting table, the automatic fire alarm went off fifteen minutes after the fire department, signalled by a street box, had arrived. He told of the bodies piled up in the open elevator shaft and of the bodies jammed against the locked doors.

Both Senator Robert F. Wagner, chairman of the commission, and Assemblyman Alfred E. Smith, vice-chairman, heard Frances Perkins testify on November 14, 1911. She rather nervously explained her work as secretary of the New York Consumers League, "an organization of persons who wish to improve industrial conditions by utilizing the 'buying power' of the consumers who are banded together—that is, by pledging themselves in their shopping in such a way as to improve conditions, rather than to make them worse. . . ." She warmed up under the questioning of Abram I. Elkus, the commission's counsel, and his relentless assistant, Bernard Shientag. She spoke easily and knowledgeably of the cellar bakeries she visited from October through December of 1910, of the men who worked sixteen to eighteen hours a day, of the sweltering conditions in commercial laundries, and of the factory fires she had investigated.

During the months after the Triangle fire, she worked unstintingly with the Committee of Twenty-Five, which had evolved into the Civic Organizations' Conference on Public Safety. The chairman charged her with formulating an industrial code, together with three other key people: Carola Woerishoffer, a graduate of Bryn Mawr College, class of 1907, who worked as an inspector for the state labor department; Mary Drier who, together with her sister, Margaret Drier Robins, wife of the Klondike millionaire, had established the National Women's Trade Union League in New York; and Dr. Henry Moskowitz, a professional settlement-house worker associated with the Progressive party.

Frances's special fact-finding projects for the New York Consumers League augmented the work of the public safety group. The Consumers League was zeroing in on a campaign against the long hours of laundry workers. Carola Woerishoffer volunteered to take on a job as a laundress during the summer. It came as a heartbreaking blow when in September she was killed in an automobile accident while performing her duties as state department inspector.

In most organizations, the hard-work position is that of secretary, with many of the other positions little more than nominal titles. For her efforts on the Civic Organizations' Conference on Public Safety, Frances was named secretary, and as such, many of her recommendations for improving proposed factory legislation were included in the *Report of the Factory Investigating Commission.*

Despite an overloaded schedule and her own graduate studies, Frances accepted an invitation to teach sociology at Adelphi College. As a lecturer, lowest of the academic ranks but somewhat more prestigious than instructor, she probably found class preparations difficult, for she regarded sociology as one of those "highly speculative subjects" like economics and psychology, "subjects of which even the terminology is not yet definite," as she put it. She later expressed the view to her alma mater: "To such fields a college course should give the undergraduate nothing but an introduction. The undergraduate mind should concentrate on the scientific courses, on those courses which temper the human mind, harden and refine it, make of it a tool with which one may tackle analytically any kind of material."

One observer declared that she would have made an excellent freshman advisor. Although her suggestions were not meant to serve as "dogmatic pronouncements," Frances urged students: "Avoid snap courses; choose only the most strenuous, the most exacting; welcome mental discipline; get down to bedrock facts." In light of her machinations as a most reluctant undergraduate scholar, Frances about-faced with magnanimous bravado.

Now a bedrock fact-finding social scientist, Frances was dubbed a "fiery young idealist" by those who knew her. Her impatience with slow remedies was legendary. Although she later insinuated that her associates knew little about the legislative process, they had learned to sublimate impatience over the delays that keep a desired piece of legislation off the books year after year.

The fifty-four-hour bill that Florence Kelley had worked on, then assigned to Frances, failed to get reported out of committee in 1910. Frances's hopes for its passage in March, 1911, were dashed by a fire in the capitol that left the legislature in a chaotic state towards the end of the session. In the spring of 1912 she could count on twenty-six senators, enough to pass the bill, who agreed that children and women's weekly hours of work should be limited to fifty-four.

In the assembly chamber a floor vote exempted women working in canneries. Opponents assumed that, because of this amendment, the reformers would reject the entire bill. The Consumers League, together with other supporting groups, sent out 7,000 telegrams and fliers denouncing the amendment, but to no avail. The amended bill passed out of the assembly.

"Better take it as it is than to get no bill at all," someone advised.

"At that it is a good step forward," Frances Perkins calculated, already visualizing reamending, as many lobbyists before and after her have done.

"But it's too late now to get it to the Senate," declared a down-hearted proponent.

"Nonsense," snapped Frances Perkins, according to one report, already on her way out of the room to find "Big Tim" Sullivan, who with his cousin Christy Sullivan, also a Tammany-connected senator, was taking the night boat to New York. She persuaded him to get the amended bill on the floor of the senate.

Senator Tim Sullivan did so, but left before the roll call. Without the "Big Stick" physically present, a couple of downstate senators weakened. A quick count showed the bill was two votes short of passing. Frances flew to the telephone, learned that the Hudson River boat had not yet left its moorings, and conveyed an urgent message to the Sullivans that they return immediately.

In the meantime, according to the *New York Telegram* reporter, Louis Howe:

... Roosevelt, with his customary flair for the dramatic, refused to give up, and promised he would hold the senate floor until Sullivan could be found. He arose, said he wished to make a few remarks for the record on the bill, and—when it began to take some time to get Sullivan out of bed on the night boat for New York—switched over to a discussion of birds. The Republican leader, Brackett, protested that birds had nothing to do with the 54-hour bill. Roosevelt retorted that he was "trying to prove that Nature demands shorter hours," and went on talking until Sullivan appeared.

This last-stand pitch for the fifty-four-hour bill hardly qualified Franklin Roosevelt for plaudits as "one of its prime supporters," as

Howe led people to believe. The bill certainly was inimical to the interest of Dutchess County farmers, Roosevelt's constituents, who employed women as well as youngsters for harvesting and canning of produce. Frances was upset that this spirited young senator did not actively associate himself with the bill.

During Roosevelt's birds-and-nature filibuster, she greeted a winded Tim Sullivan, whose taxicab had broken down on the way up the hill. She later recorded that the Bowery senator told her:

> It's all right, me gal, we is wid ya. De bosses thought they was going to kill your bill, but they forgot about Tim Sullivan. I'm a poor man meself. Me father and me mother were poor and struggling. I seen me sister go out to work when she was only fourteen and I know we ought to help these gals by giving 'em a law which will prevent 'em from being broken down while they're still young.

The bill was passed—and another soliloquy added to Frances Perkins's repertoire. She could mimic ethnic and regional speech patterns along with matching body language, but could not change her own precise Bostonian accents. She must have presented a study in contrasts in her ankle-length, raglan-shouldered greatcoat and billowy plumed tricorn hat, her big brown eyes blazing as she intoned her righteous indignation over cases of social injustice in a language that sounded more English than American, and more educated than most. To her "Mother Superior," Florence Kelley, who was also refined—though capable of explosive displays of strongly worded anger—this was no problem. She was part of the editorial "we" used by Frances in her statement, "We knew from our own experience, although we rarely said so, that a primitive society in which everybody must work all the time barely to keep alive is inevitably a deficit economy." Undoubtedly Mrs. Kelly recognized the influence of University of Pennsylvania economist Dr. Simon Nelson Patten on her protegee. But she might not have realized the trepidation Frances felt as she related to her the course the fifty-four-hour bill took, and the amendment that excluded thousands of cannery workers—mostly women—from its protection. As a professional lobbyist, little more successful than most of those working in opposition to the lobbyists representing moneyed, vested interests, Florence Kelley was elated that many more thousands of women in New York State would benefit from the law stipulating the maximum hours of work.

* * * * *

In 1912 the common drinking cup was banned from public fountains, and people complained that they had to turn themselves "wrong side up" in order to drink from the faucets. The public decided that horse troughs were "a pernicious source of disease," so the street railways maintained relief stations for their horses throughout the city.

People walking the streets encountered various hazards, but fortunately women's skirt lengths had inched up off the ground. Frances Perkins marched in the great Women's Suffrage Parade that year, which Sinclair Lewis, collecting materials for his novels, described:

> . . . It was a parade of brains expressed through marching feet! It was a great thought of justice, made visible. It was—oh, let a newsboy friend of mine express it. I heard him say, after the parade, to another boy: "Say, gee, dat was some parade—all dose women walked like dey was queens!"

Girls sold a women's suffrage paper along the line of march. The suffragettes wanted Jane Addams to run as a candidate for president, to which Jane Addams merely responded that "women could take a joke, but men could not."

And although women could not vote, that did little to diminish their political fervor. The Progressive campaign of 1912 headquartered on Washington Square West, where Frances Perkins met the silk-stockinged elite of New York City, as well as settlement house and charity workers, most of whom were Progressives. Here she undoubtedly saw a great deal of Paul C. Wilson, who was working around the clock on John Purroy Mitchel's campaign for mayor.

In early summer Frances went to Baltimore for the Democratic convention. She mentioned seeing Franklin D. Roosevelt there; he seemed to be "still looking down his nose through the pince-nez." His wife, Eleanor, had joined the Consumers League and investigated the working conditions of department store girls and dress factory workers. Rexford Guy Tugwell later wrote that "Frances Perkins was among those—perhaps the principal one—who had been responsible for Eleanor's education in welfare matters." Actually, Eleanor Roosevelt also did Junior League and settlement-house work in the slums, and enjoyed excellent powers of observation. Both women reflected the generativity that comes from association with active, alert, responsive people.

For example, Frances belonged to a group called the Children of Light. This informal association functioned as a significant springboard for individual action. Speaking for the members, which included Florence Kelley, "that mother of us all," and Mary Drier, Frances explained, "That cordial, interlocking group of minds has meant much to all of us who have been welcomed to the inner conference of those who were trying to decide the best thing to do this year, and next year, and the year after, for the cause of industrial reform." Speaking for herself, she humbly acknowledged "And so, in a strange way, I am the product of that group's thought and hope, and all I have ever done is, after all, what they have done, too."

* * * * *

While it may have seemed that the social workers lived, ate, and breathed little beyond their areas of specialization, most of them were educated broadly and functioned intellectually and culturally as well as humanistically. Their awareness of the world about them diminished little, despite their fixation with poverty, politics, and injustice. Actually, in the Village before the twenties, artistic interests were *de rigeur,* and the habitues critically dissected creative writing, music, architecture, and art work as readily as they pronounced cures for the world's ills.

For some time, modern art was an enigma to Frances, but to an old friend she confessed, "Do you know how I discovered modern painting? From looking at Survage's *Landscape with a Leaf.* What a picture! The moment I saw it I was exactly like somebody who—well, after playing five-finger exercises for months, he suddenly finds music."

She undoubtedly tagged along with friends to Stieglitz's "291," which showed the most daring and experimental art of the time. A revolutionary Armory show opened on February 17, 1913. She probably felt an affinity for this anarchical art show because it displayed the Massachusetts's pine-tree flag of the Revolutionary War to symbolize the fight for artistic independence from European influence. Not surprisingly, Georgia O'Keefe was her favorite artist. O'Keefe symbolized "the new woman," free from economic or artistic dependence on men. Her highly individualistic, lyrical art style dramatically portrayed the creative forces of nature. Art shows in the Village, one after another, added to the pleasures of sidewalk promenading.

* * * * *

As executive secretary and principal factory investigator of the Committee on Public Safety, Frances represented some of the best minds and most public spirited citizens of New York City. In addition, she sought expert advice from the engineers of the large casualty companies who knew something of public safety in economic terms. She instituted a suit against the state department of labor, with Col. Henry L. Stimson, later secretary of state, as her attorney in the charges. This contributed to the legislative enactment of many bills proposed to prevent fire and accidents in industry.

She wrote an article on "the fire bills" urging support by "all thinking citizens" for the five bills recommended by the New York State Factory Investigating Commission. It appeared in the social workers' journal, *The Survey,* on February 22, 1913.

Interestingly enough, the following month's issue included an article by Paul C. Wilson of the New York Bureau of Municipal Research. Entitled "Governor Sulzer's Financial Program," it credited the governor for recognizing the need for immediate reorganization of the financial methods of the state. However, Wilson criticized as hazy the bill introduced to implement this. He hoped that the head of the new state department of efficiency and economy could improve on it so that it would be "in harmony with modern methods of public administration."

Later that year the governor faced impeachment proceedings for diverting campaign funds for his own use. The "dirty politics" involved plus evidence of New York City police corruption, contributed to the election of the city's reform mayor, John Purroy Mitchel.

Mitchel's natural talents for swift, decisive action and his ability to combine efficiency with democracy brought him many adherents. Paul Wilson was one of the many "high hat experts" Mitchel relied on instead of the customary district leaders and their allies.

Frances Perkins's relationship with Paul Caldwell Wilson at this time is mentioned nowhere in print. She knew him, as did many of her close friends—Sinclair Lewis, Mary Heaton Vorse, Henry Bruere—and she knew his reputation. He had many of the qualities that she admired intensely, although Robert Moses, Paul Wilson's associate, felt their temperaments were radically different. One of their mutual friends, Alice Barrows, evaluated Paul as one of "the most intelligent, honest and able men I ever knew." Born in Chicago, he attended Dartmouth College and the University of Chicago. His American parentage stemmed from early settlers to Pennsylvania who came from Scotland

and England. With his impeccable credentials and his brilliance, it seemed tendentious to fault him for overzealousness in his work activities.

No one spoke of Paul Wilson then or later without referring to his exceptional good looks and graciously charming social manners. This handsome man was also the most outstanding bridge player in New York City. Frances neither knew how to play bridge, nor cared to learn—but learn she did, though never with any degree of skill.

That he proposed marriage to Frances in the spring of 1913 is a matter for conjecture. The only certainty is that she felt impelled to "get away from it all," that she again needed to appraise her situation, to temporize with regard to the direction for her life. She took a trip to England.

In 1933 Sinclair Lewis's *Ann Vickers* topped the best-seller lists. John Franklin Carter, the "Unofficial Observer of the New Dealers," read much of Frances Perkins into Lewis's piece of fiction on modern American women, particularly social workers. To Carter, she was "the woman who could not be content in the presence of the social shambles and economic abattoirs conducted by the hairy-chested industrialists and justified by their lean-lipped economists."

And others who knew of Frances's trip to England in 1913 could readily visualize Frances as the thirty-ish woman visiting England as a tourist, but inevitably attracted to other aspects of English life:

> She prowled through the factory towns about Manchester (not quite so sordid as Pittsburgh), the modern rayon factories in Surrey, the missions along Commercial Road, the docks at Poplar. . . . And because she saw the workday England, the boilers and coal-pits and dynamos behind the theater lights, she loved it, and felt vastly more at home in it than in shattered abbeys. . . .Like her own America, it had problems; it fought; it was alive.

Sinclair Lewis knew other social workers—Frances would hardly refer to settlement houses as "cultural comfort stations" as did Ann Vickers. Lillian Wald, in a kind understatement, was unable to find anyone who recognized his description of a settlement house. Nor had Frances worked in a prison. But some of the vacation scene where Ann reflects on her career smacks of her introspective nature: "She would never again be thirty, sitting alone in spring sunshine on a Sussex hillside, independent of everyone so far as a human being could be, free to choose jobs and landscapes to suit herself."

In her own record of the visit to England, Frances did little more than bare her predilections for people-watching.

I brought back memories of widespread human misery so vivid that they have remained with me through all the crowded years since 1913. At that time, poverty was an inescapable part of the British scene. People who were cold because they had only rags to wear were seen on the streets—men and women with bare feet or feet wrapped in old bits of cloth, and with tattered garments pinned and tied together. One often looked into pinched, white sodden faces. More than once I saw little children staring ravenously through bakeshop windows. Drunkenness was a familiar part of the picture, for desperate people will often spend a few coppers for liquor and forgetfulness rather than for inadequate food.

Frances came home, still undecided. What was she aiming at? Did her career in social work take precedence in her life, or did she have rather normal yearnings for marriage and a family? She could not readily free herself of conventional, traditional views regarding married women working outside of the home when they did not have to do so.

Probably the most private part of Frances Perkins's life was her marriage to Paul Caldwell Wilson. It took place in the impressive old Grace Episcopal Church on Broadway and Ninth Street on September 26, 1913. The Rev. Charles Slattery officiated.

Thereafter one item, repeated like a broken record, appeared in virtually every profile and news story about Frances Perkins: "She retained her maiden name so as not to embarrass her husband with her political activities."

Frances provided one other emphatic explanation in a letter scrawled across three sheets of business-size stationery, addressed to her alma mater:

121 Washington Place
N.Y.C.
May 22, –14

To the Alumnae Secretary,
    Mt. Holyoke College

Dear Miss Secretary:
I think that you must be the person who is responsible for the incorrect way in which all mail pertaining to alumnae matters is addressed to me.

Letters from women who do not know me by sight and who cannot possibly know of or care about my marriage come addressed to me under my husband's name. I therefore think that some meddlesome person has told you to change my name on your records. I do not use my husband's name either socially or professionally and it makes a great deal of trouble and annoyance to have my mail so addressed, as it in that case does not reach me directly.

Please change your record so that it reads

Miss Frances Perkins
121 Washington Place
N.Y.C.

Sincerely yours,

Frances Perkins

In their book on Al Smith based partially on Frances Perkins's memoirs, the Josephsons tender an explanation of her adamant stand on retaining her name that has overtones of Charlotte Perkins Gilman— and of greater credibility:

Having reached the age of thirty-three, she felt it was only right to retain her own name for professional purposes, on the ground that she had begun to make a place for herself as Frances Perkins, whereas if she were to call herself Mrs. Wilson she would be set back in her career.

At the time of their marriage, Paul Wilson's career, which her name retention purported to protect, still centered on the New York Bureau of Municipal Research. One of many organizations supported by Mrs. E. H. Harriman, it had functioned as a fact-finding agency dedicated to reform since 1906. Most of the staff people had worked for the Association for Improving the Condition of the Poor. Henry Bruere, a University of Chicago professor who formerly handled welfare work for the McCormacks of Chicago, joined the New York Bureau of Municipal Research in 1911 and now headed the organization. Both he and Paul Wilson, a former student of Bruere's, supported the mayoral campaign of John Purroy Mitchel.

They numbered among the coterie of brilliant, industrious people Mitchel brought into city government after the November elections. Dr. Henry Moskowitz, whom Frances knew well, became commissioner of market: Henry Bruere became chamberlain of the city; Paul Wilson, as secretary to the mayor, handled financial and budgetary matters; the forceful Robert Moses, who ended up transforming New York into a state of public parks and beaches, was a researcher.

According to one close family friend, Paul Wilson, now thirty-seven with almost a decade of self-punishing hard work behind him, possessed an "abrupt rather crochety manner," which she believed "covered a sensitiveness and quick intuition about people and situations." Frances became dependent on her husband's excellent counsel, and he found satisfaction in providing it.

None of Frances's activities abated. As an investigator for the Factory Investigating Commission she traveled from one end of the state to the other, frequently in the company of the commissioners, including Samuel Gompers of the AFL and Senator Robert Wagner and Assemblyman Al Smith. The data they collected on man's inhumanity to man grew voluminously. They also welcomed reports on industries with working conditions favorable to employees. They sought out hard economic facts to substantiate the management-motivating argument that desirable conditions, including safe machinery, benefitted industry even more than labor.

One of the commissioners, a real estate broker, disagreed with many of Frances's views, particularly those having to do with the number of square feet necessary for each employee to work in safety. "She is a professional agitator," he exclaimed, a label picked up by others who objected to her stance.

It was a stance strengthened by a sense of injustice when the owners of the Triangle Shirtwaist Factory, indicted on first and second degree manslaughter charges, were acquitted by a jury. During 1914, out-of-court settlements of twenty-three suits brought against them resulted in an average payment of seventy-five dollars per dead employee.

In 1914 she also found herself touted as a "revolutionist," a term other antagonists hurled at her through the years. This title harked back to a feminist meeting at which she and others addressed a large gathering in "New York's overgrown soapbox" known as Cooper Union.

One writer derisively reported that the other speakers did not know what they were talking about and delivered a dismaying "mass of quixotisms." But, according to the story, Frances Perkins had no doubts at all—"It meant REVOLUTION." Direct quotes from her speech proved it: "Feminism is revolution, and I am a revolutionist. I believe in revolution as a principle. It does good to everybody."

If these were Frances Perkins's words, it can be surmised that they reflected the Ambrosial Harper Scotch Liqueur from Leith with which she, her husband Paul, and a friend, Henry Bruere's brother Robert, had celebrated just before the meeting. The occasion became a part of the repertoire of old family reminiscences.

That summer the Wilsons had a full household. Their mutual friend, Mary Heaton Vorse, with a new baby, "little Joe," moved in so that she could be near her husband, Joe O'Brien, while he was in Presbyterian Hospital.

They continued where they had left off in their all-night discussions, on Cape Cod, of child abuse, inadequate schools, and the new administration. Now they also fulminated over the war in Europe, whether or not the United States needed to prepare for it. Mary Heaton Vorse remembered: "We still believed that one could vote down a world conflagration, and make motions about hurricanes. We believed . . . that it was in the power of individuals and nations to decide whether to take part in a world upheaval or not."

Paul Wilson and Frances Perkins had many other visitors. Some came with their problems. Alice Barrows, excited about a work-study-play plan to relieve school congestion, solicited Paul Wilson's help in dealing with a recalcitrant board of education. She apparently knew Wilson well:

He hated pretense and bombast but was quickly responsive to a straight-forward approach. Knowing that what he would want were facts, simply stated, I told him briefly about Wirt's [the educational consultant] diffi-culties. After a few questions, he gave a little grunt of impatience and said, "All right, I'll attend to it."

Later that year, Lillian D. Wald was appointed to the committee set up by Henry Bruere to investigate unemployment problems. Frances Perkins worked with her on this, and she would later rely extensively on the procedures recommended for a community attack on the problem: "fact finding; stabilization of seasonal industries; adequate public employment service; public works planned ahead to take up the slack when private industry sags; unemployment insurance; vocational guidance and training; relief; and emergency employment." Much of Frances's future work incorporated these concepts. She observed that year the futility of demonstrations by the unemployed. The great mass meetings such as the International Workers' Conference in Carnegie Hall yielded little more than ill will and antagonisms based on misunderstandings. The meetings at Union Square won for the unemployed fines, prison sentences, and the brutal bludgeoning of participants.

* * * *

In 1915 Frances was, as she put it, "literally and figuratively 'on the run.' " She felt that the New York State Legislature was incredibly reactionary and seemingly bent on repealing or amending to death most of the labor laws she had spent the previous five years getting on the statute books. At the time she wrote her class letter, the legislature had six days to go before adjournment. All she and her fellow reformers hoped for that year was to hold their own so that "perhaps women and children in New York will still have the little protection against long hours, fire hazards, and unsanitary conditions which we've been able to get." The Factory Investigating Commission made its last report to the legislature with recommendations that went beyond those in the thirty-two bills it had managed to pass since the Triangle Fire of 1911. The 1915 legislature did not act on the recommendations that year, or the next, or the next.

At times, Frances felt that she worked at nothing but the myriad details that went into making up state law. She found herself closely tied to a work routine, but she had yet to lose her ability to expand the hours to fit in those activities that interested or enriched her personally.

In 1915 people still felt war could be averted. Notable among these was her friend and mentor, Florence Kelley. With her other Friends of the Light, Frances took part in the Woman's Peace Movement.

Frances and her husband both furthered the interests of aspiring artists. On one occasion they held an auction to help a young writer stave off starvation. And she was "keeping up with the post-Impressionist school of painting"; this probably meant in terms of understanding the newest artists under discussion and the refinement of her own skills with palette and brush.

Frances's alliances suggest something of the multi-faceted inconsistencies of her character. She would later be shocked and indignant over the extramarital activities of some of the men in Roosevelt's administration, yet she took pride in working on behalf of Isadora Duncan's dancing school. Isadora Duncan epitomized modern, unconventional womanhood, by among other things, bearing two children out of wedlock.

Frances Perkins enjoyed decorating and periodically rearranging her home at 121 Washington Place. She added to its charm with fine colonial furniture and immaculate upkeep.

On the care and nurture of her husband, she feared that her school friends suspected the worst. "I know that many of you believe in your hearts that I live in a sleeping car and let my husband eat delicatessen food out of a paper bag. No, really I don't," she assured them. "I have a comfortable, though old fashioned house, and there always appear to be plenty of competent professional household workers who want to take care of the house for me and my man." She really felt that she had never enjoyed as many creature comforts before in her life, although she admitted to never knowing in advance what she was having for dinner or when her workroom would be cleaned up.

Like many New Yorkers, she had a little country place. She called it "a shack in the country," and because it was close in, she could get there every Saturday afternoon. Long Island, flat and unkempt with scraggly sumac and shrub oak, hardly compared with the rocky, rolling Maine shoreline, but on the edge of Long Island Sound she could enjoy the miles of beach, ocean waters tame enough for real swimming, and the isolation. In the winter she walked in the woods; in the summer she swam. This, she felt, kept her alive "to the part of life that dies so quickly in this dirty, foolish, town."

In 1916 Frances became pregnant and cut back on her expenses and activities. A Waverly Place neighbor, Floyd Ward Johnstone, remembered how they "used to budget their income to see if there was any chance for luxury—and the many interesting almost all night talks over the problems of the world. . . ."

New neighbors, George Caylor and his wife, Tema, moved into 125 Washington Place, just a few doors from Frances's place. The relationship with the Caylors was casual; "they sometimes passed the time of day on the street," but that was all. By the time the Caylors moved away in 1919, George suspected something was amiss, and noted, "It was from this time on that Frances Perkins resented intrusion."

Susanna was born on December 30, 1916. The *Mount Holyoke Alumnae News* somehow printed this announcement in April, 1917: "BIRTH—To Frances (Perkins) Wilson, a daughter, Penelope, born in January, 1917."

Shortly thereafter Frances undoubtedly penned one of her scathing letters to the alumnae association. The next issue in July made haste to publish an emendation:

Frances Perkins has for some time been doing work of great public importance in her position as Executive Secretary of the Committee on Safety of the City of New York.

She has never assumed the name of her husband, Mr. Wilson, and therefore the form in which the notice of her daughter's birth appeared in our April issue was a deplorable mistake. The name of the daughter will be Perkins-Wilson until she is grown. Then she will adopt either name that she chooses, "when she first registers to vote."

The last quotation might have seemed unduly optimistic to Mount Holyoke alumnae scattered around the country, but the following year women in New York were granted the right to vote in New York State.

On April 19, 1917, the United States entered the "War to End Wars." Frances puttered around her home; she enjoyed her child. But being a mother did not mean she could abnegate her responsibility to her country. She accepted the position of executive director of the New York Council of Organization for War Service. She coordinated the activities of various groups and agencies, demonstrated her talents as an administrator, and authored a monograph, *Women as Employees.*

Years later, Paul Wilson wrote to their friend, Howard Brubacker, then in the editorial department of *New Yorker* magazine, ". . . I was so excessively busy day & night from late 1905 through 1918 that many interesting people & matters were neglected. . . ." One of these neglected matters was his health; he became a "chronic invalid." Many people conjectured on his condition, everything from acute alcoholism to a complete nervous breakdown, but Frances, even in letters to close friends, merely referred to "his being ill," or gave an optimistic prognosis: "His own sympathetic and friendly personality is beginning to assert itself over his own troubles."

Frances Perkins liked to remember "those happy hopeful fruitful days when we were all young." If there was a grimness to those days, she didn't say.

VI

Pounding the Democratic Drum

January 1919. "FANNY PERKINS, FORMER WORCESTER GIRL GETS $8000 JOB AND STARTS A RUMPUS" proclaimed the headlines in her hometown newspaper. A provocative story followed:

> A Worcester girl, Fanny Perkins, has set New York State topsy-turvey. She didn't mean to do it.
>
> She is presumably the innocent cause of the political turmoil of which Gov. Alfred Smith is the center, but his naming her as state industrial commissioner at $8000 a year, started something that voters in the state are clamoring to bring to a finish.
>
> The job is the highest salaried that any woman has had under the state government, and it may mean a fight. It is the first appointment of a woman under the new political conditions in the state, and it has already thrown a monkey wrench into the works.

Frances certainly saw the industrial commissionership as an opportunity—the unprecedented salary almost quadrupled the national average family income. But she feared the opportunity might be construed negatively by Florence Kelley. In their work for improved legislation and enforcement through the Consumers League and the public safety commission, they were critical and objectively aloof from government. This position would make her a part of the government.

The newly-elected governor, Al Smith, promised that he would defer announcing her appointment publicly until she discussed it with her employer. Frances arranged to meet Mrs. Kelley at Pennsylvania Railroad Station, where she was due to catch a train. They took a table in the restaurant, and a tremulous Frances blurted out the news. She remembered that Mrs. Kelley's "eyes opened wide, her mouth opened, tears ran down her cheeks as she said in a shaky voice, 'God's holy name be praised!' "

Objections to the appointment came primarily from the Associated Manufacturers and Merchants and from the state Federation of Labor. The manufacturers' representatives claimed that if Frances Perkins succeeded Louis Wiard, a manufacturer, to the position "the employers of the State will be in the same position that we once were as a country—taxation without representation." Labor representatives, with two of their own already on the industrial commission, argued that she simply was not the right person to interpret the compensation laws and labor problems that come before the commission. They avoided mentioning her sex.

A belligerent governor defended her. "The appointment of Miss Perkins will be confirmed all right, make no mistake about that!" With perhaps some political sensitivity for the newly-franchised members of her sex (New York women won the right to vote in 1918; in 1920, women could vote in every state), he emphatically declared: "There are millions of working girls in this state and the industrial commission for that reason, ought to have a woman in its membership. Having settled the question of appointing a woman, I could think of no one better fitted by knowledge and ability than Miss Perkins."

The opposition dealt the final blow, delivered by Republican Senator G. F. Thompson. He claimed Frances Perkins did not represent employers, employees or the women of the state. "She represents nothing except agitation," he railed. "In fact agitation has been so closely linked with her name that she would not change it when she got married!"

All of the Democrats present at the February eighteenth legislative session confirmed Frances Perkins's appointment, joined by thirteen Republican senators; the final vote was thirty-six to fourteen in favor.

One peccadillo still needed absolution. The governor had asserted, "No politics whatever entered into this appointment. I do not even know whether Miss Perkins is a Democrat or a Republican." A Democratic district leader checked the records and promptly reported to the governor that Miss Perkins was not registered as a Democrat.

When the governor called her to his office, she admitted the same thing herself. According to the Josephsons' account, Smith persuaded her that being an independent had its disadvantages, that one could accomplish more with the backing of a party organization. She appreciated the fact that the New York Democrats were "doing those things" that the reformers believed in, though she suspected that they wished the reformers would be more "reasonable."

Frances came from a definitely Republican family and conservative town; she openly admired former President Theodore Roosevelt, a Republican. When people over the years asked how she came to be a Democrat—assuming she was—she extolled the virtues of Al Smith or Franklin D. Roosevelt or a particular piece of legislation for which the Democrats were responsible, whatever suited her fancy.

Picasso once said that "Art is a lie that makes us realize truth." Frances's fabrications may well have been an art form rather than a reflection of her Hull House "fulin' "-the-press orientation. Unfortunately, unless she spelled it out, few people caught the symbolic meaning of her message.

For example, following her 1936 Roosevelt campaign speech to Holyoke Democrats, Frances answered a reporter's question on why she was a Democrat with some nonsense about how, when she was a student at Mount Holyoke, another student, Amy Moore, organized a Democratic club and offered her a chance to pound the drum in the Democratic band. "That, and that alone, was the reason why she first espoused the Democratic party, she smiled,"—and so the matter-of-fact reporter reported.

This particular version of her conversion to the Democratic party, unlike many of Frances's stories, does not appear in print repeatedly. Undoubtedly, it was a spur-of-the-moment improvisation. Her alliance with the Democratic party enabled her to spread her own gospel. And that she did. On this particular occasion, instead of the expected "rip-snorting attack on the Republican party, or a flag waving defense of the New Deal," her animated talk extolled "the essential divinity of the common man." It stressed the necessity of making it possible "for people outside the main stream of production to share in the benefits of modern civilization." It condensed Dr. Simon Nelson Patten's lectures into a rousing seventy-minute speech.

In effect, Frances believed that politics was merely a means to an end, and the basis for her membership in one party rather than another was little more than happenstance.

Not everyone countenances non-partisanship. When asked to endorse Frances, a Mrs. Grovenor Allen demurred:

> I can think of nothing I would rather do than add to the love concerning Frances Perkins. But alas, she escapes me! She is the most impolitical person in the world. . . . She told me that she was not even an enrolled Democrat when he [Smith] appointed her.

Her retarded development as a political partisan in no way impaired her relationship with two highly significant Democratic women, Mary (Molly) W. Dewson and Belle Lindner Moskowitz.

Frances knew Harlem-born Mrs. Moskowitz as a settlement worker on the East Side of Manhattan. She also knew Mrs. Moskowitz's first husband, architect Charles H. Israels, who worked with her on the public safety commission just before his death. Now married to Dr. Henry Moskowitz, commissioner of markets during Mayor John Purroy Mitchel's administration, Belle Moskowitz was the saint of the immigrant Jewish ghetto, the patron saint of aspiring, gifted Jews, and the hard-driving down-to-earth saint who had personally adjusted over 10,000 labor disputes relating to the dress and shirtwaist trades. She had also been a prominent Republican until attracted to the social ideals of cocky Al Smith.

Her overweight frumpy-housewife appearance, with dark hair twisted into a knot on top of her head, belied her intellectual acumen. After Frances Perkins introduced her to Al Smith, Belle made some constructive suggestions for running his campaign, joined the campaign headquarters staff, and, after his election, moved to Albany where she became the governor's most trusted advisor. According to Lela Stiles (who worked for eight years with former journalist Louis Howe, subject of *The Man Behind Roosevelt*) the newspaper men would say "Let's go up and see Belle and see what's on Al's mind today."

Governor Smith cautiously went along with her brainstorm, the Reconstruction Commission, to reorganize state government to meet the post-World War I needs of its citizens. The legislature—Republicans constituted the majority in both houses—demonstrated its disinclination to go along by failing to vote appropriations for the commission. Regardless, members of the commission worked without pay and in some cases, raised funds for a staff. Frances Perkins already knew a number of them personally: Abram Elkus and Bernard Shientag, who were on the Factory Investigation Commission, and Robert Moses from Mayor John Purroy Mitchel's office. One of their tax reform measures saved the state millions of dollars.

Frances Perkins's principal activities on the industrial board had her reporting to the chairman, John Mitchell, one of the first members of the United Mine Workers and its president since 1898. The other commissioners were Edward P. Lyon, James M. Lynch, Henry D. Sayer and, serving as secretary of the commission, Edward W. Buckly. The dynamic, idealistic attorney, Bernard L. Shientag, served as counsel to Frances Perkins, judging by a memo he wrote her in 1919.

The industrial commission acted as the final arbiter of justice in Workmen's Compensation cases. The original act, which passed in 1913 with help from the Factory Investigating Commission, had been emasculated by the 1915 legislature. Now through the governor's direct intervention, a strong measure passed prescribing that cases be handled by the Workmen's Compensation Bureau. Frances recalled cases handled without the intervention of the bureau in which workers were sorely cheated. When she questioned one worker as to why he had accepted a picayune settlement that hardly reflected the permanent nature of his work-related injuries, he naively explained, "The insurance company people were all educated, and so I thought they had to be honest." With the new law, equitable judgments could be made.

Matters of equity frequently required Solomon-like judgments when parties to a dispute were close to the point of explosion. Commissioners would be assigned the delicate task of defusing these bomb-like altercations. Frances hardly had her shoes dampened as commissioner when Governor Smith reinforced his conviction as to her suitability by naming her to settle a vicious strike at the Rome Brass and Copper Company in upstate Oneida County's leading industrial town, Rome.

In relating the experience, Emily Smith Warner, Governor Smith's eldest daughter, notes that Frances Perkins did not yet enjoy universal fame—that was yet to come. The town was in a turmoil. Caches of explosives were on hand, as well as state militia.

> The company officials with whom she was now called upon to deal, however, were shocked at the very thought of discussing their labor problems with a woman. However, there was nothing else they could do, and after Miss Perkins had presided at a meeting to which she had called representatives of both the company and the union, one of the company's officers was so impressed by her ability that he asked the company's attorney to learn from Father "where he found that woman."

Frances also found herself responsible for suggesting and developing legislative proposals for Governor Smith. She looked for information and guidance from the research director of the National Consumers League, Mary (Molly) W. Dewson.

Wellesley-educated Mary W. Dewson, a tall, rather stately woman, possessed an outward serenity that covered a controlled whirling-dervish mind.

Although their personalities didn't exactly mesh—both women were big enough to discount this—Frances Perkins looked to Mary Dewson as an invaluable resource person:

> I conferred with her constantly on legislation, not only with regard to wages but with regard to the hours of labor for women, child labor legislation, Workmen's Compensation, corrections and additions to the basic factory act of the State of New York, and other such matters; in particular, industrial homework or "sweatshop work" as we called it, was then a highly abused form of manufacturing in New York State.

Frances particularly appreciated Mary Dewson's clear thinking. "She reasoned logically from the existence of very low wages and the low purchasing power and low standard of living—to poor health, poor education, and a poor life." Frances ascribed to her the broad humanitarian philosophy shared by many of Frances's associates.

* * * *

Adolph Berle, characterized as "the hope of the Social Gospel of creating a Kingdom of God on earth," lived at the Henry Street Settlement and Frances spoke with the ardent young idealist from time to time. He made a special point of introducing her to James T. Shotwell, a professor with an overriding, proselytizing conviction regarding the merits of the International Labor Organization. Professor Shotwell described the genesis of the organization, and explained that its name was a misnomer: "What was created was an international economic organization to deal with labor problems."

The ILO actually derived from the International Association for Labor established by private individuals in Brussels in 1897. The group was successful because of the conviction "that they were serving a lofty aim which would benefit humanity." It aligned itself with the League of Nations, and initially membership in the ILO was a prerequisite for membership in the League.

Professor Shotwell eagerly argued for America's participation in the

ILO. Samuel Gompers of the AFL numbered among the proponents, but despite his professed "voluntarism," the business community failed to see "... that labor had declared its readiness to cooperate with capital in a new enterprise on a world-wide basis, and in a way which promised advantage to capital through the elimination of unfair competition and the increased buying power of backward nations."

Employers, however, denounced the organization as under Bolshevistic influence, even though Russia didn't belong. Members of Congress labeled it "revolutionary." The U.S. Department of State purportedly feared even responding to official letters from the League Secretariat, let alone the ILO.

Professor Shotwell won an enthusiastic supporter to the concept of an international agency setting standards and holding up ideals of sound, humane labor conditions on a worldwide basis. Frances would end up being credited with bringing the United States into the International Labor Organization.

But in 1919 when the ILO held its first meeting in Washington, D.C., chaired by the first secretary of labor, William B. Wilson, it was viewed by some as a "pitifully futile attempt to enlist American interest in at least one activity of the League of Nations."

Industrial physician Dr. Alice Hamilton recalled that the meeting "was distinctly uncomfortable for us Americans. The hostility toward our foreign guests was not even thinly disguised and no amount of cordiality in private could make up for the rudeness of many of the public speeches."

To Frances, the ILO's poor initial reception represented a challenge. In one way or another, in talks and press releases, Frances would bring up the subject: "The International Labor Office, established under Article 13 of the Treaty of Versailles, probably symbolizes the most important and significant change in world conceptions of international relations that has been written into the documents and archives in several hundred years." She was paving the way.

* * * * *

In 1920 Al Smith again ran for governor, and undoubtedly Frances was recruited by Belle Moskowitz to help with the campaign. But the Republican presidential candidate, Warren G. Harding, and his vice-president, Calvin Coolidge, brought a preponderance of Republican victories in their sweep across the country. Judge Nathan L. Miller took over the next two-year term of office as governor of New York State.

As is the case with office holders and their political appointees after their term of office, Frances Perkins had to find employment elsewhere. Because of her interest and earlier experiences, she accepted the position of director of the Council on Immigrant Education. At Hull House in Chicago and during her two years in Philadelphia, she frequently dealt with highly exploitable, eager-to-Americanize immigrants.

Postwar immigration had grown from 24,600 in 1919, to 246,000 in 1920, to 652,000 in 1921. Many of the immigrants landed in that great "melting pot," New York City, at a time when industrial conditions were less than favorable. These alien workers undermined the wages of other workers; compared to their former circumstances, starvation wages seemed high. Many were single men who competed for a few years with men who headed households, then returned to the "old country" with the savings that stemmed from frugal, celibate living.

In May, 1921, Congress enacted the first law since the 1882 Oriental Exclusion Act to limit the number of people that could immigrate from the countries of the Old World. But the impact of the flood tide was already felt.

Frances Perkins was concerned with the assimilation of these foreigners into the ways of a strange new world. They often drifted to the sections of the city that had become enclaves of various nationalities: the Scandinavians in Bay Ridge, Brooklyn; the Germans in Yorkville, upper Manhattan; the Italians on the East Side of Manhattan; the Irish in Gramercy Park, Manhattan; the Jews of various national origins in Flatbush or Boro Park, Brooklyn, or parts of the Bronx, or lower Manhattan; the Poles in sections of Staten Island.

A humanistic progressive era had been superseded by a vicious, name-calling, frenetic national consciousness. Large corporations such as United States Steel stirred up racial hatred so that workers would not attempt to unionize.

Again, Frances was in a hotbed. The bigotry of her beloved country sickened her. Someone had to battle with this monster, and somehow she was in the midst of the fray, as she would be again and again on behalf of the immigrants to this country.

There were some working *against* improvements in the human condition, or at least this was the evaluation given of the suffragists who were fighting for legislation to bring about full equality for women. The social workers who had crusaded for the women's vote had also fought the battle for women's protection. They feared that equality mandated by law would rescind the laws and codes that had improved the wage-earning woman's lot to some extent. Even after men received the same protection, these women looked at laws governing marriage, child support, and the crime of rape, and determined that equality meant disaster for the vast majority of women.

Frances Perkins, representing the National Consumers League, spoke vigorously against the blanket equality bill proposed by the National Woman's Party. The very exclusive Southampton Colony of Long Island gave a tea in her honor, during which she outlined the dangers of equality in terms of "the poor working girl." This type of audience—where women derived their status from the position or wealth of their husbands—responded to her humanistic arguments.

* * * * *

In 1922 the Women's Division of the state Democratic party under Belle Moskowitz pitched in with vigor in Al Smith's campaign for governor. Frances Perkins, Eleanor Roosevelt, and countless others made their voices heard throughout the state. And Smith's gravel-voiced, East Side accents—Frances claimed, "I never heard a sentence that didn't pass!"—made the greatest impact, as he debated everything from the conservation of the state's power resources to the rights of labor and the need for low-income housing. The "Happy Warrior" won the election handily.

Toward the close of 1922, Frances joined with other members of Smith's inner circle, Governor Smith, and his family, in the return to Albany for the inaugural festivities. Back in New York City, where the state department of labor and many other state offices were located, she resumed her position with the industrial board.

Under Governor Miller, the state department of labor underwent a reorganization that prescribed a three-member industrial board; this, together with the department, was under the industrial commissioner, sometimes referred to as the commissioner of labor. Bernard L. Shientag was named industrial commissioner, a choice exemplifying Smith's rejection of the political "spoils system," favoring instead the most qualified person he could attract into state government.

Particularly before and during the legislative session, a group of interested, knowledgeable people—trade union women, Consumers League members, representatives of the Child Labor Committee and the

New York Association for Labor Legislation—would get together with Frances and Bernard Shientag "to plan strategy and tactics with regard to special social and labor legislation in which we were interested." Frances recalled that, as a representative of the Consumers League, Mary Dewson's experiences with the Massachusetts wage boards "largely formed our attitude on minimum wages, wage legislation and administration."

Few women were part of that small segment of the population that enjoyed unprecedented prosperity over the years from 1923 on. The Russell Sage Foundation declared that between 10 and 12 percent of American wageworkers—men and women—were always looking for jobs. Frances believed there was the "dawning realization that unemployment was a constant industrial phenomenon which industrial depressions merely exaggerate and dramatize." She could see the need for permanent, effective employment offices. As she walked along Sixth Avenue, "I saw men lined up before those shabby stairs, searching the battered bulletin boards, and I knew that what was true of New York City was true also of Philadelphia, Chicago, San Francisco and the other great centers of production."

* * * *

In 1924, like many others who graduated from the "youthful revolt" era, Frances joined in the exodus from a gradually deteriorating, honky-tonk Greenwich Village. She now lived at 308 West Ninety-fourth Street, near Central Park, and traveled daily to her offices at 124 East Twenty-eighth Street.

She planned to spend August of 1924 with Susanna in Damariscotta, take a trip to Castine to visit friends, Polly Porter and Mary Dewson. In a note to Mary she wrote that she wanted her to take on a New York Women's City Club job, but admitted that there could be problems "getting on with a bunch of women. . . ."

This last statement reflected stereotyped thinking regarding the inability of women to work well with each other. That Frances picked it up is one of those anomalies reflecting the inconsistencies of human beings. Although for some time Frances had been working almost exclusively with men, she had enjoyed the most positive experiences with Florence Kelley, Lillian Wald, and women in the trade unions. Even as she wrote that statement, as the permanent president of the class of 1902, she was planning the 1925 reunion with her former classmates. To these women she could never express adequately the full measure of her "love and loyalty." Of "Gilly," whom she hoped to appoint as reunion manager, she wrote, "I would always rather have Gilly manage me than anything else I can think of."

Frances lavishly praised women with whom she worked and contributed to their advancement at every opportunity. In the state department of labor she particularly admired Lillian R. Sire for her courage and resourcefulness. Since 1924 Mrs. Sire had been directing the Bureau of Labor Welfare, which functioned as a form of small claims court, seeing to it that workers received the wages due them. People running summer hotels in the Catskills were notorious for failure to pay their help at the end of the summer, claiming financial hardship. Or they paid with bad checks. Unbelievably, while it was a felony to make payment for goods with a bad check, there was no penalty for paying wages with a bad check. This held true right up to September, 1931, when corporations that failed to pay wages were subject to heavy fines—if they were solvent; they usually weren't.

Because the Supreme Court declared federal child labor laws unconstitutional, reformers supported a constitutional amendment that would permit Congress to regulate the labor of children under eighteen. Frances worked with Mary Dewson and Florence Kelley on the ratification committee headed by Grace Childs. They all counted on Governor Smith's endorsement but were sorely disappointed. In his message to the state legislature, the governor recommended a referendum.

Influential opponents—the president of Syracuse First Trust & Deposit Company and the publisher of the Syracuse *Post-Standard* —organized the New York State Citizens Committee for the Protection of Our Home and Our Children. As a result, for the next ten years ratification of the amendment, introduced in every legislative session, failed. This would be another endurance contest in which Frances outlasted her opponents. In Washington, D.C., federal regulation of child labor eventually found favor as a New Deal weapon against depression unemployment.

To the New York Consumers League, it seemed that the opponents to social change had strengthened their forces. At their anniversary meeting in 1925, they reviewed the League's permanent victories over twenty-five years. But Florence Kelley lamented:

... that was before the National Manufacturers Association and the National Industrial Conference Board and many other great national organizations for slowing the national pace got their stride. . . . Everything we undertook was far easier and more glowingly hopeful then than it is now.

Frances Perkins probably felt that Florence Kelley relied too heavily on voluntary reform emanating from middle-class enfranchised women. Mrs. Kelley's epitaph would someday read: "She made everyone brave,"—not the least of these, Frances Perkins, who struck out in her own way to bring about the changes for which the Consumers League fought so diligently.

In 1926 Governor Al Smith appointed Frances the chairman of the industrial board to replace retiring John Higgins. The other two commissioners were Richard Curran of Rochester and Richard Cullen of New York City. Bernard Shientag had also moved on, and she would normally have reported to the new industrial commissioner, James A. Hamilton. Unfortunately—or fortunately—Hamilton, a professional politician, showed a disinclination to become involved in state department of labor matters. Frances assumed many of his responsibilities, including that of reporting to the governor on labor problems. Many of the supernumerary duties she took on were possible because of the invaluable assistance of her secretary, Frances Jurkowitz, called Miss Jay.

One way Frances could bring about the improved labor conditions that the Consumers League had so long tried to achieve was through the voluntary compliance of employers who themselves helped set up the codes with which they agreed to comply.

The commission also determined the policies and principles on which a referee based decisions in connection with claims by employees or employers. If the claimant was dissatisfied with the results of the public hearing, the person could appeal the case. The next hearing would be before the commission, and the judgment of the commission would be accepted as final. The commission covered the entire state. It sat regularly in Buffalo, Rochester, Syracuse, Utica, and Albany, the largest upstate cities, and as needed in the smaller towns. For the commissioners, this meant living out of a suitcase and traveling on trains which, before reaching the terminal in each of these cities, passed through the ugly squalor of neighborhoods with homes unfit for human habitation.

Frances kept in touch with Lillian Wald, writing her periodically for her views on employment agencies or nursing regulations. Whenever

Frances could make it, she would try to get to the Henry Street Settlement for Tuesday dinners, which started at 6:00 P.M. From 7:00 or 7:30 on, the residents discussed various social concerns.

Frances belonged to the exclusive Cosmopolitan Club. The club had a long waiting list, and it was difficult for just anyone to become a member. In November, 1926, Frances wrote to Lillian Wald, asking if she would recommend Mrs. Henry Bruère (Jane) as a candidate. Frances asked that Miss Wald's letter of recommendation emphasize the "candidate's brains and temperament" rather than her good manners and kind heart.

Frances hobnobbed with New York's high society. This was inevitable for a significant member of the governor's circle. Often on her trips to Albany, she stayed overnight at the governor's mansion, enjoying the pleasure of his warm family life. Quite naturally, she was invited to the biggest social event of the year, the spectacular wedding of the governor's eldest daughter, Emily.

Now, as chairman of the industrial board, a cut above her previous "woman's first" in New York State, Frances qualified for occasional local press coverage of her success as a woman. Typically, one female reporter reminded her of the women who complain "from the depths of their overstuffed divans," that they would like to do something, but what is there that they can do? Frances's spontaneous answer: "Doing means digging your nails in and working like a truck horse." She also expressed the conviction: "We make the most of our own opportunities. They seldom make us."

When asked about her next ambition, Frances leaned back in her swivel chair and laughed. "I'm like the young man who enters the ministry. I wait until I'm called. I have never sought a job. The job simply beckons me. It is there to be done, so I do it. Some one must, you know." This phrase became one of her favorites. Actually reporters visited her infrequently as she was doing little more than her job, which is what most people were doing. And that's not newsworthy.

An editor invited Frances to write on opportunities in industrial relations for inclusion in the book *An Outline Of Careers for Women: A Practical Guide To Achievement.* Frances directed the article to ambitious women—and to the less ambitious whom she recognized that ambitious people depended upon:

. . . for those who do not wish to make the effort to achieve the heights—and there are many who with perfect reason prefer to walk in comfortable gardens on level planes rather than to scale the side of the mountain—the rewards and the interest that come with work well done in the less responsible positions in this field are very great.

For those who wish to take the trouble to spend their energies and their youth in the solution of one of the greatest problems in the world—namely, the adjustment of the mechanistic environment of this modern industrial civilization to the needs of human beings—to them lies open one of the greatest of opportunities for human service.

Her alma mater diligently tracked her record as one of its out-standing graduates. At Mount Holyoke's ninetieth commencement in June, 1927, an Honorary Master of Arts degree was bestowed upon her. This also marked the twenty-fifth anniversary of her graduation from Mount Holyoke.

Over the years Frances Perkins had attracted many friends, and also even more admirers. Belle Moskowitz may well have overshadowed Frances in Governor Smith's eyes, but the people Frances worked with, the people who worked for her, and those who observed her in action—and later talked about her performance to others—undoubtedly reacted much as did an expressive reporter in the *Manchester Guardian:*

To watch her at work in her court, whether in New York, Albany, Rochester, Buffalo or Syracuse, reviewing compensation appeal cases is an interesting experience. She is always alert, never off her guard, never inattentive, never out of humor. The people never become mere "cases" to her, and she has an uncanny power of finding the human chink in the professional armour even of an insurance company lawyer. I never sat under a judge who was better at getting at the facts, nor swifter in apprehension of their relevance. She has won every inch of her way to the high office she now holds by service, efficiency, and a remarkable combination of courage and humour.

Her work on the Workman's Compensation Board brought her to the attention of the everyday working man, manufacturers, farmers, and corporation lawyers. The legislative functions of the industrial board gave her visibility to the politicians. Frances was wont to say that she was "just doing a job that needed doing." She sought personal anonymity, but she was made conspicuous by her high-powered industriousness.

* * * * *

In 1928 Bernard Baruch and Joseph P. Kennedy—the "smart money" —were pulling out of the stock market. But that was in no way responsible for the unemployment statistics appearing on the governor's desk as early as February. New York, the largest industrial state in the union, invariably suffered instantaneous and pronounced reactions to shifts in the economy, while other states noticed little. Governor Smith ordered his industrial commissioner, James A. Hamilton, to investigate the possibilities of some form of public works program to relieve the unemployment situation. Probably neither of the men was aware of Frances Perkins's work with Lillian Wald and Henry Bruere on unemployment problems during Mayor John Purroy Mitchel's administration.

Anyway, Frances had her own little imbroglio to contend with. The State Industrial Survey Commission publicly charged the Workmen's Compensation Bureau with "irregularities." The governor invited Professor Lindsay Rogers of Columbia University, as a commissioner under the Moreland Act, to investigate the allegations. They centered on administrative problems—not directly the purview of the industrial board—but Frances Perkins worked with Professor Rogers, and they straightened out what they could.

As the year progressed, unemployment grew more serious, but by the summer of 1928, interest had turned to the forthcoming presidential election. Frances, recruited to campaign on behalf of the popular Al Smith in the first contest for the presidency by a Catholic, learned again, as she had as a youngster visiting Boston, and as a social worker in Philadelphia and New York City, that America the Beautiful could be America the Brutal when it came to unmitigated, unthinking prejudice. In the homes of leading Democrats in the South, she savored the traditional Southern hospitality, but on the podium she winced while standing up to the expletives and decayed vegetables hurled at her. Touring the South with the still beautiful, gracious, former Southern belle, Mrs. Dana (Irene) Gibson, Frances had ample opportunity to observe pathetic, rural shacks and large numbers of people without shoes on their feet. But then, in her beloved New York City over a million people occupied housing that had no indoor toilet facilities, no bathtubs, no light, no ventilation, and no privacy. People did wear shoes, though folded newspapers frequently covered a hole in the sole.

Shaken by the flagellation of her favorite politician, she attended the New York State Democratic convention in Rochester and vividly remembered the phone calls to Franklin D. Roosevelt, who was continuing his physical therapy for polio in Warm Springs, Georgia, urging him to run for governor. The slate that the flamboyant mayor of New York City, James J. Walker, finally presented to the delegates listed Roosevelt for governor and Herbert H. Lehman for lieutenant governor. Lehman, a philanthropic banker, numbered among Lillian Wald's frequent visitors at the Henry Street Settlement.

The letter Frances dashed off to the gubernatorial candidate on October eleventh suggested her father's influence, with its emphasis on Greek philosophy regarding the ideal State:

> Your nomination and acceptance are in the great tradition of Plato—the best of our citizens serving the State at personal sacrifice and for no glory but that of the State. It is a long time since American political life has produced such a situation—and your election, which is certain, will bring a wholesome uplifting quality to our political life. We shall be a better people because of your sacrifice.

She was acutely disappointed when the returns clearly showed that Smith lost the presidential election to Herbert Hoover; however, Roosevelt won the election for state governor by a small margin.

Basically an apolitical person, she felt relieved to have campaign pressures removed so that she could get on with other things. In the course of her work with the industrial board and political campaigning, she came to know many businessmen, some of whom she regarded as even more "enlightened" than the social reformers from whom she had learned so much. The men responsible for making profits to keep their companies going understood the problems from the inside out, and she respected their judgment.

One, George F. Johnson of Endicott-Johnson, she characterized as possessing "a high degree of social spirit"; he regarded his employees as "working partners," and urged that corporations give a yearly report of "stewardship" as expressed in average earnings of the workers. Frances became involved in his plan for arriving at more definite facts on workers' earnings and savings, and the number of individuals supported on earnings. That December she also tucked into her mental file the proposals for reducing unemployment presented at a small meeting at Greenwich House by Gerard Swope, the president of General Electric, little realizing they were virtually a blueprint for the National Recovery Administration (NRA) that would materialize during the next presidential administration.

VII

The Largest State Department of Labor

"It began in 1928..." according to Eleanor Roosevelt and Lorena Hickok in their book, *Ladies of Courage*. Molly Dewson, head of the Democratic women, "practically made a career out of promoting Frances Perkins ... she went to Warm Springs to see New York Governor-elect Franklin D. Roosevelt to suggest he place Frances Perkins in the gubernatorial cabinet as State Industrial Commissioner."

Bess Furman, journalist par excellence, tells the story more graphically:

> Molly said ... "the minute he was elected Governor of New York, I went down to Warm Springs, by Eleanor's arrangement, to ask him to make Frances Perkins the Industrial Commissioner of New York State."

> I said to him: "You have a woman on the Workman's Compensation Board who would make you a marvelous Industrial Commissioner."

> "I think so myself," said Franklin. You know he likes to think he thinks up things himself.

> "Well, I want to back you up on that idea," I said.

Rexford Guy Tugwell, an astute economist and protégé of Dr. Simon Nelson Patten, recorded his impressions:

> Frances Perkins, whose position until then as chairman of the Industrial Board had been a semi-judicial one, was, however, asked to go on with Franklin as Industrial Commissioner—administrative head of the department. This, for Frances, was an unexpected promotion. She was, in fact, his

concession to the feminists and to the welfare workers who had joined in urging that he retain Belle Moskowitz.

Although Franklin D. Roosevelt had been physically crippled some years before by polio, his intellectual radar remained unimpaired. He was probably more attuned to what was being said about Frances Perkins than the *Manchester Guardian* reporter—and his immediate predecessor, Al Smith. Roosevelt noted for the record ". . . I kept sixteen of his eighteen Department heads, but he was furious because I put Miss Perkins in place of old man Hamilton, who had been a complete stuffed shirt as head of the Labor Department. . . ."

Al Smith's rejection of Frances Perkins was in no way meant as disparagement; he sincerely feared that the many men in the department, the industrial commissioner's subordinates, would balk at taking orders from a woman.

Frances Perkins did not number among those fanatical Roosevelt devotees who Robert Moses believed exacerbated the differences between Smith and the new governor. She felt a strong pull on her sense of loyalty to Al Smith—he took a chance on her when she was an unknown woman—and to her dynamic colleague, Belle Moskowitz. She knew very little about this polished, aristocratic, governor-elect's sympathies on social reform.

She actually was better acquainted with his wife, Eleanor, and his mother, Sara Delano Roosevelt, having been invited on occasion to visit them at their picturesque Hyde Park mansion overlooking the Hudson River. Sara Roosevelt, often critical of visitors, apparently warmed up to her daughter-in-law's contemporary; Frances fit in with the upper class quite readily. Eleanor enjoyed Frances's fun-loving spirit and her gift of mimicry and marveled at her ability. They both had husbands incapacitated in very different ways—which may have figured in the direction their lives took.

Franklin Roosevelt invited Frances to visit Hyde Park shortly after the election. Following the customary social preliminaries, he brought up the main purpose of her visit, the industrial commissionership. Frances reflected briefly on her predisposition to continue on the industrial board with its relative freedom from administrative detail. She then warned of the ineptitude and corruption in the state Department of Labor, laying the blame on Democratic party appointments, and unequivocally declaring her incapacity for political pussyfooting. She stressed the need for reorganization of the department so as to eliminate the impediments to the effective handling of workmen's compensation cases and the administration of the factory act. She spoke of improved legislation protecting women and children employees and codes governing mercantile establishments. She made it clear that Al Smith's appointment of a woman to high office ten years before was more courageous than Roosevelt's venture in this direction. One thing she didn't say was "no"; her grandmother's counsel of so long ago—if someone opens a door, go through—was ringing in her ears.

The governor's announcement of her appointment brought plaudits from the League of Women Voters and the Women's Trade Union League, who regarded Frances as "a representative of enlightened and forward-looking citizenship in public life." They faithfully refrained from references to gender. The *New York Times,* on the other hand, commented: "As a representative of her sex in high office, Miss Perkins would have a chance to clean the page sullied by Mrs. Knapp."

Women in politics enjoyed a reputation for scrupulous honesty, with one exception. A former home economics professor and university dean, Mrs. Florence E. S. Knapp, while in office indulged in the common practice of directing some state funds toward her family's well-being. Frances Perkins would have a chance not only to clean the page sullied by one lone woman, but by many men.

Letters of congratulation poured in from all over the country. Frances's able secretary answered them all. In one case a woman from the division of factory inspection struck Frances as somewhat too effusive: "The long trail is ended. The goal is reached." On this note Frances penciled, "Miss J—Heaven is my home!!" The secretary sent out a standard acknowledgment.

That intrepid group, the League of Women Voters—informed lobbyists bucking vested interests in parts of the United States long before citizen action groups became popular—added a little reminder to their congratulatory letter. It seems Frances Perkins let her membership lapse. She promptly wrote a check to cover her dues.

Frances's twelve-year-old daughter, Susanna, was present when Justice Bernard Shientag administrated the oath of office on January 15, 1929. Shortly thereafter nearly 1,000 people honored Frances Perkins at a luncheon in New York City's Astor Hotel. Apparently so moved at the sight of all these well-wishers, she set aside her prepared speech and spoke on the most personal level recorded. In essence, she described herself as symbolizing the efforts of the many who shared "the idea that social justice is possible in a great industrial community," and her own "modest success" as reflecting "the intelligent support, the honest reporting and great good-will" of the people with whom she worked, as well as her "happy personal life." She took exception to Albert Edgar Wiggam's recent statement: "Intelligence is that thing which enables people to get along without education; and education is that thing which enables human beings to get along without intelligence." To have capital and labor working for the social good requires the "marriage of intelligence and education," and she trusted that the state Department of Labor would demonstrate the benefits of this union.

After expressing the desire that industry become a positive social force and asking for help, cooperation, and advice from all, she concluded:

> I will not ask you to share my responsibility. That I know is mine and mine alone. I must decide and I must stand by my decisions. I must be made or I must fall by their wisdom and intelligence. I do ask you to lift up your hearts that I be made both wise and watchful, so that only good shall come. And when I am left alone in the last analysis to make my decisions on important matters, I shall not be alone either, for "I shall lift up mine eyes unto the hills whence cometh my strength and my salvation."

As for the New York State Labor Department, it now had its largest appropriation. She assured the audience, "I am a thrifty woman, and I shall try to spend it thriftily. I shall try to get as much for that money as it is possible to get in service." With undue optimism, the new labor commissioner declared that "industry in general is prosperous and therefore ready to cooperate in developing out of good conditions and high wages and short hours . . . the cure for over-production and under-consumption and poverty and all the industrial ills that go in its train."

After the applause died down, people crowded around the head table, each wanting to shake her hand, to convey good wishes or share a recollection of former days. Quite some time passed before the crowd dwindled, and a little old lady with a shawl covering her bent shoulders timorously emerged. It was Mary of the janitorial staff. For all but two of the past ten years she had cleaned Frances Perkins's office and had quietly adored its occupant. Knowing this, a kind person had given her a ticket to the luncheon. Somewhat embarrassed and confused as the remaining group looked at her, she bowed her head and curtsied.

According to one of the onlookers, "Immediately both of Miss Perkins' hands flew out to that humble, awe-struck figure. 'Why, Mary, how wonderful to see you here!' "

This was the Frances Perkins that the common man on the street—the laborer, the factory girl—would know affectionately as "Ma Perkins of the Poor People's Department." It was the human touch. It was caring. And it was one of many contradictions to Mary Dewson's judgment that old-fashioned New Englanders are incapable of warmth of expression; "by and large they stand aloof." In their reserved relationship, she claimed, they established a cooperation "of the head, not the heart." Shortly after the luncheon, Frances dispatched a note to Mary Dewson:

Dear Molly:

I cannot tell you how much that luncheon which you arranged for me has meant in my life and I want you to know not only that I am grateful for all that you did to make it a success, but that it has given me a new insight into the beauty of loyalty and chivalry between women. How fine it is to play the game together all these years, isn't it?

Never fail to call on me for anything I can do, either for you or for your schemes.

Your faithful and loyal friend,
Frances P.

****

Frances Perkins headed the largest state department of labor in the country. Its 1,800 employees did business with more than 3 million people a year. She was vitally involved with each of its departments: the Workmen's Compensation Bureau, which adjusts claims made in connection with industrial accidents; the Division of Industrial Relations, which mediates employer-employee disputes and strikes and handles claims for unpaid wages of men and women, mostly foreign-born, who otherwise would have been defrauded by their employers; the Division of Women in Industry, which checks on working conditions of women; the Division of Inspection, which enforces laws pertaining to factories and stores, housing, sanitation, fire and accident prevention, and child labor; and the Bureau of Industrial Hygiene, which disseminates information on health hazards in industries and prescribes measures for preventing occupational diseases. Heading this complex of bureaus and divisions was no small job.

In New York State at that time there were about 70,000 manufacturers, 75 percent employing less than 50 persons. This multitude of small businesses, many of them shoestring operations, hired no scientific management consultants, marketing researchers, or paraphernalia commonplace to large industries, of which there were relatively few at that time. Frances therefore saw as a principal function of the New York State Department of Labor that of providing information on the techniques of industrial welfare and human relations. Oftentimes these small factories could not afford the latest in safety equipment, and so Frances provided a "speakers bureau." These lecturers went directly to the factory workers and told them how they could avoid accidents on the job.

Frances had a personal interest in industrial safety and was anxious to find ways to reduce the "human factor" responsible for so many tragic accidents:

> ...People who are exposed to dangerous machinery day in and day out, month after month, during weariness and strain and all the ups and downs of human life, have got to develop some new power of co-ordination which will enable them automatically to carry out their work in a safe way.

Still performing the role of factory investigator, she personally questioned a fifteen-year-old boy who had lost his hand on one of the guillotine paper cutters used by printers. Why had he rested his hand on the table under that cutter? It was absent-mindedness; for a moment he forgot where he was. Frances urged educators and psychologists to work out "simple habit principles which can be taught" so as to reduce the margin of risk in high-speed industry.

In some cases, the nature of the work precluded the possibilities of satisfactory safety measures. The worker breathes in lead and benzol when spraying paint, yet the efforts of industry, in conference with the industrial board, produced no satisfactory solutions to the problem. In the dry-cleaning business, with its constant threat of fire and explosion, the trade association worked out a code providing safety measures with which the industrial board concurred. Forty-five percent of the men engaged in excavation and tunnel work suffered from silicosis, and since the state's labor law exempted this industry because it didn't classify as a factory, cooperative efforts to reduce the dust from rock drilling had to be encouraged. This, too, was achieved through the conference method, with contractors talking to industrial physicians, engineers, and ventilation experts brought in by the Department of Labor in order to arrive at a solution.

The industrial commissioner realized that the canning industry in no way responded to "the big-stick method" of the law. At the beginning of the 1929 canning season, Frances called in representatives of the industry for a major conference. They promised to eliminate child labor from the canning industry, and some of them kept their promise.

Policing all of the industries in the state was an impossibility. Frances knew, "So long as government's only role in industry is the policeman, there is scant hope of permanent results." If only the abused worker would complain. She sent to the newspapers press releases that urged people to write to the industrial commission if they knew of labor law violations. Although her inspection force was undermanned, she promised to take an inspector off routine work to run down special complaints.

But jobs were getting scarce and layoffs common. And a shortened workweek meant no money with which to pay the rent. Many workers did not know the laws that protected them, and even if they did, they would hardly hazard a complaint that might jeopardize their jobs.

The unemployed faced the worst hazard of all: starvation for themselves and their families. In April Roosevelt set into motion the first state-organized system of relief for the poor. It recognized that the magnitude of the problem was making it impossible for communities, on a private charity basis, to care for their own. Relief, of course, was recognized as a temporary emergency measure until other means could be devised to restore purchasing power to the ever-increasing numbers of unemployed without any financial resources at all.

Frances had been keeping tabs on the unemployment situation through Eugene Patton, the state Department of Labor's chief statistician. Week after week the situation worsened. In June she set up an advisory committee chaired by Arthur Young of Industrial Relations Counselors, Inc. to make recommendations for a state public employment service. The federal government's employment offices were a farce. In addition, the Federal Employment Index—an indicator of employment trends—never jibed, as New Englanders would say, with the data collected by the largest industrial state. Some people suspected that President Herbert Hoover "edited" the federal figures before making them public.

Sinclair Lewis wrote of Frances's position that it was "considerably weightier than that of the King of Norway or Sweden or the President of the Irish Free State." This commentary appeared in *Pictorial Review* under the title "Is America a Paradise for Women?" It faced a rebuttal by his most recent wife, Dorothy Thompson, who logically argued that the exceptional case did not make America a paradise for women, to counter Lewis's naming Frances Perkins as evidence of the unlimited professional opportunities open to American women.

Lewis renewed his friendship with Frances and proudly presented his famous journalist wife. They were now living on West Tenth Street in Greenwich Village. Frances recalled, "I had dinner at their apartment several times and they dined with us." (The use of pronouns is interesting, for it suggests that she accepted invitations on her own behalf, but when people came to her own home, they ate with other members of her household. Whether that included her husband or not is speculative; his illness had forced him to give up all forms of employment and he spent long periods hospitalized.)

Frances found Dorothy Thompson to be a most interesting person—more so than Lewis—and they would see each other on occasion in later years at the White House. As rather different, outstanding personalities, they never got to know each other well.

Frances restricted her social life to informal suppers at her apartment with a few friends, or dinner at the home of the governor or some prominent industrialist or financier. She had even less time for her Consumers League and settlement house friends. She worked often until nine or ten at night and felt the need to relax. "For it's only when we're relaxed that the thing way down deep in all of us—call it the subconscious mind, the spirit, what you will—has a chance to well up and tell us how we will go." She enjoyed reading Chaucer with her daughter, "for nothing re-creates one more thoroughly than retasting old experiences with the young." Like many career women who feel guilty about the hours spent away from home, she tried to make precious and special the time devoted exclusively to her child. But invariably she gave vent to the remonstrances common to all parents: "How can you expect to be a civilized member of a civilized world if you don't put your things away?"

* * * * *

A civilized world? On "Black Thursday," October 24, 1929, many people wondered if the world was civilized. Rich people became poor, and the poor? Their number increased, as it had been increasing. Many history books mark Wall Street's long overdue, head-on clash with reality as the beginning of the Great Depression. Frances knew better.

A stock market crash is not a depression. A crash is only the sudden disappearance of the market for stocks and bonds. A depression is the slow disappearance of the market for commodities which stocks and bonds represent—steel, coal, clothing, beef, automobiles, telephone calls, cold cream, houses, books.

There was no instant slump for the wage-earner at the crash, as there was for the security holder. It had been a dividend crash and he had no dividends. The worker did not think, "My Tel and Tel, which I bought at 198 as a real chance is now down to 76. My United States Steel preferred, the best heritage any grandmother could leave me, is now 45."

The stock market crash accelerated the general decline in the economy. A census during the first week of November in Buffalo, a mighty industrial city located near the brink of Niagara Falls, showed that for the 12,331 enumerated males eighteen years old or over, 176 per thousand were unemployed or underemployed, and for better than half, the unemployment had lasted for more than ten weeks. Over the state, factory employment alone from November to December declined by 4 percent. The statistics that Frances Perkins pored over, and that she could articulate as readily as her "human interest" cases, spelled depression in bold letters. That December, usually a high employment month because of the Christmas season, the employment figures were lower than for any December since 1914, when the state Department of Labor first started collecting data.

On January 22, 1930, newspapers across the country headlined President Herbert Hoover's confidence-boosting assertion that gains in employment heralded an economic upswing. Frances read the *New York Times* in her chauffeured car on the way to the office. The cheery news horrified her. Figures for the first fifteen days of January rested on her desk. Something was amiss. Frances visualized the reaction of the unemployed and their families and immediately decided the children should know that their fathers were unemployed through no fault of their own.

She called for Eugene Patton, the chief statistician, and together they projected New York State's figures to the rest of the country. They phoned Ethelbert Stewart, head of the Bureau of Labor Statistics in Washington, D.C., for information. There was no way the president of the United States could be right.

She called in reporters and explained her press release with its conglomeration of statistics to them. On January twenty-third, the newspapers headlined that Frances Perkins had taken "sharp issue" with the president on his claim of a decline in joblessness. She was quoted as questioning how the president and secretary of labor had gotten figures on the "last ten days" in January—from January 10 to January 21; certainly not from her office, which collected data from the country's key industries and manufacturers located in the state. The *New York Times* quoted her as saying, "Whoever supplied the President with his information may have made a telegraphic canvas and reported on the basis of answers from several employment agencies." She illustrated that the taking on of help by silk mills in Binghamton, New York, "is an encouraging sign, but absolutely meaningless in relation to conditions in the State as a whole."

The newspapers included her statistics on the eleven major industries that reported for the first half of January. Only four showed slight (2.8 percent and less) increases in employment. Because of the spurious accuracy of jobless headcounts, she artfully hedged reporters' blunt questions with a run-down on the census in Buffalo.

In Washington, D.C., Senator Copeland of New York read the story in the *New York World* and received unanimous consent to have it reprinted in the *Congressional Record*. At about the same time a phone call came into her office from the governor of the state. A state official does not contradict the president with impunity. But Roosevelt promptly squelched her profuse apologies with an ebullient, "Bully for you! That was a fine statement and I am glad you made it." He also admitted that if she'd asked permission to have the truth published, he might have said no.

President Hoover's well-meaning attempt to "restore confidence"— which he sincerely believed was a first step to recovery—had been foiled by a contumacious woman. No one defended his figures; no one challenged hers. Herbert Hoover's reactions to Frances's expose did not reach her ears. She was, however, reminded of the incident some five years later when the University of California conferred honorary degrees on them both, and Hoover refused to stand next to her for photographers.

U.S. Senator Robert Wagner sought amplification of the newspaper stories. She painstakingly explained, "Our index of manufacturing employment is now based upon the average for the 36 months from January, 1925, to December, 1927, as 100. On this basis the employment index in manufacturing for December, 1929, was 94.2." The department also collected information from twenty-three cities in the state on the number of building plans filed and their estimated cost. From November to December, the number declined insignificantly, but the valuation decreased by more than 50 percent. Figures from the state's employment offices also served as good economic indicators. She noted that "in New York City alone the number of workers registered for each 100 jobs was 214 in November, 1929, and 222 in December."

She claimed lack of authority to quote the Welfare Council of New York City, "the official clearing house for nearly 1,000 private relief agencies," but she felt certain that they regarded "the present unemployment situation in New York City as severe, with no signs of improvement up to date." Senator Wagner had her letter printed in the *Congressional Record* of January thirty-first.

Every month the industrial commissioner could be sure of a couple of cases dealing with eager job applicants bilked by fly-by-night, fee-collecting employment agencies. Local licensing bureaus could not squash these hope-peddlers as they moved from one city to another. The department was able to recover some thousands of dollars each year taken from job applicants referred to nonexistent jobs, or to jobs from which they would be fired by unscrupulous employers in league with the agency. Frances sought to integrate the work of good private agencies with a general employment clearing house under the supervision of the state Department of Labor. She also set up a Junior Jobs Division for youngsters between the ages of fourteen and seventeen who needed employment to survive along with others.

Jobs, she knew, could do more to restore confidence than anything else, because they restored that most important missing ingredient, purchasing power. She pleaded with manufacturers to avoid layoffs as much as possible. She suggested that they produce "for stock" in off-seasons. Along this line, the upholstery concerns offered special discounts during their slack season. She tried to promote the immediate repair or improvement of facilities so that laborers and craftsmen could be employed. Of course this moral suasion had little positive impact. As Joseph Stalin once said to H.G. Wells, "No capitalist is going to lose money to serve the needs of the people."

She devised plans for getting little children out of the job market. By

1928 the state's labor law had prohibited the employment of children under age fourteen in trade, business or occupations, with certain exceptions. During 1929 and 1930, the New York Child Labor Committee conducted an investigation of the scallop sheds on Long Island. They found children eight years old opening scallop shells after school until ten o'clock at night. The Cannery Shed Law originally had not covered these sheds. Frances issued an order that placed them under the law. She met again with members of the canning industry, and they reassured her that child labor was virtually eliminated. It was agreed that, in emergencies, canners could work employees up to twelve hours a day and sixty-six hours a week, but they would file applications showing their need and their maintenance of minimum standards. Actually the production of new efficient machinery ended up having a more salutary effect on the elimination of child labor and long hours than all of the laws and codes put together.

For some time employers, economists, and social critics talked of some form of insurance that would tide over working people between jobs. Roosevelt showed interest in this, but little historical information was available. In July Frances sent him a note suggesting that he "go cautiously when talking about unemployment insurance by that name. Unemployment reserves is safer and more educative for the present." Of course, to the Republican leadership in the legislature and the National Association of Manufacturers terminology made little difference; they were opposed to anything that might increase the cost of doing business in the state. At the Democratic state convention, Governor Roosevelt recommended that their platform include a proviso to create a commission to make a study of unemployment insurance and of the stabilization of employment.

During the 1930 gubernatorial campaign, Molly Dewson became more active as a political campaigner than ever before. For the first time, she worked with James Farley, a fortyish, seasoned politician, both amiable and industrious. She reported to him, "Frances Perkins wants us to have a committee to work with the intelligentsia for many of them have been confused by the press as to Roosevelt's record during his first two years as Governor." Farley laughed at this—he would never regard Frances as much of a politician, although he admired her as a capable, trustworthy person—but he tolerantly gave Molly Dewson the go-ahead if she really felt it was worth bothering with one and a half percent of the population.

As was expected, the incumbent governor won the election with a substantial margin that amply betokened the citizens' confidence in him.

Frances's political activities had been substantially circumscribed by the demands of her position. However, she delighted in hearing that Grace Abbott, chief of the Children's Bureau in the U.S. Department of Labor, had been named as a possible successor to the second secretary of labor, James J. Davis. Newspaper articles and letters from distinguished citizens pleaded with President Hoover to appoint this "conspicuously eligible" woman to his cabinet. Frances Perkins spoke at a major conference sponsored by the National Consumers League. The league enthusiastically endorsed Grace Abbott as labor secretary.

During this period, unfortunately, Grace Abbott indulged in unhappy pronouncements on the nature and extent of the depression that ran contrary to Hoover's things-will-right-themselves optimism. On December ninth, the appointment went to William N. Doak, a self-made former union man who shared Hoover's conviction that federal paternalism—even during the economic emergency—was "not only retrogressive, but dangerous."

Grace Abbott stoically resumed her duties. Her supporters, chiefly feminists, simmered silently. The women's movement languished again as it had in 1920 when President Harding failed to honor his promise of a woman in his cabinet. Women's gains since the Nineteenth Amendment gave them the right to vote and since Congress created the Women's Bureau in the Department of Labor, were statistically negligible. The yellow jonquils of the suffragists withered in a workaday world that limited women for the most part to subordinate positions.

Out of the melee came a pejorative description of the qualifications needed by a U.S. secretary of labor:

A Secretary of Labor must be something of a stuffed shirt, with a gift for making long-winded speeches about nothing in particular. He must have a genius for inaction, a positive flair for never doing anything to offend anyone. On the one hand, he must avoid any work or action that might tend to alienate a segment of the so-called labor vote and on the other hand he must be ever so careful not to give labor enough of a break to arouse criticism from employing corporations which can be depended upon for political contributions.

A Secretary of Labor ought to be able to dig up a union card out of his old papers but he must have piled up enough money and property to realize that this is the best of all possible worlds, and that changes are always dangerous.

When business depressions come along he must be able to rise up and blame them on the Senate, the Bolsheviki, the Democrats, or somebody, and when the several million persons are unemployed he must be able to proclaim that a few hundred thousand are merely taking a voluntary vacation and that everything will be alright in a week or two.

By virtue of sheer size, the New York State Department of Labor could be viewed as an ideal, small-scale model for the federal department. Its commissioner did not meet the criteria for secretary of labor that came out of the 1930 speculation on appointments for that office.

*****

At the opening of the 1931 legislative session, Governor Roosevelt reiterated the need for a compulsory unemployment insurance system and an insurance program to provide for the aged. The Old Age Pension Law passed the previous year functioned as a form of poor law for those over age seventy. Roosevelt believed that with contributions to an insurance program starting at an early age, the dole system could be eliminated.

Sidney Hillman was called on to testify on behalf of the Mastick-Steingut workmen's compensation bill. As president of the Amalgamated Clothing Workers of America, he could point to the experience in the Chicago men's clothing industry, where such a fund added less than a penny to the cost of production.

Although Frances recognized that old-age insurance and unemployment compensation did little to ameliorate the unemployment problem, she spoke on behalf of both. And again she witnessed the clout of a recalcitrant Republican-dominated state legislature.

Frances didn't learn patience; she learned that impatience yielded nothing. And the time spent waiting could be spent honing the intellectual weapons for a stronger defense at the next opportunity. She could make speeches to persuade the voters—the assemblymen's and senators' constituents—as to the inherent soundness of these programs. Unemployment insurance, she constantly emphasized, was not a cure for unemployment. "Unemployment is a symptom, not a disease. Its elimination depends on our ability to define and deal with economic maladjustments that produce it." This approach paralleled the one she later adopted to explain industrial strikes. To cure symptoms as opposed to their cause, she elaborated, serves as a temporary remedy. It is important for the person who itches to get relief immediately for the itch, but if it is a persistent condition, he would be foolish not to search for the cause.

She stressed that "all forms of social insurance should so far as possible, be kept impersonal in their administration," and advocated that industry foot the bill for unemployment insurance as a cost of doing business. "The argument that the benefits will 'mean more' to the workers if they have contributed directly to the fund" she deemed a sentimental consideration. "Our experience with workmen's compensation doesn't indicate that it has any basis in fact." In a talk before the National Conference of Catholic Charities in Wilkes Barre, Pennsylvania, she indirectly responded to the hard-core individualistic critique:

In years past thrift was the people's best protection against the inevitable slack period. And thrift remains an excellent fortification of the individual. Much of the forced thrift that was practiced in other times had tremendous hardship attached to it. It was the kind of thrift that is accompanied by undernourished children, widespread illiteracy, by squalid and unhealthful conditions of living—the very things that our American civilization has been striving, indeed without complete success, but nevertheless valiantly striving—to overcome.

One speech she especially enjoyed giving that spring—quite unrelated to the unemployment problem—made it possible for her to renew old acquaintances. The venerable Jane Addams of Hull House was to receive the M. Carey Thomas Prize of $5,000 from Bryn Mawr College. Frances became infatuated with Bryn Mawr's Quaker atmosphere and lush, green hilly countryside just a short distance from Philadelphia. And she especially enjoyed visiting with Jane Addams and her old friend, the progressive world-renowned educator, John Dewey. Grace Abbott of the U.S. Department of Labor's Children's Bureau and Mrs. Carrie Chapman Catt, the remarkable feminist and founder of the League of Women Voters, were also on the program.

Back at her job, the industrial commissioner took the New York Child Labor Committee to task for its lack of vision. At the instigation of Florence Kelley, the committee supported a bill that would raise the minimum working age from fourteen to fifteen. But few significant people could be convinced that an extra year of schooling would benefit the children. Frances charged that the committee's failure stemmed from the fact that it had

...done very little toward presenting for popular consideration a program of what might be done with these early adolescent years that would in the end give to society and to the children themselves a much greater return than if those same years had been spent at low wage repetitive jobs which very likely serve as training to prepare the young person for a lifetime of low wage repetitive job holding.

Frances wanted the committee to envision "what tremendous social gains we stand to make through carrying out a program of proper training for life during those very impressionable early adolescent years."

Her own impressionable adolescent, Susanna, attended a private school and was preparing for college. The years passed so quickly. In April Frances had celebrated her fifty-first birthday—or was it her forty-ninth, making her three months younger than the governor? Over the years she associated with many people who had died at a much earlier age. People in public life suffered not only from the stress and pressure put on them, but from threats from deranged individuals unable to cope with opinions radically juxtaposed to their own. Mulling these things over in her mind while a train rhythmically chugged its way back to New York City, she found herself uneasy, filled with unexplainable premonitions. She hastily evaluated her co-workers and the next day scrawled across four sheets of personal-sized stationery an ominous message to Mary Dewson:

June 23, 1931

Dear Mary,

I've often thought that in case I were knocked out Franklin would look to you to help him reset the Labor Dept.

You don't know the names of the *best* people & most reliable & those who have a good point of view & should be in positions of greater responsibility. So here they are, written on the train yesterday.

With love and complete trust in you as a sort of moral executor.

Francis P.

P.S. I'm *O.K.* nothing iminent. Just New England forehandedness. I care more about this dept. & what it can do for the working people in N.Y. than for most anything else.

Mary Dewson, quite touched by the message, may have construed it as a foreboding stemming from momentary depression or fatigue, but for the next quarter of a century, subsequent industrial commissioners would learn that the New York State Department of Labor was Frances Perkins's special baby, and she would provide continual unsolicited advice on its tender, loving care.

*****

Frances found herself with an unusual opportunity to speak at the International Unemployment Conference scheduled for September in Amsterdam, Holland. For over two years her work had left her with no free time. While on the other side of the Atlantic, she could study the practical workings of unemployment insurance in England. The governor concurred. In addition, she planned to tour the British Isles with her daughter, Susanna.

The England she visited in 1931 in no way resembled the country she had visited in 1913. She glowingly reported:

> I went from town to town, through one city after another, and never saw people in rags or shoeless. I did not encounter that drawn look that comes from years of underfeeding and despair, except on the faces of a few aged unemployables . . . people on the streets have good, warm "durable" clothes these days and they all have shoes.
>
> . . .The only drunken person I saw in England this summer was an American girl in a hotel lobby.
>
> . . .The "pubs" were well filled but even on Saturday nights in the poorer sections of large cities I saw no "drunks."

The poor publicity and cross-cultural misunderstandings regarding the British Dole, a system of extended benefits for those who since World War I had been minimally employed, made it necessary to distinguish it clearly from unemployment insurance. One advantage of the British system, she noted, is that it gives the facts making it possible to determine the nature of its problems—industrially unemployables versus the unemployeds—a distinction our charity and relief agencies did not make.

Many British employers, of course, wrung their hands over the dole. Frances Perkins would then ask, "Well, what should be done? Should it be abandoned?" The answers were never in the affirmative.

"After all, it's saved England," was the usual reply. "I don't know what we could have done without it." Another said, "Well, if it went through one generation, I don't think we'd notice it. For two generations I don't believe I'd worry. Three—there I'm not so sure—you have only to look at the British upper classes."

She remembered particularly sitting in a referee's court in England where some doubtful claims were being reviewed:

> The procedure is informal. The claimant tells his story in his own way. The three referees ask questions about any points which are not clear, and they summon witnesses if they feel that further testimony is needed. None of the claimants whose cases I heard were represented by counsel. Most of them were unskilled workers, but they were able to make a clear statement, and they were fully aware of their rights under law. One man, for instance, had a fairly involved situation to describe in explaining why he had not accepted a job offered through the local office. If the facts were as he presented them, he was justified in refusing the employment under his trade-union regulations and was entitled to benefits. The referees asked a few questions to clear up one or two details, then allowed the claim.
>
> "But aren't you going to check his story?" I asked, a good deal surprised.
>
> "That hardly seems necessary," the referee replied, "After all, the man himself knows better than anyone else what his union regulations are and how the work offered him conflicts with them."

Frances had worked with immigrants over so many years, she knew their ways well, particularly those of the plain laboring man. Unlike the workmen in England who answer all their lives to the name their parents gave them, immigrants were arbitrarily assigned names that officials on Ellis Island could spell, or that the working boss could pronounce. Frances, whose innate interest in human beings made it effortless for her to master unusual names as well as remember the countless faces that came before her, encountered this immigrant phenomenon often.

> . . .In this country, as a matter of convenience, Guiseppi Catalano may be Joe Carter on one firm's records, Jim Lane on the books of another employer. In administering the workmen's compensation law in this state we have found many wage-earners who, with no intent to deceive, have changed their names with almost every job. Their own names are hard to pronounce, confusing to spell, and a shortened version of the real name is used by the "boss" and by fellow-workers.

If we were ever to develop any form of social insurance program in the United States, she knew we had to devise "some ready and reasonably fool-proof system of identification." Otherwise, there would be no way of knowing that the man whose family called him Theophilus Sotiropoulos is actually Tom Paul who lost his job with the textiles plant last month who is the Tim Store "let go" by the finishing factory the year before.

Social Security numbers would, of course, take care of this problem. The only exceptions were hundreds of people who bought wallets in a five-and-ten-cent store and, finding a mock Social Security identification card in the wallet's clear plastic window, proceeded to use the number that appeared on the card. These people simply didn't understand the purpose of Social Security and having an account identified by a number belonging exclusively to them.

It must have amazed her that so many people knew so little of their rights as workers, and as citizens; nor did they understand their obligations. She was especially conscious of this when her Division of Women and Children submitted a report to her on the effect of the Double Compensation Law. This law penalized those employers who hired children under working age, and its intent was not only to discourage child labor, but to assist the youngster who became handicapped as a result of an on-the-job accident. The division's research showed that the awards tended to be squandered or used by the family for its own purposes. With the exception of only four cases upstate where guardians had been appointed, the money awarded did not go for the vocational training that could have provided some security for the handicapped youngster.

Earlier in the year, some vicious attacks were again made on her and the operation of the Workmen's Compensation Commission. Rose Schneidermann of the New York Women's Trade Union League published in the newspapers a resolution castigating the "irresponsible people" who made the attacks:

. . .we are profoundly suspicious of the intentions and actions of people who are showing such a sudden and deep interest in the Workmen's Compensation Commission, which interest they failed to show in the past when it might have been most valuable . . .

Frances could have only felt heartened by the pledge of support that followed:

Resolved, that the Women's Trade Union League hereby assures the New York State Commissioner of Labor, Frances Perkins, of its confidence and faith in her integrity as commissioner, her entire devotion to her task, her ability and willingness to right all wrongs wherever possible if submitted to her fairly and honestly . . .

Criticism could be viewed as a challenge—and there could always be an element of truth to the charges. Frances plunged into the job of eliminating the administrative boondoggling that seemed to delay some workmen's compensation cases—and those who worked with her learned, if they hadn't already, that she had a "holy hardness" about her. She had the satisfaction of finishing out the year with a report that the Workmen's Compensation Commission has satisfactorily handled 26,000 cases more than in the previous two years. This was accomplished without any additional budget and without additional personnel.

In the process Frances found herself at odds with one of her aides who spitefully wrote an excoriating letter that got into the hands of the Accident Prevention and Safety League, an association of window-cleaner employers. So the new year of 1932 started again with allegations against her. The association filed charges with the governor claiming that the state's insurance fund "was administered with waste, extravagence, favoritism, delay, discourtesy and intimidation," and requesting an immediate investigation. The press, somewhat tired of extolling the virtues of the top woman in the state, played up the charges, then chose to ignore the 262 pages of typewritten testimony and 226 exhibits that Frances pulled together. The association's only "evidence" was the letter written by the aide with whom Frances had long since cleared up the misunderstanding. Nor did the press find interesting the fact that the charges had stemmed from infighting between the many small, highly competitive operators in the hazardous window-cleaners' trade.

Next, the newspapers accused her of rejecting "the flippant fancies of the flappers." The New York *Tribune* editorialized: "Strange doctrine this in 1931! Miss Perkins seems to have lost her usual salty realism." In her attempt to iron out seasonal unemployment in the women's wear field, she apparently failed to notice that "middle-aged women" no longer existed.

On February seventeenth her friend and guiding light, seventy-two-year-old Florence Kelley, died. Frances, who looked upon death as the beginning rather than the end, eulogized the founder of the National Consumers League with sharply-drawn reminiscences that explained this vital, dedicated woman as a warm, loving human being with the human tendencies to lose her temper and to appear less than fashionable in her dowdy clothes. Frances kept her memory warmly alive in her frequent speeches on social progress.

Frances Perkins, hardly an arbiter of fashion in her tailored blouses and dark skirts, now twelve inches from the floor, discovered the phenomena of "the five-dollar dress." For a time, consumers who still had some income purchased excellent merchandise at below-cost prices. The retailers, forced to clear their shelves, brought in cash in any way they could through large-scale mark-downs. But then they restocked the shelves with goods manufactured to lowered price lines. Where, according to Frances, fifteen dollars had been a fair standard price for a dress, the five-dollar dress appeared in the windows of little shops on Madison Avenue and in the towns all over the country. Frances wrote an article on the five-dollar dress for the *Survey* that newspaper reporters later found cause to mock.

Already it was evident that the press was anathema to her, possibly because of her New England background; New Englanders believed a lady's name appeared in print when she was born, married and died. Or it might have been Jane Addams's long battle with reporters. Or the fact that the most interesting thing about Frances to so many of the men and women who interviewed her was her sex, which she regarded as totally irrelevant, or what she slept in—who in the world could be interested in her long "old-fashioned" nightgowns or the twin bed she claimed for herself? But this was the human interest that reporters needed for their profiles.

One reporter asked her why she obviously derived so much personal satisfaction from her job. Her answer did little for sensational journalism:

I had constant contact with what was going on. Such things were a matter of day-by-day accumulation. If a new machine was being tried in some factory, I would hear of it very shortly and probably see it before tests were completed. I went into the workshops and saw for myself that the workers were being well or badly cared for. They came to me with their stories if things were going wrong.

According to all reports, Frances worked her staff hard, but since she worked harder, they couldn't complain. On the contrary, her charisma was such that they felt inspired to commit themselves to the same holy charge that seemed to drive her on. She used a rather effective ploy; she let them be their own taskmasters. Yet they were ever mindful that no detail escaped her attention, and their reward would be her praise, generously and graciously bestowed.

When she was asked to testify at hearings being conducted by U.S. Senator Robert M. LaFollette, Jr. of Wisconsin, she alone, according to a brilliant young economist, Isador Lubin, dramatically translated the statisticians' portrayal of the economic breakdown into terms of human well-being. She spoke as though she knew each of the one and a half million people unemployed in the state personally. Together with the millions of part-time workers, they sustained, over the past two years of depression, a wage loss exceeding $1,600,000,000. To offset the suffering caused by this loss of income, only $35,000,000 had been available through private and public agencies dispensing relief.

She emphasized: "No charitable relief is given until every personal resource, in the way of property and personal belongings, friend borrowing from friend, and all that sort of thing, has been exhausted." To the many families almost impoverished by unemployment but not yet on the level of destitution, she explained, the loss of income had mandated a level of living so low that malnutrition and depletion of health were inevitable. She predicted that the full effects would be seen in several years, when the crisis was all over.

She told of the sweatshops' resurgence and housing in Manhattan:

> ...old, worn out, dirty, dark room tenements, which a few years ago had been practically abandoned, have now come back into a period of prosperity. The people who had moved out into the Bronx and other sections of New York City, into newer parts of the town, are now finding their way back to the old-law tenements.... Two or three families crowd into four- or five-room apartments. That, of course, has always had in the past very undesirable social results.

She painted a very black picture. Welfare recipients were getting $2.39 a week, and some people were too proud to accept it. Frances knew women who worked a full six-day week for $1.50. Newspapers were called "Hoover blankets," the only cover for people who slept in the parks.

She vigorously supported passage of Senator Robert Wagner's bill for "a complete, well supported federal-state employment service," adding, "In this state, we expect and hope to receive increased appropriations from the next legislature for the development of our state public employment bureau and we shall be ready to meet that appropriation with effective work."

She had already experienced first-hand the disadvantages of a strong centralized government. A few months after the "reorganization" of the U.S. Employment Service, she had read in the newspaper that a new branch was to be opened in Rochester. She immediately wired John R. Alpine, the supervising director of the federal service, protesting that "Rochester already has the largest and best equipped public employment service in the state." Supported by private funds as a demonstration center, the Rochester facility was conducted by the state cooperating with the city's Public Employment Center. She urged that "if federal money is to be spent on employment work in New York, a new office be opened in some district now without such service—such as Watertown, Jamestown, Glens Falls or Utica—or else that the new force be added to some existing state employment office in which additional help is needed, such as Syracuse, Albany, Brooklyn or Long Island."

When she received no response to her pleas, she finally called in the press:

In Elmira, a small town in which the state is now conducting an employment office which meets the needs of the town, the U.S. some months ago, without consulting officials of the NYS Employment Service, opened a new office. Now, according to the newspapers, they are contemplating opening a competing office in Buffalo . . . The NYS Employment Service is always ready to cooperate, but how can we cooperate when we don't know what is going on?

A reporter asked Frances Perkins, "What do you regard as the most serious of the problems demanding attention?" Her answer reflected the assimilation of facts and figures, of conferences and committees, encompassing many minds, including, admittedly, that of many university professors:

Out of the welter of problems facing us today, it seems to me that the human one of no work, no wages, no buying power is really the most crucial. Our present social organization rests upon industrial mass production, and mass production has as its corollary mass consumption.

But mass consumption in its turn means that the wage earners must be able to buy. When the family pocketbook is empty the neighborhood stores are empty. They cannot buy from the wholesaler or manufacturer, and the manufacturer cannot buy from the basic industries that supply him with tools and raw materials. The wheels stop, more workers are laid off or cut to lower than subsistence wages, so that they are also forced to stop buying.

Like the ripples eddying out from the pebble dropped into a pool, the circle grows until it has reached every part of the social structure. A general paralysis ensues—the lawyer, the physician, the artist, the music teacher are as much affected as is the wage earner. The spring of economic life dries up at its source.

She, together with many others, realized all too well that implementation of the mass consumption concept could not be achieved by traditional means or even by the token measures taken by her as industrial commissioner. As a matter of fact, vagueness characterized the campaign promises made by the Democratic presidential nominee, Franklin D. Roosevelt, whose "New Deal" slogan headlined well.

Frances, along with many others, contributed ideas and materials for his campaign speeches. She noted that he would transpose a statement she had written, such as "We are trying to construct a more inclusive society," into the homier, "We are going to make a country in which no one is left out."

She did not take to the hustings as she had four years earlier on behalf of Al Smith. Periodically, she contributed some ideas to campaign headquarters or got together facts for the governor. She listened to Roosevelt's speeches over the radio—she'd finally had one installed in her bedroom. She also listened to the election returns on the radio, and concluded:

The election in the Fall of 1932, in so far as it had a conscious and emotional significance, was a vote against the depression—a bewildered people, viewing the chaos in which their lives were staged, voted overwhelmingly for what they called a "New Deal." And by that they meant apparently exactly what the term meant in its original card playing sense, a different arrangement of trumps and aces in different hands.

Roosevelt's campaign workers were ecstatic over his election, the not least of whom, Mary W. Dewson, who revelled in the praise bestowed on her and Eleanor Roosevelt for gearing up the Women's Division of the Democratic party. Frances heard glowing reports of their success in bringing out women's votes. She rarely thought of herself as a feminist these days, but she found it exciting that women were increasingly outspoken, involved and committed.

Although peripheral Women's Division activities pivoted around Frances Perkins, she had no part in them. They resembled the surreptitious planning for a surprise party where the person for whom the surprise is intended feigns obliviousness to the unusual goings-on, the too-loud stage whispers, the knowing grins—and then gawks in open-mouthed amazement when the occasion arrives.

New York State Industrial Commissioner Frances Perkins with Eleanor Roosevelt, wife of Governor Franklin D. Roosevelt, and Mrs. Percy V. Pennypacker, President Chataugua Women's Club, January, 1931.

VIII

A Woman in the Cabinet

In 1932 most women laundered family clothing bent over corrugated metal scrub boards with bars of caustic brown soap. They shelled peas, snipped string beans, boiled greens and soup bones for hours, and stored leftovers in a wooden icebox for use the next day. They shopped daily if they had money or credit, or twice a week with inadequate home relief grocery orders.

Women working outside of the home held menial, poorly paid jobs. If the job was worth having, women, particularly married women, faced abuse on charges that they deprived unemployed male breadwinners of much-needed income.

Only an economically advantaged minority patronized commercial laundries and delicatessens, and a few outspoken feminists among these had marched in suffragist parades, worked behind the scenes during political campaigns, invested in education and sought to excel in a man's world. Some lived in settlement houses with the poor, fought for legislation to eliminate sweatshops, supported the factory girls' strikes against long hours and low wages. And for themselves and their able sisters, they sought equal opportunity and recognition through appointment of a woman to a presidential cabinet position.

Their bombardment began with Franklin D. Roosevelt's landslide victory in the presidential election of November 8, 1932. The chairman of the National Woman's party wrote to the president-elect warning him that her counterparts were "justly impatient and deeply concerned lest American women be ignored further." She also reminded him of the "glamorous opportunity to distinguish his administration for all time" by being the first to give women recognition. Mrs. Ogden Reid, vice-president of the *Herald-Tribune*, challenged the New York State

Federation of Women's Clubs by asking if women were afraid to take top positions. Novelist Fannie Hurst exhorted clubwomen to demand that a woman receive a place in the new cabinet.

One noted scholar, Dr. Lorine Pruette, went so far as to advocate a "real New Deal Cabinet" composed *entirely* of women. In a half-page spread complete with a gallery of photos, the *San Francisco News* quoted her as saying:

> If we're really going to have a New Deal the first qualification for executive office ought to be a concept of social justice—and that's where these women come in.
>
> They don't know administrative technicalities? Listen! Women have been embroidering the altar cloths while men said the mass in public life and in politics long enough! Therefore, why not place women where their well known "broader social viewpoint" can mold policies to be executed by others adept in routine technique? That would be a "new deal."

Roosevelt never openly sought to win women's votes by promising high-ranking appointments for representatives of their sex. It would have been politically unwise to raise the issue while one out of every three family breadwinners suffered from unemployment or a shortened workweek with reduced pay. At the polls, voters demonstrated their loss of faith in the incumbent president, Herbert Hoover, who was futilely assuring the nation that prosperity was right around the corner. The Democratic candidate for the presidency, New York State Governor Franklin D. Roosevelt, had promised them a New Deal. In Roosevelt's words, "The forgotten man, the little man, the man nobody knew much about, was going to be dealt better cards to play with." In his unprecedented speech accepting the nomination, Roosevelt also assured a new deal for "the forgotten woman." He did not elaborate, however, and left the entire women's end of his campaign to his wife, Eleanor, and Mary (Molly) W. Dewson.

A human dynamo and gifted organizer, Molly Dewson headed the envelope-licking, door-knocking, speech-making Women's Division of the Democratic National Committee. She proudly boasted:

> We women were given our own money to spend exactly as we thought best—and Louis Howe later said Eleanor and I made the same amount of money go twice as far as the men.

We had our own campaign literature written by and for women. We carried
on a huge correspondence with precinct workers. . . .

Dewson's associates prepared "rainbow flyers" on major campaign
issues so that local workers could speak authoritatively on vital
concerns. With characteristic exuberance Molly Dewson exclaimed,
"And oh, the joy of being competent! There is nothing like it to put
ginger into workers."

Even before Roosevelt's nomination, Louis Howe, Roosevelt's
gnome-like political strategist, promised Dewson, "If we're elected,
we'll take care of you in Washington." She had no personal aspirations,
however, and whenever Roosevelt applauded her efforts to bring about
his election, she told him, "Only one thing I'll ask of you, and don't
give me the answer now—Frances Perkins as Secretary of Labor!"

The political life of Mary W. Dewson, a tweedy, buxom woman,
centered on furthering social justice through women in politics. She had
learned, ". . .many things I thought might never happen, happened
through a little planning and some pleasant persistence."

Hers was not a generalized bid for recognition of women's equality.
Dewson promoted Frances Perkins, the industrial commissioner of New
York State, for very definite reasons:

> This is not an act of friendship on my part. Frances and I were never personal
> friends. I just believed that here was the golden opportunity for pushing
> ahead the labor legislation program for which I had worked for so many
> years. I am convinced that certain women . . . have been more successful in
> getting progressive labor laws passed and more effective in their administra-
> tion than any men ever have been or could have been.

In her campaign to secure the appointment of Frances Perkins,
Dewson encouraged key people to write to Roosevelt on behalf of the
industrial commissioner. She dashed off letters to every woman leader
she knew in the nation—many sounded like the promotional copy of a
huckster. To Clara Beyer of the U.S. Department of Labor, she wrote:

> Go to it for Frances Perkins. Get your State Labor Department leaders to
> write Governor Roosevelt at Warm Springs. Anyone outside New York State
> who has standing and a letterhead would be fine. Otto Beyer himself would
> be great. The Brookings School economists who have gone to other states are
> good material. *Now* is the time.

Frances Perkins and Mary Dewson at the swearing in of Charles V. McLaughlin as first Assistant Secretary of Labor, January 20, 1938.

In another letter Mary Dewson averred:

> ...there is no woman in the offing in this country who will be of cabinet timber and I allege that once in a while the great mass of unorganized women workers should have someone at the head of the labor department of the cabinet who understands their problems as well as the men's. And Frances Perkins will be dead to labor before FDR leaves Washington and so it's now or never.

Edwin E. Witte, who would develop much of the Social Security program, wrote the president-elect about having had the pleasure of meeting Miss Perkins in London the year before. They were both studying unemployment insurance, she for New York State, and he for the Wisconsin commission. Mary Gilson, an economist at the University of Chicago who had participated in the governor's conferences, wrote Roosevelt about hearing Perkins speak in Cleveland, and claimed that enlightened industrialists "think her great."

Only a few expressed their reservations. Although Daniel C. Roper, who would be secretary of commerce in Roosevelt's cabinet, wrote approvingly of Frances Perkins, he added, "I have, however, been surprised to find the number of women who oppose putting a woman in the Cabinet at this time . . . on the ground that they think it is too early for such recognition." Women had won the right to vote in 1920, but most people still felt that "a woman's place is in the home."

Cordell Hull, then a senator from Tennessee, brought out two other considerations in his response to Molly Dewson:

> ...I have the most favorable opinion of the lady to whom you refer, Miss Frances Perkins, of New York. Her economic labor statistics are far more accurate than those of the Labor Department here in Washington.

> I have no idea as to the number of Cabinet Officials Governor Roosevelt may have in mind that would come from New York. This phase, coupled with the other one that the Labor Department was originally created for and largely at the insistence of the labor unions would seem to comprise the only two impediments or difficulties in the way. Personally, and apart from possible labor complications, I feel entirely in accord with your views. In any event, I shall gladly join you and others in emphatically bringing this matter to the attention of Governor Roosevelt.

Of the ten cabinet members to be named, James Farley, national chairman of the Democratic party, who became postmaster general, and

William H. Woodin, secretary of the treasury, were New Yorkers. Frances Perkins claimed New York State by adoption, and her residence negated her Massachusetts origin.

To appoint a nonlabor person, and a woman at that, to head the Department of Labor would openly court antagonisms. Organized labor took credit for the creation of the cabinet post twenty years before and regarded the secretary of labor as its representative in the administration. The head of the American Federation of Labor, William Green, let it be known that he backed Dan Tobin, a member of the International Teamsters Union and past-chairman of the Democratic Labor Campaign Committee. Another American Federation of Labor man, the suave, talented Edward McGrady could also claim labor's support. An outstanding record of labor reform prompted rumors that Senator Robert F. Wagner of New York might be acceptable to organized labor. Rexford Guy Tugwell, one of the president-elect's "brain trust" advisors, believed that Frances Perkins "had no claim in the going regard to become Secretary of Labor," the post for which her role as industrial commissioner best equipped her.

Molly Dewson persisted despite the opposition. She collected newspaper clippings endorsing Frances Perkins and sent them to Roosevelt. She wrote him a chatty note describing a game of "cabinet-making" played at a celebrity-studded dinner. She mentioned quite incidentally that Frances Perkins was unanimously selected for the Department of Labor. She took special delight in the *Herald Tribune's* report:

> Just before the end of the campaign the Massachusetts Progressives for Roosevelt League, headed by Professor Felix Frankfurter of Harvard University, chose Miss Perkins in an open communication as an example of the type of Cabinet officer whom they would like to see Mr. Roosevelt select.

An article speculating on patronage in New York State under Roosevelt's successor, Governor-elect Herbert H. Lehman, declared that the Democrats were convinced the industrial commissioner's post would be vacated because she would move to Washington. The *New York Times'* rundown on 160 "favorite sons" from every state in the union named three women. Frances Perkins was among them.

While hopes for equal opportunity for women continued to see-saw with each rumor, the key figure in these speculations stayed remotely in the background. Frances may have relished a political skirmish on behalf of others, but her genuine concern for the problems of the poor and the exploitation of the "working class" had long since preempted her youthful ardor for "women's rights." When Molly Dewson spoke of her plans one evening as they walked along Madison Avenue to a Schrafft's restaurant, Frances reacted with an emphatic, "But Mary, Franklin would never do it."

Fortunately, the resolute Molly Dewson expected neither praise nor encouragement. Years before, she had equated Frances Perkins with Rudyard Kipling's lines on aloofness: "This is a picture of the Cat that Walked by Herself through the Wet Wild Woods waving her wild tail and walking by her wild lone."

Frances Perkins was both independent and a realist. She refused to waste time or energy needlessly, and Molly Dewson's ambitions for her seemed predestined for failure. Just a couple of years before she had observed the futility of this type of venture when Grace Abbott failed to be named secretary of labor by Hoover.

Roosevelt had boasted to her that he would take more chances on appointing women and demonstrate more nerve about improving their status than did Al Smith. Frances fully expected him to live up to his boast, if only to establish the precedent during his presidential administration. However, she held to her conviction that Molly Dewson's efforts would fail. For one thing, she sympathized with organized labor's possessiveness regarding the Department of Labor. She considered herself a social worker, not a "bona fide labor person." For another, she was perfectly content devoting her working hours to helping the poor, no matter what their status, in a position that afforded countless opportunities for achievement. As a result, she first discouraged, then ignored, Molly Dewson's behind-the-scenes endeavors on her behalf.

At a labor meeting Frances addressed in Columbus, Ohio, Clara Beyer of the Bureau of Labor Standards in the U.S. Department of Labor described Molly Dewson's activities, and Frances reiterated her negative views. Back in Washington, Clara planned for Frances to join Grace Abbott of the Children's Bureau early in December for a state labor officials' conference on child labor. Clara saw this as an opportunity to promote Frances's appointment in Washington circles, and cautiously wrote Frances about a dinner party in her honor.

Frances's reluctance to give voice to the rumors is evident in her response: "I would be delighted for you to give me an entirely personal dinner provided there would be no publicity and no talk about the matter that you discussed with me in Columbus."

The conference of state labor officials started early Saturday morning, December tenth, with the tall, erect, vibrant Grace Abbott presiding. Some people still hoped, as they had in 1930, that this prairie-born woman of pioneer stock would be named to the president's cabinet, even though she was a Republican. Frances and Grace Abbott shared a common nonpartisan concern for the abolition of child labor.

Frances told the group that "to countenance child labor at a time like this is to sanction extending the depression into the lives of the next generation." Well fortified by facts and figures, she declared, "No amount of statistics and no number of bulletins can take the place (to a child) of a lamb chop and a glass of milk at the right moment."

In the discussion that followed, Joseph M. Tone, the labor commissioner of Connecticut, told Frances that she had done such a good job in enforcing child labor laws in New York that enforcement had become more difficult in Connecticut.

"We get your refuse," he explained, and then said that "raiding sweatshops is like raiding speakeasies." The sweatshops he described "had peepholes, making necessary raiding squads at both front and back doors."

That evening, the gentlemen of the press were holding their annual Gridiron Club dinner for the president and cabinet members. At Clara Beyer's instigation, the women of the press held a dinner in honor of Frances Perkins. Clara knew that a number of influential members leaned toward the National Woman's party's equal rights position and felt that if they had an opportunity to speak with Frances they might change their slant.

The next day Clara brought Frances to the home of Chief Justice Brandeis of the Supreme Court and his wife. They had both expressed an eagerness to know Frances better.

That evening Mrs. Harriman gave a dinner for her that included members of the Gridiron Club and other influential members of Washington society. Clara assured Frances, "I have made it clear to Mrs. Harriman that you are not a candidate for the position of Secretary of Labor, and that the dinner is to be merely a tribute to you as an outstanding woman."

Although perhaps justified, Frances Perkins's skepticism was not shared by all. Sidney Hillman, president of the Amalgamated Clothing Workers of America, considered rumors of her appointment well founded. He arranged a meeting with her through Dr. Leo Wolman, a mutual friend and noted labor economist and statistician.

Actually, Sidney Hillman needed no introduction. He had won nationwide attention during the Hart-Shaffner, Marx strike in Chicago in 1910. Frances Perkins recalled meeting him shortly afterwards at the home of Belle Moskowitz who, before her alliance with Al Smith, promoted the careers of promising young Jews. Perkins remembered Hillman as an agreeable, modest, tight-lipped gentleman who seemed somewhat surprised at his own success.

At this meeting Hillman presented his ideas for solving the unemployment problem. They impressed Frances Perkins and she said so. But she made it clear that little could be done at the time, or even after he followed up their discussion with a memorandum he wanted her to bring to the attention of the president-elect.

Shortly after the election, Frances Perkins announced that employment had increased 2.8 percent, bringing the increase from July to 11 percent. As an item in the back pages of the newspapers, the industrial commissioner's announcement caused little elation; the employment index still stood 41 percent below October, 1929, the date of the stock market crash. The statistics that came across her desk again reflected the economic doldrums in December and, perhaps, inspired a sentimental, four-page Christmas message to Franklin D. Roosevelt:

Dear Franklin

I incline to prayer when I think of all that the humble and lowly and hurt of this land are expecting of you. So my Christmas gift to you will be that my Christmas Communion will be made for you with the intent that you may be given grace to keep your heart aware of the beauty and strength of these submerged lives and receptive to the inspiration for concrete ways of giving them the "breaks." Joy in the humble homes and the laughter of courage, hope and happiness on the lips of the working millions is the vision, and you dear friend are perhaps the tool to be used for this lowly purpose.

Roosevelt acknowledged her note on his last day as the governor of New York:

Dear Frances:

Thank you for that awfully nice letter of Christmas greetings. You are quite right in all that you say, and my hope is that I can accomplish something worthwhile for the man at the foot of the ladder.

This is my last day as Governor of the State. I shall see you at dinner but please let me take this opportunity of telling you how grateful I am for the fine work you have done these four years. I know of the difficulties you have met, and the fine way in which you have handled them, and always with your mind set on doing the most good for the greatest number. I know you too must have a tremendous feeling of satisfaction in what you have accomplished.

You know my best wishes go to you for the New Year.

Always sincerely yours. . .

They both wrote—and spoke—the same language, aptly described as employing "terms redolent of the sturdy Protestant Anglo-Saxon moral and intellectual roots of the Progressive uprising."

On that last evening of 1932 Frances Perkins joined the Roosevelts for dinner at the executive mansion in Albany. Afterwards, together with George S. Van Schaick, the commissioner of insurance, and his wife, she stood beside Eleanor and Franklin Roosevelt as they said good-bye to the servants. Roosevelt lightened the sad occasion by jauntily sporting his black high hat and exuding jubilant spirits. They went on to the Governor's Inaugural Ball.

* * * * *

Shortly after the election, Franklin Delano Roosevelt announced publicly that he would decide on his cabinet some time in February. As gossip abounded, he reiterated his warning that rumors were to be ignored. He seemed impervious to Molly Dewson's persistent needling. Apparently, although he could be persuaded to make appointments on the basis of good politics at lower levels, when it came to top-ranking, policy-making positions, only ability and his own personal confidence in the appointees counted.

Roosevelt told a trusted advisor, Raymond Moley, that he was seriously considering Ruth Bryan Owen, daughter of William Jennings Bryan, for a cabinet appointment. She, like her famous father, enjoyed a reputation as a gifted speaker. She had served two terms as a congresswoman from Florida—and her exceptionally attractive appearance would be an asset for a "symbolic woman" in the cabinet.

The president-elect discussed various other people under consideration, but somehow Frances Perkins's name did not come up. He was well aware of her background, progressive views, efficiency, articulateness, and intelligence, which had led him to appoint her the industrial commissioner of New York State four years earlier. He admired her courage against odds and her unstinting efforts to cope with the plight of citizens plagued by an economic disaster unparalleled in history. Her performance reflected a total dedication to her work. Roosevelt agreed in principle with Eleanor Roosevelt, who maintained:

> When Molly Dewson backed her for Secretary of Labor, she wasn't backing any novice in the business of politics and government, any fluttery feminine do-gooder. If any woman in the world was equipped by experience and ability to be the first woman Cabinet member, Frances Perkins certainly was.

Other people concurred, and, urged on by Molly Dewson, they wrote Roosevelt, until the stack of letters extolling Frances Perkins's virtues could not be ignored. He finally told Molly Dewson, "It's surprising how many people want Frances for Secretary of Labor. I never realized her hold on the public mind."

FDR realized, as Eleanor Roosevelt later wrote, that the turmoil had to be contrived; state industrial commissioners do not get national publicity. But by not letting on, he left Dewson believing, "This was the one time I was deceptive with Roosevelt."

In January, 1933, Franklin D. Roosevelt ranked legally as a private citizen; his term as governor was ended and he had not yet been sworn in as president. Congress passed the Twentieth Amendment, which decreed, in effect, that he would be the last president-elect sworn into office on March fourth. This "lame duck" amendment would keep defeated legislators from making laws and bring future presidents into office on January twentieth.

On February fifteenth Joe Caylor received a telegram from Frances Perkins. He still lived in Philadelphia. She asked him to meet her at the Broad Street Station and ride with her out to Bryn Mawr. She wanted very much to see him, according to his brother, George Caylor. Joe replied that he would be delighted. George's memoirs tell nothing of the gist of their conversation while on the train, undoubtedly because Joe was extremely close-mouthed about personal matters.

It was not atypical of Frances to use traveling time for various purposes, such as interviews with reporters, many of whom admitted to basing their articles on virtually undecipherable notes caused by the motion of a train or taxicab, or for conversations that she wanted free of interruptions. Frances had kept up a steady correspondence with Joe Caylor, and although it is not known if they had seen each other during the twenty-eight years since she had worked for the Philadelphia Protective Association, there was a strong bond. Undoubtedly she needed some objective counsel regarding the rumors of her possible appointment as secretary of labor.

New rumors speculated as to how she would react when the cabinet position was offered to her. Elizabeth Brandeis wrote to Clara Beyer: "Could it be that Miss Perkins is going to refuse? That would be a terrific disappointment. Isn't it possible to get *some* organized labor support for her?"

On the morning of February twenty-seventh, the president-elect's secretary called to ask Frances Perkins to come to his East Sixty-fifth Street city house that evening. There are variations on exactly what took place after her arrival. According to her own recollections, Frances found a stocky blond man with a cherubic face waiting outside Roosevelt's second floor study. When Roosevelt came out he said, "Frances, don't you know Harold?"

"Shall I just call him Harold or do you want to tell me his last name?" she asked.

"It's Ickes," he laughed. "Harold L. Ickes." Roosevelt used first names, even on short acquaintance, as was the case with his new secretary of the interior.

The paths of Ickes and Perkins had never crossed, yet they had followed the same paths. She had become involved with Chicago's Hull House about a year after Jane Addams, the matriarch of social workers, was called on by the Russian Jews of the settlement house neighborhood to protect them from a feared anarchist massacre. Jane Addams sought out a young lawyer, Harold Ickes, known to have radical sympathies, to help her fight for legal justice. He would be the only cabinet member to outlast, by a few months, Frances Perkins's record tenure in office.

Frances Perkins followed Roosevelt back into his study where, without preamble, he declared: "I've been thinking things over and I've decided I want you to be the Secretary of Labor."

Rather than feign surprise, she launched into a carefully prepared dissent. First she explained that Governor Lehman counted on her to continue the work so necessary in New York State. Next, although she agreed that a woman should be appointed to the cabinet, she argued that it should be the right woman in the right position. An appropriate secretary of labor might well be one of the remarkable women associated with the labor unions whom Roosevelt already knew.

FDR listened patiently. She could outtalk him if she felt the need, and he was definitely fascinated by her ability to express her ideas clearly and precisely. He shared her dedication to social justice and the idealism and sentimentality that sprang from the progressivism and the *noblesse oblige* of the well endowed.

The facts she recited with animated expressions and graceful hand gestures sounded familiar. He let her finish before he used his trump card. Her duty to the despairing people of America required that she accept the appointment, he said. Roosevelt counted on the effectiveness of this approach, and he got the expected reaction. Liberal idealists found a call to duty impossible to resist.

He anticipated her next maneuver. When he had tapped Frances Perkins to serve as industrial commissioner, she had first spelled out the conditions under which she would consider accepting the appointment. She repeated the ritual.

Much was being said about including a "symbolic woman" in the cabinet, but she could not be expected to function as nominal head of the U.S. Department of Labor. Both of them had long suffered over the problems faced by a country in the throes of a disastrous depression. The Department of Labor needed to spearhead drives to conquer the enemy: to solve unemployment problems, to expand the activities of the Bureau of Labor Statistics so that the magnitude of the problem could be accurately assessed, to revitalize the employment offices, and to exploit every device so that those who wanted to work could do so. The people of America needed security, freedom from want, and, in the war against poverty, she saw herself as something more than a critical bystander.

Theirs was an easy give-and-take conversation. Roosevelt liked Frances Perkins as a woman because she did not trade on the fact that she was a woman—or a wife and mother. Roosevelt noted the perky tricorn hat, her trademark, topping a small oval face framed with wavy brown hair, which showed no signs of graying although she was his age, in her early fifties. Her eyes were her most striking feature; they seemed disproportionately large, with the fiery glow of polished tourmaline.

"Child labor laws . . . workmen's compensation . . . relief programs to allieviate immediate distress . . . social security." Yes, yes, he agreed. They had attacked these problems in New York State; now they would be operating on a national level.

As she got up to leave, he grinned broadly, saying, "I suppose you're going to nag and nag me until every one of these things is an accomplished fact." The nod of her head showed determination, though she could still grin broadly at her own seriousness.

As Frances Perkins rode back to her apartment, she reviewed their conversation. She had forgotten one important matter, the International Labor Organization. Ever since its first meeting in Washington, D.C., in 1919, she had held the conviction that fair labor standards could not be limited to this country. The United States, by its membership and participation, would some day contribute to the welfare of the working people in every developing country of the world.

That would come later, of course. Now the immediate situation impinged on her consciousness as she again saw people, some well dressed, pawing through garbage cans for scraps of food. What had happened to the land of opportunity, the land her forefathers had sought out two hundred years before, when today, families were without sufficient resources to keep themselves alive?

*****

Inauguration Day, March 4, 1933, was fast approaching. President Hoover's outgoing cabinet members paid ninety dollars to have their black leather-and-mahogany chairs moved from the White House, crated, and shipped home as souvenirs.

Into the Cabinet Room workers carried ten new chairs, each with a shiny metal nameplate designating a cabinet office. The secretary of labor's chair stood last, at the far end of the solemn line-up—not, as some journalists implied, because a woman for the first time in history would be sitting there, but because the Department of Labor was the last cabinet office established. Seniority and rank dictated the precise positioning of each chair around the table.

People speculated on the unprecedented seating of a woman at the cabinet table. Some were fearful that "this feminine stowaway would surely sink this ship of state." Others suspected that the appointment reflected the influence Roosevelt's wife had on her husband. Eleanor Roosevelt denied contributing in any way to his decision, adding that Frances Perkins was her husband's choice but "I was delighted when he named her and glad that he felt a woman should be recognized."

A pleased Molly Dewson also discounted her influence, attributing other factors for bringing about her objectives:

No matter how much Dan Tobin and the other labor leaders pressed him, I am sure he would have appointed her Secretary (even) if I had never taken the precaution to claim, half jokingly and at proper intervals, that it was my price for the political work I did. He thoroughly enjoyed breaking tradition by appointing a woman to the Cabinet and he was too practical a politician not to avoid lining up with either the AFL or CIO by appointing a Secretary from either side . . .

This last point warrants consideration. The rivalry between craft unions and industrial unions complicated the "political job" of cabinet-building. Rexford Guy Tugwell, economist and presidential advisor, finally conceded that Perkins's appointment was perhaps a "necessary evasion of a choice between competitive leaders," illustrating a "principle Franklin felt and acted on whenever he could. . . ." Actually, Roosevelt determined at the outset that unorganized as well as organized labor should be represented in his cabinet. Frances Perkins as an active, experienced protagonist of workers, unionists, immigrants— the masses of impoverished people—represented a logical choice.

Roosevelt showed a predilection for associates who were "talky, sympathetic, idealistic," who had a sense of humor and did not bore him. And while he may not have overtly sought commotion in appointing a woman to his official family, he was aware that a member of the opposite sex would produce an electric charge in the group. Roosevelt did not like things to be dull.

To many people, the greatest significance in Perkins's appointment to the president's cabinet was that it established a precedent. As a Boston newspaper put it, "It may remain unbroken through long years to come. In other words, there may never again be a President's Cabinet composed exclusively of men."

Survey, the social workers' publication, happily reported that newspapers made little mention of the new cabinet member's sex. Rather, reporters emphasized her admirable qualifications for the position, which, the *Survey* editor concluded, was in keeping with Perkins's career.

Some congressmen were not as benevolent. Newspapers, reporting the reaction of two "lame duck," Republican congressmen to the cabinet appointments noted that criticism centered on Frances Perkins and William H. Woodin, secretary of the treasury. Woodin came under fire because of a $40,000 donation to the Roosevelt campaign fund and his aluminum interests, she because of her sex.

One congressman deprecated her appointment as "a widespread gesture" for the benefit of "the mothers and sweethearts of the

nation." Another twitted that Frances Perkins would encounter difficulties because of her signature. He cited Controller General McCarl's
ruling that in signing pay checks, federal employees must use their legal
names. The name Mrs. Paul C. Wilson would have to appear on the
payroll if Frances Perkins wished to collect her $15,000 cabinet salary.

Representatives of New York State defended her. One boasted of her
record as an official of the Labor Department of New York State. "No
record could be better," he declared, and "in using her maiden name
she is within her legal rights under the laws of New York State."

"I know Frances Perkins," another congressman continued, "and I
know of the fight that was made in Albany for decent living conditions,
for labor and for other industrial reforms, and the leader in that fight
was Frances Perkins."

Personally affronted by the appointment of a nonunion person, and
a woman at that, the president of the American Federation of Labor,
William Green, bitterly threatened that labor would never be reconciled
to Roosevelt's selection. Frances handled the denunciation with equanimity: "Mr. Green and the American Federation of Labor are entirely
within their rights."

She had expected union-leader protest and wondered how violent it
might be. "I am glad they expressed themselves openly and frankly. It
creates a more wholesome situation and I do not in any way regard it as
an expression of ill-will against me."

She described Green as "a man of great integrity, vision and
patriotism." And with a curious admixture of humility and the
self-confidence that allows for admission of reliance on others, she
explained, "Inasmuch as Mr. Roosevelt will call a special session soon
after his Inauguration there will be many matters for me to talk over
with Mr. Green and the representatives of organized labor. And I
certainly shall do so. If they cannot find the time to come and see me, I
will hasten to see them."

Green, however, hardly represented the true feelings of rank-and-file
union men. They had long seen their representatives become enamored
of the "mahogany table" and lose sight of the workingman's objectives.
Unions all over the country assailed William Green and wired messages
of enthusiastic approval to the president-elect.

Roosevelt's successor as governor of New York, Herbert H. Lehman,
reacted to Frances Perkins's "promotion" by confessing that he would
keenly feel "the loss of her talents and long experience." Having
retained her as industrial commissioner, an appointive position, because

of her exceptional abilities, he could only exclaim, "Would that she were twins!"

Frances Perkins entertained a similar wish as she worked frantically to ready everything for her successor. She passionately loved the New York State Department of Labor and would maintain a deep interest in its activities all of her life. The day before her departure for Washington, she appeared before the assembly in Albany to make a final plea for progressive labor legislation and reiterated the need for unemployment reserves in industry, and a minimum-wage law to cover women in other than factory occupations. She shook hands with Mark Daly of Associated Industries, a powerful opponent of her efforts to improve conditions for working people. The *New York Times* glowingly editorialized: "Few women in high office have been tested in the fires through which Miss Perkins has passed. Social justice is more than a shibboleth to her; it has been the maxim of her life."

Frances Perkins's first mass press interview the next day went badly. Her face flushed visibly. She toyed nervously with a pencil and then a pen. The twenty reporters crowding around her desk ignored her patent displeasure with personal questions. Finally, she explicitly requested that they abstain from exploiting those of her family not in official life. The women reporters particularly showed little interest in the problems of unemployment on which she was prepared to speak at length. Their questions struck her as trivial and irrelevant.

Some she answered with "Is that quite necessary?" The question in back of many people's minds finally came up: "How do you feel about being the first woman to sit in the Cabinet?"

"Well, I feel just a little odd." By now she was wondering how she was going to attend to all the details necessary for her departure. She impatiently twiddled with the eyeglasses hanging from a black band around her neck.

"And how will you sign your pay checks?"

"I will do what the President instructs me to do. I have been confirmed in office by the Senate in this State six times. On each occasion I signed Frances Perkins."

The questions continued: "Will your family go with you to Washington?" "What dress will you wear for the Inaugural Ball?" "What are your hobbies?" "Will you engage in social life in Washington?" "What are your pet hates?"

She quite incidentally mentioned an aversion to telephones, automobiles, airplanes, radios, and anything that makes a noise. In a rapid aboutface, the next day the *New York Times* indignantly editorialized, "What right has the Secretary of Labor to hate four modern big industries that give employment to millions of people?" Caricatured as suffering from "technological exasperation," she found the prying of reporters insufferable and her introduction to life in the goldfish bowl of public office less than fortuitous.

The Secretary of Labor, Frances Perkins, wearing her trademark, a cloche version of the tricorne hat, 1933.

IX

The "Poor People's" Department

According to one historian, "She had been incongruously given that most masculine of departments, the Department of Labor, redolent of big men with cigars in their mouths and feet on the desk. . . ." Another wrote:

Up to 1933, the Department of Labor was a happy hunting-ground for superannuated labor union officials and the headquarters of some of the dirtiest deals in the history of the United States. The alien-deportation racket alone was an open sewer and the immigration service in general was a disgrace to civilization. In a capital where there was a faint suggestion of bad drains in every government department, the Labor Department stank.

Past history had left the United States Department of Labor with a scurrilous reputation, not totally warranted. Frances not only learned the full history of the agency she headed while rummaging through the files, but at the slightest hint of interest, she would give an academic rundown on its historical background that astounded labor men as well as bureaucrats who made light of this relative newcomer in federal government.

Frances readily empathized with those who had engaged in the uphill struggle to bring the U.S. Department of Labor into existence. When she took over, it was twenty years old, but a half-century had been invested in its inception.

Early in 1868, William H. Sylvis, president of both the International [iron] Moulders Union and the National Labor Union, outlined a labor program calling for "a new department at Washington . . . the head of said department to be called the Secretary of Labor and to be chosen directly from the ranks of workingmen." Sylvis's death the following year, the demise of the National Labor Union in 1873, and Congress's reluctance to create new departments despite urgings of agriculture and business in their own behalf, resulted in a compromise development of state bureaus of labor statistics.

After much haranguing in the Forty-eighth Congress, a labor-appeasing bill establishing the Bureau of Labor Statistics within the Department of the Interior was signed by President Chester Arthur on June 27, 1884. The commissioner of the bureau was "to collect information upon the subject of labor, its relation to capital, the hours of work, and the earnings of laboring men and women, and the means of promoting their material, social, intellectual and moral prosperity."

During the Southwest Railway strikes of 1886, President Cleveland realized the desirability of enlarging the bureau so that it might investigate causes of disputes and serve as arbitrator. In 1888, Congress provided for a three-man arbitration board to check interstate labor disputes. Although used for only one investigation, this board increased the prestige of the bureau, and in 1888 the Bureau of Labor Statistics became an independent department without executive status.

In 1896 bills urging the establishment of a Department of Commerce, and reducing the Department of Labor to bureau status within it, brought vigorous interest and protests, but in 1903 the bills were passed by a Republican majority that was apparently blind to the divergent views of labor and capital.

The year 1906 brought with it the appointment of business-biased Oscar S. Straus as secretary of the Department of Commerce and Labor, Theodore Roosevelt's labor-antagonizing open-shop stand, and the National Association of Manufacturers-influenced Congress. The American Federation of Labor increased its political activity. In 1908 the Democratic party pledged "the enactment of a law creating a Department of Labor, represented separately in the President's Cabinet. . . ."

In 1910 the Democrats gained control of the House and the AFL promoted the selection of Congressman William B. Wilson as chairman of the Committee on Labor. This former secretary-treasurer of the United Mine Workers helped prepare what would eventually become the Organic Act. The Department of Labor introduced by Representative George Sulzer of New York was reported in 1911 by the legislative committee to have no opposition.

The Senate passed the bill quickly. President William Taft hesitantly signed it, convinced that the nine existing departments were adequate for the "proper administration of the government."

On March 4, 1913, former Representative William Bauchop Wilson took the oath of office as the first secretary of labor under President Woodrow Wilson. Secretary Wilson's background and interests, as well as those of Frances Perkins's other two predecessors, were reflected in the department that she took over twenty years later.

As secretary of labor, Wilson concerned himself with developing trade union relationships and settling labor disputes. He served the eight years of Woodrow Wilson's administration.

On March 5, 1921, President Warren Harding appointed James J. Davis secretary of labor. It is generally conceded that Davis oriented the Department of Labor "in such a way as to gain the confidence of the business community with which he was identified." Under President Calvin Coolidge he emphasized the immigration aspect of the department's program, an emphasis continued by his successor.

In 1928 President-elect Herbert Hoover favored for the cabinet position his campaign labor advisor, William Nuckles Doak, vice-president of the Railway Trainmen's Union. William Green opposed this non-AFL selection, so Secretary Davis—whom Hoover conceded "was good at keeping labor quiet"—remained until his resignation to run for the Senate. He served for nine years and eight months.

His resignation spurred high hopes that Grace Abbott of the Children's Bureau would be appointed, but instead William N. Doak took the oath of office on December 9, 1930, as the third secretary of labor. A professed "Republican who believes in evolution not revolution," Doak apparently relied on restricting immigration and naturalization as a means of alleviating the depression that deepened every day he was in office. Doak was relieved of his post on March 4, 1933, after two years and three months, by the newly-sworn-in president, Franklin Delano Roosevelt.

*****

On that first Monday, March 6, 1933, the secretary of labor found it rather amusing that her predecessor, the Honorable William N. Doak, insisted on sitting at the left-hand side of her desk. A thin-lipped, close-shaven, starch-collared gentleman, he watched everything she did through his wire-rimmed eyeglasses. She thought it a well-meant gesture. Probably he heard before anyone else her comparison of Washington, D.C., cockroaches with those she had seen elsewhere, and viewed her tidying the desk, brightened by a bouquet of red roses sent by the Mount Holyoke class of 1902. When Doak wasn't present, his freshly painted, shiny, full-length portrait glared at her from across her desk.

The doors in the long hall leading into her office popped open like lids on a jack-in-the-box revealing department heads vying for a first glimpse of the new woman labor secretary. There was much consternation over how she should be addressed. Customarily a cabinet member is "Mister Secretary." The answer seemed obvious to her. She replied tersely, "Call me Madam."

Although "ma'am" is still used as respectfully as "sir" in the South, in many parts of the country "madam" suggested the phony deference of obsequious store clerks, or worse. Those accustomed to saying "Mister Secretary" not only found the new title difficult to roll off the tongue, they smirkingly joked that "Madam Secretary" sounded—well funny.

"Fannie the Perk" loved a good joke herself, even if she was the butt of it. In this case, she probably had forgotten her experiences with prostitutes in Chicago and Philadelphia, and that the women who operated brothels were colloquially called "madams." Oveta Culp Hobby, during her brief stint as secretary of the Department of Health, Education and Welfare, avoided this little fiasco by calling herself "Mrs. Secretary." The term "Ms." had not yet been coined although Southerners commonly used "miz" as a prefix for a married or single woman's name.

"Miss Jay," Frances's steadfast, devoted secretary Frances Jurkowitz, quickly implemented measures intended to conserve the time and energy of the secretary of labor, as well as to save her embarrassment. She immediately issued a directive specifying that no publicity or statements on the Department of Labor would be permitted without the secretary's approval.

As a result, one reporter answered the question, "Is FP a good executive?" with "Perhaps not. She is kind of bossy. Nobody in her department, for instance, can give out information without her okay. It got so bad one employee quipped, 'A fellow asked me for the time of day, I couldn't tell him because I didn't have Madam Secretary's okay'."

On one occasion when a Mr. Dudley Pendleton wrote an article about the labor secretary, Miss Jay quickly determined the source of the "personal touches" for his article. Frieda Miller of the New York State Department of Labor was peremptorily chided: "I know that you acted in the best faith, but the article and personal references were perfectly awful. I am sure you will agree with me that these people should be referred directly to us."

Frances relied heavily on Mary LaDame, a gracious, able woman who gave up her work in New York City to serve as an assistant. But it was Miss Jay who saw to it that no one simply popped into the secretary of labor's office. Years later Frances Perkins's associates still winced recalling the gauntlet they had to run in the front office before gaining admission to the inner sanctum. Many felt that this contributed as much to the poor public relations burdening the secretary's office as a lack of understanding of the public relations function. Many department heads wondered why the secretary of labor retained Miss Jay. Frances, basically a sensitive person when it came to human relations, could not have been oblivious to rumblings about her old-time secretary. Possibly Frances realized she would often serve as the president's scapegoat, and she would need her own, Miss Jay. Miss Jay protected her from countless intrusions that would have diminished her effectiveness.

Frances found many devices whereby she could convey to those who worked with her, her sincere interest in their efforts as well as in them as human beings. One was by closing off the private entrance to her facilities. This meant that she rubbed elbows with her rank-and-file employees, and her phenomenal memory for names and faces did much to establish *esprit de corps* throughout the complex that constituted the Department of Labor.

Secretary Perkins's *Survey* article on "The Cost of a Five-Dollar Dress" inspired gossipers to observe that female employees were wearing smocks rather than their bargain dresses, for fear of displeasing her. This was undoubtedly short-lived. The staff quickly learned that other matters relating to the *modus operandi* of the Department of Labor were of greater significance. She made it clear to her staff:

> . . . if an inquiry comes in upon which we have no information they are not to reply to it in the usual stilted Government official's letter, "We are sorry but we have no such information;" they are to say, "We will get you the information.

And if it cannot be had without going to the Library of Congress and all of the departments of Government and all of the universities in this country and Europe, if it cannot be had without going out into the sweat and the toil and the turmoil and the difficulties of our ordinary industrial life, we will go there to get it if it is possible for us to get it.

It was soon said of her, "She expects a great deal of Mortal Man. . . ." The chauffeur she inherited was the first to agree. He resigned after a few weeks because "he was tired." The evening of his resignation, he went with his old boss, William Nuckles Doak, to a wrestling match by way of celebration.

A few months later, *Time* magazine interviewed the new chauffeur assigned to drive her official car. Asked if he had any complaints, D.B. Flohr answered: "Say! You can put this down. She's the sweetest little woman in the world to work for!"

Secretary Perkins did not stint in her own efforts on behalf of the Department of Labor. She was busy at her desk before 9:00 A.M.; she frequently lunched at the desk, and often returned to it after a 7:30 P.M. dinner to work until midnight. Ironically, she was concerned with shortening the working day of labor.

Only a few people knew that her day had started at 7 A.M., when she took communion at an Episcopal church in which Henry Wallace, the secretary of agriculture, served as acolyte. She told reporters that from 9:30 to 10:00 A.M. she went over the mail received in her office, from 10:00 to 10:30 she conferred with state officials on local labor problems. From 10:30 to 11:30 her bureau heads reported to her. A typical working day might also include a press conference from 11:30 to 12:00 noon and from 12:00 to 12:30 P.M., individual appointments. She said she usually ate her lunch from 12:30 to 1:00 P.M. while going over the afternoon mail. From 1:00 to 2:00 labor representatives brought their special problems to her, or she dealt with labor disputes, or made recommendations to the various division heads on policy matters. On Tuesdays and Fridays, and later only Fridays, she attended cabinet meetings at the White House. On other days she might meet with the Public Works Board. From 4:00 to 5:00 the Executive Council or some other recovery or relief group would meet with her. From 5:00 to 7:30 she held informal conferences on special governmental relief problems. She generally took dinner between 7:30 and 8:30 in the evening, and this, too, could be an informal conference. If her daughter was in town, she would pick up her mother in her little sports car. Frances invariably returned to the office and worked on correspondence and reports until 10:30 P.M.

She gave credit to her scientifically constructed swivel chair for minimizing the fatigue of long days at the office. It encouraged correct posture.

She invited one guest, "Sit in it yourself and feel how it fits." She quickly added, "And don't think for a minute it's a 'woman executive's chair.' Why, all my masculine Assistant Secretaries have been getting chairs like it since I started the fashion!"

The chair illustrated her perennial interest in scientific management for increased productivity. It could not offset the countless crises that played havoc with her daily itinerary. Rather impolitically, she ignored a deluge of cocktail party and dinner invitations, not yet aware that acceptance would at least have indicated an intent to be present. Invitations to accept honorary awards, to serve as keynote speaker or guest of honor were accepted warily.

The Bureau of Immigration and Naturalization had been established in the Treasury Department in 1891. In 1903 it was shifted to the Department of Commerce and Labor, and in 1913 the bureau became part of the newly-formed Department of Labor, primarily as a measure to insure appropriations and personnel. The Bureau of Immigration, whose 1700 employees made it the largest bureau in the Department of Labor, and the Bureau of Naturalization became separate entities.

Frances Perkins's historical review of the Department of Labor made it all too clear to her that the reason the department had failed in its true function was because her predecessors and their assistants concentrated on immigration problems and had time for little else. As she put it, "Immigration problems usually have to be decided in a few days. They involve human lives. There can be no delaying." And under William N. Doak, delays were minimal. He boasted, ignominiously, in his *Annual Report* of 1932, "The past year has been one of unremitting and devoted work in the deportation of aliens . . . (who violated) one provision or another of the immigration laws." Incipient union leaders, agitators and organizers of foreign birth invariably were found to be in violation of "one provision or another" and quietly whisked away. A former New York City realtor, Murray Garsson, headed the Immigration Department's "secret raiding squad" consisting of twenty-one "detectives."

On Tuesday, March seventh, Frances called in Peter F. Snyder, an assistant to the secretary, to find out about the authority of the secretary of labor vis-à-vis the commissioner general of immigration. On March ninth the assistant presented her with the amendments to the immigration laws since their enactment, with her responsibilities and those that were delegated clearly delineated in red and blue pencil.

Having determined her legal rights and responsibilities under the law, Frances Perkins's first official act was the elimination of "case fixing and terrorization of aliens," which included extorting money on threat of deportation from ignorant immigrants whose status was completely legal. The squad's "zeal for the chase" involved the services of approximately one thousand immigration inspectors.

In its "Profile" of Madam Secretary, the *New Yorker* magazine presented this interpretation of Frances Perkins's disbanding of the squad:

Mr. Walter Pollak, the constitutional lawyer, suggests that this, her first official act, bears an informing cyclical relationship to a five-hour speech delivered by James Otis, her most eminent forebear, before the Chief Justice of Massachusetts in 1761. James Otis denounced the practice of empowering British officials to search places for smuggled goods as "the worst instrument of arbitrary power, the most destructive of English liberty and the fundamental principles of law that ever was found in an English law book," since they placed "the liberty of every man in the hands of every petty officer." A good deal more of the speech is quoted in the Wickersham Report on Deportation published in 1931.

"The Wickersham Report will be my Bible," said Frances Perkins upon assuming office. "Hereafter the deportation laws will be enforced with due regard to human values, international amenities, and economic conditions within our own and other countries."

To her way of thinking, there was an urgency about the Immigration Bureau that mandated her immediate attention. But as though she had some foreboding that immigration problems would bring her personal catastrophe, she let it be known to the president that she regarded the location of the Immigration and Naturalization Service in the Department of Labor as "more a matter of historical accident and convenience than of necessity." First, of course, she would get the service in order, then she hoped it could run itself. She held the firm conviction that full responsibility for passing final decisions on deportation and admission of aliens should not rest with the secretary of labor or her assistants, but rather with the specialist, the commissioner in charge.

In June she had the president send an executive order to Congress to facilitate the consolidation of the bureaus of immigration and of naturalization in the interests of efficiency and economy. The president already knew of her intent to make the new Immigration and Naturalization Service "virtually autonomous," with the exception of general policy and certain appointments.

Colonel Daniel MacCormack, a Scotch-American retired Army officer in his mid-fifties, had been appointed the commissioner of immigration in 1932. Little authority had been invested in him, and any decision he made could be vetoed by the secretary of labor, the assistant secretary, the second assistant secretary, and the two assistants to the secretary. She retained MacCormack—a resourceful, commonsense humanist—and instructed her assistants "to respect his decisions and wishes in immigration and naturalization matters." A year later she requested the president to issue an executive order to legalize what was already a *fait accompli*. Also she sought to have MacCormack's title changed to commissioner general and his salary raised from $8,000 to $10,000 a year in the light of his responsibilities and his successful execution of them.

With the help of Turner W. Battle, her executive assistant, she quickly introduced her democratic town-hall-meeting methods by calling a conference in which fifty men and women were invited to discuss conditions at Ellis Island. Once New York City's immigrant receiving depot, it now received ferryloads of deportees from all parts of the country. To the social workers' publication, *Survey*, this reflected Frances Perkins's "willingness to temper justice with mercy, to administer the law with regard to the humanities." An Ellis Island Committee of Ten was formed to see to it that the Immigration Service incorporated humanitarian considerations.

Humanitarian considerations were far from negligible. Adolph Hitler had begun his reign of terror as chancellor of Germany in January, 1933. The German immigration quota was already full; German Jews were unable to get passports from their government. Few visas were being issued by the State Department because of strict adherence to the immigration act provisions having to do with immigrants' liability to become public charges. The news to the editor of the *American Hebrew* and others who sought to allow entry of the children of German Jews was most disheartening. Offsetting this was a liberal policy regarding extending visitors' permits. Often the president spoke and wrote to Frances Perkins about his concern for the "real hardship cases." Because they had to work within the framework of the law, she could only respond, "The problem, however, is a difficult one and we are studying and investigating each case thoroughly." For some people, deportation was tantamount to the death sentence executed in a Nazi concentration camp. MacCormack informed the branch and division heads of the service that the secretary of labor felt that the most important function was not only to enforce the law, but in addition the service should be "a truly helpful institution for all having business with it." As a consequence, a folder on immigration at the Roosevelt Library is filled with letters praising the service. One from a counsellor-at-law is typical: ". . . your helpful letter is one of the few I have received from a Governmental department indicating willingness to go beyond academic answers."

Attempts made by the secretary of labor to have the Immigration and Naturalization Service removed from her jurisdiction met with complete failure. Other problems, economic matters primarily, held the president's attention. Not until 1940 would the service become part of the Department of Justice, and then the press would treat the shift as indicative of Frances's guilt by default.

While Frances Perkins's number one responsibility was the U.S. Department of Labor, she served simultaneously in a less-heralded capacity as a member of President Roosevelt's "inner cabinet." This meant her counsel was sought regarding national policy frequently not directly pertinent to her department; it meant a broader perspective than if she had just functioned as the militant advocate for the wage earners of the nation. According to Rexford Tugwell, a "brain trustee" who was named assistant secretary of agriculture, none of the cabinet members could represent exclusively the special interests of the departments he or she headed.

The fiftieth anniversary publication of the Department of Labor subtly alludes to its being short-shrifted as a consequence:

Examined critically, it is evident that the Secretary's thinking was not initially concerned with the Department of Labor, its functions and administration. Her interests covered a far larger realm of discourse. She thought of the role of government as a whole as the avenue through which people might bring about the changes they desired. Consequently she was as much concerned with legislative enactment as with legal interpretation, as much with the development of governmental agencies outside of the Department of Labor as with strengthening the Department itself, as much with what the individual States might be able to contribute as with what the Federal Government should do.

In effect, Frances Perkins was more concerned with functional than with administrative matters. People interviewed years later concur wholeheartedly in their judgment that in no way was she an empire builder. This, of course, sat poorly with the heads of some of her divisions who strongly felt, and not without justification, that they could not expand activities in many obviously vital ways without appropriations for additional personnel. Their memoirs reflect a narrower division-centered view than Frances Perkins could afford to share.

As the historical review of the department notes, "She had the full support of the President." This meant that "she served as one of the chief focal points in the Administration for the ideas and constructive proposals of numerous outstanding thinkers throughout the world . . ." Further, she supported the president, even if it meant sacrificing her time and energies to his projects rather than to priority items on her own agenda.

*****

What was the economic situation that the secretary of labor saw in those first days in office? Her own evaluation is a poignant yet controlled understatement:

The record must begin with 1933. Economically the country was on the ragged edge of nothing. Unemployment was in its worst phase . . .

In 1933 wages were falling rapidly. There was a steady increase, throughout the late twenties and early thirties, in the number of people dependent upon private and public charity.

With the coming of depression the average earnings of wage earners dropped from $1,475 in 1929 to $1,119 in 1932. With this as the average, it is not difficult to imagine how small became the wages of those below the median in the economic scale. Pay checks of $2.00 and even less for a 60-hour week were known. There came the dark day of the bank holiday and it was evident that credit along with wages was falling.

The spiral was downward and accelerating. It had to be stopped and reversed. The realization came that we must at once restore employment, through either public or other means. Other alarming problems were present. The sweat shop was flourishing, long hours at meagre pay were the rule, oppressive child labor was on the increase. But all these had to be dealt with later. First, men must be put to work.

Roosevelt had an idea for putting men to work that he tested on Frances during their first weeks in office. If it had shortcomings, he could trust her to tell him so, critically and constructively. She listened to his plans for a national reforestation program—the Civilian Conservation Corps—and she immediately knew the Department of Labor could not handle such a program alone. Even the recruitment of personnel presented a problem because the U.S. Employment Service was practically defunct. The president told her to revive it. He thought all kinds of unemployed men could work in the woods for a stipend on which they could survive more satisfactorily than in the cities. Frances pointed out: "It would mean putting into wholly unfamiliar jobs men with no knowledge of the woods nor any inclination for that kind of work. Further, it would take in men in all gradations of physical health, a large percentage of them unsuited by environment or temperament for the jobs required of them."

He agreed that the matters of selection and placement, of education and compensation, would be left up to her. He also agreed that the Army knew more about camp construction and care of the men and that the Department of Agriculture's Forest Service and the Department of the Interior could map out the conservation program.

On March fourteenth, he sent a memorandum to Secretary of War George H. Dern, Secretary of the Interior Harold L. Ickes, Secretary of Agriculture Henry A. Wallace, and Secretary of Labor Frances Perkins, with the simple statement, "I am asking you to constitute yourselves an informal committee of the Cabinet to coordinate the plans for the proposed Civilian Conservation Corps."

The speed with which Roosevelt's simple idea was implemented astounds anyone familiar with the legislative process. To Frances, who had spent five years getting the fifty-four-hour bill passed in New York State, it seemed incredible.

At her first press conference she announced to the reporters that the Department of Labor had no news to report. Things were in the offing, of course, as she was working with the president on his two new organizations, one of them a Civilian Conservation Corps that would put young men to work in the woods. She had dropped a bomb.

William Green of the AFL, looking for his chance, immediately opened fire on her. He assumed, as did many others, that the idea for the CCC emanated from her, and he told the world that what this antiunion woman proposed actually represented "forced labor," that the one dollar a day pay would undermine the wage scale of all workers.

Labor leaders William Green and David Dubinsky escorting Frances Perkins to a benefit performance of "Pins and Needles," Washington, D.C., December 5, 1935.

Frances told him the one dollar a day was actually relief money.

"Nevertheless," Green responded, "it is wages—they are getting it as wages."

"It's called wages only to save face," said Frances.

He refused to endorse the bill, which surprised and disappointed the president.

On March twenty-third Frances testified on behalf of the proposed conservation program. From the gallery where they viewed her, reporters later wrote, "In her debut before Congress . . . standing in the glare of Kleig lights . . . Madame Secretary made such a favorable impression that many a hostile vote was won over to the White House plan." William Green testified against it, to no avail.

On April fifth, shortly after the Seventy-third Congress authorized the emergency conservation work, President Roosevelt signed his Executive Order 6101. Immediately the U.S. Employment Service began the process of selecting and enrolling 25,000 unmarried young men.

In June, 1933, for the first time in history, a cabinet member and a first lady held a joint press conference. Eleanor Roosevelt and Frances Perkins announced the formation of a CCC camp for unemployed young women in New York and New Jersey. Earlier, at Eleanor Roosevelt's request, Frances Perkins had her staff check on the employment opportunities for women in horticulture. Although around 200,000 young "wandering women" needed employment, the federal or state tree and plant nurseries could only offer work two months a year.

Of the thirty dollars a month the young people aged seventeen to twenty-three were paid, twenty-two dollars a month went to enrollees' dependents or were retained by the government until they left the corps, after a minimum period of six months or a maximum of two years. Eight dollars a month for spending money presented relatively little hardship, as enrollees received a complete outfit of clothing, food, shelter, medical and dental care, and necessary transportation without charge. Leaders earned up to forty-five dollars and their assistants a maximum of thirty-six dollars a month.

On April seventeenth the first 200-man camp was set up at Luray, Virginia. By June 30, 1935, the CCC employed 1,242,000 men, including 32,000 Indians and 8,000 enrollees from American territories.

As a result of the Reorganization Act of 1939, the CCC became part of the Federal Security Agency. Over the next few years many camps were absorbed into the military defense program, while others continued in forestry and fire prevention work until the project's termination on April 15, 1943.

Years later Frances would classify the Civilian Conservation Corps as "one of the most effective experiments in the history of social welfare." She proudly boasted, "Thousands of families had been eliminated from local relief rolls. Enrollees regained self-respect and self-confidence, benefited physically from their work and mentally through educational activities." Decades later prosperous-looking, dignified gentlemen in their forties would stand in line after her lectures to personally give testimony to what the CCC had meant to them in terms of their survival. These stalwart "first-citizens," moved by her words and more so by their recollections, talked to the little lady then in her seventies, with reverence in their voices, and tears streaming down their faces. A young local reporter viewing the maudlin spectacle would feel repugnance and avoid mention of this in her article, which was appropriate, as the adulation and gratitude these men felt was very private and personal.

*****

The CCC constituted a small part of her first one hundred days in office. The conference of labor leaders that Frances Perkins described at the first meeting of the cabinet materialized on March 31, 1933. Clara Beyer reported, "Miss P's conference went over in fine shape. She won the labor group in remarkable fashion." Following the conference, according to another onlooker, a labor chieftain pressed her hand and said, "You are a 'wiz.' " Those who overheard it were convinced of the sincerity of the tribute.

The conference brought out the need for some form of federal unemployment relief that would not be used to supplement sweatshop wages. It emphasized the need to eliminate child labor, the curtailment of hours of labor, and the establishment of a minimum wage pegged to a basic level of living. Boards should be established to settle labor disputes, and the government should purchase from firms that had satisfactory working conditions. Public and semipublic buildings should function as educational centers for the unemployed.

Actually the ten-point program that the meeting "produced" originated with the competent people in the Department of Labor. Frances used this opportunity to press her view that "the reforms, while in effect on an emergency basis, were of basic importance in the national

industrial and economic life and many should be made permanent."
Not until she had left public life did Frances Perkins candidly describe
this and similar conferences:

> The suggestions from labor leaders were practically of no consequence, in the
> early years, being limited to such ideas as permission for the unemployed to
> sleep in public buildings, the improvement of soup kitchens, and the
> immediate abolition of child labor. . . . It indicated how frustrated they were
> and how unable they had become to think in terms of the great public problem
> because of the tenor of the depression. The best suggestions came from
> people from the Department of Labor who had been thinking long about
> some of these things.

The most important effect of the first labor leader conference was
that Frances Perkins won the labor leaders to her side, at least for the
moment.

During Hoover's administration, Senator Hugo L. Black of Bir-
mingham, Alabama, introduced a bill, based on "the stagnation principle," limiting the hours of work to thirty. Still pending when Roosevelt
came into office, the bill would do little to solve unemployment
problems. For political reasons, the president felt that mild support
should be given to the bill, with amendments relating to a floor under
wages and modifying the number of working hours in various industries. Frances Perkins proposed some of the points made by Sidney
Hillman when he had visited her some months before her appointment.

On April 25, 1933, Frances testified before the House labor committee on Black's thirty-hour bill. Among the spectators were Eleanor
Roosevelt, the first president's wife to attend a congressional hearing on
a labor bill. She also brought White House guest Ishbel MacDonald, the
daughter of England's Prime Minister Ramsey MacDonald, and their
mutual friend, Mary Dewson. Frances, following the line prescribed to
her by the president, proposed amendments to make the Black bill
workable. She admitted to the committee members that spreading the
work with a thirty-hour law in no way alleviated the problem of
inadequate purchasing power. Minimum wages needed to be established
for businesses involved with interstate commerce so that a reasonable
level of living could be assured. She added that minimum wage
provisions should cover all workers so as to "put a bottom to the fall of
wages." The Senate passed the thirty-hour bill fifty-three to thirty.

Frances Perkins's lack of enthusiasm for it went unnoticed. The press
charged that she proposed to give herself the "powers of a czar over

industry," that her views expressed "left-wing radicalism" and "Soviet-ism," and that she was a "Mrs. Hitler" and "a super-manager of American industry." Her bad press was the price she paid to retain for the administration the amity of Senator Hugo L. Black, who would be named to the Supreme Court by President Roosevelt in 1937.

Within days of her testimony two letters arrived at her office threatening her life. There was some concern as to whether or not she should make a scheduled speech at a dinner in Philadelphia. She did so with twenty-five policemen standing guard while she spoke. She explained that her modest plan was intended to make the Black bill workable. The *New York Times* wrote that she was "astonished and amused" that her plan should be regarded as a demand for "broad and sweeping control of industry."

On the positive side, Frances generated support from labor and civic organizations for the Wagner-Peyser Act setting up a national employment service. This, she noted, "fulfilled a need which had long been felt by the most disadvantaged group; it offered a welcome alternative to the system of privately operated employment agencies, many of which were notorious for their unscrupulous practices. . . ." The earlier federal employment service functioned in only twenty-three states. By the end of 1933 almost every county in the nation would have an office that helped recruit labor for the public works programs as well as the CCC. The Wagner-Peyser Act also established a federal advisory council consisting of representatives of employers and employees who formulated policies and discussed problems relating to employment. The secretary of labor personally selected the twenty-two representatives of the public and fourteen each from organized labor and management.

A major function of the president's cabinet was bringing in knowledgeable people to assist the administration in "doing something" to swing the economy around. Frances brought, among others, Harry Hopkins of the New York State Temporary Emergency Relief Administration and William Hodson of New York City's Welfare Council to see the beleaguered president. They worked with Senators Wagner, La Follette and Costigan on the Federal Emergency Relief Administration, a first step in the "economic pump priming," which materialized on May 12, 1933, with Hopkins as the administrator. It was a temporary measure about which Hopkins admitted, "The money, spent honestly and with constant remembrance of its purpose, bought more of courage than it ever bought of goods."

Supplanting the FERA, the Civil Works Program provided work rather than doles. Harry Hopkins selected the projects with the cooperation of local agencies as well as of politicians. Imbued with the principles of work relief programs, he became convinced that they obviated the need for unemployment insurance.

As she had in New York State, Frances Perkins still advocated an unemployment insurance system. At every opportunity she promoted the idea that the states set up reserves to displace the bread lines: "a systematic, honorable method of tiding over a slump period for those who want work and lack it." She firmly believed that "the cost should be assessed as one of the industrial hazards for which industry itself must provide." The "drying up of purchasing power" is something industry can ill afford; yet it is coincident with economic insecurity.

"Big Business" promptly tagged her prolabor as she boldly asserted that "employers have a certain social responsibility in the conduct of their industries. . . ."

> As a Nation we are recognizing that programs long thought of as merely labor welfare, such as shorter hours, higher wages, and a voice in the terms and conditions of work, are really essential economic factors for recovery and for the technique of industrial management in a mass-production age.

The secretary of labor did not place the entire burden of industrial reform on business. She threw out a challenge to the laboring man as well: "The test of adjusting our industrial life . . . [poses] . . . a new responsibility for constructive leadership on the part of labor."

Frances Perkins's most significant contribution to the welfare of both organized and unorganized labor took form in section 7 (a) of the National Industrial Recovery Act, harbinger of the Wagner National Labor Relations Act. It decreed: "Employers shall comply with a maximum hours of labor, minimum rates of pay, and other conditions of employment approved or prescribed by the President." The National Recovery Administration (NRA) codes set up on an ad hoc basis eliminated many social abuses.

Organized labor received a spur in title I, section 7 (a) that provided employees with the "right to organize and bargain collectively through representatives of their own choosing" as well as circumscribing joining a union as a condition of employment. Frances Perkins observed that John L. Lewis and Sidney Hillman were the first to latch on to section 7 (a) to reinforce their unions:

> John L. Lewis' union on the eve of the passage of the NRA, was down to rock bottom. Lewis himself had few men he could lead. Hillman's union was not as threadbare in membership but it had little money in its treasury. He

proceeded to carry on a suspension basis thousands of people who were out of work and could not pay their union dues. But both men saw that Section 7 (a) of NRA gave them the tremendous legal lever to lift their unions to new heights of strength. This was not true of other leaders in the American Federation of Labor who were either ignorant of the full meaning of Section 7 (a) of the NRA or too indifferent to utilize it.

Frances categorized Sidney Hillman as "one of the few labor leaders who could think," and had him placed on the Labor Advisory Committee of the NRA under General Hugh Johnson. Dan Tobin of the AFL was another of the labor leaders she and President Roosevelt consulted frequently; he numbered among those later sent to study conditions in England.

*****

The secretary of labor had occasional bouts with an affliction known facetiously as foot-in-mouth disease. On May 22, 1933, she addressed the Welfare Council of New York City:

> ... I have said in the last few weeks ... that if the minimum rates of pay and the hours of work could be fixed in the Southern mills and in the Southern employments generally, that those who wanted to get rich quick ought to buy a shoe factory for people who may have their wages for the first time in a generation come up to the level of living wages. ... a social revolution can take place if you put shoes on the people of the South.

A similar "shoeless South" remark, based on her earnest enthusiasm for building up the job market, threw the press in a tizzy. Reporters quoted every Southern legislator they could reach. Most defended the "barefoot boy with cheek." Senatory Bailey of Georgia, with pseudo-righteous indignation, sonorously declared, "Why, even the mules down South wear shoes." Another was astounded: "Imagine the wear and tear on the sidewalks of every village in Alabama if a good 50% of the pedestrians were shod in hard leather ... It would have a dumfounding effect in mills or at farm festivals."

Bess Furman, an Associated Press reporter, in *Washington By-Line* reviewed what she regarded as a milestone among Frances Perkins's early press conferences. Frances showed the reporters her shelves where over two thousand proposals for economic recovery were stacked. Most of them, she explained, fell into one of six categories:

First, those wanting government to take over all industry and operate it for the benefit of the people.

Second, those advocating some sort of subsidy, loan, or allowance to private industry for the purpose of re-employing a certain percentage of those out of jobs, with a fixed line of wages, and a limit to profit during the period of federal encouragement.

Third, plans for setting up industrial boards similar to the War Labor Board to speed up the industrial process—these boards not to take over, but to act as arbiters on production, wages, and hours.

Fourth, plans based on the conception of a permanent future of combining agriculture and industry—resettling the people of this country on thinly settled spots, and having near them a small industry, where farm life and farm living might be combined with some cash wages. Her own comment on this was: "The kind of a plan I like to discuss myself in front of a fireplace— interesting but no good next month because it doesn't come to grips with the problem."
[sic]
Five, an enormous program of a great variety of public works, and great reclamation projects, making over the surface of the land.
[sic]
Six, re-establishing of barter plans in a big way. This she saw only as "a makeshift and better than not eating."

Bess Furman noted that both the people at Associated Press and at United Press felt that Frances Perkins's press conference was the most outstanding of any in Washington. Unfortunately, the ballyhooing press got more mileage out of the "shoeless South" story and for years incorporated it into their articles on the first woman cabinet member.

Rather sensitive impressions of Frances Perkins's first months in office were recorded by Margaret G. Bondfield, the first woman cabinet member in England, also charged with the portfolio of labor. Her article, "Revolution in the U.S.A.," recorded for the *Survey Graphic* her visit to Washington, D.C., in the summer of 1933. She found that the Department of Labor was housed in temporary quarters as was her own Ministry of Labor in Whitehall.

. . . but there the likeness ends. Instead of a duke's mansion, with its marble staircases and painted ceilings and rabbit-warren of little rooms, it is extremely utilitarian and unadorned. The Secretary herself severely tailored in black with a touch of white, has shared the fate which seems to fall upon women Cabinet Ministers of being in the center of the storm, and in her case, with some extraneous disturbances which she might have been spared.

Her praises for Frances Perkins were eulogistic:

> As a guide to the "revolution" she was superb. It was fascinating to watch her imperturbably calm in the tempest of excitement, steering her barque of policy between the Scylla of an unfounded optimism and Charybdis of a pessimism which whirls around *laissez-faire.*

The U.S. secretary of labor's knowledge and understanding of the British system of unemployment insurance astounded her; she sympathized with the view that the American program had to be based on American conditions as well as on shifting public opinion. As the labor minister saw it:

> From all sides it amounts to an attack upon the old idea of American individualism; there is a recognition of the fact that the wage scales have never been so high as to give reserves to the workers to tide them over periods of unemployment.

The legislation whizzed through the Congress at a head-spinning rate. In retrospect, Frances Perkins admitted making many mistakes: "One error was that I expected vigorous, clear partisan opposition, long analytical debates, modifications, intelligent and constructive proposals from the opposition, and instead our bills sometimes went skimming through before we had a chance to perfect them."

*****

Ike Hoover, the chief usher of the White House, taught the cabinet members how to survive shaking thousands of hands without mutilation. Frances quickly mastered the art of gripping a person's hand lightly but firmly between the knuckles and fingertips. This spared her wrist from pumping and her palm from crushing as it virtually incapacitates over-enthusiastic handshakers with 100-pound fraternity grips. Like Eleanor Roosevelt, Frances found that in the moment the person was gently drawn past her, some interesting fact or kind sentiment would be expressed that would make the crowd filing by more than just a blur of faces. The handshaking ritual accompanied every banquet, reception, tea, and honorific occasion; she claimed that she did not find it an ordeal.

The secretary of labor took no offense in the protocol that decreed that the cabinet members' wives ranked above her at social functions. Even though she had earned her position, she headed the last department to be established. On the other hand, women senators had precedence over senators' wives. She learned that at least once a year her attendance was expected at a luncheon meeting that the senators' wives held weekly. Also, she must give a luncheon for the president's wife.

She discovered that as a cabinet member, she preceded senators and foreign ministers at social functions, but she was supposed to call on them rather than vice-versa. This proved difficult, and senators who wanted to speak to the secretary of labor not infrequently "cooled their heels" in her front office like anyone else.

Matters of protocol concerned her less than social amenities disconcerted the many men with whom she dealt. If she arrived last for a cabinet meeting—which happened at times—all of the men except the wheelchair-bound president felt obligated to rise from their seats. The labor union men could no longer prop their feet on the desk nor employ vocabulary presumed to be offensive to a lady (little realizing that she not only knew street language, she could use it for shock value if necessary).

As a change of pace, Frances enjoyed getting together with "the girls" occasionally. Eleanor Roosevelt arranged the get-togethers over lunch every few weeks. She recognized that the two of them derived minimal pleasure from "the perfunctory side of social life in which people come together first and foremost as a duty, though by good luck, it might often prove to be a pleasure as well." She and Frances shared gripes and inside news with Isabella Greenway, a member of Congress from Arizona, Caroline O'Day, a representative-at-large from New York, and Lady Lindsay, the British ambassador's American-born wife.

More often, the social functions Frances attended were large, full-blown, formal affairs. The first of many took place on March 24, 1933, in the magnificent crystal chandelierred ballroom of the Hotel Commodore in New York City. Fourteen hundred guests paid homage to her integrity, courage, and vision. Through her many years under the unrelenting glare of the spotlight, the tributes periodically bestowed so lavishly on her would help mitigate the ugly criticisms meted out from other sources. On this occasion, her daughter Susanna and four of Frances's classmates from Mount Holyoke's class of 1902 were present. Eleanor Roosevelt set the mood with her anecdote:

A Senator called the President the other evening while I was sitting in his room, and after a few moments of conversation the telephone was put down and a broadly smiling President remarked "For the second time a chairman of a committee informs me that our new lady member of the Cabinet has made the best impression of anyone that they had had before them in a long time. She had completely won them over to her comprehensive knowledge of her subject and her clear exposition." He added, "It is pleasant to have one's judgment approved in such a cordial way."

In June, Goucher College, a women's college in Baltimore, Maryland, conferred upon her the degree of doctor of laws, complete with hood, diploma, all the pomp and circumstance appropriate to commencement exercises, and a glowing citation by the sponsoring professor of economics, Dr. Elinor Pancoast and by the university president, Dr. David Allan Robertson.

Later that month she went to Madison, where University of Wisconsin President Glenn Franks concluded glowing introductory remarks with:

Because having achieved national leadership by the compelling power of a superlative capacity, the accident of your being a woman has lifted womankind above that separation of sex which has, over the centuries, exiled so much feminine genius from the councils of government, I am happy to confer upon you the honorary degree of Doctor of Law.

The 6,000 people in attendance gave a thunderous ovation as Frances Perkins crossed the platform. She somberly credited the University of Wisconsin faculty, particularly Professors Ely and Comstock, with turning her mind toward the field of social welfare through their writings. She was followed by Pulitzer-Prize-winning poet and author Edna St. Vincent Millay, who acknowledged that she felt "proud to be on the same platform with so distinguished a stateswoman as Miss Perkins."

For this particular function the secretary of labor had arrived in Madison early enough to allow time to visit with the economics and sociology faculties of the university, to garner opinions and ideas from as many progressive academic people as possible, and to update her Simon Nelson Patten economics background. She invariable derived some secondary benefits from her travels; in this instance, some free education. Elsewhere she might indulge her penchant for visiting art museums.

Frances looked to the universities particularly for feedback on her own progressive ideas—and for subtle propagandizing. That August, for example, she addressed the Institute of Public Affairs at the University of Virginia on "compulsory reserves against the ordinary hazards of industrial unemployment. . . ."

She stressed that "If such a system is to succeed, if it is to be a benefit instead of a burden, if it is to be kept away from the entanglements of dole features, it must prove a going enterprise." Equally important, she asserted, "politics must be kept from entering into its definition of benefits and its administration."

She visualized a group of states setting up an authority "along the lines of the Port Authority of New York and New Jersey, a public body with the advantages of a corporate organization." This had to be a compulsory system. "The managers of industry would be exerting themselves to reduce their premiums just as they became interested in safety devices to cut their premiums under various state workmen's compensation laws." In other words, "an incentive for the stabilization of employment" would be provided.

The secretary of labor's many speeches on unemployment insurance served to educate those whom she knew were most likely to communicate with their representatives in Congress. She anticipated legislation going into the hopper soon.

*****

People couldn't help wondering about Frances Perkins's home life when she wasn't working or traveling. Isolated dribbles of information indicate that she maintained a fourth floor apartment at 1239 Madison Avenue in New York City. Two days after she took office, the family's dog, Balto, a reddish-brown, stubby-tailed Irish terrier, ran away from home. This tidbit rated a *New York Times* story complete with picayune details on the dog's height and the tricks it could do. Balto returned home.

Frances employed a man full time to take care of her invalid husband while he was able to live at home. Susanna, labeled a "sub-deb," was finishing high school and had been accepted by Bryn Mawr College. Frances saw both her husband and daughter on her frequent trips to New York for business as well as pleasure. She kept her husband posted on her many activities and occasionally he provided counsel that proved useful in maintaining her perspective.

In Washington, D.C., she shared with Mary Harriman Rumsey a handsome corner home on P Street in nearby Georgetown. The daughter of a railroad tycoon and sister of Averell Harriman, Mary

Rumsey had been widowed some eleven years earlier when Charles Cary Rumsey, a polo-playing sculptor, was killed in an automobile accident. She had raised their daughter and two sons, managed their estate, and developed an interest in scientific farming and the cooperative movement. As a debutante she had helped found the Junior League with its emphasis on good works and had known Frances Perkins as a young social worker frequenting the settlement houses.

Mary Rumsey apparently knew everybody in Washington. According to Queens College economics professor Persia Campbell, who would become the New York State consumer counsel in the fifties under Governor Averell Harriman, Mary was "always a picturesque figure, an impulsive and erratic organizer, but persistent in the pursuit of her ends, and with great driving force."

NRA's General Johnson, not overly enthusiastic about including a Consumers Advisory Board on the National Recovery Administration, specifically requested that his friend Mary Rumsey chair the board. Although initially naive as to the full scope of her assignment, Mary Rumsey's innate interest and ability, plus the assistance of her consumerist house companion, Frances, enabled her to find her bearings and frequently stand up to the obstreperous General Johnson. She promoted the formation of consumer groups across the country, and encouraged them to report consumer concerns to her.

Because of her *entrée* to the White House and the respect she engendered, she was a wise choice for the first consumer's voice officially introduced into federal government. The Consumer Advisory Board suffered a tragic setback when she died suddenly following a horseback riding accident on her Virginia estate in December, 1934.

The extent of Frances Perkins's shock and bereavement is not known. Certainly attending to Mary Rumsey's effects in their shared home was a sad task. Some time later Frances realized she had no proper photograph of her friend, and she wrote to the family asking for one. Many years later she warned her own admiring secretary that she had better not put off getting Frances's autographed photograph because one could never know when it would be too late.

While his sister was alive, Averell Harriman visited often. He recalled Frances Perkins as being very forceful without being controversial. She had incredible political understanding and tended to persuade rather than be demagogic. He felt that she achieved a great deal in a quiet manner, and he remembered her vibrant personality and ready grin.

*****

In the fall of 1933 at the annual convention of the American Federation of Labor, its president, William Green, declared with genuine sincerity, "I am pleased beyond expression to present to you Miss Frances Perkins, Secretary of Labor." Frances invariably experienced the stage fright that guarantees a superb performance. She wanted to win the goodwill of all these men, officers and delegates of labor unions and local chapters, who looked at her so expectantly.

Her lengthy talk, a straightforward progress report, brought in the ten points recommended by the committee that had met with her on March thirty-first. At the instigation of the labor unions, she pointed out, the Department of Labor's program was rapidly fulfilling the "aspirations of the old fashioned trade unionist," under the label "a free economic plan for recovery."

She made her lengthy discourse palatable not only by her animated delivery, but by interspersing intellectual content with the anecdotes she related in spell-binding, climax-building, pseudo-serious tones. In most cases her elaborate tale dramatized a significant concept rather obviously.

Her speech emphasized the unity of members of a great democracy, that what working people (namely union members) want is what all people find right and necessary. In effect, she was carefully, cautiously sowing seeds to bring about reform in labor union structure.

She elaborated on the new spirit of unity and of action abroad in the land under the president's inspiring leadership. "The worker, the employer and the consumer are united at this moment in cooperating in a drive against the forces which have brought want, despair and misery into so many homes in the last few years." In response to her plea for positive whole-hearted, constructive cooperation, the president of the AFL, William Green, who just a few months earlier had declared that unions would never be reconciled to her appointment, pledged:

> I want to assure her with all the sincerity I possess, in answer to her plea, that this great American labor movement will give to her and those associated with her in the administration of the Department of Labor, full, complete and unreserved support. And if she gets into a fight with those who would seek to hamper her in her work or limit the activities of this Department, call upon the hosts of labor and we will supply millions to help you.

After the speeches, two delegates, Nathanial Spector and Max Goldman of the Cap and Millinery Department of the United Hatters Union, presented her with a black felt hat. In contrast to her usual tricorn, this swashbuckler had a brim turned up on one side and down on the other, decorated with two bows and a silver buckle. In her note of thanks to them, she said that she never realized that she could wear such a becoming hat. And like her tricorn, it would be a symbol of a great and growing union.

In the late fall of 1933 she spoke at Atlanta University on the deplorable situation faced by the "colored laborer." The newspapers cited her as regarding of the utmost importance the building of better homes for "colored families" in Atlanta, and expressing special interest in the proposed housing project for them in the neighborhood of the university.

X

Working for "That Woman!"

Elizabeth Brandeis scribbled a postscript to her letter of March 12, 1933: "It must be thrilling to work under your new chief. By the way, who is to be head of Labor Statistics?"

By return mail, Clara Beyer responded:

Feathers are beginning to fly around the Department of Labor. The whole atmosphere has changed since March 4. I wish you could see the men who threatened to resign if a woman was appointed; they are crawling on hands and knees. So far no changes in personnel have been made. Miss Perkins is wise in looking over the field and also in learning something of the work of the Department before she moves in this direction. I have heard no rumours as to the head of Labor Statistics. Lubin wants the job, but that does not necessarily mean that he will get it.

Frances Perkins saw little justification for firing experienced, knowledgeable personnel simply because of their political affiliation or to accomodate the patronage system. The indomitable Mary Anderson who had succeeded Mary Van Kleeck, the first director of the Women's Bureau, in 1919, and the friendly Grace Abbott, who had followed the first Children's Bureau head Julia C. Lathrop in 1921, continued their efforts without interruption. The department's librarian remained Laura A. Thompson, who had held the position for a decade before the Department of Labor became a separate entity. Also retained were Hugh L. Kerwin who had served as the director of conciliation since 1917 and Samuel J. Gompers, Jr., chief clerk and superintendent since 1918.

The secretary of labor made countless new appointments. She recruited Charles E. Wyzanski as solicitor of the department, making him third in command. They first met in April, 1933, the afternoon of the day she testified on behalf of Senator Black's thirty-hour bill. He later gave this overview:

> Amidst panic and confusion worse than any I have ever encountered, she was sensibly concentrating on the recruitment of personnel whose capacity (sometimes as yet not fully proven) and industry, integrity, and independence could be relied upon to formulate and administer the plans of those sectors of the New Deal that were either in or tangent to the Labor Department. When one now reviews the roster of appointments for which she was responsible, the list of persons to whom she freely delegated vast responsibilities, what a splendid list it was! For the chairmanship of the National Labor Relations Board, Lloyd Garrison and later Francis Biddle; for Commissioner of Labor Statistics, Isador Lubin; for heads of special labor tribunals, Governor John G. Winant of New Hampshire and Chief Justice Stacy of North Carolina; for lawyers, Thomas H. Eliot (later Chancellor of Washington University, St. Louis), Professor Charles Gregory of the University of Virginia, Gerard D. Reilly (later a member of the NLRB), Professor Henry M. Hart of the Harvard Law School; the present Solicitor General, Archibald Cox; for important administrative posts, Arthur Altmeyer, Grace Abbott, Kathryn Lenroot, Mary La Dame, Frances Jurkowitz—the roll stands as a challenge for comparison with any department of government at any time in our history.

Each one on the roll could tell a tale of Miss Perkins's gaiety, charm, and courage. How warmly she encouraged them. How greatly she trusted them. With what personal attention she followed their family and individual development.

Wyzanski and many others attest to her unswerving loyalty to those with whom she associated ". . .so long, but only so long, as each was true to the best in himself as his own vision saw the best."

Mary Dewson on the other hand, analyzed Frances Perkins's personnel practices from the perspective of a behind-the-scenes politician. She attributed Frances's time-consuming deliberations on personnel changes to "uncertainty as to her own judgment of persons." Frances, she suspected, also disliked having to adjust to other human beings. While little evidence supports this critique, it is true that she was disinclined to discharge a person who proved unsatisfactory; she loathed admitting, even to herself, that an individual had not lived up to her expectations. And she preferred having a position vacant to having an inept individual create a mess from which that person's successor might find extrication difficult if not impossible.

On one occasion, Mary recommended Ethel M. Smith, a member of the Women's Trade Union League, for a position in the department, and Frances, who liked this friendly woman, agreed that she would try to find a place for her. But for the most part, Frances rejected having people foisted on the department because of their affiliation with a labor union or the Democratic party. She let both Mary and Postmaster General James Farley know this in no uncertain terms.

Mary Dewson, to whom Frances owed her own position, was personally incensed. She felt:

> ...Miss Perkins did not have to show her contempt for the patronage system. Her alternatives were to do something constructive about it, or to go along with it and concentrate on her main objectives. As that keen-minded old thinker, Florence Kelley of the National Consumers League, used to say, "Don't fight on all fronts at once. You will collect for the main issue additional enemies but no additional friends."

Senator Joseph F. Guffey was another who took offense at Frances Perkins's "lack of interest and cooperation in matters of patronage." And as Mary Dewson claimed, Frances was not like Thomas Jefferson "about whom we must deduce opinions." You could always reach Frances by telephone, and she would say what she thought, somewhat too decisively.

From her first day in office, Frances had been under pressure to replace Robe Carl White as assistant secretary, a position he had held since 1925. The person suggested to her by Postmaster General James Farley, among others, was Edward F. McGrady of the American Federation of Labor. She knew that the AFL actually wanted McGrady in the top position as secretary of labor. But would putting him second in command placate the labor unions? And was that sufficient cause for making the appointment? James Farley, an impressively big man who headed the Democratic party, a rugged gum-chewing man who proudly proclaimed that he was an honest politician, naturally took offense at Frances's failure to act on his recommendation. Yet his admiration for Frances as a person of incredible integrity in no way diminished. Although as a fellow cabinet member he found her at times a trifle too voluble, he unstintingly acknowledged her prodigiousness and her ability and willingness to accept blows that he felt should have been aimed at others. He could not force an assistant secretary on her.

On July 14, 1933, Frances sent a telegram to that oldest of friends, Joe Caylor of Philadelphia, asking him to come to Washington Saturday morning: "I should like to talk to you and will appreciate it very

A note from the President attached to this unidentified newspaper photo of Frances Perkins and James A. Farley read: "After all these years of trusting you I believed that I could let you go to Chicago without a chaperone. You really must not let the camera men catch you when you are so truly coy! F.D.R.," July 16, 1940.

much." Although his brother George's memoirs indicate nothing about the nature of the meeting, Sarah, Joe and George Caylor's sister, believed that at one time Frances offered Joe an undersecretaryship in the Department of Labor. The timing suggests that the sister's suspicions were not unfounded. According to Sarah, Joe refused the appointment on the grounds that he didn't want to work for the federal government.

In the next telegram retained in Joe's file, dated August 8, 1933, Frances invited him to become a member of the Federal Advisory Council. Joe met with other members of the council at the Mayflower Hotel on Monday, the fourteenth. In a letter dated August twenty-first, Frances thanked Joe for a note she had received from him, and for his suggestions about a radio address.

Joe's files contained nothing more until June, 1939, when Frances wished to reappoint him to the advisory council as his term had expired. Arthur J. Altmeyer, who had now succeeded Robert Hutchins to the chairmanship of the council, also urged Joe Caylor to continue as a member because he particularly valued his recommendations on the development of the Social Security programs.

The Federal Advisory Council position paid no salary. However, travel expenses were reimbursed. It meant that Frances could occasionally see Joe Caylor, still a bachelor and possibly her "first love." If romance still lingered in her heart, absolutely no one knew of it, and his name is conspicuously absent from everything pertaining to her. If she had desired a discreet and secret romance, she chose well. Joe Caylor left no evidence. One of her confidantes claimed that Frances's sexual drive was completely sublimated, so that a platonic friendship—the kind that men and women do have, despite gossip-mongers who would attempt to distort such relationships—probably was the basis of their meetings, as well as an overriding interest in labor problems.

Joe Caylor may have been just one of many people whom she trusted enough to consider for the position of undersecretary. On August third, Robe Carl White submitted his resignation. Frances accepted it on the tenth, but with his assurance that he would stay on for a time to assist her.

When Edward McGrady was made assistant administrator of the National Recovery Administration, Frances saw something of his ability in handling labor matters. A tall, trim, suave gentleman, he spoke quite bluntly, intelligently, and to the point. Frances, who had reason to suspect that union leaders had arrived at their positions through qualities other than intellect, found herself impressed by McGrady's performance, particularly after he deftly handled strikes by the workers at the Frick Coke Company and the Pittsburg Coal Company. Shortly afterwards at a meeting of the cabinet, Frances had the opportunity to exchange a few words with James Farley. With her usual candor she told Farley that she had been wrong about McGrady. On August eighteenth, his appointment as undersecretary of labor was made official by her communication to the president.

Edward McGrady served the Department of Labor so effectively, one *Saturday Evening Post* feature writer accused Frances of jealously seeking to have him fired at the earliest propitious moment. Actually, Franklin D. Roosevelt's files contain numerous memoranda from the secretary of labor heaping praise on McGrady in connection with his various activities and requesting that the president congratulate McGrady personally for his successes. A number of these congratulatory messages she drafted herself for the president's signature. With great reluctance she accepted McGrady's resignation because of "compelling personal obligations" some four years later.

To illustrate Frances's dawdling over a personnel decision, Mary Dewson used the case of Arthur J. Altmeyer, who had terminated as chief of the Compliance Division of the National Recovery Administration in 1934. Mary and Clara M. Beyer decided that Altmeyer was just the person to serve as Frances's assistant secretary of labor. Mary recommended Altmeyer, whom she'd known while she was with the National Consumers League and he with the Wisconsin Industrial Commission as chief statistician. Frances agreed to consider Altmeyer, but failed to specify a time frame. Clara Beyer reported that Altmeyer, running out of patience, was tempted to accept an appointment at the University of Wisconsin in Madison.

Mary persuaded Altmeyer to wait another day. Before breakfast the next morning she telephoned Frances with the announcement, "I am coming over to see you. It's very important or I should not get you or myself up at this hour." Frances appointed Altmeyer to the assistant secretaryship, but in 1935 when he joined the Social Security Council as chairman, she did not replace him.

Considerable outside pressure was exerted on the secretary of labor regarding appointments, as this note, a precursor of the eventual personality clash, indicates:

August 5, 1937   The White House, Washington
                        CONFIDENTIAL

MEMORANDUM FOR THE SECRETARY OF LABOR

I hear John Lewis is miffed because you have not answered his letters, especially the one about filling the vacancy of Assistant Secretary of Labor.

                                               F.D.R.

She didn't knuckle under. Not until 1939 did she fill the position briefly with Marshall E. Dimock, then in 1940 with Daniel W. Tracy, whom she promoted a year later to undersecretary of labor. The assistant secretary's position remained open during her remaining years in office.

Whatever the reasons, with possibly one exception, she was not overtly under pressure from President Roosevelt. With his "well-developed sense of rumour," he passed on what he heard to her, then took her explanation at face value. On one occasion in 1934 he wrote her, "Complaint is made that a lot of old Davis appointees in Pennsylvania are still running things. Can you do anything about it?" She in no way interpreted this as a *carte blanche* order to dismiss people appointed years back by a predecessor, Secretary Davis. Rather, her investigation turned up only one Davis carry-over. She wrote the president that reports showed him to be one of the best and most capable employees in the service; he had demonstrated his competence particularly while working on the steel strike. That ended the matter.

The one seeming exception came out during interviews with former Department of Labor employees years later. W. Frank Persons was named director of the Re-employment Service, a temporary system of registration and placement set up to facilitate the immediate induction of the unemployed into public works. Apparently a "presidential appointee," Persons "felt his oats" and the secretary of labor "couldn't tell him anything."

Frances Perkins believed in assigning responsibility and authority to others, a creative energy-unleashing device she learned from her commander-in-chief. The director of conciliation, Hugh Kerwin, for one, proudly recorded in his first report that "a great majority of the cases submitted to the Department's representatives were settled without the necessity of a decision by the Secretary of Labor." She liked to oversee the operations, and if a person did the job as expected, her intervention was unnecessary. When errors were made, however, she assumed full responsibility for them.

One person she became heavily dependent upon once she decided to appoint him was Isador Lubin of the Brookings Institute, a former student of the iconoclast economist Thorstein Veblen, and a remarkable young statistician. At his first meeting with her in 1930 when she had testified at Senator Wagner's hearings on welfare, he had set his sights on being associated with her. He was tapped to head the department's Bureau of Labor Statistics, which Frances insisted be completely overhauled with the assistance of the American Statistical Association so that state industrial commissioners need not suspect the validity of its data as she had done.

In December, 1933, Isador Lubin was questioned on his authority to collect cost-of-living data, later the basis of the Consumer Price Index, and received vindication from Congress. He prepared the monthly press releases that explained the statistics his bureau collected and invariably stood by the secretary of labor's side prepared to answer questions during most of her sessions with the press. A charming, affable man, he played an ameliorative, supportive role, and simultaneously increased in stature.

In an interview many years later, he recalled how she always referred to the things "we are doing." This applied even when he erred seriously during the Christmas season of 1933 by sending out a personal letter of thanks to cooperating government officials, complete with holiday greetings and imprimateur. The director of the budget and comptroller were furious. Frances Perkins simply said to him, "Lube, we made a mistake."

Isador Lubin knew that she was very religious, but learned that she did not have a bias about religions. When he recommended Jake Perleman for an important job as head of the Wage Division, she asked, "What do you know about him?" Lubin mentioned religion.

"What has that got to do with it?" she asked. "If he is the best man for the job, take him."

Thirty-five years later, tears still filled Isador Lubin's eyes as he recalled the sudden death of his wife Ann in 1935. Senator Rifkin had phoned Frances's office to tell her. She insisted that Lubin not go to his home, but rather to her assistant's apartment. He arrived there at 2 P.M. At about 6. P.M. she came to the apartment. "I have just come from church where I prayed for Ann's soul." Her words of comfort meant much to him: "She treated me like a son."

In turn she depended on him as much as she depended on anyone. It must have been a blow, when, according to Isador Lubin, "In March, 1941, the President stole me." It didn't help matters that he was still on her payroll, and the department didn't get reimbursed.

Over eight years and more he came to know her as well as anyone could. Her early exposure to socialistic doctrines notwithstanding, he felt that she never was a socialist. "She had faith in our system." Also, she firmly believed in states' rights. As a consequence, he claims, "We are still paying for it," in connection with state unemployment insurance laws with their inexplicable, questionable, state-by-state differences in payment scales and eligibility requirements. He feels she misjudged the situation, yet Congress refuses to change the standards.

He recalls that she had little to do with day-to-day detail. She did maintain interest in what the various bureau heads were accomplishing. "At the end of the first year she asked what we ought to be doing next year and the year after."

He remembered that when Perleman came in she put the regulars in the back room. She encouraged him to be imaginative about wages and productivity. She didn't want him to be hamstrung by ideas of what was impossible. She thought if he worked with just three or four people he could get more done.

She warned, "Don't think about how big a job it is!" And she told him to remember "Certain things have to be done immediately." Yet she balanced it with another reminder: "You won't go to Hell if you don't solve the problem today."

Her job required an inhuman exercise of self-control. She restrained her anger with employees whose attitudes she found narrow-minded and stupid, with trade-union people who refused to cooperate. She could have acted the part of a man as she had in college plays. She raised her voice on occasion; she sounded dogmatic as she expressed her antagonism against unfairness, but regardless of her true feelings, she favored the role of genteel lady for the most part, in keeping with the prestige of her position.

She developed many friendships with employers, and while she may not have been exploitative by nature, she occasionally resorted to leverage, using the "good guys" against the "bad guys." She sent for Isador Lubin on one occasion when Goodyear Rubber Company employees were ready to strike. The heads of Goodyear were in her office, and in the back room she had the heads of Sears Roebuck.

To Goodyear she said, "If you won't be decent, Sears won't buy your tires." She told Lubin she had Sears in the back "just in case."

Goodyear didn't know it. According to Lubin, "She often used people in the business world to persuade others." Of course the strikes she averted made no headlines.

He remembers her aphorisms: "What did you do today that you didn't do yesterday?" "We are trying to save the world." But they were okay. "The people she worked with were a big family—close friends."

He respected her intellectuality with one exception: "Fundamentally, she was not daring enough." This is one reason why the Civilian Conservation Corps could never conceptually be credited to her. She later recognized it as a daring, successful sociological experiment. Its failure would have been laid on her head, but she could not be credited with its inception. She would not take a chance politically. And although many people labeled her a revolutionist or radical, the truth of the matter, according to Isador Lubin, was that "she had her feet on the ground. She was not a zealot."

Regarding racial discrimination, her actions give the clearest evidence of her stance. In March, 1934, she took on Lawrence Oxley as special assistant. Years later he could still remember Chief Clerk Samuel Gompers, Jr., telling him to take his papers to Frances Perkins's office. Miss Jay told him that the secretary would like to have him stay for a moment.

Frances Perkins extended her hand. "Mr. Oxley, we are awfully glad to have you join our family." A major assignment involved a national study of organized labor and the black worker. His qualifications for the assignment were impeccable. Born at the foot of Beacon Hill in Boston on May 17, 1887, he had studied two years at Harvard University, and in World War I was commissioned first lieutenant in the infantry and served as morale officer with the general staff. As special investigator with the War Department Commission on Training Camp Activities, he traveled across the country. Now he would be the first black man in an executive position in the Department of Labor.

The secretary of labor chatted with him generally, then said, "I want you to know we all make mistakes. While you are with us you are going to make mistakes." Looking at him straight on, "The first time, we will just forget it. The second time, I will go along with you. The third time it is your mistake."

According to Clara Beyer, the truth was that if anyone made a mistake Frances simply took the blame. "Word never got to anyone on the outside that a person on her staff had erred."

On one occasion, upon Oxley's return from St. Louis where he had spoken at Christ Church, Miss Jay called him to come to the office. When he arrived, Congressman Cochran of Missouri was seated across from Secretary Perkins. He didn't put his hand out so Frances Perkins said simply, "Mr. Oxley, have a chair." The congressman proceeded to explain that "his man in St. Louis" had said that Lawrence Oxley made some statements at Christ Church to which he objected. Frances Perkins called the library for a clipping that described the meeting and what Oxley said. It included his charge that white people were getting all the public works program jobs.

The congressman insisted that Oxley said other things.

"Who is your man in St. Louis?" asked Perkins, reserved, diplomatic, and cautious—her usual manner.

"I am not willing to divulge his name," was the response.

She showed him the clipping. "Would you take the word of the reporter?" She sounded angry. She turned to Oxley, "Did you say what the man said you did?"

Then to the congressman, "I will take the word of my man here."

"All right, Madam Secretary, but I will take action on this," retorted the congressman as he charged out the door.

"Mr. Oxley, I want you to forget this absolutely. I have dealt with Congressmen before."

According to Oxley, "She had no patience with mediocrity, but a gentle way with the neophyte." He frequently drafted material for her to use. She would look it over and point out its failing.

"You don't leave me any place to step back." She checked out his letters, caught him when he stated a fact unequivocally and suggested that he preface his assertion, "With all the information we have on hand it would appear. . . ."

He particularly remembered her reminder, "Facts alone are inadequate. Facts in their related order are powerful."

She would want to see him after he'd been out of town making a speech or conducting an investigation, but he could be sure it would never be between 9 A.M. and 5 P.M. He could count on her being free at 6:30 or 7:15. "She had a long day, but she would sit so calmly, patiently. Her eyes and eyebrows spoke louder than anything she might say." And she listened.

*****

The matter of industrial strikes beleaguered Frances Perkins's entire administration. She had been in office just a few weeks when the "children's strike" in Pennsylvania called attention to the thirteen, fourteen, fifteen and sixteen year olds employed in the manufacture of men's shirts and pajamas. Their spontaneous walkout protesting the pitiably small wages they received demonstrated to Frances Perkins "how low that particular industry had fallen."

To bring the cotton textile industry up to a level of "fair practice" under the first codes developed for the NRA was a monumental task. To Frances the arguments, the compromises, were necessary: "It was a way of democracy; it was a way of common sense; it was a way of morality."

Before the hearings on steel, she went up to the "steel country," to Homestead, Pennsylvania, the center of strife for decades.

To go through a great steel plant is a thrilling experience. There is no such blazing light in Fourth of July fireworks as when they tip the great containers and let out the white-hot steel; there are no more beautiful colors than the violet and rose tones that steel takes on as it cools—and perhaps no more strenuous place to work than at the open-hearth furnaces where steel is made.

And while she paraded through the plant, the former factory investigator barraged the company representatives with questions. "What are the hours?" "What are the wages?" "What constitutes a week of employment and how much employment is there in a year?" "How about accident insurance and unemployment insurance, and do you carry pensions for the workers?" "What about age limits?" "What is the present accident rate? And what are the safety devices to keep it down?"

She then went to Duquesne to see the blast furnaces and the runs where liquid steel was poured into forms for ingots and then flattened into sheets. Here, too, she asked her questions.

She particularly wanted to speak to the workers themselves. A parish pastor offered her the rectory; it was small, but she could speak to representatives chosen by the workers. These people called her "Miss Secretary" or "lady"; later, reverentially, they nicknamed her "Ma" Perkins because she cared about them, and she listened just as her own grandmother used to listen, and they felt "she was fair."

Desperate pleas for help came from individuals, and then from labor groups who discovered that section 7(a) of the NIRA was not an open-sesame to union recognition.

One of the labor leaders came to exclaim in frustration, "If only they would take us for granted"—meaning the employers—"if only we could be taken for granted for once, so that we would not have to use every ounce of our energy to fight for our existence. Then we could make the constructive contribution to the affairs of this particular industry which is so needed and which only the labor groups can make, because only the labor groups know intensely what are the problems and needs of this industry." Employers' nonrecognition tactics could be brutal, as this telegram illustrates:

THOUSANDS OF PEOPLE STRIKING IN COTTON FIELDS IN SAN JOAQUIN VALLEY. THE FORCES OF LAW HAVE PERMITTED THE RANCHERS TO BE ARMED WE ARE BEING THREATENED TO BE MOBBED AND OUR CAMPS RAIDED BY GUNMEN AND OUR WOMEN AND CHILDREN MURDERED. WE ARE ADVISED THIS VIOLENCE IS TO OCCUR TOMORROW MORNING.

C.H. ERNEST, CHAIRMAN AGRICULTURAL WORKERS INDUSTRIAL UNION.

On October 9, 1933, she wired California Governor James Rolph, Jr. Regional offices of the Conciliation Service were put into action. A spirit of cooperation had been established by the president through his governors' conferences and by Frances Perkins through her meetings with state industrial commissioners.

Franklin D. Roosevelt frequently found himself forced to defend his administration's position on labor disputes. At his press conference of November 8, 1933, he first emphasized the need to get people off the relief rolls and into regular employment, then responded to the inevitable question on strikes:

And yesterday, at the Council meeting, the Secretary of Labor reported that—and for the long-faced gentry throughout the country this will come as a terrible shock—reports that a survey of industrial disputes, made on a basis of comparisons the last previous comparable period, 1921, when we were beginning to snap back out of the post-war depression, shows that in the six summer months of 1921 there were 1453 strikes and lock-outs, and in 1933 there were 900. In the 1921 period 895,000 employees were involved in those strikes and lock-outs. In the same period this year 584,000 were involved. The Secretary of Labor said that this indicates, of course, that there is no need for the public to become in the least bit alarmed over present disputes. On the basis of man hours, the number of actual working hours involved, the comparison is even more favorable because, of course, in 1921 the average day's work was a great deal higher than it is today.

A reporter pointed out that the *Annalist* said Labor Department figures failed to show that strikes were rapidly rising in number in 1933, while they were decreasing in 1921. The president replied:

> Well, let's give the other side in order to make it fair. . . . This year there were strikes called for "test purposes," to get immediate entrance of the National Labor Board into the situation. . . . There were "friendly strikes." For example, garment unions affecting 40,000 people . . . done with a distinct objective, agreed to by the employers (to eliminate sweatshop competition) and employees.

> Then there is another thing which must be remembered always. In periods of rising prosperity and greater employment you always have an increase in the number of strikes for the very obvious human reason that an individual who is employed doesn't strike if he can possibly help it when unemployment is rising because if he strikes and it doesn't work he has no chance to get a job and he is thinking about the food for the family the next day. Therefore it is a pretty encouraging thing to see people who have the guts to stand up for their own rights and it means that they feel that they can get employment somewhere else if they are thrown out.

Privately Frances Perkins and her staff labeled some of the strikes " 'nonsense strikes' because you couldn't find out what it was that the workers wanted."

Section 8 of the act creating the Department of Labor empowered the secretary "to act as mediator and to appoint commissioners of conciliation in labor disputes whenever in his judgment the interests of industrial peace may require it to be done. . . ."

The case details of government activity in labor-management relations are conspicuously absent from the Department of Labor's early *Annual Reports*. The first merely notes that 9 cases had been successfully mediated; Frances Perkins's twenty-first states that 774 cases were adjusted.

In effect, section 8 of the act saw little service beyond the railroad and shipping industries, and generally the government involved itself minimally, by intent, in labor disputes before the passage of the Wagner Act of 1935.

Exactly twenty years after the establishment of the Department of Labor, Frances Perkins was the first secretary of labor with a college degree in lieu of a union membership card. She made labor leaders uneasy until, according to Eleanor Roosevelt and Lorena Hickok, they realized that "she was doing the job a Secretary of Labor is supposed to do—looking after the interests of labor—a rather new experience to them."

In keeping with the intent of the act, Frances emphasized promotion of the welfare of *all* the workers, not just union members, and abhorred the union leader's view that nonunion workers were "riff-raff."

The feeling still prevailed that legislation favorable to labor might eliminate the need for unions, but union growth was obviously being stunted initially by lack of explicit government sanction of collective bargaining, and a vital concomitant, government protection. Collective action on the part of workers was not in itself illegal, but the devices used by the private-property employer group to fend off demands of employees were implicitly sanctioned by the courts. Work contracts were for the most part unilaterally determined. Realistically, the company unionism that grew up around World War I denied collective bargaining.

In 1933, with twelve to fifteen million people unemployed, few workers could afford to pay union dues, even when they were working. Generally debts had accumulated, many related individuals depended on a single income, and rents were still high while wages were mercilessly rolled back.

The National Industrial Recovery Act developed as emergency legislation to relieve the depressed situation. Its significance in terms of labor standards improvement rested in section 7 (a) providing workers with the "right to organize and bargain collectively through representatives of their own choosing," while simultaneously disallowing joining a company union or labor organization as a condition of employment.

On August 5, 1933, President Roosevelt set up a National Labor Board with Senator Robert F. Wagner at its head. That same month in Homestead, Pennsylvania (site of the violent Carnegie strike lost by the union in 1886), the secretary of labor found the basic right to freedom of speech being violated. Under these circumstances, negotiation of contracts, conceptually and practically, was in the realm of the improbable and ridiculous.

The Franklin D. Roosevelt files contain countless cases such as that of a Pittsburgh steel company where all employees automatically received a Republican ballot for voting purposes. The president of the company told the Pennsylvania Commission of Labor that out of five or six thousand employees in his plant, 112 were members of the union; therefore, 112 Democratic votes would be cast. As a result of a Washington-inspired investigation conducted by Governor Pinchot, the town's votes numbered five thousand Democratic. For the first time, a noncompany mayor and police chief were elected to office.

For some time the labor board operated effectively, settling strikes through a procedure known as the Reading formula. This called off the strike, required that workers be reinstated without prejudice or discrimination, and that an election to determine collective bargaining representatives be supervised by the National Labor Board. The freely chosen representatives of the workers were authorized to negotiate contracts with employers.

The refusal of the Weirton Steel Company and the Budd Manufacturing Company to honor the Reading formula dramatized the innocuousness of the board as a law enforcing agency. On Executive Order, Public Resolution No. 44, status, prestige, power and authority were bestowed on the National Labor Board, but employers chose to ignore this caveat also.

R.R.R. Brooks in *As Steel Goes . . .* posits the generally held opinion that section 7 (a) "gave very little real protection to labor's right to organize in the industries where employers were determined to fight it." The specialized Automobile Labor Board was equally ineffective.

Fearful of a similar board set-up, the steel union men who had suffered "espionage, discrimination, discharge and black list" because of their union proclivities, warily agreed to a meeting at the Department of Labor. It typified many "stormy sessions" in which the secretary of labor took part.

A rank-and-filer's account reads: "McGrady and Ma Perkins said the Iron and Steel Institute insisted we were after a closed shop. . . . We didn't want anything more than union recognition. Miss Perkins kept saying that she wanted to help us, but that as long as the Institute kept talking 'closed shop' there wasn't much she could do."

The rank-and-filer's reference to the secretary of labor as "Ma Perkins" was no snide allusion to the radio soap opera in which the heroine, "Ma Perkins," listened to sob stories and solved everyone's problems. The term was intended as disparagement by certain of the intelligentsia and the anti-Roosevelt press, but this subtlety was lost on rank-and-filers who had found a friend in the head of the so-called "poor people's department."

In the saloon, pool parlor, or union hall where the workingmen congregated, as much hoping for job leads as socializing, there was agreement: "Sure, big businessmen don't like her . . . she's trying to get the workers a fair deal out of the New Deal. And the big labor bosses don't like her because she keeps their grabby hands out of the union koffers. She's a very special lady who is helping all of us!"

The March, 1934, automobile strike, which openly ignored the National Labor Board, and the June, 1934, steel crisis demonstrated the need for better governmental machinery to settle disputes. The workers themselves were confused as they read flyers from the American Federation of Labor claiming that "the Government only gives A.F. of L. hearings . . . an employees' organization is a company union and illegal."

The general public was disturbed. Letters poured in, many condemning the radical union members for furthering the disasterous depression, and others taking a stand similar to that of the renowned educator, John Dewey:

My dear Mr. President:

. . .I wish particularly to associate myself with what is said about the necessity for collective bargaining by means of the organization of labor under its own direction, and free from even the appearance of dictation and control by employers—an appearance that always accompanies "company unions" and is only too often a reality and not an appearance. A public declaration from you on this point would in my best judgment do more to clear the atmosphere and dissipate uncertainty than any other one thing.

Self-government in industry is impossible on a one-sided basis. It cannot be brought about in a desirable way by Governmental action and pressure without an undue regimentation to which you as well as public ideas in general are opposed. It demands the cooperation of labor acting freely on its own account.

That recovery depends upon the securing of mass purchasing power is a principle on which your administration has educated the public mind. The sure and direct way of accomplishing this end is the complete unionization of labor.

Respectfully yours,
(signed) John Dewey

Obviously any action taken by the president would have been condemned.

While the steel negotiations were going on, the San Francisco longshoremen's strike of May, 1934, mushroomed into a general strike by July. According to Rexford Tugwell, Frances Perkins alone correctly evaluated the West Coast tie-up as "a spontaneous demonstration to vindicate the right of collective bargaining."

While the president's other advisers were urging him to cut short his trip on the U.S.S. *Houston*, she cabled him: "ONLY DANGER SAN FRANCISCO STRIKE IS THAT MAYOR IS BADLY FRIGHTENED AND HIS FEAR HAS INFECTED ENTIRE CITY." She felt his unscheduled return would only "start the very panic it is necessary to avoid."

The president's answering telegram, which he first wrote out in longhand, read:

"U.S.S. Houston

(July 16, 1934)

For Secretary of Labor—

Thanks your estimate of situation. If other means fail you might offer complete arbitration all employers and all unions involved on three conditions first work to be resumed, second inter union agreements to be mutually suspended third decision of arbitrators to bind all parties for a definite period as long as possible. Stop. If you think advisable you can issue any statement or offer as coming from me or with my approval. Stop. It occurs to me the country as a whole may not understand the history of the strike and that with any statement you may want to clarify the issues publicly Paragraph Confidential Please consult with Hull and Cummings as to our authority to maintain food supply in affected areas and with this concurrent maintenance of traffic and order.

Paragraph. I am inclined to think after Howe's radio today (sent at Perkins' request) it is at present best for me not to consider change my itinerary. Stop Keep Howe in touch Stop Wire me Monday.

Roosevelt

The president's faith in her judgment is evident in his unequivocal statement, ". . .you can issue any statement or offer as coming from me or with my approval."

A description of the human being heading the Department of Labor during those grueling summer days and nights appeared in the *New York Times Magazine*, August 5, 1934:

Long-distance calls, nervous, rushing secretaries, conferences with labor leaders, consultations with assistants and hurried bites to eat, right in the office, marked those days and nights. At times the wonted tricorn hat, as famous in its way as Al Smith's brown derby, was tossed on a table beside

Madame Secretary's great desk. At times her large lustrous black eyes look tired and lines showed themselves at the corners of her expressive and mobile mouth. Sometimes her arm would ache and tingle from holding the telephone to her ear as she received reports from the troubled areas; sometimes she was almost ready to drop from exhaustion; yet she stuck to her job in a torrid and almost deserted city. Working at top speed, appreciating fully the gravity of the situation, Frances Perkins always had time for a smile. Coupled with her serious outlook upon life is an abundant sense of humor.

The longshoremen overruled the opposition of their leader, Harry Bridges, to arbitration; union recognition was won.

On August fifteenth, Frances Perkins drafted a note for Franklin D. Roosevelt to write to the undersecretary of labor, Edward F. McGrady, thanking him for the fine job he did in San Francisco.

Some informal requests for the deportation of Harry Bridges as a "labor agitator" had come to the department, but the Immigration and Naturalization Service's routine check indicated no police record or other grounds justifying deportation. On August fifteenth, shortly before the culmination of the longshoremen's strike, the bipartisan National Labor Board had become the nonpartisan National Labor Relations Board by resolution of Congress. Frances Perkins had complained to the Honorable Colonel Marvin H. McIntyre, assistant secretary to the president: "We are all anxious for the government to have a united front in the handling of labor disputes. It is unfortunate when several agencies act in the same dispute independent of one another."

The National Labor Board had functioned independently under the NIRA. However, as with the code-making functions, reliance on the Department of Labor was necessitated by the department's "virtual monopoly on technical competence." To avoid duplication—it already had vital information on hand—and to avoid confusion, Frances Perkins wanted the new National Labor Relations Board placed under the jurisdiction of the department. In the interests of economy and efficiency, the president appeared to agree with the secretary of labor.

Clara Beyer wrote to Grace Abbott, then in Nebraska: "Apparently the determination of labor policy is at last lodged with the Secretary of Labor. The President is turning over to her the setting up of machinery under the compromise Wagner Bill. If she plays her cards skillfully, she has an opportunity to re-vitalize the National Labor Board and her whole conciliation machinery."

Lloyd K. Garrison was resigning from the chairmanship of the National Labor Board. The two other members of the board, Harry

Millis and Edwin S. Smith, warned his named successor, Francis Biddle, that the secretary of labor was stripping him of the power of appointment and budget control. According to Frances Biddle:

> There had evidently been a misunderstanding. Lloyd Garrison, telling me about my work, has assured me that part of its attraction was that I should run my own show, reporting to no one but the President, working of course in close co-operation with her—a co-operation from which he had greatly profited—but that I should in fact be my own master in matters of policy and personnel.

Oddly enough, although Biddle threatened to refuse the widely publicized appointment, thereby embarrassing the president, he appreciated the logic of Frances Perkins's argument. The president, in his inimitable fashion, arranged a compromise. According to Biddle:

> . . .This particular compromise was an abandonment of principle, which the Secretary had on her side. She argued persuasively to the President, who kept nodding as he listened to her with his usual patience. He was rarely impatient with Miss Perkins, of whom he was very fond. The pattern of the New Deal, she insisted, was spreading irresponsibility over the earth, with no co-ordination of shape. Proper organization meant lines of responsibility running up and down, not sideways. If the Board reported directly to the President it would mean that it would in fact be responsible to no one; or, worse yet, he would have another burden, comparatively unimportant, on his overburdened back.

The merits of her discourse notwithstanding, Biddle adamantly insisted that the quasi-judicial board would have status only if it were independent. Biddle claimed:

> Roosevelt hated to make sharp decision between conflicting claims for power among his subordinates, and usually decided them like an arbitration: each side should have a slice. Now run away, both of you, and be happy, and don't bother me any more. . . .

The matter was far from closed. In May, 1935, the Supreme Court decided the Schecter Poultry case, making the National Industrial Recovery Act unconstitutional. Frances Perkins numbered among those involved with labor problems "on the alert to salvage as many of its good features as possible." She had always viewed the steps taken by the NRA as temporary expedients. From her point of view, "one avenue which had served a temporary need was closed; another making the gains permanent was to open." The most important point: "The labor protectives contained in Section 7 (a) of the Act were to be improved and become permanent national policy."

On February 21, 1935, Senator Wagner had introduced a labor disputes measure that was to establish the National Labor Relations Board as the "Supreme Court" of labor relations. Wagner agreed with Frances Biddle that the Department of Labor looked after the interests of labor and so could not function with the impartiality necessary. Biddle held the conviction, "To succeed in the long run the Board must have the confidence of industry as well as labor and of the country at large."

Frances Perkins again argued that "The New Deal was already proliferating into a tangled wilderness without paths leading anywhere. . . ." As the only administrative official testifying before the committee on the Wagner bill, she hammered at the point that the secretary of labor formulated the government's labor policy and reported to the president, so the board belonged where the conciliation service was already housed.

When taken to task for coming around to the secretary's point of view, AFL President William Green apologized with, "But she kept fixing me with her basilisk eyes!" And of course there was the "masculine deference to the mightier power of the female of the species." At any rate, his testimony sounded wishy-washy: "Labor is a bit sentimental because it feels that the Department is set up for labor."

And that was the problem. Commissioners from the Conciliation Service had long found it expedient to omit reference to their affiliation with the Department of Labor, because managers erroneously felt that organized labor controlled the department. Actually a committee consisting of Sumner Slichter, William Leiserson, and William H. Davis had recommended that the Conciliation Service, a non-law-enforcing body, be removed from the department for that reason, but this did not occur.

The day the Wagner Labor Disputes Act passed the Senate, Frances Perkins wrote to the president:

The House Labor Committee expects to be ready to report the Bill on Tuesday. The House Committee will offer a Committee Amendment to the Bill, placing the Labor Relations Board in the *Department of Labor*. This is what we have agreed ought to be done. Senator Wagner as you know, is opposed to it and wants an independent Board. Mr. O'Connor of the Rules Committee will be seeking your advice with regard to giving a rule to bring the report of the Committee to a vote, and I want to underscore the necessity of *insisting upon the Board being in the Department of Labor.*

The final outcome reverberated through the press to the nation. The "Capital Stuff" columnists for the widely-read New York City tabloid, the *Daily News*, on July 5, 1935, pulled no punches:

The President of the United States is a gentleman, and a gentleman never, never draws off, measures his distance, and then deliberately gives a lady a swift boot to hasten her departure.

And so Frances Perkins, Madam Secretary of Labor, first of her sex to sit in the Cabinet, ranking distaff representative of the New Deal, can never accuse her old Albany pal, F.D.R., of being no gentleman.

But on the other hand, Ma'am Perkins knows today that the political boys, to put it coarsely, have pulled the plug on her. In other words, she's all washed up so far as sounding an authoritative note in the Administration's delibera-tion on labor problems are concerned.

. . .This was made clear today when the President signing the Wagner Labor Disputes bill, politely but definitely moved Secretary Perkins out of the picture.

The president's formal statement purportedly spelled out the secre-tary of labor's defeat: "The National Labor Relations Board will be an independent quasi-judicial body. It should be clearly understood that it will not act as mediator or conciliator in labor disputes." That it "cut the ground from under the feet of Madame Perkins" had as much basis in fact as references to her imminent resignation because she was "no longer No. 1 Woman 'n the New Deal Administration."

The mediation and conciliation agencies remained in the Labor Department, and as was anticipated, according to *Survey Graphic* some years later, "even such ordinarily well-informed writers as Dorothy Thompson and Arthur Krock were confused about the authority and procedures of these governmental agencies."

Many employers and their associations defiantly ignored the Wagner Act. In 1937 the Supreme Court upheld the act and the right of the National Labor Relations Board to bring to the federal courts cases of failure to comply with a "cease and desist" of an unfair labor practice. The NLRB had an erratic career; judging by criticism over the years, it simultaneously "protected labor organizations and labor leaders against the public" and made "consistently pro-management" decisions.

With the enactment of the Wagner Act of 1935, the United States government was committed to the encouragement and protection of the practices and procedures of collective bargaining. The National Labor Relations Board was charged with certifying employee representatives to bargain in "good faith" with "good-faith" bargaining employers.

With the exception of certain union security provisions (finally in the Labor Management Relations Act of 1947), the government merely suggests terms of agreement. The final decisions and outcomes of collective bargaining rest in the hands of labor and management.

*****

Frances accepted with alacrity the invitation to address the fifty-fourth convention of the AFL in 1934 for reasons she explained at the outset of her laboriously-detailed speech:

> One of the best things the American Federation of Labor has done, so far as I am concerned, is to have the Fifty-fourth Convention in the City of San Francisco, for at least it has taken me almost three days to come here, and they have been three days of indescribable peace, comfort and security. Mr. Green knows it is practically the only vacation anyone in the Department of Labor has had in the last year and a half.

She went on to explain what had taken place under the New Deal administration, confessing that it hardly represented "the millenium on a silver platter." She mock-scolded:

> All we Americans have a habit of expecting the millenium overnight, and we are apparently confirmed in our habit of expecting the millenium out of a law, out of a statue or out of some particular official or group of elected officials. It takes longer than a year or two, it takes more co-operative effort than can be represented by just one or two officials to really put into effect the hopes, the ideals and the highest aspirations of the people of the United States of America.

Her synopsis of the depression, the National Industrial Recovery Administration with its labor board and collective bargaining provision, strikes, and unemployment insurance, closed with a euphoric promise of a millenium in the form of "programs of social security which have been referred to by the President in a message to Congress":

Programs which will look toward stabilization of incomes to the aged, programs which will look to the assistance of those who are put in the poverty class because of invalidism and illness over which they had no control, programs which will look toward the development of continuing and continuous work, programs based on social needs—in short, a program headed toward the development of this country in the interest of all of the people of the country, a program headed toward the prevention of erosion, a program headed toward the full utilization and production of our river courses, our waterways, our water supplies, a program headed toward the utilization of our land and water for social purposes; a program headed toward the utilization of our great open spaces for the real recreation and the proper use of leisure by the American people, free from the devastating effects of long hours and low wages.

Her speech could be interpreted as a superannuated defense against the criticisms of the impatient liberals. According to Francis Biddle, Paul Ward of the *Baltimore Sun* had taken to broadcasting his disenchantment with the secretary of labor with persistence. He "found that Miss Perkins with her 'ramrod back,' her almost pathological abhorrence of publicity, and her 'middle-class mind,' could talk endlessly with professors and social workers about the 'inevitability of gradualism' but had little to say in the policy decisions shaped by the President himself in the application of his 'Boy Scout technique' to the class struggle."

By many, Frances Perkins was regarded as the most "liberal" and "progressive" of Roosevelt's cabinet, terms frequently used as disparagement. Babson, in his exposé *Washington and the Revolutionists,* excerpted newspaper articles to come up with a brief run-down on Perkins's goal:

More pay, more comfort, more security, more peace of mind for the ordinary worker. What is a fair wage? "Enough to permit a worker to call a doctor when his baby is sick without going on half rations for a month after." Unemployment insurance? "Many corporations dipped into their surpluses and reserves during the last few years to meet their dividend payments. Would it not be equally wise and just to make some of these reserves available for meeting payments in lieu of wages for employees who must be laid off from time to time" Consuming power? "If we see the wage which goes to the investor is less because the wage which goes to the worker has got to be greater I think you'll hear all over this country 'aye' from people who will be glad to make the sacrifice." Miss Perkins sums up her philosophy thus: "It's time to treat ourselves to some civilization even if it requires revolution."

These goals, radical for the time, earned Miss Perkins the sobriquet, "That Woman!"

At least "That Woman!" could not be charged with "driving like a woman." On September 13, 1934, Assistant Secretary Turner W. Battle wrote in a letter to the president's secretary, McIntyre, that the secretary of labor ran off the road in an unavoidable accident and wrecked her car. It would cost $1200 to put the automobile in running condition. She was awarded $4000 for a new one.

Frances Perkins not only never drove a car, she never learned to drive. However, it would never do to say the chauffeur ran off the road in an unavoidable accident. Shortly afterwards the *Washington Herald* reported:

> The Secretary of Labor, Miss Frances Perkins, has a shining new official car in place of the rather old one used by her Republican predecessor. And it is unlike the rest of the official cars in that it displays no department seal on the door, nor has it the siren blast of the White House nor the Postmaster General's.

The lack of a department seal did little to keep the reporters from dogging her footsteps. Clara Beyer enjoys telling how, at one hotel where Frances Perkins was staying while in the midst of labor negotiations, the press of photographers and reporters made it almost impossible for her to open her door. She managed, and then in stentorian tones proclaimed, "Gentlemen, did you know that Miss Greta Garbo is on this floor, just three doors down." She got to her meeting on time.

*****

Shortly after Frances Perkins took office she told *New York Times* reporter Alice Rogers Hager about her plans to bring to Washington the heads of state departments of labor so that she could keep informed on what was taking place at the state level. She felt that the work done in the states need not be duplicated in Washington, but rather "we should utilize it and make it available for the information of the whole country."

At the first of these meetings she queried the participants about the structure and status of their labor departments, their laws protecting women in industry, whether or not their budgets enabled them to enforce the laws they had on the books, their workmen's compensation provisions, and the laws they were working to get passed.

In 1934 she awarded a red ribbon to the labor commissioner who had gotten a minimum wage law passed, a blue ribbon for a child labor law, and so on down the line. The first year in office the labor commissioner of Pennsylvania received none and boasted that the next year he would make up for it. True to his boast, the next year fifteen ribbons were strung across his chest. According to Clara Beyer, the first year Governor Green of Rhode Island was in office, he decided the state needed to catch up on labor legislation. He personally came to Washington for assistance from the Department of Labor staff in developing a program. The following year his industrial commissioner's chest flaunted a rainbow of ribbons. Observing the fanfare, Rose Schneiderman reported, "Maybe you think that the boys weren't pleased with those ribbons. Indeed they were. I know because I attended all of the conferences which continued throughout the Roosevelt administrations."

At the October, 1935, convention of state labor officials, in Asheville, North Carolina, Edwin S. Smith, a member of the National Labor Relations Board who opposed placing the board in the Department of Labor, followed Perkins's speech with the statement: "I have frequently felt that if by some magical process Miss Perkins' personality and her enthusiasm could be subdivided into a thousand parts . . . that in a very few years we would be much further toward the goal of industrial civilization. . . ."

At the 1935 AFL conference in Atlantic City she reminisced back to the previous year when she traveled across the whole United States. From Atlantic City to San Francisco

> . . . is a long way in mileage and sometimes I think it is a long way in thinking, and the great obligation of the people who live in this generation is to bring about unity between the people of all the United States, to bring about unity between the people who work for wages and all of the groups so that all of the East and the West and the North and the South will cease to have special meanings and that we may develop a national and democratic consciousness—conscious not of power in competition with other nations, but conscious of the power of the people of the community to cooperate with each other for the enhancement and development of a civilization in which they all can share.

At this convention she told one of her celebrated anecdotes about a Chicago meat packer who before the depression had made money, but now was having difficulties. He finally put a rabbit sausage on the market. When Frances Perkins met him she said:

"That's very nice; I am so glad you are doing well and your place is working full time and your people are all working. But, dear me, how do you get enough rabbits for your sausage?"

He said, "That is very simple; out here in Illinois we have lots of fields and woods. People shoot them and snare them and the farmers catch a few, and in recent months they have taken to raising them on rabbit farms. They bring them in and we buy the rabbits."

I said, "That is interesting; I'm glad to know it, but still rabbit meat is pretty light and there isn't much of it. Don't you have to dilute it or mix it with something else in order to make a good substantial sausage?"

"Yes," he said, "we do."

I said, "What kind of meat do you use?"

"We use a little horse meat," he said.

I said, "Oh, that's interesting." And then out of sheer interest I said, "What are the proportions, how much do you have to use?

He said, "We make it fifty-fifty, one horse to one rabbit."

In the American system of mutuality and cooperation the relative value or merit of any one group can't be readily assessed. The important point she believed is the "acceptance of the principle of equality of bargaining power."

The thorough coverage of this convention by the press set it apart from others; seemingly the nation recognized the significance of labor to the economy.

President Roosevelt, with Frances Perkins and other cabinet members, reviews the fleet, May 31, 1934. James A. Farley (directly behind Frances Perkins) wrote in his memoirs that Perkins was "a misunderstood and unappreciated woman, who made no little contribution herself, even if one were to count nothing but the blows she took for others."

XI

"May Susie Wash the Dishes?"

"She has flouted every respectful notion of how the first woman Cabinet member should behave," complained a *Collier's* magazine writer after Frances Perkins's first year of office. His philippic described her as abrupt, chilly, and impersonal. Worst of all, Madam Secretary made herself virtually inaccessible to the "boys on the Hill"—Washington vernacular for the Congress. By way of return, according to the writer, as part of her "hazing," the legislators cut the budget for the employment service, in which she placed so much faith, by 2 million dollars. The journalist wondered why she used vinegar instead of molasses to catch flies, while half-heartedly acknowledging, "She has what in a masculine member would be characterized as 'guts'—and few members dare indulge in that luxury."

It was common knowledge that she stood up to the "barrack-room vocabulary" of General Hugh Johnson, the NRA's major domo. She also told a congressman during a hearing, "Your questions don't make any sense at all!"

This wasn't a matter of masculine guts, but rather exasperation with those who seemed bent on hindering rather than helping her work. She violated the stereotype of women as all sweetness and light, and made no apologies. She had a job to do; that some called it "a man's job" mattered little. The job left no time for pandering to the whims of the uncommitted or posturing for the press.

On one occasion, during the brief five minutes she had allocated for reporters' questions, one of them asked the secretary of labor if she found her present work more demanding than her former job as industrial commissioner.

"Not the work, the conversation," she replied.

Actually Frances could hold her own in any conversation, but unlike some profusely fluent, erudite speakers, she wrote prolifically as well. While many government officials employ ghost writers for articles and speeches, Frances collected necessary data from her staff, then dictated copious notes. She edited ruthlessly, sometimes retaining only one sentence on a page. A sentence certain to be deleted, "I am a missionary at heart," appears frequently in her first drafts, but not in finished manuscripts.

When she couldn't get her educational messages across through the press, she used the media for articles she wrote herself. In public speaking the length and complexity of her sentence structure rivaled those of Marcel Proust. In writing, she favored the pithy statement. Her article "Women Want to Know about the N.R.A.," requested by the editors of the Pictorial Review Company, opens: "Depression is a word of despair. Recovery is a word of hope. Recovery is the middle name of the great national enterprise by which the American people are seeking to overcome depression."

To illustrate the NRA codes, she cited the cotton textile industry as abolishing night work and child labor, with a maximum work week of forty hours and twelve-dollar weekly wages in the South and thirteen dollars in the North. About this significant beginning she wrote, "Human values began to emerge in industry. Perhaps like the Sabbath, industry was made for man and not man for industry."

She found that many people were astonished to learn that the moral aspiration for the welfare of working people was also an economic law. "This was a new idea—that the line of prosperity was a circle and that we all might be in it."

The Protestant work ethic had so long been the marrow and bone of American society, people wondered about all the leisure time a forty-hour week would provide. As an economist, Frances Perkins visualized improved standards of living through increased consumption:

> Leisure makes possible not only the bus rides and the movies but breeds demand for the clothes to go with them, the games to play, the books to read, the music to listen to, and all the other host of activities which draw the picture of money moving from hand to hand. . . .

The *Survey* magazine chose to print one of her more barbed utterances on leisure: "Some people who have plenty of leisure are worrying about how others will use theirs when it comes to them."

She expressed her particular "worry" in a *Good Housekeeping* magazine article:

I am not concerned with the way the working man and woman will choose to spend their leisure, but I am concerned that it will not be exploited. . . . A new problem is the exploitation of leisure—a problem of some seriousness—because leisure time represents the part of life which ought to be in the control of the individual. . . . The right to choose is not the same as the opportunity to choose.

The last statement reflected a concern that decisions might be based on what will pay a profit. She valued recreation, which to her meant re-creation, yet leisure appeared to be anathema to her.

Anyone reviewing her activities over the year preceding the publication of her book *People at Work* in 1934 must wonder when she found the time to write it. The 287 pages of simple prose describe the history of the American industrial revolution in warmly human terms, including the changes that affected the lives of wageworkers through the twenties and into the depression. Probably some chapters had been drafted before she took office and much served as prolegomena for the New Deal.

The John Day Company, its publisher, received letters commending the book from notables such as John Dewey, Alfred E. Smith, Lillian Wald, and John R. Commons. Another of Frances's friends, Mrs. Robert W. Bruère, wrote her that "236 reviews of the book have been received—all favorable but two, and there the criticism was on the ground that you were not radical enough. It is a great grief to the publishers that no one has knocked the book—they say it is such good publicity."

Actually, the criticism was acerbic rather than scandalous. Lewis Gannet could only complain in the New York *Herald Tribune* that Frances Perkins "reveals herself in *People at Work* as an honest optimist." He amplified:

. . .With her spirit no one will quarrel. But when she says that we can reach the goal by bearing in mind that what we want is "the good of the majority," "reasonable returns to capital," "fair" rates to labor, and "just" prices to the consumer, captious critics are likely to arise and remark that the whole quarrel is about the definition of those amiable but amoeboid words.

In the *Saturday Review of Literature*, Suzanne La Follette found Frances Perkins's patriotism and partisanship galling as "topping for the mess the country is in." Worse yet, the book's author reflected the attitude of a social worker ". . .and that is quite enough of an obstacle to helpful analysis of the mess we find ourselves in." The *Nation* magazine also accused the author of exhibiting the obvious stigmata of the social welfare worker. . . Something more than welfare legislation, more than democratic idealism, more than good-will and brotherhood, and more even than the Department of Labor may be required to advance the "good life" for the working people in terms of the "Good Job."

In a profit-oriented, mixed free enterprise economic system, social workers ranked low in prestige. A popular mock-definition of the time was "A social worker is a woman who sees a silver lining in anybody else's cloud."

For years to come critics would derive satisfaction in depicting the secretary of labor as "merely a social worker." But in the same year her book came out, Roger W. Babson designated her "the chief revolutionist" in the president's "revolutionary program," and dedicated his volume *Washington and the Revolutionists* to Frances Perkins, secretary of labor.

Roger W. Babson had also written books about the three labor secretaries who preceded Frances Perkins. His chapter entitled "That Woman!" may well have been the most complete biography of Frances Perkins written up to that time. The author became a unique advocate for a woman as the secretary of labor:

Certainly there is no position in the Cabinet for which women are better fitted than to serve as Secretary of Labor. This does not mean that the Secretary of Labor should always be a woman, but it does mean that the position should be held by a woman at least a third of the time. Not only has the Department of Labor two or three divisions which deal almost exclusively with women and children, but women are constantly becoming a greater factor in industry, finance and commerce.

*****

From the beginning to the end of the New Deal administration, programs and projects developed in a dozen directions simultaneously. Labor—as earners, consumers, or both—was an integral part of these and appropriately the secretary of labor's voice was heard on most of these matters. Frances Perkins served on the President's Emergency Committee on Housing together with Harry Hopkins, Henry Wallace, Rexford Guy Tugwell, Averell Harriman, and chairman Frank Walker. The Home Owners' Loan Act of 1933 provided for long-term mortgage loans at low interest rates to help home owners who were delinquent in payments to remain in their homes. On January 24, 1934, the Emergency Housing Corporation was established with the secretary of labor its sole stockholder.

By mid-1936, 1,017,821 home owners had availed themselves of low-cost loans that added up to an overwhelming $3,093,451,321. By 1942 almost half of these loans would be repaid. Frances later observed that these impressive figures merely indicated good business practice, but told little of the human pathos "inherent in the employment and credit situation that prevailed in the depression years out of which the Home Owners Loan Corporation was born."

In the summer of 1935 she alerted her key people to be on the lookout for the right person to head up housing activities. Although Hoovervilles—shanty towns similar to those outside of Bombay, India— were becoming less visible, slums persisted.

Opposition to slum clearance projects came from many congressmen and their constituents who feared that the bulk of federal monies would go to the large cities—particularly New York City—where the most decrepit, overcrowded, rat-infested, and substandard housing blighted large areas. Frances, who had spent so much time in these slums, knew how they pressed down on the children, making full physical and mental development virtually impossible.

Her interest in the nation's children never abated. In June, 1933, *Parents'* magazine featured her one-page article on child labor entitled "Our Crime Against Children." The editor also included a paragraph urging readers to write to their state governors if their states had not yet ratified the child labor amendment to the federal Constitution. Up to that time only Arizona, Arkansas, California, Colorado, Montana, North Dakota, Ohio, Oregon, Washington, and Wisconsin had done so.

For a quarter of a century Frances numbered among those reciting Sara N. Cleghorn's "The Little Toilers." How well she knew it by heart:

> The golf links lie so near the mill
> That nearly every day
> The laboring children can look out
> And see the men at play.

To all who would listen she described the sweatshops with little bodies huddled together stripping cigar leaves, the smell and slime of the scallop sheds, the trucks in which children were hauled like so much cattle out to the fields for picking, the toddlers handing yellow pinheads to mothers making artificial flowers in their homes hour after interminable hour. These children could neither read nor write; they couldn't name the state in which they lived. And they saw little value in knowing these things.

In 1916 social workers thought they had seen the end of child labor with Congress's passage of the Keating-Owen bill which prohibited interstate shipment of goods produced in violation of the child labor law. Hardly two years later, the Supreme Court declared the law unconstitutional with its decision in *Hammer* v. *Dagenhart.*

In 1924 by a joint resolution of Congress an amendment to the Constitution was submitted to the states reading: "The Congress shall have power to limit, regulate and prohibit the labor of persons under 18 years of age." This enabling act was viewed by many not only as a violation of state's rights, but of family rights.

Catholic organizations particularly feared that Congress would control family life. Articles captioned "May Susie Wash the Dishes?" cautioned on the dangers inherent in the amendment. Although Frances usually refused to defend herself against personal attacks by the press, she reacted spontaneously against articles attacking the child labor amendment and penned poignant "letters to the editor" that appeared in newspapers across the country alongside those written by everyday citizens.

The president of the Carnegie Foundation for the Advancement of Teaching charged that her crusade for ratification of the child labor amendment was "an extra-ordinary proceeding for an administrative official" and provided evidence that women in politics tend to be "sentimental rather than thoughtful."

Frances set her sights on having the amendment pass in 1934. In January President Roosevelt, in his opening message to Congress, jumped the gun by proclaiming that child labor had been abolished. The Congress applauded, but Frances Perkins feared that the president had really "bollixed things up." She recognized that while child labor had abated under the NRA codes, the termination of the NRA would also end the temporary surcease. She promptly wrote a detailed plea for renewed vigor in obtaining ratification of the amendment. Many newspapers printed under her by-line her article refuting popular misconceptions associated with the bill.

Every speech, whether to the Wellesley College Institute for Social Progress or to the National Business and Professional Women's Association, and regardless of the topic assigned, incorporated her views on the amendment. She ignored political considerations, which the White

House could not do. The Children's Bureau study of child labor conditions in the newspaper and periodical publishing business went directly from the Department of Labor to the White House for use by the president at his discretion.

The head of the Children's Bureau, Grace Abbott, brought to the secretary of labor's attention reports on the rising tide of malnutrition among children. One out of every four examined in various parts of the country were seriously undernourished. Dietary deficiencies or borderline malnutrition characterized others. In the coal-mining sections of West Virginia and Kentucky, 90 percent of the school children were underweight.

Frances immediately called into Washington representatives of the state departments of health, medical societies, private national health organizations, agencies dispensing relief, and other charitable groups. Together with specialists from the Children's Bureau and other related departments of government, they determined ways of locating and meeting the needs of inadequately fed children.

Frances's concern for children took another direction. Although repudiated by the National Woman's Party for her opposition to blanket equality for women, she brought about a little-heralded piece of legislation that ended discrimination based on sex that affected children in the matter of naturalization. She personally agonized over bill H.R. 3673, which the House of Representatives finally passed on April 25, 1934, and the Senate passed on May 10, 1934. This for the first time placed men and women on an equal basis as to the naturalization of a child born outside of the United States. It meant that an American-born woman's child could automatically, upon application, become a citizen of the United States just as an American-born man's child could. The law also provided an alien husband of a citizen wife with the same privileges formerly extended only to the alien wife of a citizen husband. In effect, the bill used the term "citizen" without reference to sex, thereby placing men and women on an equal basis.

*****

"The fact that I'm a woman is incontrovertible," Frances Perkins acknowledged in a *Fortune* magazine article. Outside of her job activities, people repeatedly reminded her of what she had achieved despite being a woman. She found it more than slightly disconcerting. "I consider myself a good feminist, but I want my work recognized because it is work, not because a woman did it," she explained to her social work friends.

She was in good humor the day *New York Times* reporter Alice Rogers Hager interviewed her:

> I asked Miss Perkins if she felt under a handicap in dealing with her position and its problems because she is a woman.
>
> "But," she protested, laughing, "I'm not the person to answer that. You see, I'm so accustomed to being a woman that I never think about it. Except in climbing trees, it never bothers me."

From then, when contending with this trite, tiresome question, Frances's flip answer became, "Only in climbing trees." She insisted, as have numerous other successful women, "I really believe most people make the mistake of over-estimating the difficulties a woman meets."

A number of women who made it to the top of their professions gradually discounted the discrimination that limits the opportunities for their counterparts. Some also discovered that instead of a handicap, being a woman could be an asset. Their views on sexual discrimination end up straddling a limp high wire, leaving them teetering one way and then the other.

Frances Perkins's sometime associate, Dr. Alice Hamilton, wrote of the problem of her time in her biography:

> In the United States a woman finds it harder to gain entrance to the medical schools than does a man, much harder to get her internship in a first-class hospital, and difficult if not impossible to get on the staff of an important hospital.

Yet in her very next paragraph she boasts that she never personally suffered from the difficulties that women doctors have to overcome. No bars were erected to keep her from her laboratory work, from joining scientific societies and speaking and publishing as freely as if she were a man. In addition, she claimed:

> And when I went into industrial medicine I often felt that my sex was a help, not a handicap. Employers and doctors both appeared more willing to listen to me as I told them their duty toward their employees and patients than they would have if I had been a man. It seemed natural and right that a woman should put the care of the producing workman ahead of the value of

the thing he was producing; in a man it would have been sentimentality or radicalism.

In the light of her singular achievements, she forgot the difficulty of finding an internship after her graduation from the University of Michigan Medical School. Then after finally gaining admission to one of the German universities for advanced studies in her field, she suffered the indignity of begging to attend lectures, then being seated in far-off corners to avoid her contaminating male students. When she reached the eminence of an appointment to the faculty of Harvard Medical School—"the stronghold of masculinity against the inroads of women" —she was denied the customary faculty privileges of using the Harvard Club, receiving a quota of football tickets, and marching in the commencement procession and sitting with her colleagues on the platform. (Her printed commencement invitation, which she was expected to ignore, tactlessly included the proviso that "under no circumstances may a woman sit on the platform.")

As the only qualified candidate in industrial medicine available to Harvard University, she could have demanded equal rights for herself, thereby establishing the precedent for other women. But in many minority causes where individual members of the group have managed to cross the barriers, the urgency of the cause diminishes for them. They reason that because they made it to the top, anyone can. The help sought by those they left behind is not forthcoming.

As a young suffragist, Frances had marched in parades and spoken ardently in favor of equal rights for women. But around 1925-26, when the National Woman's party urged that wage-earning women "depend not on protective legislation but upon taking their place in the American labor movement as workers, not as women," her own views calcified. While suffragists sought expanding economic opportunities for ambitious and intelligent women, she developed into a "social feminist" with the social worker's focus on underprivileged, disadvantaged women employed for wages desperately needed to support themselves and their families.

One analyst of women's status hypothesized a correlation between severe emotional disorders and feminist militancy, having observed that "social feminists as a group were better balanced than hard-core suffragists." Certainly the conservative social feminists did not shock the sensibilities of society as did Frances's distant cousin, Charlotte Perkins Gilman. At a time when it was far from fashionable or ladylike to discuss world-wide dissemination of birth control, she had asked:

When pacificists gather together to seek the cause of war, does anyone mention babies? ...With all its lamentable accompaniment of license and misbehavior, an intelligent limitation of a population to the resources of a country is one of the most essential requirements for any hope of world peace.

Shortly after World War I she addressed herself to dissatisfied students of that time:

This new century of ours, still gasping from its hideous baptism of blood, has imminent possibilities of swift improvement. If our so ostentatiously revolted youth would outgrow their infantile delight in "self-expression," playing with their new freedom as a baby does with its fingers and toes, and see their real power, their real duty, things would move.

Charlotte Perkins Gilman was impatient not only with youth and the world, but with women. She wrote:

This is the woman's century, the first chance for the mother of the world to rise to her full place, her transcendent power to remake humanity, to rebuild the suffering world—and the world waits while she powders her nose. . . .

Frances Perkins was neither powdering her nose, nor expecting the mother of the world to rise to her full place. Her vision extended only to the here-and-now problems of the majority of working women. When *Survey* magazine asked her in 1926, "Do women in industry need special protection?" she gave a resounding "yes," and explained:

The program of industrial legislation for the protection of wage earning women was initiated because of observed and striking facts; namely, the overwork, exploitation and unhealthful surroundings of the working women who crowded into factories in the latter part of the nineteenth century.

She found that without laws "conditions tended to sink to the old levels of exploitation" primarily because most women worked in factories employing under fifty people; these do not use and develop scientific management methods, and they are not unionized. (In New York State, this applied to 71 percent of women factory workers.)

She feared that the equal-righters overlooked two important facts:

. . . *first*, that as industry has become more finely differentiated and divided the best economic opportunities for women as wage earners have developed in specialized trades and occupations where women are preferred and usually excel men in skill and competence; and *second*, that industrial work rarely offers opportunity for a satisfying career.

The work provides "economic independence but it is not a career."

Again, dealing with the situation as she saw it then, she reminded the suffragists:

Industry is very largely a man's world, arranged and operated by men and with its conceptions of comfort and convenience based on man's physical structure, habits and social status. . . .The woman wage earner enters a misfit world. The laws which reduce her fatigue by limiting hours, requiring seats, prohibiting night work and guaranteeing her a living wage are all aids to her in her struggle to work with health and happiness and to compete fairly with men who have by habit and greater experience most of the advantages in any competitive struggle.

While men had organized to effectively improve conditions for themselves, in New York State only 13 percent of the working women belonged to trade unions, and the slow progress made over a 10-year period indicated it would take 129 years, 2 months and 26 days to organize them all. "Self-protection through unionization is a slow method for those who live and work today."

Why don't women join unions? She found that the majority assumed they were working temporarily; also their wages were insufficient to allow for union dues. Many were young and not far-sighted enough to realize the values of collective bargaining.

Frances Perkins recognized that some women felt the laws shackled them, hamstringing their ability to compete with men. Eighteen women printers in New York made a *cause célèbre* over the night work law that kept them from their jobs, but when exempted, only three returned to night work. Frances's memories reinforced her convictions:

No one who has known a town in which the women work on the night shift and the men on the day shift—can forget the pathos of sleepy women, haggard and drawn, frying potatoes and scolding children throughout a day broken only by snatches of sleep in a chair by the stove.

A rebuttal to which she was impervious—reformers are peculiarly resistant to reform—came from Professor Elizabeth Faulkner Baker, a Barnard College economist who argued that most of the protective legislation was needed equally by men. She too pointed to the fifty-four-hour work week and prohibition against night work that limited the women printers, and added that prejudice against the women had been so great over the years, most of them had sought employment elsewhere anyway. Eighty-three percent of the women streetcar conductors lost their positions and seniority because of the protection laws. She observed that "cramped and tired scrubwomen" in the large office buildings were disappearing because electric machines were taking their place with men operating them; not because it was hard work, but because more work could be done quickly, and the pay was better.

Professor Baker claimed that men boosted protective legislation for women feigning "instincts of chivalry and decency," whereas their principal objective was to eliminate women from the field. And although she agreed with Frances Perkins's major arguments, she discounted protectionists' theory that the minorities adversely affected by protective legislation were unimportant relative to the "usual sacrifice made for the optimum good." These minorities, she noted, are at women's industrial frontiers, and concluded, "women's sharp need for protection has abated."

Frances was not the only anti-equal-rights feminist who persisted in looking to the law to provide some measure of equity. Rose Schneiderman of the Women's Trade Union League was convinced that the equal rights amendment to the Constitution would nullify "all the laws affecting women workers for which we had struggled for so many years." She went so far as to say, "On a number of occasions we charged the Woman's Party with being supported by the National Association of Manufacturers, allegations they never denied." Eleanor Roosevelt shared Rose Schneiderman's sentiments.

But not all of the laws on the books aimed at fair treatment of women. Eleanor Roosevelt was particularly irked by the attitude toward the employment of married women. She couldn't understand why no one questioned the right of a rich boy to hold a job. "He may have failed to see the connection between bread and work, while the great majority of married women who work are constantly conscious of it," she claimed. The Economy Act of June 30, 1932, mandated by law that married women be dismissed from government service.

Most of the act had been repealed except Section 213 dealing with married women. The bill for its repeal, H.R. 5051, had been reported favorably by the Civil Service Committee of the House of Representatives, but it never got beyond the consent calendar. Frances Perkins urged the president to recommend its passage to the Congress. Noting that women's organizations, including the General Federation of Women's Clubs, favored abrogation of the act, she took a tack close to the president's own interest: "The legislation has really not accomplished any genuine economies but has promoted considerable discontent and furnishes a convenient talking point for those who are unfavorably disposed toward the Administration." She also persuaded him to eliminate the amendment preventing appointment to the Civil Service "where the combined family income after such appointment would exceed $4,000."

Discrimination against married women in government hardly compared to the problem of exploitation of household employees. Heywood Broun had facetiously remarked, "But the day is at hand when the houseworker will no longer be content to be treated 'like one of the family.' He has a right to demand something bettter than that." Actually, household employees constituted one of the major groups of women wage earners in the country—approximately 1 million in 1934, according to Mary Anderson, head of the department's Women's Bureau. The Department of Labor joined forces with the YWCA and the National Committee on Household Employment in calling a national conference in Washington to work on the problems of household employees.

Some thirty years later Frances Perkins still insisted, "Women need household help if they are going to work."

"But who can afford it?" asked Dr. Gwen Bymers, a consumer economist at Cornell University. "With wages so high in other fields, it's impossible to hire people for housework at wages women's own salaries can afford."

Frances looked to increased cooperation among all members of the family and to new equipment making household maintenance simpler as a solution to this particular problem. She personally had always relied on well-paid servants who were committed to her and her family, because of the demands made on her time extending beyond a nine-to-five regimen.

Many writers of the day insisted on making Frances Perkins "fit" the common stereotype of the woman official as portrayed in a 1936 article "Ladies in Politics: The Gentle Experiment." Women in political positions were supposedly "like prim old-maid schoolteachers of our youth: precise, rule-bound, unimaginative, opening the office promptly at the appointed minute and closing it just as promptly. With superiors they are obedient and reliable; with inferiors they tend to be fussy and exacting." Because she didn't "fit," she was castigated for flouting "every respectful notion of how the first woman Cabinet member should behave." And only rather begrudgingly was she cited as an exception to the woman's suffrage movement, which had "proved to be like those reforms that promise everything and accomplish nothing."

The failure of women to achieve phenomenal success after their enfranchisement of 1919 made the jeremiads of the antisuffragists seem painfully ridiculous. During the thirties one woman writer suggested amelioratively, "Suffragists never really thought that women equipped with the ballot could work miracles over night and correct all the evils men had permitted to creep into politics. . . ." She added, most women agreed with a Mrs. Poyser, "I'm not denying the women are foolish. God Almighty made 'em to match the men."

Obviously it was a man's world, and women had been sitting in the bleachers as observers for too long. "Men were the players, the coaches, the umpires, the linesmen, the water boys. When it suddenly became clear that the gate receipts depended somewhat upon us, men began to make chivalrous and very awkward gestures." In the political arena, the tokenism hardly reflected the impact concerned women had on social legislation.

It was in this area that Frances Perkins actively promoted "woman power." Her files contained scores of speeches on the abolition of child labor, workmen's compensation, old age and unemployment insurance, public works, industrial health and safety, the right to organize and bargain collectively, the extension of vocational education and vocational guidance—but invariably she was drawn into the problems of women.

When the American Association of University Women invited her to speak on "How Women Achieve in Government," she apologized with "—I knew at once that you would not expect me to speak on that subject, or at least you would not expect me to answer any very profound questions with regard to it. To get to the 'how' of anything, as you know, is a most difficult job." She then pegged her talk to the University Women's theme, "social responsibility goes with the privilege of education."

She had just come from the funeral of the former Children's Bureau director, Grace Abbott, and the description of Grace Abbott's career served as both a eulogy and an illustration of social responsibility.

It is no fun to accept ridicule and abuse. . . You will remember the days when speeches were made on the floor of Congress asking what right that "old maid" had to tell people how to bring up their children. You will remember how Grace Abbott and Julia Lathrop had to take it; they gritted their teeth privately but they walked out smiling, just as though nothing had happened. Grace Abbott had that quality, and it is essential to anyone who would go into public office. We have a rough and tumble democracy, and I am glad we have; it is part of an expression of life, part of the way we keep our public officials from dreaming too many dreams.

Frances Perkins still held to her dreams of eliminating poverty and hoped to direct the sound thinking of these educated women to the problems:

We must think of this responsibility as constructive, not corrective. Our nation is not yet complete; our democracy is not yet complete. If we are to grow, and develop, and meet the demands of the times, we must be creative. . . .

Occasionally described, somewhat fatuously, as "surprisingly feminine for a feminist," Frances found her leisure time too scarce to allow for a reading of the much-discussed book by Virginia Woolf, *A Room of One's Own*. She finally asked one of her staff to abstract the book for her. She could only agree with Virginia Woolf's caveat: "It is fatal for a woman to lay the least stress on any grievance; to plead even with justice any cause; in any way to speak consciously as a woman." One of her nationally broadcast radio addresses echoed Virginia Woolf's admonition:

. . .I don't believe that political action should be taken by woman as a sex. I think the reason why legislation for workers has made such recent advances is due to the fact that public opinion has become conscious of the rights of workers as individuals. In the same way, women wage earners will make their most important advances by calling attention in every channel open to them to their economic injustices and relying on the education of public opinion to right them.

Clearly not as a woman but as a human being seeking justice, she had differed volubly with General Hugh S. Johnson of the NRA over matters such as the overt discrimination against women wage earners in many of the codes. She literally stormed at him, wrote him lengthy letters and distributed carbon copies of her charges to influential people. She especially objected to the obfuscation of the code's statement: "Where women perform in all respects the same kind and amount of work as men, they shall receive the same wages." The industry codes spelled out lower minimum wages for women than for men, and this sentence, she charged, "gives the impression that women are to be paid on the same basis as men, while in fact such a result will not be obtained."

Frances knew the score all too well. It took no clairvoyance to anticipate the many fine distinctions that could be made between the work of the man and that of the woman so that the woman would not be paid the same higher rate. Frances made her rancor known: "I deplore the growing tendency for the codes to set up a differential in rates based on sex, and I particularly object to the wording which will give the definition a false appearance of fairness."

Eleanor Roosevelt shared Frances's indignation over the unjustifiable wage differentials. She invited General Johnson and Frances Perkins to luncheon at the White House, where her disarming charm succeeded in persuading the obstreperous General Johnson that, if nothing else, wage discrimination based on sex at least could be eliminated.

Discrimination takes many forms, but the difficulties Frances Perkins encountered over the years could be regarded as neither more nor less than if she had been male. In the upper echelons of business, government, or academia, she might have contended with others who presented opposing views as stridently, or who sought to outdo her, or coveted her position, or exaggerated her failings regardless of sex.

Frances developed a voice that could not be drowned out by the volume men frequently resort to in lieu of substance, and although she disapproved of the practice, she could interrupt any man who interrupted her. She did her homework, and competed with any and all when it came to having facts and understanding at the ready.

At the same time she showed enough genuine humility so that men and women preferred their help to her willingly and graciously. She co-opted others for the causes in which she believed and for which she worked. Frances Perkins was not a woman among men; she was a person with a purpose and point of view working with many people with purposes and points of view.

If Frances uttered a cross word, menopause would be blamed now that she was in her fifties. Male bosses' irritation is customarily ascribed to arguments with their wives. The "conventional wisdom" shows little depth of analysis. Few subordinates fully appreciate the extent of the demands, the harrassment, the interruptions, the interminable crises heaped upon crises, the long hours, the time-consuming amenities and the incessant role playing—the denying of one's self—that are part and parcel of the top executive's performance. Rare is the supernumerary who copes with all with aplomb and subliminal equanimity.

While Frances had no spouse to cook dinner for "the boss and his wife," or to plan cocktail parties, or shop for her secretary's Christmas present, or send her clothes to the dry cleaners, or remember family birthday cards and gifts, or handle the myriad duties that wives handled before better than 50 percent of them took on full-time employment, she learned to deal with these details as countless single men and women and one-parent families have in the years before and since.

Frances enjoyed a number of advantages over most people: exceptionally sound health, a high energy level, excellent coordination and organizational abilities, self-discipline, will power and an unfathomable reserve of religious faith and conviction. Actually, only a firmly entrenched sense of decorum kept her from climbing trees.

She openly defied society's folkways in only one significant way: the refusal to change to her husband's name upon marriage. A Lucy Stone League had promoted the retention of a woman's given name as a matter of principle in 1921, but it did not come to the fore again until 1932 when the candidacy of Elsie Hills ("legally" Mrs. Albert Levitt) for the Connecticut House of Representatives was questioned because of her refusal to adopt her husband's name.

Because of her national prominence, Frances received a number of enquiries on the legalities involved. One came from Judge Lila M. Neuenfelt of Dearborn, Michigan, who had married and planned to run for election again. The secretary of labor admitted that she herself had received no formal information regarding her right to use her maiden name. From time to time lawyers had advised her that she was so entitled, citing several cases that maintained "the common law right of a person to change his name in good faith and for an honest purpose."

*****

The head of the Department of Labor's Women's Bureau quickly discerned that she could not judge a woman's potential support of the woman's movement by whether or not the woman assumed her husband's name. An unmarried woman herself, Mary Anderson had been appointed by the department's first secretary of labor, William B. Wilson, to the position of assistant director, under Mary Van Kleeck, of the World War I Women in Industry Service on July 8, 1918, at a salary of $3,500. She became director of the Women's Bureau on June 5, 1920, when the Congress approved the bureau as a permanent addition to the Department of Labor.

The Women's Bureau started out hamstrung by discrimination. Senator Reed Smoot of Utah had put a proviso in the appropriations bill specifying that not more than two people of the Bureau's staff could earn more than a $2,000 a year salary. He believed "no woman on earth was worth more than that." To Mary Anderson's protests the senator responded that with unemployment after the war, positions would be sought after at any salary.

The bureau chief worked under Labor Secretary Wilson, then Secretary Davis, but she felt that Secretary Doak really "went to town" for the Women's Bureau. Initially her reaction to Doak's successor was positive:

> When Frances Perkins came in as Secretary of Labor, we were all jubilant, because we thought that at last we would have someone who really understood our problems and what we were up against and would fight for us. I felt that I had a friend to whom I could go freely and confidently, but it did not turn out to be that way.

Because of her conscientiousness, Frances Perkins inadvertantly closed the door on that friendship barely a month after she had taken office. The president had urged his cabinet members to operate their departments as frugally as possible. (Vice-President Nance Garner would later compliment Frances Perkins on being the only cabinet member to abide by the president's economy measure.) Aware of her ability to eliminate wasteful expenditures and to exercise strict control over financial matters, Frances naturally suggested that appropriations granted by Congress for the Women's Bureau be under the secretary's jurisdiction so that the funds could be allocated most usefully.

Mary Anderson was devastated. Obviously the new secretary of labor, as a neophyte in federal service, was unaware of the dangerous implications of such a precedent. Mary Anderson could see the very existence of the Women's Bureau jeopardized if it was ever under the thumb of some unsympathetic secretary of labor. She persuaded Frances that the groups who had worked to establish the bureau would be mortified. She offered to rechannel funds to purposes designated by the secretary of labor and to put members of her staff at Madame Perkins's disposal.

Mary Anderson, completely out of sympathy with Frances Perkins's budget management proclivities, concluded, "Fortunately, nothing more came of this suggestion, but I must confess the memory of it made things difficult for me from then on."

As a specialist in the women's field, Mary Anderson knew without a doubt: "Perhaps the most familiar and exasperating problem of any working woman is the famous (or should I say infamous?' 'pin money' theory." The assumption that women workers had no family responsibilities was the chief cause of their low wages relative to those received by men. Women's Bureau investigations showed the enormous extent to which family welfare depended wholly or partially on the earnings of wives and daughters. But it happened to be a die-hard theory about which this Swedish-born, labor union-oriented director of the Women's Bureau—who had always required more than "pin money" to support herself and other dependent family members—felt very strongly.

Frances Perkins unthinkingly churned up the issue by mentioning in the department's *Annual Report* the number of women who work for "a bit of extra spending money." Frances confessed that a newspaper-woman had already taken her to task for the phrase. Mary Anderson's tone can be imagined as she retorted: "I can well understand that, because these newspaperwomen know from their own lives that it is not the case. Long before the Women's Bureau was started, we had that theory to contend with and we knew that it was a terrible charge to make about working women. I thought we had laid that ghost [to rest]."

Frances again caused Mary Anderson distress when the proposed Wage and Hour Act included a stipulation that standards of minimum wages and maximum hours have no classification on the basis of age or sex. Gerard Reilly, solicitor of the department, included in the testimony he prepared for the secretary of labor just two lines on the subject. When newspaperwomen asked what Madame Perkins was going to say about the same minimum wage for workers of either sex, Mary Anderson could only promise, "Well, I know it is in her testimony and she will speak about it but you will have to wait and hear what it is." To Mary Anderson's infinite dismay, Frances skipped over the all-important two lines.

After the hearing the newspaperwomen bombarded Mary Anderson for an explanation of the omission. The Women's Bureau chief threw up her hands: "God knows! Go up and ask her."

Then Senator Robert LaFollette asked Frances the leading question regarding women getting the same minimum as men. To Mary Anderson's relief, the answer was "Yes." As she was leaving, Frances half apologized, "I fixed that all right, didn't I? It was such a long statement that I couldn't read it all."

Mary Anderson's analysis of Frances Perkins's lack of support reflects a sweet reasonableness:

> All through the time she was Secretary of Labor, I think Miss Perkins rather minimized the importance of women's problems because she knew that a good many of the representatives of organized labor did not like her very well, partly because she was a woman and partly because they thought of her as a social worker and not a real labor person. So every time there was a chance to single out women, she leaned over backward not to do it. I understood her difficulties and sympathized with her, but just the same it was discouraging not to have more enthusiastic backing.

Mary Anderson's files contain countless expressions of appreciation from the secretary of labor and Frances Perkins's files contain copies of her many letters to President Franklin D. Roosevelt requesting increased funding for the Women's Bureau of the Department of Labor. She urged his support for additional appropriations on the grounds that "the labor legislation which has been enacted has broadened the scope of the Bureau's work. Certainly a substantial increase in the appropriations for the Department must be made if we are satisfactorily to discharge our responsibilities." Simultaneously she scrawled alongside her signature assurances to the president that she was "striving loyally to keep the budget requests down."

*****

Two academic experiences highlighted the year 1934. The University of California at Berkeley invited her to give the annual Charter Day address on the occasion of its fiftieth anniversary—the first woman to be so honored. She would also be receiving an honorary degree together with Jane Addams and former-President Herbert Hoover.

Photographers wanted the three honorary degree recipients to pose together for pictures, but Herbert Hoover had a number of reasons for declining to be photographed with anyone but Jane Addams. Not only had Frances Perkins assailed his unemployment statistics while he was president, but he regarded her as an extremist.

After making her speech on behalf of independent, democratic labor

unions to negotiate with employers, Frances quietly asked Jane
Addams, "I do hope I didn't say anything to annoy him."

"I saw you were skating on thin ice," Jane Addams responded, "but
you needn't have worried; he was asleep most of the time."

The newspapers made much of the fact that a University of
California alumna, Miss Martha Ijams, refused to serve as hostess of the
annual alumni dinner because of Frances Perkins. Her excuse: "It seems
to me entirely·out of place that the first woman to be so recognized (as
Charter Day speaker) should be a mere politician." Frances Perkins
ignored the slur.

Jane Addams titillated the Hull House residents with her tale of the
incidents. When asked if Martha Ijams was not a rather silly woman, she
is said to have replied:

> Why, not at all silly. She said what she thought and said it very clearly. I can
> understand her point of view. What I can't understand in a Californian is her
> inhospitality. I mean to a guest. To ideas, I don't suppose Californians are any
> more hospitable than the rest of us.

On November ninth Frances delivered the Founder's Day address at
her alma mater. She eulogized Mary Lyon, Mount Holyoke College's
founder, and characterized ". . .greatness as being the ability to put into
action the high visions which she conceived."

"We must be doers, not mere verbalizers," she exclaimed, noting that
over 50 percent of America's idealism had never been translated into
practical terms. With technology comes the "more abundant life," and
the "problem is now to achieve the balance which was the essence of
Greek civilization and which is so desirable in all life."

"Never in the world's history would I rather be twenty than right
now," she admitted, because the opportunities for social vision had
never been as vast.

Frances was named a trustee of Mount Holyoke College, which
would be celebrating its centennial in 1937. But she would never
forgive the school for appointing a man, Roswell G. Ham, to the
presidency to succeed Dr. Mary E. Wooley, who had joined Mount
Holyoke during Frances's junior year, 1901. Over her ten-year term as
trustee, she was extremely critical of what she called the "Ham period."

We Can See It Better With the Naked Eye

A typical cartoon showing Frances Perkins, this one from the New Orleans Times Picayune, *November 5, 1934.*

XII

From the Cradle to the Grave

The magnitude of the problems being faced in government and in the nation made women's equality a rather low-priority issue. On June 19, 1934, the Emergency Appropriation Act for Fiscal Year 1935 was approved with $899,675,000 allocated to the president for carrying out certain acts of Congress including the National Industrial Recovery Act. Roosevelt requested that an unobligated balance of $1,965,595 be allocated to the secretary of labor, with $1,000,000 going to the Employment Service to meet the needs of the National Reemployment Service. Frances Perkins actually required $3,000,000 immediately for services and payment of overdue salaries.

Miracle cures for the depression continued to proliferate, many so far-fetched that a social worker with the Brooklyn Bureau of Charities dourly observed, "Civilization cannot progress without prophets but there are some voices crying in the wilderness that belong there." Huey Long's "Share the Wealth" scheme and the Townsend Plan to provide for the aged gained adherents at an accelerated rate. Congress felt the pressures.

The president reflected on his own ambitions for national "cradle-to-the-grave" insurance protection with two visitors from England, Sir William Beveridge and Sir Henry Steel-Maitland. For a spell Frances Perkins only touched on the subject lightly with him. But intermittently he was encouraging Senator Robert Wagner and Representative David J. Lewis to push a tax bill for unemployment insurance, which pleased Frances. When the newspapers failed to report on action in Congress, she prodded the president with a letter written on April 17, 1934:

> Don't forget this, will you? You wrote a letter which has gone all over the country and everyone has relied on that as an indication that it will go

through. It is probably our only chance in twenty-five years to get a bill like this, and I don't know of anything that will start unemployment insurance except this. It is very important—do please telephone the Chief Performer on the Hill at once that this must come of Committee and be passed.

The Wagner-Lewis bill ended up as a bellwether indicating the need for greater study and a more comprehensive program.

In the spring of 1934 Frances found it propitious to remind Franklin D. Roosevelt of his promises to her when she had accepted the appointment as secretary of labor. He required little persuasion; these ideas had been part of his 1930 gubernatorial campaign platform and a reason for sending Frances to England to study the unemployment insurance program the British had been operating under since 1911. Besides, he was thinking ahead to his 1936 reelection campaign.

Early in June, 1934, the president gave notice in his message to Congress that the following January he would be presenting "a series of proposals intended to ward off in future years the corroding insecurity which economic collapse had made evident." He wanted these "systematic programs for the *prevention* of poverty" to be considered "before the lessons of the depression began to fade."

On June 29, 1934, Executive Order 6757 created the Committee on Economic Security. To this committee the president appointed the secretary of the treasury, the secretary of agriculture, the attorney general, the federal emergency relief administrator, and as its chairman, the secretary of labor. Professor Edwin E. Witte of Wisconsin, whom Frances had met while studying unemployment insurance in England, was named executive director.

So little money was available to the committee, Frances Perkins "borrowed" economists, attorneys, statisticians, clerical help, and equipment from every department in government that she could. Most of the cabinet members enthusiastically supported her, especially in light of the importance the president placed on the program. Two experts on social insurance systems in every part of the world were recruited from the International Labor Organization. Harry Hopkins made $125,000 available from the Works Progress Administration (WPA) for research on unemployment. A "National Conference on Economic Security" was arranged for November fourteenth and fifteenth at the Mayflower Hotel. Together Edwin Witte and Frances Perkins wrote a speech for the president.

The forenoon of November fifteenth, the unemployment insurance section of the newly-appointed Advisory Council on Economic Security met at American Red Cross headquarters. The members included many people Frances Perkins had known over the years: Mary Dewson, Gerard Swope, Paul Kellogg, former New Hampshire Governor John Winant, as well as Marion B. Folsom, Grace Abbott, William Green, Assistant Secretary of the Treasury Josephine Roche, and others. After University of North Carolina President Frank P. Graham called the meeting to order, Frances explained that the council would advise the Committee on Economc Security collectively and individually on all aspects of the program being developed. She warned that the council's deliberations were to be given no publicity and that all information regarding the committee's proposals were to be treated as strictly confidential.

Paul Kellogg, editor of the social workers' journal, *Survey*, was elected vice-chairman and Edwin Witte secretary. Witte then presented "Suggestions for a Long Time and an Immediate Program for Economic Security" reflecting the thinking of the many individuals he and Frances had conferred with frenetically over the weeks. He stressed that these were "merely to form a basis for discussion and did not represent the definite decisions of anyone." Unlike many consultants called to Washington who find they function primarily as funnels for administrative propoganda, the council would be more than a rubber stamp endorsing predetermined proposals.

At the White House reception the next day the president gave his prepared speech. According to J. Douglas Brown, who became chairman of the advisory council, "Since neither Ed Witte nor Secretary Perkins possessed the zeal for old age insurance which had by now possessed our staff group, the President's address focused on unemployment insurance and played down the early likelihood of any old age security program. . . ." Ignoring the fact that the old-age provisions required the greatest selling effort to the public and the Congress, Brown's staff provoked newspaper comment. According to Brown, "By the time the newspapers reached Warm Springs, where the President had gone for the weekend, the telephone wires to Secretary Perkins became hot. The Secretary soon communicated the President's displeasure to Ed Witte who in turn hurried to the (staff) office. . . ." The old-age section of the program was no longer understated.

During Christmas week the committee got together at Frances Perkins's Georgetown home at 8 o'clock in the evening. The servants were instructed to tell anyone who came to the door that she was "not at home and to close the door in their face." Telephone service was turned off.

"I provided one bottle of spirits only—for five or six people, the principal members of the committee—no assistants, no aides," she remembered. They debated until 2 A.M. the merits of a federal versus a state system of unemployment insurance. She claimed that she regarded the federal system as "much more efficient," but state administration of unemployment insurance won out because "it was more likely to pass."

On January 4, 1935, just over six months after the president had set up the committee, the president addressed Congress, and four bills were dropped in the hopper, by Pat Harrison and by Robert Wagner in the Senate, and by Robert L. Doughton, chairman of the Ways and Means Committee, and David J. Lewis of the House of Representatives. The cabinet committee met again before submitting its final report to the president on January 15, 1935. Two days later he transmitted the report to Congress with his recommendations. On January twenty-first hearings began before the House Committee on Ways and Means and on the next day before the Senate Committee on Finance.

Lobbyists, students of government, and the·legislators themselves, know that following a piece of legislation can be a full-time job. The "Chronological Summary of Activities of the Committee on Economic Security and Development in Social Security Legislation" suggests that everything else must have stopped while this was going on.

After many days of committee hearings, debate in the House and Senate, consideration of amendments, House-Senate conference committee meetings, and preliminary conference reports, the conference committee filed its final report on August eighth. The House accepted the report without record vote, and the next day the Senate accepted the conference report without record vote.

To the president of the United States and the secretary of labor, these were more than events and dates torn off a calendar pad. Frances kept the president informed on virtually every statement made at every hearing, every whisper in the cloak room, and every bit of luncheon gossip she heard. Her almost daily memoranda to Franklin D. Roosevelt indicated the direction proposed changes were taking that would affect the final product with which the president's name would be associated.

For months Frances had also been "educating" the American public on the significance of the Social Security program, through speeches, articles over her by-line in newspapers and magazines, and radio addresses. She made sure that the constituents of the senators and representatives were well informed on the basic concepts.

On more than one occasion she played the role of Daniel entering the lion's den. For example, at the sixty-second annual meeting of the New York Board of Trade, 600 luncheon guests at the glittering Hotel Commodore relaxed for the grand finale of the program. They had just unanimously resolved to oppose any form of federal and state unemployment insurance and to promote legislation to outlaw strikes and lockouts. The honored guest speaker, listening attentively to the business of the meeting, carefully planned her line of attack. Heavy-handedness was out. Frances Perkins was the missionary seeking to convert the heathen.

One by one she covered the points made in the resolution. Regarding labor-management differences she stated: "The settlement of differences by compulsion sounds a little strange to my ears. If we had such laws we would be making the United States of America into a different country. It might be a better country, but it would most certainly be different from the democracy in which we live."

Patiently she admonished the audience on the weakness of separate employer unemployment reserves, noting that her proposal for a general pool would be "cheaper because its administration will be simpler and less expensive. There would be none of the hazards of having one fund exhausted while another, through no fault of any one, was intact." And the important point she emphasized, "It would provide equality of security for workers of all classes." Then like any well-trained salesman, she talked in terms of her audience's paramount interest: "Unemployment insurance would be a boon to industry, because the payment of benefits to those who otherwise would not be able to buy would tend to stabilize the domestic market on which industry is largely dependent."

The *New York Times* referred to the "gentle, good-humored chiding of Frances Perkins," the approach she deemed necessary to her concluding request that the board cooperate in the "accomplishment of the sort of program its members had condemned."

Of course not everyone was persuaded to accept the "socialistic program" she promoted. Some felt compelled to share their negative reactions with their representatives in Congress. And one representative in particular took it upon himself to inform the president.

On January 26, 1935, Maury Maverick, congressman from Texas, wrote to Franklin D. Roosevelt:

Secretary Frances Perkins is the subject of a letter to me. Enclosing a copy to you from one John B. Trevor, in which he indicates that Miss P's record is "deplorable."

You need no advice, inasmuch as you are well satisfied with Miss Perkins. However, as a new Congressman, having observed her record for many years, I believe she is the best Secretary of Labor we have ever had—and not "since" anybody else. The Secretary has COURAGE, knows that civil liberties MUST BE PRESERVED, and that a kindly attitude is the best. It is commendable that she is not to be moved by the flub-dub and the clap-trap of so-called "patriotic" organizations.

Roosevelt responded briefly on February 2, 1935: "I, of course, go along one hundred percent with your sentiments with respect to Miss Perkins."

The president, too, witnessed some "patriotic" reactions that led him to tell a press conference that he sometimes felt that the representatives of business organizations did not fully reflect the sentiments of their members. It seemed that representatives of the American Bankers Association, after muttering that they did not approve of the aged starving or the poor losing their jobs, turned their backs and walked out during the discussion of unemployment insurance. Insurance companies, fearing they would be driven out of business, also opposed the old-age program that meant for the first time in history people could plan for retirement independent of the largesse of their children, that they could seriously consider insurance programs and annuities to supplement the foundation provided by government with their collective funds. But to some, this did not jibe with the American free enterprise system.

The label "communist" was hurled at Francis Perkins more than once, directly or by allusion. During the congressional deliberations, she had been invited by Suffragan Bishop Charles K. Gilbert of St. George's Protestant Episcopal Church to occupy the pulpit to explain the government's Social Security program. Frances summarized the provisions for old-age pensions, unemployment insurance, and the protection of children in destitute families. Following her talk a young woman in the audience inquired loudly:

"Have you read Karl Marx's *Manifesto*?"

The secretary of labor did not have an opportunity to respond. The woman promptly added:

"Karl Marx's *Manifesto,* page thirty, proposes the same program that you have just outlined. How can you support such a program when you know that it is the same as Marx's?"

According to the journalist recording the unusual exchange, Frances Perkins retorted: "I am supporting it because I'd rather see it a reality than on page thirty."

By way of contrast, it would be most gratifying to read in a publication like the esteemed *Wall Street Journal* a positive evaluation of one of her talks:

> Secretary of Labor Frances Perkins, on Saturday performed a feat practically unprecedented so far as officials of the Administration are concerned. Speaking at the annual dinner of the New York County Lawyers Association she offered a seven-point program for social security to which none of her hearers took exception. As Under-Secretary of State Castle put it—"As one Tory to another I must agree with Secretary Perkins."

> Stabilization of industry to prevent unemployment, wage payments and rates on the highest level consistent with stable profits, hours of work as short as possible, "thoughtful management with a social consciousness" to enable combination of these things, industrial expansion correlated to the same ends, "civilized relations" between employers and employees based on adequate organization of the latter, and, finally, systematic provision against loss of individual earning power from age or any other cause of disability;—these constitute the Secretary's proposals.

> If these ideals are Tory, we are all Tories; if they are Liberal, we are all Liberals; if they are Socialistic, we are all Socialists. In short we are all agreed upon the desirability of the millennium. This is not said in a spirit of cynicism—not at all! Secretary Perkins was not talking mere dreamstuff. What she said was not empty of practical content. But the message it carried was addressed—consciously or unconsciously, it matters little which—more directly to her own colleagues than to anyone else.

In its last point regarding her colleagues, the article referred to her substitution of the "spirit of cooperation for the spirit of class war." Actually many social workers disassociated themselves from a social security program that held promise of reducing the poverty that gave them employment.

Jane Addams of Hull House was not one of these. She wrote to the president congratulating him on the many fine things he had accomplished toward Social Security and advising him to put the new Old Age Pension System "into the hands of the new Social Insurance Board, and the mothers' pensions given to the Childrens' Bureau." She added, "I know that you share our desire that they may be taken as quickly as possible away from the connotation of 'relief.'"

The matter of where to place Social Security had been ticklish, with Frances Perkins visualizing it all contained most efficiently and economically in the U.S. Department of Labor. On the one hand the

From left to right, E.A. Witte, Robert L. Doughton, Sen. Alben Barkley, Sen. Robert Wagner, an unidentified observer, Secretary Frances Perkins, Sen. Pat Harrison, and Rep. Lewis of Maryland watch as President Roosevelt signs the Social Security Act, August 14, 1935.

president had advice such as that from Jane Addams, and on the other, countless memoranda from the secretary of labor, and finally a copy of the chart she had shown him "giving the relationship of the various bureaus of the Department of Labor to the proposed Social Insurance Board if situated in the Department of Labor."

When congressional hearings suggested that her proposals might be a stumbling block, she graciously advised the president not to press placing old-age insurance in her department. Many years later she gave vent to her true feelings:

> It had been anticipated that the Social Security Board and its operation would be in the Department of Labor. That indeed would have been logical. But as soon as the matter got into Congress it became obvious that it was the same old story. Neither the Congress nor state legislators wanted money to go to the Labor Department. There is always the feeling that a Department of Labor will be soft on workers, that it will be too much influenced by working people and their point of view.

On August 14, 1935, the president approved H.R. 7260. The president passed out pens to key people, but ran out when it came Frances Perkins's turn. He called for a special pen. She was also to be honored by being issued the first Social Security number and card. This honor she hastily declined. She was not about to reveal that the Department of Labor and the FBI had a record of her birth date as 1882, which meant she pretended to be fifty-three rather than fifty-five; she would continue to minimize her age by two years for another quarter of a century. Others in a similar predicament would later discover that Social Security sympathized with people who subtracted from their ages until they wanted to prove they actually were sixty-five and eligible for Social Security; job discrimination based on age had long been a major problem in this country.

Those who had made the Social Security program a reality, who had dealt with matters of taxation for its earmarked funding, who had projected costs and eligibility requirements, who had compromised about exemptions to coverage, recognized that the program provided a base facilitating sound financial planning by citizens, and that it was subject to review, change, and additions for the disability and health insurance provisions they sorely wanted. In the meantime, the next stop had been to get appropriations to start the program and to appoint a Social Security Board. Senator Huey Long, in one of his final performances as devil's advocate against the New Deal administration, managed a filibuster that meant the appropriations bill failed of enactment. On August twenty-seventh, the Committee on Economic Security moved into the Department of Labor building. John G. Winant was summoned from Geneva, Switzerland, to assume chairmanship of the autonomous, unfunded Social Security Board.

On Labor Day, 1935, Frances Perkins gave a talk over a national network on the newly passed Social Security law. The controlled emotion in her voice gave life to her straightforward description of the program's objectives. As a radio script, it read badly, but with her intuitive feeling for emphasis and pause, her conclusion sounded like a proclamation:

> The passage of this act with so few dissenting votes and with so much intelligent public support is deeply significant of the progress which the American people have made in thought in the social field and awareness of methods of using cooperation through government to overcome social hazards against which the individual alone is inadequate.

Some years later she heard the president discussing the Social Security program over the radio. On her personal stationery, interestingly enough monogrammed "W," she handwrote the message:

> How nice of you dear F.D. to mention me "with thanks" in your radio speech on Social Security.

> It's like you of course but somehow it was very warming & gratifying to have you remember and appreciate what I did to make possible that program which I venture to think may have more weight than any other item on our "application for entrance," in persuading Saint Peter to stamp our visas.

> Thank you faithfully for your friendship & your "pat" & most for your courage to keep on going.

Although many people credited her with the Social Security program, she made a sincere disclaimer: "It represented the thinking of 150 of the best minds in the country." She was only one of many contributors.

Maternal and child health and welfare provisions of the act were administered by the Children's Bureau, headed by Katherine Lenroot. The newly established Social Security Board, headed by Winant, had responsibility for the unemployment insurance provisions. Frances influenced the selection of many people to the board and helped steer its course, according to Mary Dewson, another of its members, with a hand held too firmly on the rudder.

On one occasion some members of the Social Security Board came to

Frances Perkins's office to confer with her. Frances showed the effect of having too often chaired meetings, of being in the fore, of having people look to her for leadership, and in a way common to many top executives, department heads, college deans, and organization presidents, she held the floor with a soliloquy that allowed for no interruptions. Mary Dewson, fully sympathetic with a speaker's propensity to be carried away by her own eloquence, finally tapped her arm and gently interjected, "I have an idea I should like to contribute, and Mr. Wagenet, head of the Department of Unemployment Insurance, wants to make a few points."

The next day, knowing that Mary was again in the Department of Labor building, Frances sent for her. She profusely apologized to Mary with a show of emotion that clearly revealed how Frances had personally agonized over her lapse of good manners and her presumptuousness. Frances gave ample lip service to the give-and-take of the open forum; she was a good listener. But she increasingly, to her own chagrin, succumbed to the role of center stage. Mary Dewson later recorded in her memoirs:

> She was intellectually arrogant but perhaps she realized her sense of intellectual superiority, and her impatience with less brilliant minds and less gifted speakers had given her some unattractive habits when talking things over in groups. With a single person whom she respected her expository and argumentative habits were above criticism. But in a conference I never saw her try to discover how far the other persons had thought through a problem so she could let them have credit for the distance they had gone, and then continue from that point with a few clarifying words.

Mary feared that Frances's command of language had descended into volubility. Frances recognized this herself, as she was called on to speak before every kind of group imaginable. She complained to Mary, "No one can make a good talk on the same subject over and over again." A number of her labor speeches were on the tip of her tongue, and sometimes three-quarters through one she would inadvertantly start at the beginning of another. She knew short speeches were the best, but found it difficult to abstract from her vast accumulation of data. Fortunately, her delivery in a rich, variegated voice, accentuated by animated facial expressions and graceful hand gestures, enthralled those hearing her for the first time.

One person claimed, "Her sweet-tempered calm derives partly from knowing the inexorable logic of events, partly from self-study, completed and dismissed." Frances purportedly admitted, "By now I've either cured my faults or given them up as a tough job." Her intimates knew this was far from true.

*****

Over virtually the same period of time covered by the development and passage of the Social Security legislation, Frances Perkins set up a Division of Labor Standards. At the recommendation of the state labor commissioners who had come to Washington for her meeting, the division outlined as its objectives: "to study specific and local problems and make recommendations on industrial sanitation, health and safety, security, wages, working hours, housing, adult and vocational education, community opportunity, and many other factors which bear upon the lives of our workers."

The division operated without congressional appropriations until 1937, but Frances Perkins managed to get a great deal of mileage out of the limited funds her budget could spare. The division filled a vital service in what Dr. Alice Hamilton designated "the dangerous trades." Dr. Hamilton's story illustrated the struggle to enlighten industrialists who were willing to sacrifice human lives for their own profit, and the secrecy surrounding industrial hazards.

On one occasion Dr. Hamilton received a wire: "Epidemic of insanity has broken out in rayon plant. Doctors do not understand. Can you help?" Evidently carbon disulphide insanity had resulted from exposure to fumes given off in the manufacture of viscose rayon. Dr. Hamilton needed documented proof, but found it impossible to interest state authorities. She finally went to Frances Perkins. According to Dr. Hamilton, "This was not the sort of work the Department of Labor was supposed to do but when I put the situation up to Secretary Perkins and V.A. Zimmer, head of her Division of Labor Standards, they agreed to let me do it, provided I could get the cooperation of the state departments of labor."

By lending the prestige of her department to the study, Frances ran the risk of incurring the antagonism of the rayon producers, who had successfully kept secret the dangers faced by churn men and spinners so as to avoid paying compensation. Rayon, the first significant man-made fiber, had become "big business" in the thirties because of its relatively low cost. Progress in eliminating the hazards to workers went slowly, but after three years, viscose rayon works were made safe through new methods devised by engineers. Dr. Hamilton bestowed a rather typical accolade on the Department of Labor:

> Since the autumn of 1935 I have been attached to Secretary Perkins's Department as Medical Consultant, and I have no hesitation in saying that this Department, especially the Division of Labor Standards under V.A. Zimmer, should be given a large share of credit for the improvement now seen in the dangerous trades. The public does not realize how greatly the Labor Department has expanded and developed under Secretary Perkins, but I, who have known it since its foundation in 1912, have seen it pass through a promising childhood and a troublesome adolescence, to its present capable adult self. The careful, steady spadework carried on in the different states, all of them sovereign states with their own standards or lack of standards, is the least spectacular but I think the most rewarding part of the campaign against industrial accidents and diseases.

The Division of Labor Standards was also assigned to administer the apprentice training program. On June 27, 1934, the president issued an executive order empowering the secretary of labor to set up a Federal Committee on Apprentice Training because employers could not afford to train workers at the wages prescribed under NRA codes. During its first year, committees set up in forty-three states had progressed so well that after the Schechter decision terminated the NRA, the program was established on a permanent basis in cooperation with the National Youth Administration.

In the spring of 1935 the Works Progress Administration research on depression youth documented the unhappy statistics that about 3 million youngsters, one out of every seven aged sixteen to twenty-five, were on relief. Of these, fewer than 40 percent had schooling beyond the eighth grade. Less than 3 percent had entered college. Most distressing of all, large numbers of young people in final desperation had literally become hoboes. The transient service of the WPA in a single day in May 1935 counted 54,000 young people registered at its camps and shelters. Large numbers who had become tramps on the highways and on freight trains were unregistered and uncounted.

The WPA study actually verified Frances Perkins's observations. Her speech-making activities provided peripheral benefits in that they got her out of her "ivory tower" third floor offices in Washington, D.C., and into the streets, and in this case, the railroad yards. She particularly recalled those in St. Louis where the railroad had brought in the wandering youngsters—"hungry, ragged, nothing to do, a little wild naturally after their experiences, and they were having accidents on the railroad all the time." The railroads provided what they could by way of shelter and food, then appealed to the country to help the youngsters to return to their homes, to help get work for them.

Frances asked one boy why he had left home. His lachrymose answer:"I couldn't bear to take the food out of the mouths of the kids. I had to get out and fend for myself. I thought I could make out all right, and Ma could feed the kids with what I would eat." Another explained, "I thought, well, perhaps if I go to the next town I'll get a job."

Executive Order No. 7086 of June 26, 1935, established the National Youth Administration as part of the WPA under the Emergency Relief Appropriation. A part of the program provided work training or part-time employment for needy students.

Because of what she had seen and heard, Frances felt justified inquiring into the activities of the Federal Board for Vocational Education. On June 12, 1934, she asked Clara Beyer of the Division of Labor Standards for information on whether the board was industry minded and what it was doing about employee training. Then again she asked about a meeting scheduled for November 14, 1935, and wrote Clara, "Will you see me about this meeting and coach me for it? I want you to come with me, too."

Her memo to Clara included an afterthought: "Can you do any electioneering beforehand for the Secretary of Labor as chairman?" Her desire to arrogate this responsibility to herself reflected a conviction that interagency cooperation was desirable, and unnecessary duplication of effort was not.

It turned out that Clara could handle this assignment. On October 6, 1937, Frances also reappointed Clara Beyer as chairman of the Federal Committee on Apprentice Training.

The Division of Labor Standards enjoyed the advantage of having a secretary of labor who had worked with young people, who knew their vulnerability to exploitation. In addition she had spent years working with the Consumers League and the Triangle Factory Fire Commission on matters of industrial safety. This particular expertise was brought to bear in connection with the new Department of Labor building nearing completion on 14th Street and Constitution Avenue, NW, about five blocks from the White House. Except for a few details, she was thrilled about the move. Dedication ceremonies took place on February 25, 1935.

Frances had wanted cork flooring instead of asphalt tile installed, but somehow was overruled. On learning that the floors were dangerously slippery, she immediately had them resurfaced. With due respect to the architects who designed the handsome new building, she ordered tests to correct some improper lighting. Industrial safety did not apply only to factories. Poor lighting in working areas induced fatigue and contributed to accidents.

Her own spacious office reflected the dignity and the stature of her cabinet position. In addition, a small comfortable sitting-dressing room adjoined her office. From its balcony could be viewed not only the Department of Agriculture greenhouses across Constitution Avenue, but the gleaming Washington Monument. Just beyond the grass-covered park from which it rises, thousands of Japanese flowering cherry trees outline the Tidal Basin. Not visible from the balcony were the omnipresent slums that marred the beauty of Washington, D.C.

Another of the perquisites of high office was her own private elevator. However, periodic checks on the private elevator showed that it was getting little use. It seemed that Frances Perkins wanted those brief moments waiting for the public elevator, then riding to the third floor, to exchange pleasantries with the department's staff.

Only on rare occasions did Frances Perkins indulge in a purely social luncheon with her women friends. Somewhat more often she lunched with the elegantly groomed, charming Senator Robert Wagner, the immigrant son of a German janitor, who people said "radiated goodness." Most often Frances ate a sandwich routinely brought to her desk. But one time she decided to visit the dining facilities in the building, where most of the department's employees ate. She discovered to her horror that ropes in the cafeteria delineated eating areas for white people and blacks.

In an office of the United States government, which she naively and idealistically viewed as exemplar for a democratic nation, this common, accepted practice of segregation absolutely sickened her. She immediately ordered the ropes removed and issued a directive prohibiting segregation in the U.S. Department of Labor, purportedly the first federal agency to do so.

Fortunately she was probably spared from realizing that integration did not immediately result from a prohibition of segregation. Black employees were as disinclined to mingle with the white as the white were with them. More active measures—the promotion of qualified black personnel—would bring about the integration she felt appropriate to a democracy, and the actions she took, with the warm support of Eleanor Roosevelt and her friend Mary McLeod Bethune of the

National Council of Negro Women, were decisive steps in that direction.

Frances Perkins's concern for the welfare and morale of the department's employees, regardless of color or sex, extended to minute details. Her associates say that one time she visited the cafeteria on the pretense of getting a cup of coffee. One taste verified the gossip she had overheard. She trotted off to the concessionaire. "You improve this coffee or get out!" the former Consumers League activist told her in no uncertain terms.

Despite the publication of consumer exposé books and the inception of a consumer product testing organization, the consumer movement enlisted few adherents. A jest making the rounds was that youngsters wanted, instead of fairy stories about a prince, dragon, and beautiful princess, the story about an NRA official who killed a profiteer and rescued a consumer.

With her Consumers League experience and her concern for the quality of life, Frances should have been a militant consumerist. She credited herself with bringing consumer representation to the NRA, and enthusiastically assisted in Mary Harriman Rumsey's work as director of the Consumers' Division of the NRA. A Department of Labor history noted, "Its Director was adviser to the President on consumers' problems and reported to him directly," the first time in the nation's history that such recognition had been given to consumer affairs. By executive order, the division became part of the Department of Labor on December 21, 1935.

Possibly because of the trauma over Mary Rumsey's untimely death, or because consumer matters were associated with women—housewives and home economists—or because she was already spread too thinly, Frances failed to promote this division, and even neglected mentioning it in her annual reports. Steeped in the economic theory that equated consumption with income, she overlooked the importance of consumer ability in the marketplace as a significant variable affecting the level of living that wages could achieve. Of course, as she had personally noted, "More than two-thirds of the goods disposed of in this country are bought by those whose incomes are less than $2000 a year." Improved purchasing power came first.

Many of the Consumers' Division functions would eventually be picked up by the labor unions themselves to help insure that higher wages meant improved levels of living for their membership. With no objection from the secretary of labor, the Consumers' Division was absorbed by the Department of Agriculture in August, 1938.

*****

The United States joined the International Labor Organization on June 22, 1934. A quarter of a century later, Frances Perkins, upon hearing how old friends and coworkers at an ILO reunion dinner applauded her, wrote to her former division head, Clara Beyer, now retired:

> I have always been very grateful that I had the opportunity to take the U.S.A. into the International Labor Organization. I hope I have written it all very carefully in my memoirs, that is, the "how" we did it. I think it's a little early to tell all, but when I am gone someone will find it.

Either she had forgotten that she had written a chapter on the ILO called "Approaches to World Order" in her book, *The Roosevelt I Knew*, with a convincing run-down of her behind the scenes machinations to bring the United States into the ILO, or there was more to it. Former "brain truster" Adolph Berle who had introduced Frances to the concepts of the ILO while a resident of the Henry Street Settlement House, praised her faintly: "The top person gets the credit, but the layers below show the currents that brought things into existence." According to C.W. Jenks who became principal deputy director general of the ILO headquarters in Geneva, Switzerland, "Without Frances Perkins, the U.S. membership in the ILO would never have been taken. She gave the ILO full support, and enlisted others."

Jenks had the impression that President Roosevelt and Secretary of State Hull suspected that the ILO represented a backdoor entrance to the League of Nations. He added, "Hull did see it as a first break with U.S. isolationism," the isolationism reflected in the Congress denying President Woodrow Wilson's request for U.S. membership in the League of Nations.

Frances Perkins, on good counsel, gradually won the Senate Committee on Foreign Relations to the idea of ILO membership. Her carefully prepared message to Congress asking for its authority to permit the executive to join the International Labor Organization, anticipated every objection that could be raised, with emphasis on the organization's independence from any other international body or peace treaty.

At its conference in Geneva on the day the ILO accepted the membership of the United States, a number of Americans attended as "observers," as had been the case in previous years, but the secretary of labor's many commitments precluded the possibility of her attending. She regretted this because she gained useful ideas from the scholarly exchange of information with experts from other countries.

On his visit to the capital, the British economist John Maynard Keynes, whose analyses of national income and the marginal propensity to consume would appear the following year in his treatise on *The General Theory of Employment, Spending and Money*, shared with her his views on the multiplier effect of public spending. Quite aside from scholarly pursuits, Keynes had a preoccupation: the study of hands, and had particularly noticed those of the president. He might well have noticed Frances Perkins's hands, which many writers described as singularly beautiful. She used them expressively, and indulged in the vanity of bracelets on each wrist which not so accidentally attracted attention to her hands.

Around this time C.W. Jenks met her for the first time. He was visiting shortly after the United States became a member of the ILO. They were both at a small offbeat dinner party given by a Professor Rapard, director of the Institute of Higher International Studies. The professor favored "free enterprise . . . keeping things moving as they should." He admitted to some skepticism about the New Deal. Frances discoursed on the importance of sturdy initiative.

"You are the last person I expected to hear this from!" exclaimed the professor. She explicated the long-run objectives of various employment programs instituted by the administration. The professor never quite grasped her interpretation of Franklin D. Roosevelt's CCC, NRA, WPA, and Social Security programs, but he agreed with her rationale for universal labor standards so as to prevent international competition based on exploitation of workers.

In 1935 American representatives attended the ILO conference for the first time as delegates; the government provided a six dollar per diem. Frances Perkins, again unable to leave Washington, arranged for a small ceremony preceding their departure on the US Line's SS *Manhattan* on May 22, 1935. She alerted the delegates to inquire about as many phases of economic security, old age pensions, and unemployment insurance as they could. In closing she reminded them, "It is from the exchange of knowledge and suggestions on these topics that the United States will develop not merely a sounder national policy in the field of social legislation, but also a greater understanding of and sympathy with the problems of other countries."

Grace Abbott, as one of her final tasks before joining the University of Chicago briefly before her death, was assigned by the secretary of labor to present a resolution on behalf of working women. Grace Abbott felt considerable reluctance about voicing this resolution before the many ILO members who believed that industrial work for women should be completely abolished, but it had been prepared by Mary Anderson of the Women's Bureau, and Frances felt compelled to have it presented. The ILO adopted the resolution.

Instead of a pleasant ocean voyage, Frances Perkins faced the excoriation of people like Representative Tinkham of Massachusetts, who charged that through the "contemptible trickery and gross fraud of Secretary of Labor Perkins, the United States in effect has been drawn into the League of Nations." Tinkham set himself up as a vigilante overseeing American involvement with the ILO; he predicted that through Secretary Perkins's "audacious intrigue . . . the independence of the United States will be destroyed, the will of the American people thwarted, and the United States inevitably involved in the next European conflict." By comparison, the Senate Appropriations Committee's objections to ILO membership fees seemed moderate.

In the spring of 1936, participation in the women's division of the Democratic national convention in Philadelphia under the leadership of Mary Dewson—practically as many women delegates and alternates were present as men—added to the secretary of labor's already overburdened workload. Although the renomination of Roosevelt and Garner was assured, Frances's speech had to be politically letter-perfect. Her staff prepared it with care, and to the resounding cheers of the women, she instead delivered an extemporaneous tribute to Eleanor Roosevelt's love of the human race:

> She has therefore gone out through the length and breadth of the land, in the face of unfavorable criticism, not only to meet the people of the country personally as a friend, but also to utilize that contact, and make herself a channel through which their need, their hopes, their desire could be carried directly to places where solutions could be found to their problems. She has been gallant, courageous, intelligent, and wise.

> Many women in this country when they vote for Franklin D. Roosevelt will also be thinking with a choke in the throat of Eleanor Roosevelt!

*****

Frances had a couple of good reasons for going abroad the summer of 1936. One was that she knew that her speaking schedule before the

November election would be extremely heavy. Previously, providing for the care of her chronically ill husband, Paul Wilson, had tied her down. He had been living at her New York apartment with a manservant in attendance. Now, after several tries, he had finally adjusted to staying at a hospital. Frances wrote a mutual friend that she was going to Europe "not only with his consent but at his vigorous suggestion."

On July sixteenth she wired Roosevelt:

THE PRESIDENT: MY COAST SEEMS CLEAR FOR A HOLIDAY WHICH I RATHER NEED STOP WILL IT BE ALL RIGHT WITH YOU IF I GO TO EUROPE JULY TWENTY-FIRST FOR ABOUT FIVE WEEKS

The next day President Roosevelt telegraphed back:

DELIGHTED HAVE YOU TAKE TRIP BUT THINK YOU SHOULD BE BACK BY SEPTEMBER FIRST

Finally she would get to the ILO conference in Geneva. Also delegated were John G. Winant, chairman of the Social Security Board, an astute, rather slow and deliberate speaker described as a beanstalk wearing tweeds, New York State Industrial Commissioner Frieda S. Miller, and an old friend, Robert W. Bruere. His wife Jane and Frances's daughter, Susanna, were accompanying them.

There is no record of her mentioning to the president that she had stopped off briefly in Paris, France. Here she was honored by the Congress of the International Federation of Business and Professional Women by being voted "the world's outstanding woman." She had been ranked against some remarkable people: Alexandra Kollontai, the Russian ambassador to Sweden came in second; Mme. Marie Curie-Joliet of the Curie Radium Institute was third; Amy Mollison, the British transatlantic flyer was fourth; Selma Lagerlof, Swedish novelist and winner of the Nobel Prize in literature was fifth; Eleanor Roosevelt, wife of the president of the United States, came in sixth.

In the previous session of Congress, the Appropriations Committee put the secretary of labor on the firing line with pointed questions about what the United States would get for its membership dues in the ILO. The foreign correspondent reporting by wireless to the *New York Times* speculated that "It seems a fair guess that one reason for her trip here was to determine the answer better for herself."

Another reason had to do with the textiles industry. With countries like England and Germany working a forty-eight hour week and Japan sixty hours, the U.S. textiles industry with its forty-hour week could not readily compete. Frances was laying the groundwork for an industry conference that might bring about a forty-hour work week standard in all parts of the world.

The secretary of labor was well received in Geneva. "Her stature was rated high before she reached here, and the rating has undoubtedly gone higher," said the newspapers. She was reported to number among the "rare persons in the world to whom the word statesman applies."

Her ILO trip included a visit to Austria because the president "was avid for light on European countries that might be storm centers." He wanted to know something of the effects of Nazi propaganda on the treatment of the Jews in Austria.

In 1937 Undersecretary of Labor Edward F. McGrady served as the principal spokesman for the U.S. delegation to the ILO and firmed plans for a textiles conference to be held in Washington, D.C.

In 1938 in the light of world events—German troops had taken over Austria—the ILO conference assumed particular importance, and Frances fulfilled her personal pledge to the retiring director, Harold Butler, to attend.

First she stopped off briefly in Paris where the American ambassador, William C. Bullitt, smothered her with orchids and he reported back to the president that she "seemed well and lively." He also had her to dinner together with Harold Ickes and his charming new wife—over whom Frances Perkins had raised her eyebrows in dismay because of the gossip their romance had sparked.

In Geneva, her usual polished and high principled rhetoric digressed into an exposition on John G. Winant's integrity, devotion to high purposes, and unique contribution. "We have tried him in the fire, and he has been faithful. . . ." President Roosevelt had recruited Frances to "lobby" on behalf of Winant. Aside from some political debt he may have owed Winant, the president, together with Secretary of State Cordell Hull, had deemed it sound for Winant to assume the position of director of the ILO vacated by Harold Butler.

Before resigning his position with the ILO in 1941 to assume the ambassadorship to England, Winant discussed with Frances Perkins the possibility of transferring the organization's staff to the United States. Secretary of State Cordell Hull ruled this out because representatives of Germany and Axis-dominated countries would require careful surveillance. Instead, the ILO headquartered at McGill University in Montreal.

The first half of the 1941 ILO conference was held in New York City; the second half took place in Washington, D.C., where President

Roosevelt addressed the delegation. He had already heard rumors from the assistant secretary of state that the ILO wished to discontinue E.J. Phelan as the president—the British objected to his being "militantly Irish"—and Frances Perkins's name was being suggested for the presidency. At the meeting, the British governmental delegate nominated her, with seconds from the Canadian employers' delegate and the workers' delegate of China. These reflected the organizational principles of the ILO. The vote was unanimous. Her acceptance speech was polished, high principled—and long.

The conference took place three weeks before December 7, 1941, the last the ILO would hold for some years.

Secretary Perkins and E.J. Phelan, Director of the International Labour Organiza-
tion, pose with a Philadelphia newspaper cartoon published at the time of the
I.L.O. Conference in 1944.

Left to right: William Green, President of the American Federation of Labor; Lindsay Rodgers, Assistant Director (U.S.) of the International Labour Organization; and Frances Perkins, U.S. Secretary of Labor.

XIII

"Only a two-fisted Male . . ."

"Has not the fact that this President put a woman in the Cabinet made it necessary for the next President to put at least one woman in the Cabinet?"

Frances answered the reporter's standard question with, "Not at all. It has not made it necessary to have a woman in the Cabinet. But it has made it possible."

Then the inevitable, "How do you get along with the men?"

"I have found nothing but helpfulness from my fellow members of the Cabinet."

And quite a number there were. She started out with Secretary of State Hull of Tennessee, Secretary of the Treasury Woodin of New York, Secretary of War Dern of Utah, Secretary of the Navy Swanson of Virginia, Postmaster General Farley of New York, Secretary of Commerce Roper of South Carolina, Attorney General Cummings of Connecticut, Secretary of Agriculture Wallace of Iowa, and Secretary of the Interior Ickes of Illinois. They would be succeeded by Stettinius in State; Morgenthau in Treasury; Murphy, Jackson and Biddle in Justice; Woodring and Stimson in War; Edison and Knox in Navy; Hopkins, Jesse Jones and Wallace in Commerce; Wickard in Agriculture and Frank Walker as postmaster general. Only Ickes and Perkins would hold their posts into Roosevelt's fourth term.

In their memoirs, most of the cabinet members inclined to comment favorably on Frances's virtues. Hull, for one, wrote: "Miss Frances Perkins, Secretary of Labor, has never received the full credit she deserves for her ability and public services. She was unusually able, very practical, and brought vision and untiring energy to her work."

As a practical person with few illusions about her omniscience,

Frances felt no qualms about calling on her colleagues for assistance. If James Farley or Jesse Jones had better rapport with certain members of the business community, she asked them to contact employers involved in labor disputes. She also encouraged cabinet members to use the assistance of her department and expected reciprocation from them simply because they were all working for the common good.

Generally, Frances shared a warm feeling of fellowship with the cabinet members. Every cabinet meeting began with their amiable response to the president's radiant smile and hearty handshake, and friendly greetings to each other. Feuds stayed undercover for the most part, although naturally side-taking took place, with Wallace, Ickes and then Dern lining up with her on the liberal side.

Outside the cabinet meeting room, barbs occasionally went flying when one cabinet member invaded the turf of another. Jurisdictional squabbles between cabinet members placed a reluctant president in the role of arbiter. Roosevelt either pitted one against the other or forced a compromise. These differences were usually aired with him privately, and he made the final decision, committing almost everything to executive order. Frances did not always agree with the president's decisions, but unlike some others she abided fully with their spirit and intent. Francis Biddle praised her in these terms:

> But Miss Perkins loved her old friend Franklin Roosevelt, and was loyal to him not only in act and word, but in the whole purpose and each part of her work; loyal in her heart as well as her mind, in the selflessness of her being, behind the clear-eyed view she had of him, far clearer than most of us; so that when Paul Ward suggested that her motto was "see what the boss in the back room will have," he was right, though the implication was twisted, for she stood up to the boss, but *inside* the circle of his policies.

Biddle, out of his insight on the workings of any organization, added, "It is so easy to destroy a policy, to inhibit it on the second level, the operating level, just below policy, but the level on which, in practice, policy is defined and created over the long run."

Periodically the president would remonstrate the men for what Biddle describes as "the unseemliness of washing our dirty linen in public." Everyone knew Roosevelt's remonstrances did not apply to Frances Perkins, who clearly wanted the image of the administration and its administrators to be pristine pure. When a cabinet member's advances to a young secretary in his office became known to her, she spoke to James Farley and to the secretary to the president, Louis

Howe, suggesting that they recommend that the president do something. Apparently Roosevelt found Frances's puritanical dismay amusing. When she faced him with the issue, he simply said, "I can't stop Harold."

European biographer Emil Ludwig reported that "she likes to tell how the ladies of Washington have been waiting in vain for five years to see her compromise herself in money matters, or love, or some other way." About the most lascivious gossip that hit the office grapevine alluded to her playing poker with the president, James Farley, and Senator Robert Wagner.

Although not a cabinet member, Vice-president John Nance Garner attended cabinet meetings regularly, walking out midway when bored. Frances thought of him as "a picturesque, briery, vigorous old man from Texas; slightly deaf, but not so deaf that he couldn't hear what wasn't intended for him in a Cabinet meeting."

At one of the first meetings, after listening patiently to economic reports—"he'd sat peering forward, listening with his hand behind his ear"—he blurted out, red in the face, "Mr. President, Mr. President. When we were campaigning I think we said we were going to do something for the poorer kind of people, and we better be about it. They can't wait." Frances remembered this particularly because "John Garner was no flaming radical; he belonged in the extreme right of right-wing of the Democratic party."

The vice-president thought well of Frances until the issue of the sit-down strike came up. According to his recollections, "I said to Miss Perkins, 'Do you think the sit-down strike is right?' 'Yes,' she replied. 'Do you think it is legal?' 'Yes,' she answered.

"I asked the President, 'Do you think it is right?' 'No,' he replied. 'Do you think it is legal?' 'No,' he replied."

The vice-president left that particular meeting certain that the president was about to issue a statement denouncing the sit-down strike. No statement appeared.

People frequently came away from the president with misconceived notions of his stand. The president let this happen. Frances explained, "Plenty of crackpots who had access to him brought him ideas, and he would usually handle them very amiably and say, 'That's fine, that's a good idea, that's fine.' They would go away thinking he had endorsed them. It was my unhappy lot to explain that he said 'that's fine,' just the way I say the weather's fine."

At other times the president would agree to programs he didn't fully understand. The most frequent offender, Frances thought, was Harold Ickes, "and it made the rest of us furious at him."

Possibly a Victorian sense of propriety kept Harold Ickes from clashing with Frances as he purportedly did with every other member of the cabinet. But a rather typical entry in his diary reads, "As usual, only the President listened to her. Harry Hopkins wrote me a note something to the effect: 'Elementary course in government from 4 to 5 by Professor FP.' . . .As usual, I studiously avoided being caught by Perkins' basilisk eye." (Frances's disconcertingly fixed gaze reminded a number of people of the classical legend of a fantastic lizard-like creature that the ancients said could kill by its breath or look.)

A number of the men complained privately that once Frances started talking, there was no stopping her. And worse yet, President Roosevelt appeared to be fascinated. Frances realized that her colleagues' interests rarely meshed with hers, so she consciously tried not to bore them. Years later she admitted to keeping a little notebook in which she recorded when she would discuss unemployment insurance or the Wagner bill; no more than at every other meeting. "You know, you discuss it this week, but not next. Don't wear 'em all out with your thing."

Roosevelt enjoyed teasing and occasionally his subjects took offense. Again Frances was exempt. With women Roosevelt indulged in the flattering banter that nonflirtatious people find more exasperating than complimentary. Frances knew him too well to get flustered, and socially she could exchange tit for tat with him.

Of course even a long-standing social-business relationship underwent modification in the light of the president's position. Although Roosevelt used first names on a person-to-person basis, hardly a dozen people called him by his first name after he became president. Assistant Secretary to the President Marvin McIntyre wrote that former news-paperman Louis M. Howe "was the only one of the official family who called the President 'Franklin.' It was 'Mr. President' or 'the Boss' for the rest of us." So Frances was quite surprised to have her secretary notify her one day that there was a call from a man named Franklin.

"Franklin? Franklin?" She thought for a moment.

"I don't know anybody by that name. Find out who he is and whom he works for."

Miss Jay reported back, "He says his name is Franklin Roosevelt, and he works for the United States."

Yes, she could expect this kind of thing from the Roosevelt she knew, possibly more than she confessed to in her aptly titled book. Roosevelt's son names her as one of the few confidantes to whom his father related personal matters. Some of these were not particularly confidential, such as Roosevelt's concern over his mother, Sara, spoiling his five children; his refusal to attend church "in a goldfish bowl," his description for being viewed by tourists while attending services; and insistence on burial in the Hyde Park rose garden rather than interment in a Washington cathedral. These stories appear not only in Frances's book, but are regurgitated in dozens of subsequent volumes on Roosevelt with footnote credit to the book's author.

Like many important people in Washington, D.C., Frances often went about with a retinue of assistants. Isador Lubin frequently flanked her side and supplied specific data as needed, especially when she faced the press corps. But Lubin says that she always went to the White House alone and talked privately with the president.

Obviously some of the personal confidences Roosevelt shared with her were never recorded. Rightfully, he regarded her as a discreet friend. No hint, oblique or otherwise, suggested any romantic relationship between the two. Frances was not the kind of person who made any wife jealous, and Eleanor Roosevelt certainly approved of Frances's platonic work and social relationship with her husband.

The love people said Frances had for Franklin Roosevelt, in the light of her asides over the years, appears rather to be a love for what he symbolized. In terms of the *raison d'être* for her life, Frances could be categorized as an opportunist. Roosevelt represented a means to the end she sought, namely social justice for the poor.

At the *Washington Post*'s author luncheon some time after the publication of her book on Roosevelt, someone asked how she came to know and understand him so well. The question brought back memories of a letter she wrote to her secretary when Roosevelt first became governor. She realized then that she had come to know Al Smith well over the years but not Roosevelt. She recalled writing, "I shall have to study this new Governor in order to see how we will work together. He is very different from Al Smith."

She told her audience:

And then as I thought about it I began to look back over life and see who are the people I have understood, who are the people I have studied, and they are the people who have been my superior officers. And I believe that is what we all do. You study your superior officers; you study the person you are working for; you study them not out of curiosity, but in order to appreciate their mentality, their purpose, the best side of their nature, and their weaknesses, so that you may work with them and accomplish with them and for them the thing which they really desire and hope to accomplish.

In her book, Frances conveyed the impression that Roosevelt lacked direction and planfullness, one point on which Eleanor Roosevelt, Mary Dewson, and the director of the Franklin D. Roosevelt Library at Hyde Park disagreed. Frances clearly did not consider Roosevelt an original thinker in the field of economics.

"Sometimes his notions about economics were funny," she recalled. "If you were a friend of his, you just laughed at them . . . and he could always be laughed out of them, you know."

He would get enthusiastic over someone's idea and then try the idea out on a friend. Once he said to her, "What we need to do is to reorganize the money of this country. Everything should be measured in ergs." In response to her puzzled expression, he explained, "You probably don't know; the erg is the measure of the work value, and if we can get a monetary system where the erg is the basis. . ."

"Well, I began to smell Rex Tugwell," Frances recalled, "and I began to laugh, and I asked him, 'Who was here just a few minutes ago—Rex Tugwell?' "

Then Roosevelt laughed, and said "Yes!"

Her trepidations over the president's impressionability were subtly expressed in a memorandum to him dated March 12, 1935:

I have thought for some time that you need (at least for the period Congress is in session) a political scientist right at your *personal* beck and call, to draft, to make analysis of proposals by Congress, by Administration Members, either original ones or amendments, and help you decide what is right and best so that you can utilize the existing political machinery to push it over.

You have no real defense and personal help against your associates' errors (mine included).

You ought to get analyzed information and clear statements of alternatives. Then you can decide policy and general plan to be followed. Then *your* political scientist can draft, modify, adopt, etc., this policy and see it through. Legislation must be:

1. Socially and politically proper
2. Desired by the Executive
3. Satisfactory to Congress.

Secretary of Labor Frances Perkins welcomes President Roosevelt on his return to Washington, D.C. from the Teheran Conference, December 17, 1943.

The Executive by his veto and message power is a part of Congress—the first and last word! Most really good and *wise legislation* can be *made* to fill the three above conditions. There is an art and a science to the *doing of it.* Dr. John F. Sly of West Virginia has been doing this brilliantly for the Governor of West Virginia for five years. Amazing progress has been made in a backward State. I think that he and two or three of his young assistants could be "borrowed" without more cost than expenses.

I suggest you think about this. He is exceptional and loyal to you—a real New Dealer but hard-headed and realistic. No "dreams of things to come" from him. Just do it today stuff.

A master politician, Roosevelt appointed a Committee on Administrative Management, which recommended that he have six high-grade executive assistants to help him deal with the various departments and agencies. The report noted that these executive assistants should be chosen for one qualification—a passion for anonymity.

Roosevelt wanted to cut the cost of running government, not add to it. Shortly before taking office, he'd said to Daniel C. Roper, "I'd like to see all the independent commissions brought under the general supervision of Cabinet officers. In this way their operations can be reported upon weekly. It will be in the interest of economy and greater efficiency."

With this, Frances concurred wholeheartedly and persistently. But by the end of his first term in office, Roosevelt's ideas had been modified by expedience and a realization that "the only way you can save money in the long run, 99% of it, is by cutting down government functions and doing less work."

Frances criticized his approach in submitting his reorganization committee's report as too secretive and speedy. The purposes of the business-like changes he wished to make were misunderstood. Tactically his timing was also off, as was the case with his Supreme Court packing plan which followed in February, 1937. Not until April 3, 1939, would he see the essence of his reorganization bill passed by Congress, and then the public interpreted changes affecting the Department of Labor as punitive measures taken against Frances Perkins personally.

Actually Roosevelt's most overt action against Frances consisted of deleting her justifiable but superfluous back-patting statements from letters she drafted to go out over his signature, and of letting her fight her most crucial battles alone. In addition, when the Employment Service was to be shifted out of the Department of Labor, he lacked the gumption to face her with it. Rather, he asked his wife to placate Frances. Eleanor Roosevelt also lacked the spirit for this assignment, and in turn wrote to Mary Dewson: "There is some fear that Frances Perkins will oppose it [transferring the Employment Service]. I think if you speak to her it will have more weight than if I were to do it."

Although critical of the president's shortcomings, Frances concluded that he did well in "a post of political and spiritual leadership." Looking back after World War II, she wrote prophetically:

> In retrospect, one wonders if the American people want to pay the price of having an extremely competent, straight-line administrator as President. . . .A strong straight-line administrator endowed with special power might be tempted to get the right thing done promptly and expeditiously by removing obstacles in the most efficient fashion and thus overlooking the will and true welfare of the people, since in his own mind he would be sure he was doing the right thing and best thing for the people.

Because he wanted the "vicarious experience of what was going on in an enterprise," Roosevelt at times went directly to the cabinet members' assistants or departments, which particularly irked Cordell Hull and Harold Ickes. Roosevelt's wife, Eleanor, also did a bit of nosing around the departments. According to Rexford Tugwell, this was "a practice a number of the Cabinet members resented, but some others had the wit to take advantage of her interest." Although attuned to bureaucratic proprieties, Frances frequently connived with the president's wife, which Tugwell felt proved to be to the public advantage.

Eleanor Roosevelt took umbrage with the Gridiron Club, which excluded the cabinet's one distaff member from its annual dinner for the president and the cabinet. She decided to give a Gridiron Widow's Party for women officials of government, wives of the Gridiron Club members, and for newspaper women. The first made headlines because the White House police dog, Major, bit a woman senator. The following year Eleanor Roosevelt gave a masquerade party at which Frances posed as a "brain truster" wearing an academic mortarboard and judicial robe.

Any slights to women were quickly called to Eleanor Roosevelt's attention by Mary Dewson. Dewson's persistence and persuasion touched on every area. A sharp note written by the postage-stamp-loving president suggests the extent of her women's patronage activities:

You girls have got to realize that this chiseling business on your part must stop somewhere. I have put more girls' faces on postage stamps in the last seven years than all of my 31 predecessors put together.

Incidentally, the president's reference to women as "girls" was offset by Eleanor Roosevelt, Mary Dewson, Frances Perkins, and their friends referring to the men in the cabinet and on the Hill as "the boys." One of "the boys," James Farley, during an interview twenty-five years later insisted, "Women are not pushing to get ahead the way they were then. Today they are satisfied with less."

Together with Vice-President Garner, James Farley opposed the president's campaign for a third term in office. Eleanor Roosevelt attributed this to Farley's personal political ambitions, but Frances felt certain that Farley stood on his principles. Eleanor Roosevelt's friend later wrote:

Mrs. Perkins was remarkable, Mrs. R. added, in that she never said a mean thing about another person. She would never come to the President with a story that would hurt that person with the President. That was a rare quality, especially in a woman, Mrs. Roosevelt thought.

*****

Every nation has its share of xenophobes and misanthropes. These decided that Frances Perkins was a Jewess of Russian birth, or a foundling dropped on the Perkins's doorstep in Boston's foreign quarter, or the product of a Georgia orphanage. The Associated Farmers of Riverside, California, sent out literature proclaiming her to be of Russian descent and asserting the group's resentment of interference from radical individuals. Rumors had it that she married Paul Wilson under her given name of Matilda Watski, and that she was probably married before even though she referred to marriage as an "inconvenience."

Letters coming into her office requested information on her date of birth and her ethnic background, but Frances felt that the gossip and curiosity were too pernicious to merit a response. Then she heard that a gentleman who passed himself off as a genealogist from Boston visited her sister, still living in Massachusetts. Her sister proudly recited the family lineage back to pre-Revolutionary days. According to Mary Dewson, when the man called on the sister again to determine whether or not she was an only child, she answered in good Perkins fashion that he should ask her sister, the only person in her family of public interest. He finally admitted that the Daughters of the American Revolution had hired him, a detective, to check on Frances's ancestry, and upon learning that she qualified for D.A.R. honors in good measure, still feared that Frances was nothing more than an adopted child of Jewish origin. He had been unable to locate any record of her birth in Boston in the year 1882.

Frances gave Mary Dewson the impression that her records had been destroyed, probably by fire. Mary remembered Frances saying that the carefully kept records of the physician who attended her birth were frequently relied on by the New England Genealogical Society. To cinch the matter, Frances told her, "I look like the portrait of one of my ancestors, a revolutionary orator. I have the same broad forehead and pointed chin."

Finally Frances wrote a public letter to one of the correspondents unequivocally spelling out her lineage and that of her husband. The letter, distributed to the press as a reply to the political "whispering campaign," gave her birth date as April 10, 1882, the date on all her records with the U.S. Department of Labor, the Federal Bureau of Investigation, and the Civil Service Commission—the date that appeared on virtually everything except her birth certificate and her school records. In 1960 when a group of Cornell University colleagues gave her a surprise birthday party, she admitted to a couple of confidantes that it really was her eightieth birthday, but the university's records remained unchanged. She subsequently confessed her age to Hannah and Matthew Josephson who would be finishing her biography of Al Smith, with an explanation that the confusion about her birthdate had started with a reporter. For at least ten years prior to coming to Washington, she perpetuated the "confusion."

Her statement regarding religion rings true: "If I were a Jew I would make no secret of it. On the contrary, I would be proud to acknowledge it." She clearly respected and admired the intelligence and industriousness of the many Jewish people with whom she worked. And if she remembered her earliest teaching days before leaving Massachusetts, she had especially enjoyed the people from the Jewish community.

Frances frequently felt disheartened and demoralized by the personal attacks made on her, the criticism for everything that went wrong, the blame for statements misconstrued by the press or politicians, and the lack of credit for her beyond-the-call-of-duty exertions that contributed to successful ventures. In a review of Rexford Tugwell's book *The Democratic Roosevelt,* John Kenneth Galbraith wrote:

> One of the most interesting phenomena of the Roosevelt era was the way that criticism, invective, ridicule and slander meant for Roosevelt himself landed on those around him. The office no doubt protected F.D.R. from some of the onslaught. His air of superb self-assurance, leading as it did to a certain hopelessness over the possibility of ever getting under his skin, was no doubt an even greater protection. Everyone close to him—the original members of the Brain Trust; Morgenthau, Ickes, Wallace, Hopkins, and Frances Perkins; and Eleanor more than anyone else—became a target. To be in Roosevelt's confidence, in short, was to be a lightning rod for the wrath he aroused but to which he was so disconcertingly immune.

Other writers claim that criticism did get under the president's skin. While visiting Frances's home town of Worcester around the time of the "whispering campaign" against her, he gave a speech in which he recalled how a few years earlier "the knees of our rugged individualists were trembling" when the New Deal started, and yet a few years later "some of them are even well enough to throw their crutches at the doctor."

Roosevelt hated being "nibbled to death by ducks," as he put it, adding:

> Criticism, unless constructive, is nothing but abuse. They attack what I have done, but never once do they say what they would have done or would do.

> To answer attempts to end child labor, wipe out slums, and better living conditions by yelling that is the opening wedge for a dictatorship that will destroy free speech, free press, free assemblage, and abolish trial by jury, *isn't* criticism in any honest sense of the word, but just plain, downright sabotage.

Roosevelt showed less sensitivity to the abusive criticism heaped on his cabinet members and his wife. Frances Perkins, by virtue of her sex and her pivotal position, seemed most vulnerable to incredibly malicious taunting. A year after her lineage letter received extensive publicity, Congressman Clare Hoffman still jollied up his public speeches with hyperbole referring to her as:

> . . ."the wife of someone, though God alone knows what her true name may be, and no man has yet published the place of her birth." This "tearful woman," "your Old Maid Secretary of Labor," "the first Tootsie Roll of the Cabinet," rates as "the No. 1 donkey on Dr. Roosevelt's merry-go-round" and provides "first-class comedy on the Republic's political stage."

Stephen Ragsdale made the mock plea, "Mr. President, if you believe Madam Perkins is some sort of Virgin Mary, then why not pray God that she conceive and bear us a man child to become our Secretary of Labor?"

Author Morris Bealle wrote about "Princess Pinkie," "the inscrutable Madam Secretary":

> Madam Tootsie Roll is nobody to write home about. There is more sex appeal on tap in Pangopango. The first time she walked into a Cabinet meeting she wore a hat that was an affront to the millinery industry. The thing looked like someone sat on it and she had forgotten to unwrinkle it. Seven years of Cabineteering have not changed the dainty fluff of soft stuff. She still wears that same lolapalooza of a tarbush.

Women executives at that time wore hats even in their offices if they had to make a number of calls. Men in their uniform fedoras found these a source of much amusement. Men of the press also mocked Frances Perkins's business-like black dresses: "They must have been designed by the Bureau of Standards!"

One writer, Emil Ludwig, happened to catch her late on an atypical day:

> One may guess from her anterooms—everything is spacious and comfortable, with wooden wainscoting and green leather furniture—that this department is managed by a woman. Or in what other place could I have seen a lady Secretary in a dress of Bordeaux red velvet, near whom a young man in a cap stands at the telephone smiling to her like an impudent page smiling to a distinguished lady of the court? There is in these rooms something of an inverted harem; the men go around as if they were only tolerated.

People see what they want to see, and Emil Ludwig proved the rule.

*****

If gender circumscribes ability, the ultimate test for judging the performance of the female secretary of labor had to be the handling of labor strikes that plagued the administration from beginning to end. The strikes averted because of her adeptness at dealing with significant people on both sides of a controversy gave rise to few plaudits. They rarely came to the attention of the people, the press, or the president.

During the NRA period, General Hugh Johnson would prod her, "Why should people strike now? The President is doing everything that he can do for them."

"The trouble with Hugh," Frances remarked tartly on one occasion, "is that he thinks a strike is something to settle."

Not only were working conditions in many industries deplorable, but around 1935-36 the lowest third of all American families earned an average of $471 a year, the middle third $1,076, and the top third $3,000. These averages are somewhat overstated because 1 percent of the population—families with incomes over $10,000 a year—enjoyed 13 percent of the national income.

Why did the workers strike? Frances remembered that Samuel Gompers used to say, "They organize one day, the next day they say, 'When do we get our wages raised,' and the third day they strike."

Frances determined that at first the union members struck because they didn't have a code under the NRA. Then they struck because the employers were not paying the wages specified in the code. Then, she said, "The idea that the employers wouldn't meet them when they came up with a committee was a real grievance and one that did not disappear very rapidly or very readily."

The AFL's membership had almost quadrupled under section 7a of the NRA. Frances attributed this to the people's "deep desire to belong to something that could be called a labor union and to have an opportunity to vote for representatives who would speak up about the terms and conditions of their work."

Louis Stark, a labor reporter with the *New York Times*, on his return from a weekend trip to West Virginia and Kentucky, told her, "Do you know what they're doing? It's the most extraordinary thing. They're pouring down from the mining towns into the big towns to sign up—these are real miners. In addition to that, anybody in the town who wants to signs up—man, woman, or child—signs up. They sign up in the drugstores; they sign up in the movie houses and on the streetcars."

Sometimes the success of the labor unions was not necessarily in monetary terms. For example, in July, 1936, Homestead, Pennsylvania, was open to the union members for the first time. A few years before, Frances met with steelworkers in the post office because it was a federal building that could not be declared off-limits by municipal authorities. Now the union workers were free to hold a mass meeting to commemorate the killing of steelworkers in Homestead in 1892.

On the other hand, the rift between the trade unions and the craft unions impeded progress. Frances recalled bitterly, "We attempted to heal the breach before it got too big. . . ." She formed a committee of five AFL and five CIO men who met in her office, with two of her best people from the Conciliation Service at their disposal.

The committee worked for days gathering the statistical data for each of the union federations. "And then the critical thing," she explained, "they worked up the amount of money that the AFL unions had stored away in their pension funds." The AFL would not give the CIO "access to the precious pension funds which they had built up by their own contributions for years. It was their money and their insurance fund and they weren't going to divide it. It was on that eventually, that we never could make the least bit of headway."

She found fascinating the fact that while the newspapers were screaming about the divided labor movement and some exceptional jurisdictional strikes

> the utmost peace reigned between the AFL and the CIO locally. At headquarters in Washington they would be firing verbal bombasts at each other; in the Philadelphia local they continued to work away on the everyday things they were interested in. It was the same everywhere: the local people would agree to work with each other without saying anything about it.

Getting the labor union viewpoint into committees dealing with a variety of problems presented some difficulty. According to Frances:

> You took *experienced* labor leaders who knew how to run their union, who knew how to keep things going, who knew how to make contracts, who knew when they'd got a good contract and when it needed repair; you took them right away from the union, right away from the plants and factories where they had just negotiated the contract and put them over here on a board that met in Washington four days a week. The union was bereft of their services during that period. And the union needed their services, particularly in the interpretation of the orders that came out from Washington.

Or what was just as bad, she'd be "stumped for a man to recommend" for a committee and would ask the head of the AFL or CIO to recommend someone. She discovered, "There was a very strong tendency to recommend lame ducks or relatives or excess people that they had hanging around their offices for years and didn't know what else to *do* with."

She found it embarrassing, after having asked for the recommendation, to say no, "but they were not the right kind of people." Nor were the lawyers or economists that the unions were hiring.

"I would inquire into their background. I would find they'd never worked at a bench; they'd never used a tool; they knew nothing of the feelings, the emotions, the hopes, the aspirations of the labor people.

But they were good lawyers or economists." Some could argue the case well, but from others, "you got a lot of talk . . . sort of a show-off obstructionism to something that might easily have gone through in two or three days."

Obstructionism also characterized top management people who adamantly refused to recognize labor unions by condescending to meet and talk with their leaders. To force the issue, workers employed a relatively new technique, the sit-down strike, which precluded the possibility of management hiring scabs or strike-breakers to replace them at their jobs. The sit-down strike in the automobile industry might have been classified as "creative disorder" at the outset had not law enforcement agents' attempts to bring about order instigated violence instead. The situation became further aggravated when word leaked out about a letter written by Alfred P. Sloan, Jr., the president of General Motors Corporation, questioning the extent to which the company's general policies could be subject to negotiation in the event that the United Auto Workers received recognition as the bargaining agent for General Motors workers.

Sloan refused to meet with John L. Lewis, the president of the CIO, while workers occupied plants in Flint, Michigan. He called on Michigan's Governor Frank Murphy to forcibly evict the workers and end the illegal occupation of General Motors' property. Actually the courts had not made a determination on the legality of sit-down strikes. To avoid further bloodshed, the governor surrounded the Flint plant with 1500 National Guardsmen to prevent eviction by the company's hired men. By mid-January, 1937, a truce appeared to be in the offing through the governor's negotiations with labor and company representatives in Lansing, the state capital. Unfortunately the United Auto Workers heard that General Motors planned to confer with the Flint Alliance and stopped evacuation of the plants.

The day before President Roosevelt's second inauguration, Frances hassled over the issues with John L. Lewis and Governor Frank Murphy. Before taking off for home, she wrote to the president:

I have been all day in conference with John Lewis and Governor Murphy. We have just broken up (8:15 P.M.). Lewis' position remains absolutely unchanged.

The Governor offered to surround the plants with militia while negotiations were going on if the sit-down strikers could be withdrawn. Lewis cannot agree to this. We then moved to try to bring Lewis and Sloan together. After four hours' consideration, Sloan agreed to come to Washington to confer with Governor Murphy and me but not with Lewis.

We are protecting him (Sloan) by absolute silence on the subject but I thought you ought to know.

The next day, the secretary of labor inconspicuously stole away from the inauguration stand in order to meet with Sloan and Murphy. Sloan continued his refusal to meet with Lewis while the plants were occupied.

The only power vested in the hands of the secretary of labor was moral suasion. That had failed, and rumors abounded that she wept in frustration. Actually her dander was up:

. . .an episode like this must make it clear to the American people why the workers have lost confidence in General Motors. I still think that General Motors have made a great mistake, perhaps the greatest mistake in their lives. The American people do not expect them to sulk in their tents because they feel the sit-down strike is illegal. There was a time when picketing was considered illegal, and before that strikes of any kind were illegal. The legality of the sit-down strike has yet to be determined.

When asked if the possible illegality of the sit-down strike justified the refusal of General Motors to meet with the union:

. . .I replied that in my opinion it did not. That the function of General Motors was to make automobiles and to that end to conduct its relations with its workers in such a way as to make possible the regular performance of that function—that any error or even misbehavior on the part of those workers did not impose on the company the duty of judging and punishing the offense nor relieve them from public responsibility of talking with representatives about their grievances.

On January twenty-seventh, the secretary of labor asked Congress for the right to subpoena principals in a controversy. The next day the press ballyhooed her bid for some clout in handling strikes. A reporter asked the president the question on everyone's mind: "I wondered if you had expressed to Miss Perkins any approval of the subpoena power she has requested of Congress?"

The president continued his noncommittal, low-profile stance:

This morning, when I woke up, I read two editorials on the question of the subpoena power in the Department of Labor. Now this is all background so there is no offense meant to any one paper. The *Post* this morning has what I

Man-Size Job

Voice of the People

Cartoon from the Richmond Times Dispatch, *April 22, 1941.*

would call an exceedingly intelligent editorial. The *Herald-Tribune* has a completely stupid editorial. [Laughter] So, if you will read those two editorials side by side you will get the drift of it.

The response to Frances's request took the form of a resolution introduced by Representative Clare Hoffman, a Republican from Michigan, that would require the secretary of labor to answer questions that could only have put her department and the strikers in an unfavorable light. The resolution was tabled.

Sloan intimated that he might respond favorably to an invitation directly from the president for a meeting. Roosevelt emphasized that a representative of the president had already extended an invitation. Alerted by Frances Perkins on daily developments, the president assiduously avoided public pronouncements on the imbroglio. It was therefore surprising to see in the president's files a handwritten letter from a Mr. Edward A. LeRoy, Union Club, Park Avenue, dated February 2, 1937, complaining that Frances Perkins, reduced to tears over the auto strike and the seamen's strike, should "be replaced by some practical business man, whose honesty and capability could not be doubted or assailed." Customarily, the president's secretary, Louis Howe, or Assistant Secretary McIntire would routinely respond: "This will be shown to the President and your view will be of interest to him." But President Roosevelt chose to answer in his own words:

> I hope some day that I can have a chance to tell you something of the other side of the picture because I fear from what you write that you have had only a partial view of some of the problems. I know you will realize that you cannot get anything like a complete view from reading the papers.

Many more requests came to the president's office demanding that "a two-fisted male" be appointed secretary of labor so that strikes would be handled with dispatch. The New York *Daily News* echoed the sentiment repeatedly: "Mme. Perkins, we believe, is incapable, as most any other woman would be, of settling an industrial battle between two strong-willed and angry he-men." And again on the industrial war, "We believe this war is too much for Mme. Perkins. The unwillingness of the masculine Lewis and the equally masculine Sloan to submit to a feminine umpire is a human and understandable unwillingness."

The negotiated settlement that took place on February tenth and eleventh represented a victory for organized labor, but not for the middlemen. Governor Frank Murphy lost the next election. Frances kept her position, but lost the confidence of a large segment of the public. And she could never close the door on the past.

Preserved for posterity in the *Congressional Record*, on June 15, 1937, Congressman Clare Hoffman held the floor of the House of Representatives.

Mr. Hoffman: ... Well may Franklin D. Roosevelt boast of the achievement of his purpose to beat industry to its knees. By the aid of his Secretary of Labor, who was born only God knows where, but whose destination, if the predictions of many be true, is absolutely certain;

[pause for laughter and applause]

with the assistance of his traitorous tool, Murphy, and the aid of the flying squadrons of John L. Lewis, the President has become the master of industry in Michigan and in thousands of other localities throughout our land.

...They invaded Michigan because they knew that back of Governor Murphy was the Secretary of Labor. She stands back of Murphy, and back of her stands President Roosevelt...

Congressman Dickstein asked Hoffman to yield, which he did.

Mr. Dickstein: The gentleman made a statement a moment ago that I was very much interested in. He said that the Secretary of Labor is behind Murphy. What is there that the Secretary of Labor should do to stop these strikes that she did not do?

Mr. Hoffman: In the first place, she could have kept her mouth shut and not questioned the legality of the sit-down strike.

[pause for applause]

In the second place, she could have stated, as could the President, that this· thing is unlawful. She could have called upon the President to enforce the statutes of the United States to prevent interference with the United States mails. She could have shown how the stopping of these factories and the stopping of production was a burden on interstate commerce, a subject we have heard so much about. She could have called attention to the fact that throwing hundreds of thousands of men out of employment, depriving them of millions of dollars in wages, but increased the relief burden.

Mr. Dickstein: Right there, to clear that question up, she is only the Secretary of Labor trying to enforce the laws of this Congress.

Mr. Hoffman: I told the gentleman what she could do. She has a mouth; she can talk. She did use it to call on Sloan and the General Motors officials when she wanted to interfere, when she wanted to prevent business going on.

Mrs. O'Day: Mr. Chairman, will the gentleman yield?

Mr. Hoffman: I yield.

Mrs. O'Day: The gentleman said nobody knew where Miss Perkins was born.

Mr. Hoffman: I may have displayed my ignorance.

Mrs. O'Day: The gentleman has, indeed.

Mr. Hoffman: It is not the first time.

Mrs. O'Day: She was born near Boston.

Mr. Hoffman: I have heard that she has as many birthplaces as some people have husbands.

Following the laughter, Mr. Hoffman's tirade continued with a few thousand words against the communist "Red" labor leaders that were disrupting this "paradise for the thrifty, industrious, honest, decent citizen."

*****

A long time ago Julius Caesar observed, "Men willingly believe what they wish." Hardly a week after Hoffman's attack on the secretary of labor's handling of the sit-down strike in the automobile industry, Ohio's governor, Martin L. Davey, insisted that she had instructed him to hold the heads of Republic Steel and Youngstown Sheet and Tube Company until they signed an agreement with the steel strikers. He refused:

Secretary Perkins' suggestion would be in my judgment, the exercise of the most autocratic and dictatorial powers ever attempted. In private life, it would be kidnapping. Until the courts have decided that the companies have to sign contracts or agreements I have no right to take any one and hold him. That might be all right in Germany or Italy.

The newspapers gave front-page coverage to her denial:

I never made any such unwarranted and high-handed proposal that Governor Davey summon the steel operators and hold them until they signed a peace agreement.

I merely suggested to Governor Davey, inasmuch as the Federal Steel Board reported it believed an adjustment of difficulties could be reached if the parties concerned sat down together, that the State of Ohio had the subpoena power to bring all concerned into a joint conference and thus try out the board's proposal of attempting to reach a voluntary settlement by the conference method.

As Governor Davey called out the Ohio militia to protect the rights of strike breakers, and the National Labor Relations Board charged Ford Motor Company with "malicious and brutal assaults" on United Auto Workers as they distributed union literature, the Department of Labor was working on a significant piece of legislation that would affect unorganized wage earners as well as the organized. President Roosevelt had decided that Frances Perkins could take action on the wages and hours bill that she had prepared some time before.

Through the division of labor standards' efforts on a state-by-state basis, and the Walsh-Healey Public Contracts Act, some progress had been made in establishing minimum wages and maximum hours in a work week, but coverage was limited. The Fair Labor Standards Act, as it came to be called, was introduced in the House and the Senate on May 24, 1937. Frances Perkins saw its provisions for a floor below which wages could not fall, and the regulation in effect prohibiting stretching of hours of the lowest-paid workers, as vital to a program for the reduction of poverty.

The AFL and CIO opposed the bill because they feared the minimum would become the maximum wage; besides, they wanted all wages determined by collective bargaining. Representatives of southern industries feared the South would lose its competitive advantage when no longer permitted to pay starvation wages for the production of goods in interstate commerce. When two of the bill's supporters, Senator Claude Pepper of Florida and Lister Hill of Alabama, won special elections in their respective states, the popularity of the wages and hours act on the home front became evident.

The final bill incorporated many compromises. The minimum wage in the first year would be twenty-five cents an hour, and increased annually by five cents an hour until the desired forty cents an hour was reached. The number of hours before time-and-a-half pay would be exacted were set at forty-four the first year, forty-two the second, and forty hours the third year.

With the child labor amendment still short of ratification, the Fair Labor Standards Act served as the vehicle for prohibiting employment of children under sixteen in business involved in interstate commerce. According to Dr. Jonathan Grossman, historian of the Department of Labor, the new law signed by the president on June 25, 1938, improved wages for 300,000 workers, reduced the work week for a million others, and limited the job market for youngsters.

*****

Periodically Frances Perkins received notes from the president asking her to check on Harry Bridges, a gaunt-looking wild-eyed young alien, president of the International Longshoremen's and Warehousemen's Union. The Immigration and Naturalization Service could find no grounds for his deportation.

To avoid a tie-up of West Coast shipping in the fall of 1936, she personally telephoned Harry Bridges encouraging him to cooperate by having his men continue work under a consent agreement even though the union contract had expired. Again she felt that differences would be resolved after the longshoremen and the ship companies' management "sit around a table and talk it over." Harry Bridges recalled that he persuaded Joe Curran, bosun of a Grace Line vessel (later president of the National Maritime Union) to take the ship back to its home port in New York.

The tense situation caused the president to comment at a press conference, "Just off the record, there are pretty ugly rumors about certain people who are working out there to force a showdown at this time. I don't mean Bridges and his crowd."

Assistant Secretary to the President McIntyre then added the jocular note, "Miss Perkins' 'Good boy.' The boys know that story about Miss Perkins calling up Bridges and saying, 'Be a good boy.' "

Some three decades later, in a personal letter, Harry Bridges reacted to this dialogue with, "There was no such phone call, in those terms. There was a phone call in 1936 that had to do with the tie-up in the port of Los Angeles of a Grace Line vessel." He emphasized the point, "There was no 'Bridges, be a good boy' baloney about the phone call."

Harry Bridges remembered the circumstances extremely well. His union cooperated with the secretary of labor, but then "the crew aboard the ship and myself and Mrs. Perkins were double-crossed by the Department of Commerce of that period. The Secretary of that Department brought mutiny charges against the crew—if not against all members of the crew, then against some of them (including Joe Curran)."

Frances sent Assistant Secretary of Labor Edward F. McGrady to represent her at the joint meetings between the union and the waterfront employers. Bridges said that McGrady urged an extension of the contracts for thirty days to which the union agreed, but the Waterfront Employers Association would only accept fifteen days. Negotiations broke off and all Pacific Coast ports were struck from October 28, 1936 until February 4, 1937.

During this time the Department of Labor's solicitor, Charles E. Wyzanski, believes that Frances met Harry Bridges personally and found him to be a bit of a smart aleck. But her personal reaction to the man and his manners in no way influenced her treatment of him in her official capacity.

On September 22, 1937, a district director of the Immigration and Naturalization Service in Seattle, Washington, applied for Bridges's arrest based on four depositions accusing him of being an alien radical seeking to overthrow the government of the United States by force or violence. The solicitor's office could not corroborate any of the testimony against the man.

By January, 1938, the Harry Bridges case was a public issue as a result of the Senate Committee on Commerce's maritime legislation activities. Rumors that Frances Perkins and others in the department had been threatened by Bridges were denied with her statement "that neither through fear nor cowardice were any officials of the Department of Labor at any time swayed from their duty in connection with the Bridges matter."

Before hearings could be held, an opinion was delivered on *Kessler* v. *Joseph Strecker of Arkansas* by the noted jurist, Judge Hutcheson of the circuit court of appeals, to the "effect that an alien who was acknowledged to have been a member of the Communist Party was not on that ground deportable under the immigration laws." Since "fundamental issues" remained unresolved in the interpretation of the Immigration Act—the Supreme Court had not yet reviewed the Strecker case—the Bridges hearings were postponed on the advice of the Department of Justice.

Solicitor Wyzanski tried to persuade Frances Perkins to allow the courts to settle the entire matter of Harry Bridges. But it would have violated her personal code of ethics to act the Pontius Pilate by washing her hands of the case.

The New York *Daily News* treated the developments with a light touch:

Secretary of Labor Perkins has been battered so ruthlessly for her delay in pushing the charges for Harry Bridges' deportation that reporters displayed almost unique delicacy in quizzing her after the Strecker decision in which the Supreme Court failed to fix guideposts for the Bridges case.

"Is there anything new on the Coast?" one reporter asked. Miss Perkins expressed herself puzzled by the question. Another hedging reporter tried to explain that the question was prompted by recent labor activities there.

Miss Perkins again missed the point when she interpreted the question as pertaining to the labor exhibit in the San Francisco World's Fair. Finally, a third newspaper man slyly asked: "Is there any truth in the rumor that London Bridge's falling down?" at which Miss Perkins suffered a spasm of embarrassment.

The reference to London Bridge may have been coincidental. John P. Frey, a metal trades labor union official, in his unpublished memoirs recorded that he had an informant who was convinced that Harry Bridges "never would be deported, because Bridges was in the service of the British Government—in the Information Service of the British Government! The British Government wanted to know what the United States was shipping to the Orient."

According to Frey, when the Department of Labor was asked by Congress for the Bridges papers, Frances Perkins had to report that "they had vanished." Frey believes, "That is something which is done inside of the select circle once in a while. When a case gets too damned hot, somehow there has been misfiling. Probably the furnace downstairs could tell the story."

If evidence of Harry Bridges's wrongdoing existed, Frances would probably have kept it in her right-hand drawer at the ready. According to another report, James Farley openly declared in a cabinet meeting that her failure to deport Bridges could hurt the Democratic party, and this danger should be paramount in her review of any evidence.

Joe Kennedy, chairman of the Maritime Commission, argued that "Bridges has kept West Coast shipping in turmoil to satisfy his lust for power, that it's immaterial whether he's a Communist, but that he's a trouble-maker and a pest and does not deserve the tender consideration bestowed on him by Madame Perkins."

On June 6, 1938, Representative Martin Dies, a Democrat from Texas, was named chairman of a committee to investigate un-American activities. One of his colleagues, J. Parnell Thomas, a Republican from New Jersey, stole some of the limelight with a communist witchhunt emcompassing the Federal Theater Project. Famous movie stars came under attack, including the curly-topped, dimply Shirley Temple, whose greetings to the communist-owned French newspaper *Ce Soir* made them guilty by association. When taken to task by the committee herself, Frances was emboldened to remark to Dies, "Perhaps it is fortunate that Shirley Temple was born an American citizen and that she will not have to debate the issues raised by the preposterous revelations of your Committee in regard to that innocent and likable child."

On August thirtieth, Dies sent Frances a letter demanding that her department take immediate action against Harry Bridges. She wrote back that "he, as a member of Congress, was attempting to usurp the functions of an executive department," and that action would not be taken without a "scrupulous regard for the due process of law, the clear and certain ruling of the courts, and the facts in the case."

Dies retaliated by threatening her with impeachment "if she did not enforce the law under which Bridges was deportable." The *Daily News* reported:

> Slowly but surely, the clashing forces behind the drive for the deportation of Harry Bridges, West Coast CIO maritime leader, are creating another *cause célèbre* for the history of labor, one that may be placed side by side with the cases of Sacco-Vanzetti and Tom Mooney.

But this time the victim of social injustice would not be Harry Bridges, but rather, Frances Perkins, secretary of labor and first woman cabinet member.

Frances Biddle, who became involved in a continuation of the Bridges case as attorney general, describes the 1938 period as one in which Father Charles E. Coughlin, who earned $574,416 a year for broadcasting from the Church of the Little Flower in Detroit, and the Ku Klux Klan "were fanning fires of fear, hate, anti-semitism . . . purportedly in the name of pure, white, native Americanism." The Committee on Un-American Activities, spawned in this milieu on May 26, 1938, operated without consideration of due process of law. Its inquisitions pivoted around guilt by association, with the jury a public incited by publicity. And to Martin Dies, its chairman, the most glaring example of aid and comfort to communists was the secretary of labor's refusal to deport Harry Bridges.

Action against Frances Perkins came not from the Dies committee directly, but from the first session of the seventy-sixth Congress when, on January 24, 1939, the Speaker of the House of Representatives recognized J. Parnell Thomas of New Jersey. Holding a sheaf of papers in his hand, Thomas rose and proclaimed:

Mr. Speaker, on my own responsibility as a Member of the House of Representatives, I impeach Frances Perkins, Secretary of Labor of the United States; James L. Houghteling, Commissioner of the Immigration and Naturalization Service of the Department of Labor; and Gerard D. Reilly, Solicitor of the Department of Labor, as civil officers of the United States, for high crimes and misdemeanors in violation of the Constitution and laws of the United States, and I charge that the aforesaid Frances Perkins, James L. Houghteling, and Gerard D. Reilly, as civil officers of the United States, were and are guilty of high crimes and misdemeanors in office in manner and form as follows, to wit: That they did willfully, unlawfully, and feloniously conspire, confederate, and agree together from on or about September 1, 1937, to and including this date, to commit offenses against the United States and to defraud the United States by failing, neglecting, and refusing to enforce the immigration laws of the United States, including to wit section 137, title 8, United States Code, and section 156, title 8, United States Code, against Alfred Renton Bryant Bridges, alias Harry Renton Bridges, alias Harry Dorgan, alias Canfield, alias Rossi, an alien, who advises, advocates, or teaches the overthrow by force or violence of the Government of the United States. . . .

Before the clerk could report the resolution, Representative Youngdahl interrupted. The *Congressional Record* reported:

The Speaker: For what purpose does the gentleman from Minnesota rise?

Mr. Youngdahl: Mr. Speaker, I believe this matter is of sufficient importance to require a quorum present. I make the point of order of no quorum, Mr. Speaker.

Mr. Thomas of New Jersey: Is not the point of order not in order at this point, Mr. Speaker?

The Speaker: The question raised by the gentleman is a constitutional question.

Mr. Rayburn: Mr. Speaker, the question of whether or not there is a quorum present is a constitutional one, and the Speaker has no discretion in the matter.

The Speaker: Does the gentleman make the point of order there is no quorum present?

Mr. Youngdahl: I do, Mr. Speaker.

The Speaker: The Chair will count. [After counting.] One hundred and fifty-seven Members are present, not a quorum.

Sam Rayburn moved a call of the House, which the Speaker ordered. The 373 members who answered to their names constituted a quorum, and the clerk laboriously read through the forty-page resolution presented by J. Parnell Thomas. Representative Rayburn then moved that the resolution be referred to the Committee on the Judiciary of the House for testimony.

House Resolution 67 hit Frances Perkins like a thunderbolt. Her colleagues say she reeled under the impeachment as she had never done over anything before. The impact of the long list of charges against her was devastating.

Then as now, the general public regarded impeachment as synonymous with removal from office without trial on an automatic finding of guilt. Actually impeachment means a determination that there exists "sufficient evidence of wrongdoing" to warrant a trial. Impeachable actions include abuse of public trust, an attempt to subvert the law, injury to the nation, or like actions by subordinates for whom the public official is responsible.

The highest-ranking elected official to be impeached was New York State Governor William Sulzer in 1913. The only cabinet member to face impeachment proceedings, William W. Belknap, President Grant's secretary of war, was acquitted. Frances Perkins faced the dubious distinction of being the first woman subject to an impeachment resolution.

The day House Resolution 67 was made, January 24, 1939, an eager press corps faced the president.

Question: There was a move made in the House today for an inquiry into the possibility of impeaching Secretary Perkins. Would you care to comment on that?

The President: Increasing what? [Laughter]

Question: Impeaching. [Laughter]

The President: I suppose the answer is "No, not yet."

That was the only answer he ever gave. Frances later wrote:

I didn't like the idea of being impeached and was considerably disturbed by the episode, but Roosevelt, with his complete confidence that if you do the thing that seems right to you, you'll come out all right, patted me on the back in a brotherly way and said, "Don't worry."

But worry she did, not only for herself, but for James L. Houghteling and Gerard D. Reilly. Working with Charles Wyzanski on her testimony before the House Judiciary Committee, she insisted that her opening remarks make it clear: "The responsibility for the action of the Department of Labor rests directly upon me and cannot properly be placed upon those whom the law makes subordinate to me—that is to say, Mr. Houghteling and Mr. Reilly."

She then cited her three objectives in appearing voluntarily before the committee on February 8, 1939:

. . .first, to state to you briefly the principles in the light of which I view my duty to enforce the immigration laws with respect to persons who engage in subversive activities; secondly, to state the precise facts with respect to the case of Harry Bridges referred to in the Resolution before you; and, finally, to state the precise facts with respect to the case of Joseph George Strecker, also referred to in the Resolution before you and now pending in the Supreme Court of the United States.

Her fifteen-page statement detailing the facts of the Bridges and Strecker cases, closed with her expression of faith in American justice:

. . .The immigration laws have peculiar significance to the future of our country, and it is incumbent upon those who administer them to aim at certain important goals; to preserve for this country its institutions, its ideals, and its Government safe from any foreign forces which present a clear and present danger to the continuance of our way of living; to improve rather than harm the economic and social and moral stability of our population; to promote the assimilation or Americanization of such foreign-born people as lawfully become permanent residents; and to demonstrate to such foreign born who, together with their families, are likely soon to become our fellow citizens, that our American institutions operate without fear or favor and in the spirit of fair play to the stranger within our gates as well as to the native born.

. . .I recognize the right of anyone who has valid evidence of wrongdoing to attack my record or my character and particularly in public office, and I have no resentment. This is also a part of our democratic method to safeguard against administrative absolutism. But I have entire faith and confidence in the capacity and intent of those who are in charge of the operation of our

ᴏns, not only the courts, but the Congress and its committees to
ᴛ me and to secure my rights and my reputation if I have done no
wᴛᴏ ᴀg. . .

Frances could not tell how the House Judiciary Committee reacted
to her testimony, and with a heavy heart she attended to her work. On
March ninth Clara Beyer wrote Mary Dewson:

As you can imagine, these are hectic days around here, what with the Byrnes
bill, the Wages & Hour mess, the impeachment proceedings and the CIO-AFL
peace negotiations it is a regular four-ring circus. I hope we get order out of
this chaos soon.

The final disposition of the case appeared briefly on page 4578 of
the *Congressional Record* for March 24, 1939:

Mr. Hobbs: Mr. Speaker, by direction of the Committee on the Judiciary, I
present a privileged report upon House Resolution 67, which I send to the
desk.

The Speaker: The Clerk will report the resolution.

The Clerk read House Resolution 67.

Mr. Hobbs: Mr. Speaker, this is a unanimous report from the Committee on
the Judiciary adversing this resolution. I move to lay the resolution on the
table.

The Speaker: The question is on the motion of the gentleman from Alabama
to lay the resolution on the table.

The motion was agreed to.

That was all. Not read into the *Record* was the Judiciary Committee's final report completely and unequivocally exonerating Frances
Perkins and her subordinates. It stated that based on the records, "it
would appear that the immigration authorities in Washington sincerely
attempted to do exactly what the author of the resolution now
condemns them for not doing." And in conclusion:

That, after a careful consideration of all the evidence in this case, this
committee is unanimous in its opinion that sufficient facts have not been
presented or adduced to warrant the interposition of the constitutional
powers of impeachment by the House.

The report made no newspaper headlines; no fanfare accompanied
the verdict of not guilty. Mary Dewson wrote:

If the newspaper-reading public was polled by Gallup, Roper, and Crosley very likely it would be proved without peradventure that Miss Perkins had been a failure, a burden on Roosevelt and should have resigned early in his administration. Once when I was staying at the White House I saw Frances Perkins, looking small and dejected, sitting outside the President's study waiting her turn to see him. She said "The President must accept my resignation. He would be better off without me."

About her resignation, Franklin Roosevelt merely said, "Don't talk foolish." And as long as he wanted her, she would stay. A week later her exuberant good spirits took over as she addressed an audience in Philadelphia on a favorite topic, "The ILO as an Agency of Democracy." She freely answered the unvoiced question:

We know not only that our liberties are to be bought by eternal vigilance, but they are to be bought by eternal friendliness, good will and fair play, and we are willing to play that game. [Applause.] That is why I am so glad I came this Monday instead of last Monday to address this Club. It might have been any other Monday in the last two months and I would have said much the same thing, but some of you would have put your tongue in your cheek and thought, "Does she really think she is getting a fair deal?" Now, you see, it has been proven. I have. [Applause.] The Congress of the United States, in its organized capacity, through its committees sits down and seriously studies charges that, however much I thought were unworthy and frivolous, nevertheless were painful and required that one should re-examine one's conscience, and after study exonerates me.

She added congenially, "One of the great things you learn when you go to Washington is that you may be wrong, and you have it brought home to you frequently enough so that your conscience gets some tremendous exercise." She expressed her gratification that "men of responsibility laid aside prejudices against me, against women, against partisan groups, and exercised their responsibility as Congressmen of the United States. . . ."

Hardly two days after her expression of goodwill, Representative J. Parnell Thomas broadcast nationally his denouncement of the Judiciary Committee's findings, and his firmly held opinions that "the Secretary of Labor is endeavoring to replace our immigration statutes with some sort of idealistic philosophy, peculiar to the Secretary of Labor." He urged the radio audience "to aid in safeguarding our American institutions" by demanding an investigation into the "large increase in immigration, and for the sharp decrease in deportation."

Thomas's refusal to accept the dismissal of impeachment proceedings incensed Representative John A. Martin of Colorado. The following

Monday, April 3, 1939, he rose to the floor of the House.

Mr. Speaker, the cloak of congressional immunity thrown about Members of
Congress, relieving them of outside accountability for their utterances and
acts upon the floor of Congress, is not only a very necessary but an
imperative protection of the representatives of the people in the discharge of
their duties. . . .

It is to be regretted, however, that cases arise in which the cloak of immunity
thrown about Members of Congress is not accompanied by the veil of secrecy
similar to that investing grand jury proceedings for the initial protection of
public officials from unjust and unfounded impeachment proceedings.

It is still more to be regretted when, after months of Nation-wide publicizing
of unjust and unfounded charges against a public official, the final result is
heralded by no blare of trumpets and is scarcely brought to the notice of the
public, which for months and months has been fed with promises that a
national public official would be shown to have been guilty of high crimes
and misdemeanors and of betrayal of public trust, warranting the infliction of
the official death penalty.

It is to be regretted that a case which thundered so long and loudly in the
index has dwindled to almost less than a whisper in the text.

Representative Martin went on to explain the charges cited in House
Resolution 67 impeaching Frances Perkins, the commissioner of immigration, and the solicitor, and the evidence examined by the House
Committee on the Judiciary, including that prepared by the Dies
committee, the files on the Bridges and Strecker case, the testimony of
every witness remotely connected with the charges, and the final
disposition—formal, correct proceedings briefly noted in the *Congressional Record.*

And yet, Mr. Speaker, for months the press and the air in this country were
alive with charges that the Department of Labor was exerting its official
powers to protect Communists and communism in this country, and was, in
effect, in league with Communists and communism. Had this campaign of
misrepresentation of the Secretary of Labor and Commissioner of Immigration been deliberately designed to destroy the confidence of the country in
that department of government, it could not have been more intensively and
effectively carried out.

The representative indicated that the mere act of exonerating these
public officials hardly represented justice. "All fair-minded people
should reprobate and condemn the campaign carried on against them,

more pregnant with possibilities of danger to our institutions than even the subversive forces they were charged with being in league with." And in conclusion:

The word "finis" has been written on this abortive attempt to destroy the first woman ever to have the honor of a seat in the Cabinet. In the interest of history the report should be exhumed from the tomb of a million forgotten documents and embalmed in the imperishable pages of the *Congressional Record.*

The gesture was made, but it could not undo public reaction to the move of the U.S. Employment Service from the Department of Labor to the Federal Security Agency. William Green of the AFL fully supported Frances and her futile objections to this splintering of authority. Sophonisba P. Breckenridge, now a professor of public welfare administration at the University of Chicago, wrote the president that the shift must be a great blow to the "public official of the highest ability, but a satisfaction to those who attack her because of her sex."

Shortly after Representative Martin's pleas for her indemnification, Frances Perkins saw herself cut out of the administration of the Social Security program to which she had helped give birth. On April 27, 1939, Clara Beyer wrote Mary Dewson that "the reorganization plan as it affects Social Security is the talk of the town. . . . The Secretary sent word down that the plan is acceptable to her and that there should be no attempt to organize opposition."

The press wrote with uncontained relish about Frances Perkins's continued demise in significance when the Immigration and Naturalization Service was transferred from her department to the Department of Justice, a move she had requested during her first months in office. In 1940 when the House voted by 330 to 45 to have the acting attorney general deport alien Harry Bridges—alien had come to mean spy, fifth column, sabotage—Frances's name came up less frequently. Harry Bridges busied himself spurring on activity for the war effort and running what Attorney General Frances Biddle described as one of the few unions free of corruption. In 1945 the Supreme Court ruled that Bridges was neither a communist nor subject to deportation.

In 1947 the stocky, choleric J. Parnell Thomas replaced Martin Dies as head of the Un-American Activities Committee and beefed up his flamboyant investigations of communism in the motion picture industry. Although unable to define communist, fascist, subversive, or un-American, the conservative Republican, Mason member, library trustee, and pillar of society hurled these labels freely at anyone failing to bow at the altar of American business enterprise, including the president. But a woman would be his undoing. Late in 1948 he chose to demote his secretary, Helen Campbell. She retaliated by revealing that he listed on his payroll people who did not work for him but who did kick back their salaries to him.

Righteously indignant, Representative Thomas called the subsequent investigation "a political smear . . . the dying gasp of reprisal of a defeated and discredited administration." On advice of counsel, he finally pleaded *nolo contendere* and threw himself on the mercy of the court. On December 9, 1949, in the Washington federal district court, he heard himself sentenced to six to eighteen months in prison and fined $10,000 for padding Congressional payrolls.

If Frances Perkins felt vindicated, she didn't say. Throughout her remaining long years, people tactlessly asked her what it felt like to be impeached. She answered simply, "It hurt."

Secretary of Labor Frances Perkins and Secretary of State Cordell Hull at the opening of Congress, January 3, 1940.

XIV

Rosie the Riveter

Public opinion polls ranked unemployment as the number one concern of the American people through most of 1939. When for the first time the NBC Blue Network broadcast a cabinet member's press conference a reporter, Louis Stark, voiced the question in the minds of many: "Why doesn't some government department put out accurate figures on unemployment regularly?"

Sensitive to this point raised frequently by Secretary of the Treasury Henry Morgenthau, Frances Perkins answered:

We should like to publish an estimate of unemployment, Mr. Stark, but government statistics must be not only trustworthy but easily understandable. A small change in the assumptions made in estimating unemployment gives rise to an honest difference of hundreds of thousands in the resulting estimates.

The proportion of people who want jobs keeps changing—if a breadwinner loses his job, his wife and children may look for work and when he gets a job they may get out of the labor market. To make an accurate estimate of unemployment we would have to have a complete census every time there was a drastic change in employment.

An eminent statistician once said, "You can't count the things people are *not* doing. You can only count what they are doing."

Ernest Lindley asked her, "Madame Secretary, from time to time you have spoken of self-employment. Will you please explain what you mean by this?"

Frances responded enthusiastically:

An economist said the other day, Mr. Lindley, that the future of industry lies in an expansion of the service fields of work. . . .When the Village Blacksmith of Longfellow's poem became the Village Garage mechanic he was adjusting himself to supply a new service to his neighbors in place of work he had lost.

Our Employment Service is already charting the occupations which are disappearing, and the new needs which promise to be demands for labor in a short time.

She noted that "the good old New England quality of individual gumption" notwithstanding, it was the United States Employment Service with its 1600 offices that, over a six-year period "brought together the manless jobs and the jobless men and filled twenty-five million positions in private industry and public works, from blue denim overall jobs to white-collar occupations." Frances Perkins boasted of the Employment Service's new dictionary describing 28,000 occupations, which she felt helped make workers aware of jobs that could use their training and experience.

Blaine Stubblefield expressed a common concern: "Your efforts to modify employers' disinclination to accept men over forty seems meritorious, Madame Secretary, but if there is only a given amount of work to be had, wouldn't the older men simply displace the younger ones?"

Her reply reflected the economics of Simon Nelson Patten:

Once you admit there is only a given amount of work to be done, Mr. Stubblefield, you commit yourself to a static non-growing society. With our natural resources, our capacity, our engineering and business brains, our highly efficient labor population, I refuse to admit that there are limits to the advances in our standards of living, and accordingly to the amount of work that will be available to our people. And certainly, the older worker has skills and experience which form some of our most valuable economic resources.

The reporter closed the broadcast with a personal question: "In view of your experience as Secretary of Labor, if you had known six years ago what you know now, would you have taken the job?"

"I would have taken the job even more willingly, Mr. Stubblefield."

While the American public preferred to look the other way, the president and his cabinet attempted to alert the nation to the catastrophic events taking place abroad. As early as 1939 Frances Perkins's pronouncements tended to be somewhat more serious than this one before the editors of college papers:

. . .we no longer look at life from our own isolated viewpoint—like the dear old lady in the Maine village where I spend my summer vacations who told me sympathetically when she found out where I came from, that she always pitied folks in New York City because they lived such a dreadfully long way off!

Not until December did public opinion polls show that neutrality had displaced unemployment as the greatest concern of the American people. By 1940 this anxiety heightened, providing the rationale for the president's defiance of the two-term tradition. His Republican opponent, Wendell Willkie, blighted his candidacy by declaring in a speech before labor leaders that if he became president, he would appoint a secretary of labor from the ranks of labor. After the applause abated, he added, "And it won't be a woman either!" The women of America, listening to their radios, found this a poor joke.

Long before the president's reelection, stories appeared in the newspapers about Frances Perkins's resignation. Questioned by the press, Roosevelt merely responded, "Oh, I have been reading that for almost every first of July since 1933. I guess it falls into the same category as the other stories." New York City's Mayor Fiorello LaGuardia had been considered a replacement, and after the election, Wendell Willkie. When in April, 1941, another story appeared, the press again queried the president. His answer was the same: "Just another story. It has been going on for eight years, so it's all right."

When Frances received a courteous letter suggesting that she resign because the labor situation was different from when she took the post, she wrote back, "Many people have thought I should resign, but no one ever before agreed with me so entirely about the reasons."

As the lend-lease program gained momentum, defense industries picked up the slack in employment. The strengthened job market gave courage to workers to go on strike. Letters again poured into the White House demanding that "a two-fisted male" replace Frances Perkins. One writer insisted: "This labor situation is a disgrace. Court-martial and shoot Frances Perkins and every key member of the CIO union and Communist parties." Mothers with draft-age sons vindictively charged the secretary of labor with "creating all these strikes." The prominent congressman from Illinois, Everett M. Dirksen, told the Women's State Republican Club of New Jersey:

She is lacking in the kind of perception and that quality to deal with delicate and highly controversial problems. The record of the department has not invited special respect and consideration of the people. The post should have a man with keen perception.

The newspapers blew up the magnitude of the strikes, and the president tried to put them in perspective with a memorandum prepared by Frances Perkins, which read:

1. *All Strikes.* About one-tenth of 1 percent of the workers in the country are on strike today in all industries. .1%

2. Defense Strikes. [Sidney] Hillman's office [of Production Management] advises me that 7,800 workers are on strike in situations that are significant to national defense. This represents less than two-tenths of 1 percent of the workers engaged in defense work. .2%

The president, involved with anticipating the Axis powers' next move, gave no further thought to replacing his secretary of labor.

*****

Writers covering the forties invariably dismiss the secretary of labor with a peremptory statement that she had been shorn of power. With the removal of the Immigration and Naturalization Service, the Department of Labor's size had been reduced by 60 percent. But the department's strengths had hardly rested in that division, and Frances Perkins did not mourn the absence of her name from front-page headlines.

From her special vantage point, Eleanor Roosevelt, together with Lorena Hickok, evaluated the almost surreptitious performance of Frances Perkins during this period:

She was at her best, perhaps, in the months immediately preceding World War II. With the build-up of the defense industries came appalling confusion in the labor situation. Union leaders, naturally feeling their oats in so rapidly expanding a labor market, became obstreperous and quarrelsome. Everybody who had anything to do with the defense program, including the Army and the Navy, began sending out his own special labor negotiators and conciliators, until they were falling over each other.

The chaos heightened with jurisdictional strikes between industrial and trade unions, and employers bent on having labor laws rescinded in the interest of defense production. Frances watched the dissembling of the eleven-man National Defense Mediation Board set up in March,

While Britain Sinks

Cartoon from the Richmond Times-Dispatch, *June 6, 1941.*

1941, and after six months found it necessary to advise Chairman William H. Davis that she wanted "clear and definite information to the public with regard to the means and machinery available to the handling of industrial and labor disputes. . . ." She submitted guidelines subject to modification by interested agencies.

Then, according to Eleanor Roosevelt, "Quietly and with infinite patience, Secretary Perkins worked out another conference between the labor leaders and industry, asking the U.S. Chamber of Commerce and the National Association of Manufacturers to suggest delegates for the employers." Frances recommended that Senator Elbert Thomas, chairman of the Senate Committee on Education and Labor, preside over the meetings. She knew all too well, "Labor would resent it if I did not rule in their favor, and the employers would resent it if I did!"

With her daughter married to socialite David Meredith Hare and her husband boarding in upstate New York homes when not hospitalized, Frances had sub-let her New York City apartment. When she came to the city she took a room at the exclusive Cosmopolitan Club. On Sunday, December seventh, her secretary was working with her there on the department's annual report when a call came through from the White House ordering her immediate return to Washington for a cabinet meeting. At the airport, she met other hastily-summoned cabinet members who knew as little as she did about the Japanese bombing of Pearl Harbor.

Despite the abundant warning signals, realization that the United States was officially at war came as a shock. Frances tried to pull her thoughts together. On a note pad she hastily scribbled, "There is no time to learn by experience now. We have to perform and act on what we already know to be right." On the next sheet she wrote, "Behavior must be patterned on that," followed by "No one can live better today than he did before," which she crossed out. The jottings continued:

> Great profits for industrial investment & enterprise must be given up for the duration. This is hard doctrine but necessary & it meets a response in every conscience. 2. No jurisdictional strike or stoppage, 3. No raid AFL to CIO vice versa. Divide field. 4. No obstacle to work permits for the duration. For it is all the people who are paying bills in cash & it is some of our people who are paying with their lives for the safety of the rest of us.

The remaining notes dealt with wages and hours of work.

She anticipated a dramatic change in the tenor of the industry-labor conference. After preparing the president's remarks, she sent them to his office with the customary cover note indicating that she would see him shortly before time for his presentation to "rehearse" him. The conference went well, and on December 12, 1941, Roosevelt received a jubilant note: "Sidney Hillman, William H. Leiserson, H.A. Mills and Frances Perkins agree!!" A month later, at Frances's recommendation, the president signed an executive order establishing the national War Labor Board.

While the newspapers played up time lost from defense work because of strikes, Frances attacked another culprit, industrial and traffic accidents. She pointed out to the president that in just the first six months of 1941 traffic fatalities had increased 17 percent—of which 6,000 were working men—and encouraged him to give his blessing to the efforts of the National Safety Council. In later testimony before the House of Representatives subcommittee on safety she declared:

> . . .In addition to the loss of production caused by industrial accidents must be added the human misery lying behind the 19,000 deaths and 150,000 crippling injuries during 1941. . . .This waste occurs year after year largely because the safety and health of industrial workers have been subordinated to other subjects of legislative concern.
> . . .It would seem logical that the emphasis should be put on prevention rather than post-accident rehabilitation.

In her many talks before business groups she stressed that many more million man-days of work were lost through industrial accidents, colds, and flu, than through strikes. She insisted, ". . .health and safety are as important to industry as the peaceful settlement of disputes."

When a labor strike was imminent, she received information several times a day on the progress being made to avert it. "Those days," she remembered, "were almost twenty-four hours long."

Frances once told an interviewer, "People often ask me how I feel about strikes in defense industries. I don't 'feel'. about them any more than a doctor 'feels' about an operation while he's performing it."

Years later in describing the wartime regulations that emanated from Washington, Frances cited those curbing the use of electricity by nonessential industries such as retail stores. A Harvard Law School professor prepared the notice to be posted at shop doors; it read: "The Last Individual to Leave These Premises is Kindly Requested to Extinguish the Illumination." She could just imagine Mr. Spencer Day in the grocery store where she shopped in Newcastle, Maine, reading this. She showed a copy to the president. He burst out laughing, then told her, "Oh, just reword that."

She said, "How could you reword that?"

His answer: "Word it like this: 'Put out the lights.' "

Reflecting on the wartime activities of the various federal agencies, she bemusedly concluded, "There were elements of it that were exactly like a Gilbert and Sullivan operetta as one saw the high command operating."

The Department of Labor's Bureau of Labor Statistics reported on the inexorable increase in prices and the relative ineffectiveness of the Economic Stabilization Board in controlling them. Then came rationing to see that everyone got a fair share of food and other scarce commodities, and to keep prices from soaring further because of hoarding and profiteering.

The whole field of labor underwent traumatic change. The upgrading of labor meant the training of unskilled workers, including blacks, by skilled workers, despite the opposition of labor unions fearing the dilution of labor. The employment of the handicapped began; the blind, lame, and deaf found excellent opportunities in industry. Just before Pearl Harbor, 4,000 women worked in the manufacture of airplanes; one year later 200,000 were involved with every aspect of airplane production. In one plant in three weeks' time, women workers increased production 150 percent over that of men who had ten to fifteen years of experience. As spot welders, women far outstripped the production records of men. A former Latin teacher, exasperated with the eleven steps needed to paint strips of color on a tube, blocked out three brief steps, which saved eight hours per plane. The secretary of labor called upon the local communities to help "Rosie the Riveter" solve her problems of transportation, marketing and shopping, medical care, and provision for children.

The Labor Department was accused of unjustifiable interference with war production when it objected to individuals working more than a ten-hour day seven days a week. The secretary of labor personally examined production output curves and accident and absentee rates to support her position. She pointed out the lessons learned during World War I on the cumulative fatigue from overwork.

To combat her own fatigue, Frances Perkins learned isometric exercises that she could do at her desk—when she was there. Constantly on the go, she rarely bothered to remove her hat—except when photographers caught her donning the coal workers' "hard hat" as she prepared to descend into a mine shaft.

During her visits to defense industries, she spoke to workers on the production line, trying to pick up their viewpoints, trying to understand the problem of absenteeism and turnover. One experience illustrated the fanatic fetish peculiar to the native New Englander of keeping one's private life private. Frances sympathized fully with the man who told her:

> They stopped me at the personnel office and they asked me why I was leaving, and I said, "Why, I have to."
>
> And they said, "Well, why do you have to?"
>
> "Well, I think it's best."
>
> "Why that's no reason; do tell us the reason why you're leaving."
>
> "I think it's best," he said, and walked out.

To Frances Perkins the logic was obvious: "He was an old-fashioned State of Maine man, very dignified, who wasn't about to tell the personnel staff that he had a sick wife at home and he had to drive a hundred and fifty miles each way every day and he wasn't going to do that any longer."

Frances herself boasted to an academic colleague who had unsuccessfully encouraged her to write her biography that she had even refused to tell a census-taker her sex on the grounds that it was none of his business.

Obviously Frances Perkins was not always accommodating. She opposed the War Manpower Commission as just another agency trying "to keep labor in line." Her arguments that the U.S. Employment Service could perform the necessary recruiting functions by being given additional authority and funding fell on deaf ears. The commission turned out to be one of many for which she had to provide input, but she could only say of the elaborate agenda prepared for each meeting, the discursiveness of cabinet members, and the horrendous efforts put into its operation, "I suffered under the situation, and I'm afraid that I occasionally contributed to both the mirth of the War Manpower Commission and to some of its ineffectiveness."

Some people overlooked the time factor. Frances pointed out that existing agencies "have a budget officer; they have a personnel officer; they have a head and they have clerks and messengers and stenographers. You don't have to recruit them all." She added, "It takes months, really, to set up a new agency of government," and just as long to set the rules and regulations it is to pass upon.

She recalled that an Indiana University professor felt the need to develop a roster of scientists in the country. This research activity was completed some two years after the war ended. Frances later told her students, "I don't wish to decry the research projects, but they take a little more time than is ordinarily allotted in the midst of a war."

Although she disapproved of the president's policy of setting up new agencies to meet each crisis, she found herself charged with putting them together and keeping them that way. By her own admission, this became her principal wartime job:

> At his direction I sat in on so many interdepartmental committees and held so many conferences that the Department of Labor had the air of a service agency for the war activities.

Congress increased its appropriations to the department so that it could meet the many demands made by the war agencies.

As time passed, the secretary of labor's efforts went increasingly into postwar planning. In the president's message to Congress on January 7, 1943, he stressed that not only did young people want opportunity for employment, "they want assurance against the evils of all economic hazards—assurance that will extend from the cradle to the grave." Frances put out feelers to test reactions to a more comprehensive Social Security program.

Frances also assured the president that the country was better prepared to face demobilization and readjustment to peacetime living than it had been in 1918. She stated for the record her optimistic view that the postwar transition period would go relatively smoothly "because the Roosevelt Administration has planned and legislated and administered so carefully over the past ten years."

In April, 1944, Philadelphia hosted the first meeting of the International Labor Organization since the war. The secretary of labor read a message from the president, then reinforced his plea for international cooperation in establishing minimum standards of employment and social security. On behalf of the U.S. delegation, she presented resolutions around the theme that "poverty anywhere threatens prosperity everywhere."

Elizabeth Johnstone of the ILO staff, a former Mount Holyoke classmate, recalled that a young man mercilessly taunted Frances and kept the proceedings running past midnight. Mrs. Johnstone found Frances Perkins's "firmness, courtesy and patience throughout, thereby winning the sympathy of participants" in sharp contrast to the invectives Frances used in discussing the rabble-rouser privately. Mrs.

Left to right: Harry Hopkins, Secretary of Commerce; Frances Perkins, Secretary of Labor; and Charles Michelson, Director of Publicity for the Democratic Party, at the Jackson Day Dinner, Washington, D.C., January 8, 1939.

Johnstone felt that Frances had "a righteous streak; she knew what was right and wrong." People whose countries were still gripped by the oppressors could not share her Christian benevolence toward those soon to be vanguished.

One of Frances's last reports to the president emphasized that liberal conditions for international trade hinged on a high level of productive employment in this country.

*****

Because she seemed to be a "loner," many people thought she was lonely. She actually had a variety of interests, quite a few friends including those visiting Washington, D.C., on occasion, and she took part in a number of social functions at the White House. Sometimes she joined the small group that sat by while the president broadcast his "fireside chats" and then convened in the Oval Room to read the telegrams coming in. At other times her presence was requested for formal functions.

The annual cabinet dinners commemorating Roosevelt's March 3, 1933, inauguration were held in a hotel until the war years when, for security reasons, they took place in the state dining room of the White House. The last, in 1944, may have been when Roosevelt mused over all the important people that would be killed if the Germans dropped a bomb on the White House at that moment. Then he was rather titillated by the thought, "If all of us except Frances Perkins were killed, we'd have a woman President."

At a state dinner for Stanislaw Mikolajczyk, the prime minister of Poland, Frances Perkins flanked the president together with Dorothy Thompson, the former wife of Sinclair Lewis, now Mrs. Maxim Kopf. A few weeks later the cabinet members lunched with General Charles DeGaulle and the French delegation.

Over the course of the years Frances Perkins had met world-famous people from England's king and queen to celebrated movie stars who promoted the sale of war bonds. Her countless anecdotes to students in later years included none of the glamorous aspects of being part of the White House inner circle.

A number of the events in her life were mixed social obligations. On July 10, 1944, with the president's blessing, she attended a dinner honoring former Postmaster General James Farley on his retirement from the chairmanship of the Democratic State Committee. Farley had

Frances Perkins at the 1940 Democratic Convention.

resigned from the cabinet in 1940 in protest over the president's third term.

In October, 1944, she attended the funeral of former New York Governor Al Smith. Eleanor Roosevelt represented the president at the services held in St. Patrick's Cathedral.

The following month Franklin D. Roosevelt won his fourth term of office. His assurances that he would name Frances's replacement momentarily led her to rent an apartment in New York City and to pack the books and memorabilia in her office. Her five-page documentary letter of resignation concluded:

> With one major exception all the items we discussed as "among the practical possibilities" before you took office as President have been accomplished or begun. That exception is a social security item providing for some form of benefit to persons where loss of income is due to sickness and provision for appropriate medical care for the same. I hope that this will be upon your agenda for the near future.

The letter, dated December 1, 1944, lay in abeyance for weeks, an exception to the rule that all correspondence be answered immediately. The president publicly announced, "I'll appoint anyone with the unanimous backing of the labor movement. Frances wants to get out. I'll let her if we can all agree on someone." The AFL-CIO rift of nine years made this impossible. Three days before the inauguration newspaper columnist Drew Pearson reported that the president, still undecided as to the next labor secretary, wanted John Winant, ambassador to Great Britain, but recognized that he was too valuable where he was.

The day before the inauguration, President Roosevelt told the press that at the cabinet meeting the previous week someone had asked about his administration's accomplishments over the years.

> . . .there were three of us there that had probably been thinking along the same lines, cogitating I think is the word. And one of them was Mr. Ickes, and the other was Miss Perkins, and I was the third.

> And I . . . sort of guess that all of us had come to the same conclusion, and that the first twelve years were the hardest!

Frances Perkins recorded what she actually had been thinking: the whispering campaign about the president's health was not without substance. And so, when on the eve of his inauguration he admitted that he could not let her go, she could not argue. On January 22, 1945, he formally acknowledged her letter of resignation:

Dear Frances:

I will see you as soon as I get back.

That is a tremendously interesting letter of yours and shows concisely and clearly all that you have accomplished in the Department of Labor.

There are many other things to do—matters with which you are familiar—and, as I told you on Friday, your resignation is not one of them. It is hereby declined. Indeed, it is rejected and refused.

Frances saw him a number of times after his return from Yalta, and the day before leaving for Warm Springs, Georgia, he assured her that the war would end by May. He did not live to see that day.

On April twelfth, two hours after the stunning news of the president's death, she stood in the familiar cabinet room in the White House weeping soundlessly on Isador Lubin's shoulder. She regained her composure and listened incredulously to Vice-President Harry Truman take the oath of office. A few moments later she sat at the cabinet table across from President Truman as the cabinet members discussed the wartime public's tremendous loss, and ways of furthering Franklin D. Roosevelt's aims.

Although Truman told a confidante of his intent to name a new secretary of labor, he graciously recorded in his *Memoirs:*

Miss Perkins was among the first to come and tell me that she no longer wanted to stay in the Cabinet. She said that she needed a rest. I told her that I would be happy to have her remain in the Cabinet. She was a very able administrator. I always thought she made a good Secretary. She was liked very much and trusted by labor and she was also well thought of by many of the industrialists.

Harry Truman had followed her career closely ever since she had named him the employment director for Missouri in 1933.

Before she tendered her letter of resignation, the war in Europe ended. Frances led the moving thanksgiving service for the Department of Labor employees on May eighth, V-E Day. Two weeks later her rationale for resigning was based on the need for "a variety of talents [to] be brought into the service of the government." On May twenty-third, President Truman's acceptance accompanied glowing praise for her years of service.

During her last weeks in office Frances wrote scores of analytical opinions on the shortcomings of proposed legislation, on the restriction of immigration, governmental operations and reorganization plans, and tied up loose ends and last-minute correspondence.

Daniel W. Tracy, the assistant secretary of labor, took charge of the department's final farewell to her a few days before her official June thirtieth departure. Groups of 150 department employees came at twenty-minute intervals to wish her well, shake her hand, get her autograph, then take part in refreshments from a long buffet table. By evening Frances Perkins had greeted 1,800 people. When reporters asked if she found this exhausting, she recalled how twelve years earlier the chief usher of the White House, Ike Hoover, had taught her and her fellow cabinet members to shake hands effortlessly.

The $373 collected from employees paid for the food and fruit punch, flowers, and the music of Jack Morton's orchestra, as well as gifts for the departing secretary: a standard-size typewriter, luggage, and with $37.50 left over, a U.S. war bond.

Mary Dewson worked on the committee chaired by David B. Robertson, president of the Brotherhood of Locomotive Engineers & Firemen, that arranged for Frances's testimonial dinner at the Mayflower Hotel. President Truman's telegram of regrets was read; after reviewing her achievements, it closed with: "I salute you as a great humanitarian and I thank you, on behalf of the American people, for the great work you have done so unselfishly, so capably and so thoroughly."

Senator Robert Wagner declared: "Frances Perkins was, and still is, the supreme student of social conditions and remedial social legislation. She uncovered the facts, and told us what to do about them." He expressed everyone's wish for her: "May each chapter in your endeavors be as useful to the people of America as those that have gone before."

Frances spoke of her twelve years in office as "full of satisfaction in seeing a real bulwark of labor and social conditions built so tightly it will stand, not on any ephemeral basis but on a good solid foundation."

John L. Lewis who had publicly called Frances "woozy in the head"—his wife was her great admirer—recorded in the *United Mine Workers Journal*, "We again say, despite all the criticism that has been hurled against her, she has performed her work within the confines of the limitations imposed upon her mighty well."

The *New York Times* editorialized: "Twelve years has been long

enough to prove that a woman is not out of place in the Cab, .
Frances Perkins will not be the last woman to occupy such a position."

Her last day at the office Frances placed on her desk a note for her
successor, Lewis B. Schwellenback, the president's former Senate
colleague, and detailed plans for the postwar reorganization of the
Department of Labor which would pull back into the fold the labor
functions scattered throughout a number of government agencies. She
joked about the frivolous little black sailor-hat she wore. "I'm going
into private life and this is my private hat." She had no definite plans
for the future other than spending a month or so in her family home in
Damariscotta, Maine.

When the war with Japan ended six weeks later while she was still in
Maine, she penned a letter to President Truman in her sprawling script:

> My thoughts go out to you for this time of great rejoicing. What a burden off
> your heart & mind!

> You have done all that needed to be done and done it magnificently & in a
> truly American way. Thank God this part is over!

> My felicitations and good wishes for your continuing strength and wisdom.

The president made a notation on the letter: "Bill, Please compose a
good answer. HST." The president's assistant, Bill Hassett, found
himself composing quantities of "good answers" to the letters pouring
in from Deomocratic national committeewomen, from schools of social
work, from social service agencies and others, regarding Frances
Perkins's severance from government. One from Grace Abbott's sister,
University of Chicago Dean Emeritus Edith Abbott, asked on behalf of
the American Association of Social Workers, "Is there no hope that you
will have a woman in your Cabinet?" The chairman of a Commission on
Women in World Affairs echoed the same sentiment. Others urged the
president to appoint Frances Perkins as head of a welfare department or
to the Council of Economic Advisors. The Episcopalian bishop of
Missouri and the president of Ripon College in Wisconsin urged that
Frances be named to a board to promote full employment.

When the president's assistant found himself inundated with letters
for and against the equal rights amendment, he wrote his aide, "This is
a tough baby. I would like your recommendation as to a suitable
acknowledgement for the President's signature." In handling this "hot
potato," they found themselves dependent on the comments made by

Frances Perkins to the Judiciary Committee of the House of Representatives a couple of years earlier. The statements were old, "but the best and most recent thing we have."

Actually the kind of arguments Frances Perkins presented would persist for another quarter of a century among those who believed that woman's suffrage came about because of the need to pass and maintain legislation to improve the condition of working women, and that the equal rights amendment would be counterproductive. And further, proponents of the amendment failed to realize that the promises implicit in it could not be fulfilled.

"Only the slow process of education can eradicate prejudice," Frances would explain. "Abstract equality" overlooks the role of women as mothers, the findings of physiology, psychology, and the other social sciences. Also, "discrimination" differs from "reasonable treatment of the sexes," and current practice is "deeply embedded in our patterns of contemporary culture."

Like other opponents of the amendment, she feared it would eliminate statutory rape, based traditionally on male aggression, as a crime. And husbands would be entitled to divorce on the grounds of a wife's nonsupport, and they would no longer bear the financial responsibility of maintaining wife and children. In lieu of the "bludgeon of an amendment," Frances Perkins advocated specific corrective legislation and judicial interpretation.

During the perennial controversy over women's rights, Frances removed herself by going to Europe in the fall of 1945, accompanied by her daughter, Susanna, to attend the ILO conference as a U.S. representative. In December she ensconced herself in her Washington, D.C., home at 2127 Leroy Place, NW, and started her first draft of *The Roosevelt I Knew.* She stopped work only to take the Christmas weekend in Maine, where she received an unexpected gift from President Truman—his autographed photograph and a copy of the V-E Proclamation of May eighth with his handwritten notation that this was his birth date. She worked unstintingly through April, 1946, and admitted, "I had a dreadful time writing this book." She hoped it would accomplish three things: comfort those who had lost a friend, encourage the handicapped through the example of courage shown by Roosevelt, and record for history and the world the complicated circumstances and processes by which a nation progresses.

Frances's husband, Paul Wilson, had not read the manuscript; he just knew, as he wrote to a family friend, that she needed a rest more than anything else. But when her publisher suggested that she work closely with Howard Taubman of the *New York Times* as he edited the manuscript, she never once complained of fatigue. Taubman called her "a real trooper."

XV

The Last Leaf on the Tree

Woodrow Wilson had been the first president to appoint a woman, an active suffragist named Helen Gardener, to the three-member Civil Service Commission. Mrs. Jessie Dell held the post for a year after Mrs. Gardener's death in 1926, followed by Mrs. Anna C. Tillinghast. During Frances Perkins's years as secretary of labor, Mrs. Lucille McMillin, the widow of a Tennessee governor, represented women on the commission. When she resigned in August, 1946, women's organizations were up in arms. The president's reorganization plan and the resignation of Mrs. McMillin meant that there was no woman in the government with the responsibility of reporting directly to the president.

Harry S. Truman felt compelled to take action. The morning of September twelfth he conferred with Frances Perkins. When she left the White House reporters got the impression that she did not intend to resume working for the government. They were quite surprised when a few hours later President Truman announced her $15,000 a year appointment to the Civil Service Commission, subject to Senate approval.

While some viewed her appointment as a comfortable sinecure enabling her to total up fifteen years of government service for a good retirement annuity, the *Christian Science Monitor* heralded her return "into the Administration as its No. 1 woman." She took the oath of office on October 9, 1946, on an interim basis. After unanimous approval by the Senate Civil Service Committee, her nomination went to the Senate on January 21, 1947, which took less than one minute to make her appointment official.

As a commissioner, Frances's major functions were to periodically visit the fourteen regional Civil Service offices, to make speeches, to assist in the development of competitive examinations, to work with the Loyalty Review Board, and to eliminate inefficiency and fraud by promulgating rules and regulations governing the lives of 2,300,000 federal workers.

In contrast to earlier years, the press now found Commissioner Perkins good copy. She set the pace with her first speech before the Society for Personnel Administration where she debunked their techniques "while speaking a mouthful of hard common sense," according to the *Federal Diary*. The report continued:

> The personnelists who packed the room at the YWCA loved it. They should have—Miss Perkins put on the best show in town. The Civil Service official got more laughs than a Bob Hope. Her speech was constantly interrupted by applause.

She mentioned that the Civil Service Commission with its "impressive, solid, Old World air" was strong on brevity, but did not practice what it preached. When she asked to have a voluminous document briefed for her, she got back twenty pages. After hitting at the red tape of obscure terminology and rules and regulations reflecting overorganization, she embarked on an attack on the invasion of privacy by the government. The press expressed delight that the new commissioner was "a person to be reckoned with in the Government personnel field. . . . And she'll speak her piece—there's no doubt about that."

Newspapers quickly sensed a controversy between Frances Perkins and another commissioner, Arthur S. Flemming, in the matter of questions asked on application blanks about physical defects. Frances also objected to investigators "snooping" on federal officeholders and job applicants.

"What difference does it make to us if a man entertains ladies in his room?" asked the once-puritanical former cabinet member. "How is that going to reflect on his ability to do his job?" Mr. Flemming, concerned with keeping subversives out of government, felt that the federal employee's freedom should be restricted further "by those principles which are an integral part of a developing code of ethics for the Federal service," adding, "There are few employments for hire in which the servant does not agree to suspend his constitutional rights of free speech, as well as of idleness, by the implied terms of his contract."

Frances next attacked government jargon—governmentese—which every government writer, known as an information specialist, had to learn. "You're not told to get ready," she explained at the Washington

Press Club, "you're either activated or alerted." On using "under-privileged" instead of poor, she continued, "I don't believe that's the correct word—at least they have the privilege of not having to keep up with the Joneses."

During the Korean conflict labor shortage she claimed that agencies insisted on employing only young, good-looking, good-natured steno-graphers. She claimed that "the idle, middle-class, middle-aged woman is one of the Nation's most important manpower reserves," and observed that the two best stenographers in her own department were "grouchy, middle-aged frumps" whom she found indispensable.

As a guest columnist for the *Washington Times-Herald*, she pondered over the complications of our modern way of life:

> Even the simple task of crossing the road has, in the interest of life and limb, become subject to "Stop," "Go," "Walk," and "Don't Walk" signs, with sometimes the addition of a policeman who won't let us do any of these things. And some of us try to solve our problems as though every activity of life were a traffic intersection.

In the year 1951 she found that common-sense standards did not provide answers for a puzzled employee who might ask, "Can I do this?" A conference must be called, experts consulted, an opinion delivered by the comptroller general.

> Life should not be as complicated as that. I sometimes think that we are all like the file clerk who made himself indispensable by filing everything in the wrong place and then finding it. We make our rules so complex that they must be interpreted by experts.

On the positive side, she told the personnel management people meeting in Bear Mountain, New York:

> It is a source of pride that civil service employees of the government are not charged with corruption, dishonesty, and misfeasance in office. It is important to remember that 93% of all Federal government employees are civil servants, who have come into the government through the rigid process of examination, investigation, selection for merit and high qualifications—appointed without political considerations and hired and fired according to specific rules and regulations... [This] is what *prevents* the appointment by patronage and for political considerations, avoids temptation to corruption, and secures for the people of the United States consistent service.

At the same time she agreed that "policy-making posts certainly must always be filled by people responsible to the party which has been elected on a series of pledges to the people and voters of the United States."

The Congress poses some problems, she charged, because it decides on such matters as annual leave of federal employees, and there's a massive job of readjusting when the Congress changes its mind. She wished that federal budgets could be set up on a two-year basis—"which would leave agencies free to do their work and Congress free to consider basic legislation."

Commissioner Perkins explained to the League of Women Voters the advantages of the merit system for promotion in Civil Service so that "fewer of our public servants will be beholden to a party or a person for their jobs." She advocated salaries comparable to those paid by private industry. Moral qualifications are as essential as technical ability, but she recognized that honesty, loyalty, wisdom, and good judgment are difficult to measure or test. Then she warned:

> So long as we are part and parcel of a society which lives by the wisecrack, which winks at its own shortcomings, which worships at the shrine of the quick dollar, we are not training perfect public servants. Example and public attitude are the climate in which we raise our public servants.

To the New York City Chapter of the American Association of Social Workers she observed, "No program of social assistance can be better than the individuals who do the work." She particularly reproved social workers for speaking of their fellowmen as "cases." "These people are citizens of our democracy. . . ."

The Society for Personnel Administration was admonished to stress the "art" of public service rather than the "science" of personnel. She also declared that it is not the function of government "to provide good jobs for people, but to get the work done."

The American Personnel and Guidance Association heard, "Government employment should be undertaken and regarded as a vocation, not merely as a way of making a living."

At Roosevelt College in Chicago, Frances Perkins talked about the role of government:

> Political science is not to be confused with politics. Statesmanship is not to be confused with efficiency. The Constitution of the United States is not to be confused with the budget of the United States. Government, the expression of a philosophical idea, is not to be confused with public services, no matter how valuable they may be.

If government were mainly a matter of providing public services, there would be little to distinguish one government from another, the world over. All modern governments provide them. They were provided allegedly with some efficiency, by the government of Nazi Germany. But that is not a fact which we consider when we compare that government with the government of the United States. Rather we consider their respective attitudes toward human rights. Government is a philosophical and ethical matter.

Frances Perkins's message to her successors on the Civil Service Commission reflected her own American heritage. She recommended that people going into government agencies receive a program of instruction in Constitutional principles and American history. They should know as much "as do immigrants who are seeking naturalization." That they can pass competitive exams and know little about this country, she asserted, is "a defect of the educational system through which they have come."

*****

In March of 1952 newspapers reported that President Truman signed an executive order exempting Frances Perkins from compulsory retirement on April tenth when she would be seventy years of age. Of course, since she was actually just a few weeks short of seventy-two, she had completely ignored the mandatory retirement age of seventy.

At the end of May she attended the fiftieth reunion of the Mount Holyoke class of 1902. As permanent president of the class, Frances never missed a reunion. She recalled that the 1948 reunion had been remarkable because the ladies were ordered out of the Bookshop Inn late one evening; their noise, which kept the inn's residents awake, stemmed from laughter as the former classmates tried to identify quotations from their English literature classes. Frances was asked to identify the last quotation. When she couldn't, she was told that it came from her book, *The Roosevelt I Knew.*

In 1952 sixty women came from many parts of the world to celebrate the fiftieth anniversary of their graduation from Mount Holyoke. So that no one would be disturbed by their animated conversation or laughter, their reunion banquet was held at the church, with Frances Perkins presiding as toastmistress. She reminded the septuagenarians of the time they had dashed across campus flying kites and were scolded because they were "the hope of the College." Her last night, Frances broke her string of pearls. A collection was quickly taken, and by the time Frances was back in New York City ready to embark on the H.M.S. *Queen Elizabeth* for another trip to England and to Geneva for the ILO convention, classmate Charlotte Leavitt arrived at the ship with a gift of pearls from the class of 1902.

Sitting in a steamer chair next to another classmate, Blanche Horton, she penned affectionate notes to many of her old chums. To the secretary she wrote about the reunion:

> I didn't hear one biting remark, I did not see one unkind look, or excluding act, I didn't hear one complaint or one reference to trouble or disappoint- ment or disillusionment, although every one of us has known these human experiences. Quite a feat, I think, for sixty women, no longer young, with widely varied habits, living together dormitory style, with unaccustomed rules, early rising and late noise, semi-public toilet arrangements, a triumph of adaptability and good will. I was proud of *us*. I think that this was a demonstration of the exercise of Christian love. . . .I am deeply grateful for the love my classmates show me and for the strength that love gives me.

Letters written by her husband, Paul Wilson, over the years show that his love and concern for her had not diminished. Her comments about him suggest the tenderness one has for a dependent child. Paul Wilson died on December 31, 1952. Services were held in St. Andrew's Church in Newcastle, Maine, and burial was in the family cemetery there. President Truman, finishing up his last days in office, wrote her a touching letter of condolence.

On inauguration day, January 20, 1953, Frances submitted her letter of resignation from the Civil Service Commission, effective in eighty days, to Dwight D. Eisenhower—the first Republican president in twenty years.

Her last day in office she emptied her desk drawers. Among the oddments were some twine, sewing needles, a prayer of St. Francis of Assissi—"Every government official should know it by heart," she said—and a badge from the 1948 Democratic convention.

To her secretary she said, "I'll put all my Presidents' letters together in my handbag—Roosevelt, Truman and today Eisenhower."

One of the commissioners who served with her, Robert Ramspeck, dropped in unannounced to tell her that he was sorry she was leaving. With a show of enthusiasm she explained, "It's quite an accomplish- ment to be the last leaf on the tree."

She filled out an application for a Social Security number and boasted of her new job as a guest lecturer at the University of Illinois.

One of her secretaries came in and opened her purse. "Have I got enough money?" Frances asked, then to clarify, "Every Friday my girls check my handbag to see if I've enough money for the weekend. Who's going to do that now?"

To the reporters witnessing the awkward performance, she made small talk. Her years in office had passed too quickly. "Why, it seems only yesterday that I became Secretary of Labor. So much has happened and yet time has gone so fast."

She paused contemplatively. "I was lucky to live at a time when the United States was ready for social reforms. And I was lucky to live in a period when women finally got a chance to serve in public life."

A messenger, Rudolph Valentino Williams, helped her into her coat, and she walked out of the office in time to miss the tearful exclamation of one of the secretaries, "We'll never see another person like her. She's been the most wonderful boss to work for that I've ever had."

Jerry Klutz in the *Federal Diary* noted an incredible record: "Frances Perkins never lost a single day from work because of illness in her more than twenty years here."

*****

Frances planned to write a biography of her old friend and mentor, former New York State Governor Al Smith. She excused her procrastination on the grounds that she could not fathom the rift between Smith and Franklin D. Roosevelt. Most of her time was spent as a visiting professor at a number of midwestern universities. She wrote Mary Dewson:

> Great demand for a lecture on "Roosevelt." The students, all born *since* 1933 and he is a fable—a tradition but he is alive and *moves* them. I do it pretty well. My voice still holds out and "throbs" just a bit! I get tired nowadays and have to *sleep a lot!*

Although she had made quite a profession out of her new role, she wanted to give it up. She would have liked to have moved to New York City, but could not sell her house at 2127 Leroy Place in Washington. She asked Mary, "*Repubs* don't buy. Why???"

She'd had an opportunity to attend a women's rally in Albany and was pleasantly surprised to find she had not been forgotten in New York circles. She told Mary, "they are grateful for what you and I and Alice did when we had the chance," and then with her youthful Fanny-the-Perk exuberance she exclaimed:

It was something too, wasn't it!! I sometimes pinch myself at realizing how far we came in making America Modern in the years 1910-1940. I am grateful and I know you are.

In 1955 she wrote Mary about banging herself all up: "broke shoulder, two ribs, cracked sternum and ligaments . . . bruises purple green." She had always thought she was indestructable, and because she expected to live as long as her 101-year-old grandmother, according to Maurice Neufeld of Cornell University, she denied the infirmities of age that were manifesting themselves.

She also found that her lifestyle required more money than her income permitted. She was delighted by the invitation of the School of Labor and Industrial Relations at Cornell University to serve as resident lecturer. She would live at Telluride House, a residence for students on scholarships.

When Dr. Neufeld met her at the train station, she confessed that she felt "just like a bride" moving into new surroundings. She enjoyed the students, particularly those whose questions triggered memories of her early days, of old friendships, of the New Deal era. Many of the questions were basic, such as how did the word "boondoggling" get into the general vocabulary? She knew the answer: "Boondoggling is a perfectly respectable word used in Texas and Oklahoma which means repairing or mending a harness or a saddle. If your harness or bridle breaks, you say you guess you'll put in a rainy day boondoggling." The term started when WPA projects in these states involved repairing household goods and utensils. It gradually extended to the raking of leaves in parks on the WPA project.

Semester after semester she could expect to defend the leaf rakers on WPA:

> It is possible that someone saw some old men raking leaves and doing it very badly and the conclusion was drawn that they were doing make-believe work. The only leaf rakers I ever saw were those who were too sick and old to do anything else. These were men who wanted to do something rather than nothing to get their $15.

Students dealing with new concepts in the social reform area were charmed by her simplistic view on private, voluntary charities. Her assessment of the Salvation Army reflected a Bible verse she favored as a child:

I have always liked the Salvation Army because, you know, a man can be down but he is never out. And they make a point of giving relief to the most unjust and improper people just because they are hungry. He has nothing to eat, so you give him something . . . his feet are cold, so you give him shoes. This has always appealed to me.

President Lyndon B. Johnson's "war on poverty" fascinated her because she saw it as an extremely ancient concept:

And, of course, you remember there was an attack on poverty being made at one period by the reformers. It was not just exactly as the attack on poverty is today, although as I read about this subject I remember that we used the very words, "war on poverty," over and over again, twenty, thirty, forty, fifty years ago.

. . .I saw a magazine article the other day in an old *Survey* magazine. It was signed by me—I don't recall having written it, but anyhow it was called "The Battle on Poverty." Well, I just wondered, you know, a passing thought, if President Johnson might have been reading this *Survey* . . .

Frances excelled in the history of the labor movement. She specified that labor unions were not what she would call "eleemosynary institutions, nor should they be. They have a principal job—which is to advance the wages of their own group, but incidentally a lot of other people benefit from their patterns of improved wages and such programs as unemployment insurance."

When interviewed about the labor unions' welfare funds scandal, she expressed little shock or indignation. "I never thought labor was a special class, better than bankers, bakers or any other people."

She enjoyed being called "Professor," because it gave her something to live up to. She retained her regal bearing even as she entertained fellow faculty members with her incredible gift of mimicry. Some of her irreverant remarks as she passed "cold-blooded judgment" on former colleagues were intended to shock, and they succeeded.

One of her close friends suggested that her marriage must have been a terrible burden to her. "Terrible burden, nothing!" she responded. Terrible burdens did not exist for her; disappointments, yes, but more often she could see the challenge to greater creativity, to mastery of oneself, and concluded that "it was great fun" to deal with challenges.

Some thirty years before, an old friend answered the question, "What is the true inward temper of her being?" by repeating a comment she overheard Frances Perkins make. The conversation dealt with a woman who staked her all on love, and "went to pieces over the recreancy of her lover." Frances shook her head. "I thought," she said slowly, "that at our age everybody had learned the kindom of Heaven is within." She had not changed.

Walking along the ice-covered paths of Ithaca, New York, she would take the arm of Dr. Maurice Neufeld, but insisted that it was to keep him from slipping. Even in her eighties, she knelt at appropriate times during the Episcopalian services, making no concessions to her physical limitations.

No one knew that she was suffering from arterial-sclerotic and hypertensive heart disease. She tried to conceal the fact that her vision was so poor that even reading with a magnifying glass proved difficult. Because she could not hear well, she complained, "Students no longer speak distinctly." At times she was incontinent. Dr. Alice Cooke would try to limit students' questions so that Frances's voice would not give out.

The cheerful demeanor of the aging woman endeared her to all. She joked with her secretary and greeted one and all as friends. Her memory for faces was incredible. She loved children—she visited often with her tow-headed grandson in Maine—and they reciprocated. She enjoyed two or three drinks before dinner—rye on the rocks—and would never pass up chocolate-covered mints. She disliked synthetic fabrics.

Frances Perkins particularly found pleasure in hearing that old friends and coworkers still remembered her. She wrote to Clara Beyer of her delight in reading that she had been applauded at an ILO reunion dinner, and then asked the rhetorical question:

> I endured a lot while I was in office, didn't I? But people are very ready to notice what you did when you are no longer a hazard to them. Funny but very nice!

Frances did continue with letter-writing to key politicians on key issues. In December, 1960, she wrote to Senator Kennedy recommending Esther Peterson, a position that led to her appointment as assistant secretary of labor and presidential advisor on consumer affairs.

Frances mustered up all her old energy for special speaking engagements. She had been particularly pleased with an invitation to address the International Association of Government Labor Officials meeting in Kennebunkport, Maine. Four months prior to the meeting she wrote Clara Beyer for some pointers. Knowing how well prepared Frances insisted on being, Clara sent her eight pages of notes.

As she grew older, Frances apparently lost a few inches in height. Speakers lecterns often are high enough to allow reading of notes by tall, near-sighted men. On one occasion she walked up to the lectern, heard the hand-clapping following her introduction, but could not see—or be seen. There was a pause. Then the startled audience heard a powerful voice: "Be not afraid. It is I." While the audience roared, the lectern was replaced. Frances's showmanship did not diminish with age.

In 1957 the faculty of Cornell's School of Labor and Industrial Relations surprised her with a birthday party; she seemed less than pleased. Three years later they honored her again. This time she showed her pleasure, and privately confessed to Professor Woody Sayre and some companions that it was not her seventy-eighth but rather her eightieth birthday.

A few weeks later she went to New York City to the "Living History" dinner celebration of the Research Institute of America. Fifty honored guests received gold medallions for enriching the history of a free people, and viewed themselves in film clips thrown on a gigantic screen. Frances renewed friendships and memories with James Farley, Rexford Guy Tugwell, Raymond Moley, Henry Wallace, Robert Moses, and the world's most celebrated woman, Eleanor Roosevelt.

After a summer spent mostly in Maine, Frances Perkins resumed her role as visiting lecturer at Cornell. The following year her birthday was marked by an unfortunate letter from Mount Holyoke, to which she scathingly responded:

I received a note dated April 10, 1961, purporting to greet the recipient on her 81st or was it 91st or 71st birthday. Nothing could be less welcome to this recipient or more banal as a method of "public relations."

Such letters and comments are an invasion of privacy—incorrect both as to the facts and the etiquette—and calculated to establish a firm rejection of Mt. Holyoke and all its works.

I suggest you abandon this "system of reminders to the aging" as offensive, super sentimental and useless.

Her sensitivity about age did not keep her from stipulating in her will that a gift of money from her estate go to the class of 1902 fund. A few years before she tried to find the names of all living 1902 graduates. Sixty-one still survived out of the original class of 148. Despite her own expectations of longevity, Frances informed her secretary that final instructions in the event of her death could always be found in her purse. Frances believed in being prepared for everything, including dying. She particularly specified that she wanted no life-sustaining devices employed—such as oxygen tents—when the time came.

In November, 1962, James Farley drove her to the rose garden in Hyde Park for the funeral of Eleanor Roosevelt. As United States ambassador to the United Nations, Eleanor Roosevelt had established a humanitarian reputation apart from her role as the wife of a former president.

The thirtieth anniversary of Franklind D. Roosevelt's first inauguration was also the fiftieth anniversary of the U.S. Department of Labor. Three thousand employees and labor representatives filled two ballrooms of the Sheraton Park Hotel for the golden anniversary banquet. Secretary of Labor Willard Wirtz introduced three of his predecessors: Arthur J. Goldberg, James P. Mitchell, and Frances Perkins. President John F. Kennedy was expected to arrive after everyone else had spoken—just in time for his own speech—as was his custom. But the dashing young president fooled everyone by arriving a half-hour early for the sole purpose of talking to "the grand old lady of the labor movement," Frances Perkins.

She revelled in his attention, and told him everything from the story of her peppery old grandfather dissatisfied with the bootmaker who claimed he would not live to wear out the boots, to the cockroaches infesting the old Department of Labor building when she first arrived in Washington. Because of the virtual tête-à-tête with the president, others missed her funniest remarks, but Kennedy didn't and was obviously enjoying himself.

In citing the "extraordinary record" of the Department of Labor, President Kennedy made an example of "the program which Madam Perkins put forward when she became Secretary of Labor—things which we now take for granted in both political parties which were regarded as dangerous and revolutionary and things which must be fought for in the short space of 30 years ago. They were controversial and Madam Perkins, who looked so quiet and peaceful and sweet was also one of the most controversial, dangerous figures that roamed the United States in the 1930's."

These were strong terms that the audience had to relate to the woman reporters were describing as slender and tiny—"so tiny, in fact, that, seated at the head table, the microphones brushed her hairline." Her own brief talk mentioned the department's early history when it was known as "the poor people's department."

A diminutive figure alongside the tall, angular, braid-coronaded Assistant Secretary of Labor Esther Peterson, Frances Perkins was saluted as one of the first soldiers in the war on poverty. At the thirtieth anniversary of the Bureau of Labor Standards celebrated on November 18, 1964, at the Mayflower Hotel, Esther Peterson declared that labor standards were the first weapons used in the nation's long war on poverty. Frances told the audience that she had kept a draft of the wage and hour law in her lower right-hand desk drawer—"ready for the day when the Supreme Court would broaden its interpretation of interstate commerce."

Frances continued to make speeches to teachers' associations and social workers' meetings and appeared on special programs at Cornell University, while keeping up her guest lectures in Dr. Alice Cooke's classes. When her New York City physician, Dr. Margaret Janeway, asked why she kept on working, Frances explained that she needed the money—she had enough for the luxuries, but not the necessities.

Frances caught a cold attending the inauguration of Lyndon B. Johnson in January, 1965. It hung on but did not deter her. She celebrated her eighty-fifth birthday on April tenth. When Dean Bernice Wright of Syracuse University's School of Home Economics invited her to address the convocation in May she accepted with alacrity. Frances asked that an academic robe be ordered for her in the appropriate length; she claimed to be five foot five. She agreed to wear the doctoral hood of her would-be biographer whom she had discouraged adamantly but graciously.

Frances went to see her New York City doctor about her cold and entered Midtown Hospital on May seventh—"just to clear out her lungs." In daily telephone communications, she insisted that she would be in Syracuse in ample time for the convocation.

On May 14, 1965, Frances Perkins suffered a stroke from which she never regained consciousness. She died at 7 P.M.

This was the first time she missed an opportunity to tell students about the task ahead: "It is not something to be accomplished before breakfast. It will take years, and the enthusiasm and courage of youth can do much in winning the support of public opinion." Or to challenge young people to ask themselves: "What is my duty?' ...There is always a large horizon. ...There is much to be done in other parts of the world. I am not going to be doing it! It is up to you to contribute some small part to a program of human betterment for all time."

A solemn requiem mass was celebrated at the Episcopal Church of the Resurrection in New York City. Her remains were sent to New-castle, Maine, for burial in the family plot. She requested that in lieu of flowers, donations be made to the Miles Memorial Hospital, Damaris-cotta, Maine, or the Retreat House of the Redeemer in New York City.

On May 18, 1965, a requiem mass in Anabel Taylor Hall under the auspices of the Episcopal Church at Cornell University honored her memory. Professor Maurice F. Neufeld delivered the eulogy. Frances Perkins would have admonished anyone for weeping, for as she once said, "Miss Jay, Heaven is my home."

In the center of a sitting room arrangement in the office of the secretary of labor stands a handsome old English drop-leaf coffee table that the Department of Labor acquired from her estate. Her feminine portrait looks singular among those of other former secretaries of labor hanging in the library of the new Department of Labor building on Pennsylvania Avenue. A charming pastel oil painting, it fails to capture her compelling eyes, her earnestness and vitality. Frances Perkins had refused to have the portrait done over: "Ten years after I'm gone, people will say, 'What a fine likeness.' " She was undoubtedly right.

Notes

The number preceeding each of the following notes is the number of the page to which it refers.

1 The drawn-out procedure . . . Russell Lord, "Profiles," *New Yorker*, Sept. 9, 1933, p. 22.

Descriptions of the church service appear in works on FDR and in *TRIK*, p. 139; Also FP lectures, Cornell University, e.g., Feb. 6, 1957, p. 38. The service held great significance for the president. On Feb. 28, 1938, he wrote to Clara Beyer's husband, Otto: "I believe we all began our work with greater confidence on March 4, 1933, as a result of the private service which a group of us attended at St. John's Church. . . ," SL.

"This day next year . . ." And return wire, both dated March 4, 1932, in FDRL. Roosevelt publicly declared his candidacy for president on Jan. 22, 1932, though speculation started after he won his second term as New York State governor, Rosenman, *Working with Roosevelt*, p. 56.

Because of friendship . . . Clara Beyer correspondence, Feb. 27, 1933, SL.

2 Her well-founded reluctance . . . People suspected that she was not as reluctant as she sounded; various interviews.

"At bottom, I knew . . ." Transcribed lecture, Cornell University, Dec. 16, 1957, p. 44; *TRIK*, p. 57. In a letter to an MWD biographer, March 9, 1961, she wrote that MWD "was the one that convinced me that if it was offered to me, I should accept it," SL.

Unable or unwilling . . . Photo, *Time*, March 6, 1933, p. 15; Lord, op. cit., p. 22.

FP personally ordered . . . Cal Tinney, "'Man' of the Week — Secretary Perkins," *New York Post*, Nov. 14, 1936.

Together with a friend . . . *Time*, March 6, 1933, p. 12.

At six o'clock . . . "Miss Perkins Sees New Civilization," *New York Times*, March 5, 1933, p. 21. FP inaccurately recorded the event as taking place on Sunday morning, *TRIK*, p. 152; Lindley, *The Roosevelt Revolution*, p. 70; Hull, *The Memoirs of Cordell Hull*, vol. 1, p. 167; Roper's version varies, *Fifty Years of Public Life*, p. 269.

Early the next morning . . . Lord, op. cit., p. 22.

At that first meeting . . . Farley, *Jim Farley's Story*, pp. 37-39; *TRIK*, p. 152.

Vice-president John Nance Garner . . . Undated Cornell lecture, "With the passing of the NRA . . .," p. 22.

Frances Perkins usually impressed people . . . Telephone interview, Anna Roosevelt Halsted, Washington, D.C., Jan., 1970.

She did so . . . *TRIK*, p. 153.

"You're all right . . ." "Frances Perkins, the First Woman in Cabinet, Is Dead," *New York Times*, May 15, 1965, p. 1.

5 "Success? What is . . ." Mary Graham Banner, "Does Luck Figure in One's Success?" *Forbes Magazine*, April 5, 1919, p. 923. FP claimed, "nine chances out of ten it's luck that brings success."

Frances Perkins opened the drawers . . . *Christian Science Monitor*, March 6, 1963; Carter, *The New Dealers*, p. 175; Russell Lord, op. cit., *New Yorker*, Sept. 9, 1933, p. 20.

She had learned to be practical . . . FP frequently confessed, "I am a missionary at heart"; speech of March 10, 1934, with cover letter by Mrs. Robert Bruere, FDRL. She invariably deleted this phrase from her speech drafts.

She liked to tell reporters . . . *New York Herald Tribune*, April 5, 1936.

6 Otis, a descendant . . . Warfel, Gabriel, and Williams, *The American Mind*, p. 135; Daniels, *They Will Be Heard*, pp. 26-29, 37.

James Otis's arguments . . . For the Otis quotation see U.S. National Commission on Law Observance and Enforcement, *Report on the Enforcement of the Deportation Laws of the United States*, p. 134.

Wickersham report as her bible . . . *New York Times*, March 3, 1933.

Another famous ancestor . . . Harry Clinton Green, "The Pioneer Mothers of America," in Beard, *America through Women's Eyes*, pp. 56-58, 76; Irwin, *Angels and Amazons*, p. 5.

Frances Perkins enjoyed telling. . . Benjamin Stolberg, "Madame Secretary: A Study in Bewilderment," *Saturday Evening Post*, July 27, 1940, p. 10.

One story, told repeatedly . . . Author's notes, FP speech to New York State Council for Social Studies, Hotel Syracuse, Feb. 12, 1960; also, e.g., Dorothy McCardle, "Labor Anniversary Has Significance for U.S. Women," Syracuse *Herald-American*, March 17, 1963.

7 Born in Newcastle, Maine . . . (Fred Perkins, Aug. 24, 1844–Feb. 26, 1916), Nutt, *History of Worcester and Its People*, vol. 3, pp. 231-32. Regarding Mr. Perkins's affiliations, vol. 2, p. 995; Josephson and Josephson, *Al Smith*, p. 104.

8 In later years, Frances Perkins described her mother . . . Author's notes, FP's speech, "The Impact of the Employment of Women on Industry and Business," April 12, 1962, College of Home Economics, Cornell University.

9 A number of spontaneous statements . . . *Encyclopedia Britannica*, 1966 ed., "Worcester."

. . . Plymouth Congregational Church . . . Nutt, *Worcester and Its People*, vol. 2, p. 813

10 A reporter, interviewing Frances Perkins . . . Banner, op. cit., p. 6.

11 On one occasion Fannie tumbled . . . Told by FP to the author's children: Kristine, Elizabeth, Bill, and Amie Mohr. Eight-year-old Bill, whose upper torso was encompassed in a cast as a result of a fall down a cliff, reminded FP of her own experience with a broken back, discovered after she went into government service.

"Don't waste people's time . . ." FP, "Eight Years as Madame Secretary," *Fortune*, Sept. 1941, p. 77 ff.

"She was always an original girl . . ." Babson, *Washington and the Revolutionists*, pp. 84, 88.

12 "One day we were told . . ." *Industrial and Labor Relations Report*, vol. 2, no. 2, Cornell University, N.Y.S. School of Industrial Relations, p. 12.

. . . upbringing was "pretty sketchy,". . . Cornell lectures, tape 13, pp. 2, 3.

"You must be prepared for surprises." . . . Cornell lectures, tape 13, p. 6.

"When anyone opens a door . . ." *TRIK*, p. 57.

13 . . . she did not begin to know herself . . . Cornell lectures, tape 13, p. 7.

. . . "equalitarian manners . . ." FP, "Women in Public Administration," *Journal of the American Association of University Women*, 1939, p. 13, SL.

On one occasion when visiting Boston . . . Josephson and Josephson, op. cit., p. 43.

As for elocution . . . Childs, *I Write from Washington*, p. 270; Lord, op. cit., pp. 20-23.

14 . . . took no part in the program . . . Babson, op. cit., p. 88.

Fannie Coralie Perkins considered herself tall . . . Ibid, p. 91. She possessed the beauty . . . , Nall, *Youth's Work in the New World*, p. 140.

. . . ranked as a "daring departure" . . . Irwin, op. cit., p. 279.

15 Frances Perkins did not think of herself . . . In 1929 she said she had gone to college "because it was the thing to do," C. Maud H. Lynch, "Mount Holyoke Alumna Interviewed," *Mount Holyoke News*, May 4, 1929, MHL.

She later described Miss Esther Van Dieman . . . FP, "The Teacher I'll Never Forget," *Scholastic Teacher*, Nov. 2, 1960, p. 4-T.

A course that Fannie . . . *Springfield Republican*, March 2, 1933, MHL.

One of her classmates, Alice Little . . . Babson, op. cit., pp. 85, 89, 90.

When the junior class . . . *Springfield Republican*, March 2, 1933, MHL.

16 With pell-mell merriment . . . Amy Peters Nickerson's poem in a 1948 alumnae letter, MHL.

"Be ye steadfast . . ." I Cor. XV:58; "Beop Stapolfaste" appeared in the *Yearbook*, MHL.

"I had little time to spare for my friends . . ." Lynch, op. cit.

17 Fannie spent part of the summer . . . 1902 class letter, pp. 37-39, MHL.

18 One of her young proteges . . . Lynch, op cit.; Rowland Evans, Jr., *Washington Post*, Jan. 25, 1948.

" . . . I myself saw pay envelopes . . ." FP, "My Recollections of Florence Kelley," *Social Service Review*, vol. 28, 1954, p. 15.

19 She received one job offer . . . Lynch, op. cit.

Unfortunately, the options . . . FP's Syracuse speech, Feb. 12, 1960.

"I have charge . . ." 1902 class letter, spring 1906, p. 25, MHL.

21 "College is for learning afterwards." . . . FP, "Women in Public Administration," pp. 12-13, SL; repeated in her Syracuse speech, Feb. 12, 1960.

Frances read Hartley's . . . A 1901 best seller. For the literary discovery of poverty see FP, *People at Work*, p. 39.

She agonized over Jacob Riis's . . . *TRIK* p. 10; Cornell lectures, e.g. Recording Session No. 1, Labor Union History & Administration, Feb. 6, 1957, pp. 57, 58.

22 But she claimed that Theodore Roosevelt's . . . *TRIK*, p. 10.

Theodore Roosevelt had warned: "There is nothing attractive . . ." Meyers, *Theodore Roosevelt*, p. 307.

"It was *fun* to put 'corruption' . . ." *TRIK*, p. 12.

She particularly recalled . . . FP, *People at Work*, pp. 39-40.

Dr. Taylor headed Chicago Commons . . . Josephson and Josephson, op. cit., p. 108.

The objective of these settlement houses . . . Linn, *Jane Addams*, p. 109; Sinclair, *The Better Half*, pp. 309-310; Bremner, *From the Depths*, pp. 62-63, 201.

23 Some people viewed ... Jane Addams, *Twenty Years at Hull House*, pp. 217, 225.

She recalled that the Klondike millionaire ... Genevieve Parkhurst, "Frances Perkins, Crusader," *Washington Evening Star*, Feb. 19, 1933. FP reminisced about making beds, Chicago houses with "stairs on the outside," about getting a drunk off the floor — "just neighbors coming in to help when someone was sick." Cornell lecture, Feb. 13, 1957.

Although all of her biographical records ... "Jane Addams trained Frances Perkins," Carter, op. cit., p. 175; "Six months at Hull House," *Time*, March 6, 1933. The curator of the Swarthmore College Peace Collection wrote, "Nothing has revealed through our primary sources a relationship between Jane Addams and Frances Perkins, although various biographies of the life of Jane Addams indicate at least two encounters after Miss Perkins' early years at Hull House," letter to author, Oct. 22, 1969.

24 Already a large-scale enterprise ... Linn, op. cit., pp. 209-10; Hamilton, *Exploring the Dangerous Trades*, pp. 87, 125; Bremner, op. cit., p. 62.

Hull House earned a reputation ... Jane Addams, "Twenty Years at Hull House," Beard, op. cit., pp. 326-27.

Dr. Alice Hamilton, the first ... Hamilton, op. cit., pp. 76-77.

"To Discount the Headlines ..." *Survey*, Oct. 15, 1931, vol. 67, no. 2, p. 67.

25 To Frances Perkins, Miss Addams symbolized ... FP, *People at Work*, pp. 41-42.

She could never be disillusioned ..." Hamilton, op. cit., p. 80.

In a castigating profile ... Stolberg, op. cit.

"It was she who taught us ..." FP, *People at Work*, pp. 41-42; see also Wald, *Windows on Henry Street*, p. 332.

26 "To pride one's self ..." Linn, op. cit. p. 245.

While in Chicago ... Florence Kelley's "first" as head of a state factory inspection department preceded FP's appointment by thirty-five years, Goldmark, *Impatient Crusader*, p. 36; Julia Lathrop, "Florence Kelley – 1859-1932," *Survey*, March 15, 1932, p. 677. FP's glowing description, "Industrial Work: The Factory Inspector," in Catherine Filene, ed., *Careers for Women: New Ideas, New Methods, New Opportunities – to Fit a New World* (Boston: Houghton Mifflin Co., Riverside Press – Cambridge, 1934), pp. 349-54. See Gompers, *Seventy Years of Life and Labor*, p. 486, regarding the fight for appointment of women factory inspectors.

"How many? ..." FP, "My Recollections of Florence Kelley," p. 15; FP, "A Method of Moral Progress," *New Republic*, June 8, 1953, pp. 18-19.

"... progress toward social justice ..." FP, *People at Work*, p. 285. Social workers knew little about politics, according to FP's Syracuse speech, Feb. 12, 1960.

Her classic *Women in Economics* ... Carl N. Degler, "Charlotte Perkins Gilman on the Theory and Practice of Feminism," *American Quarterly*, Spring, 1956, vol. 8, no. 1, pp. 21-39. Virginia Woolf referred to the androgynous mind; Gilman used androcentric for the same concept.

27 Charlotte Perkins Gilman, before the turn ... "The New Generation of Women," *Current History Magazine*, vol. 17, Aug. 1923, p. 736.

Mrs. Gilman initially ... Sinclair, op. cit., p. 271.

When in later years, Charlotte Perkins Gilman ... "Madame Frances Perkins," *Survey*, March 1933, p. 110.

Although a Congregational church ... Gabriel, *The Course of American Democratic Thought*, pp. 55, 316. Also Simkhovitch, *Here Is God's Plenty*, p. 173.

28 One writer speculated ... Childs, op. cit., p. 269.

"Just think how nice ..." 1902 class letter, 1906, p. 25, MHL.

"... modern ideas, fads and fancies." ... *Springfield Republican*, March 2, 1933, MHL.

"... enter the work called ..." 1902 class letter, 1909, pp. 58-59, MHL.

In the fall of 1907 ... Babson, op. cit., p. 92-93.

"This society chiefly 'researches ..." 1902 class letter, 1909, p. 59, MHL.

In a biography of Al Smith, ... Josephson and Josephson, op. cit., pp. 109-111.

29 Among her closest friends ... George N. Caylor, "Frances Perkins, 1882-1963: A Memoir," New York, July 4-5, 1965, p. 8, typescript, carbon. Gift, George N. Caylor (65M66) NYPL. (Hereafter cited as Caylor memoir, NYPL.) For a description of the Caylors, see Schneiderman and Goldthwaite, *All For One*, p. 114.

30 In his *Theory of Dynamic Economics*, ... Simon Nelson Patten, University of Pennsylvania, Political Economy and Public Law Series, vol. 3, no. 2, chapter 7.

31 He led women ... Rexford Guy Tugwell, "Life and Work of Simon Nelson Patten," *Journal of Political Economy*, vol. 31, no. 2, April 1923, pp. 153-208.

... "war bridegrooms" ... William E. Leuchtenberg, "The New Deal and the Analogue of War," in Braeman, Bremner and Walters, *Change and Continuity in Twentieth Century America*, p. 133.

"... the greatest man America has ever produced." Various speeches; also Schlesinger, *The Coming of the New Deal*, pp. 108, 299, 549.

In recommending her ... Josephson and Josephson, op. cit., p. 112.

About her studies ... 1902 class letter, 1909, p. 60, MHL.

32 Interview with Evelynn Richards, Cornell University.

The forty dollars a month ... Genevieve Parkhurst, op. cit., p. 4.

"May we be wise enough ..." 1902 class letter, 1909, p. 60, MHL.

33 Frances Perkins "jumped at the chance ..." Social work case method, Bremner, op. cit., pp. 32, 124-25. Editorial, *Survey*, May 1933, p. 208, mentions her thesis, "Malnutrition Among School Children," and that FP earned an A grade in a course on "Efficiency and Relief."

University Settlement, originally known as the Neighborhood Guild ... Bremner, op. cit., p. 183.

Frances regarded him and his wife ... Ibid., p. 183.

34 She read, studied, wrote ... Maude Aldrich letter, February 11, 1910, MHL.

Reinforcement for seemingly radical ... Simkhovitch, op. cit., p. 143. Simkhovitch served on the executive board of the National Consumers League from 1898 to 1917.

Although social workers ... FP, *People at Work*, pp. 42-43.

35 One dealt with a son ... Josephson and Josephson, op. cit., p. 112.

Of little significance ... *TRIK*, p. 9.

36 On the board of Greenwich House ... Simkhovitch, op. cit., p. 179.

From Mrs. Simkhovitch ... Ibid., p. 140.

More than any other ... The many successful men and women who went from settlements to outstanding public service careers are discussed in Chambers, *Seedtime of Reform*, pp. 255-56. New York State Governor Herbert Lehman numbered among these, Nevins, *Herbert H. Lehman and His Era*, p. 52.

37 Here an idealistic, future "brain truster" ... Adolph A. Berle, Jr., phone interview with author, Nov. 12, 1969.

She came to know and appreciate Lillian Wald ... This proved to be a useful contact. A letter of Nov. 19, 1918, shows that the Maternity Center Association of which FP was executive secretary paid fifty dollars a month for use of the Henry St. Settlement's premises at 500 Manhattan St. A letter of April 10, 1919, reveals a problem case FP referred to Lillian Wald on Jan. 27, 1926, SL.

"It cost $5,000 ..." See Nevins, op. cit., p. 78; Jerome Beatty, "She Never Gave Up: Lifesaver Lillian Wald," *Forum*, Aug. 1937, p. 70.

As executive secretary of the National Consumers League ... Minutes of the N.Y.S. Factory Investigating Commission, vol. 2, (Albany: Argus Co., 1912) p. 310.

38 It was Florence Kelley's conviction, ... FP, "A Method of Moral Progress," p. 18. Chambers, op. cit., p. 4.

Pauline Goldmark ... Goldmark, op. cit., p. 208.

In 1910 it would be hard ... "Frances Perkins, the First Woman in Cabinet, Is Dead," *New York Times*, May 15, 1965, p. 39.

"Despise not the day ..." Goldmark, op. cit., p. 209. Helen R. Whitely, "Madame La Secretary Perkins," *American Mercury*, Dec. 1937, p. 418, presented the typical anticonsumerist critique of FP's activities: "... Fanny Cora went to work for the New York Consumers' League, where she experienced the profound joy of the professional Do-Gooder in harassing small back-street concerns in the interest of the uninterested consumer."

39 But according to one ... Babson, op. cit., p. 96.

The employment of children ... Minutes of the N.Y.S. Factory Investigating Commission, Vol. 2, p. 332.

"What will we do with all the children?" ... FP's Syracuse speech, Feb. 12, 1960.

Sara N. Claghorn's poem, "Little Toilers" ... cited by Dorothy Canfield Fisher, "Child Labor Ammunition," *Survey*, Feb. 15, 1929, p. 652. FP quoted this frequently.

40 She may well have felt uneasy ... *TRIK*, p. 24, recounts her experience enlisting Tammany Hall's support for the fifty-four-hour bill.

Who thought of marriage "to get it out of the way" ... Josephson and Josephson, op. cit., p. 113.

"As I remember it, he was ..." Shorer, *Sinclair Lewis*, pp. 175-76.

41 ... "the cheap, ready-made suits ..." Ibid., p. 208.

Frances had a predilection for people ... Various interviews.

On outsiders to local life ... Simkhovitch, op. cit., p. 209.

She explained to his biographer ... Shorer, op. cit., p. 191. On outsiders to local life, Simkhovitch, op. cit., p. 209.

And for respite ... Genevieve Parkhurst, op. cit. Another version, Shorer, op. cit., p.192.

42 She did not take him seriously ... Shorer, op. cit., pp. 193, 205.

It is not known ... Vorse, Time and the Town, p. 42.

"He used to try out ..." Shorer, op. cit., p. 181.

43 She could only commiserate ... Ibid., p. 796-97.

"It seems to me a tribute ... FP, "My Job," Survey, March 15, 1929, p. 773.

44 Because of what happened ... Vorse, A Footnote to Folly, p. 39. Stein, The Triangle Fire, p. 211, says FP was visiting friends "on the other side of the Square." At a fiftieth anniversary memorial meeting, March 25, 1961, ER, FP and Rose Schneiderman shared the platform at the spot of what was once the Asch Building with fourteen survivors of the fire, p. 220.

One hundred and forty-six lives ... TRIK, pp. 22-23.

Local 25 of the International Ladies' Garment Workers Union ... Schneiderman and Goldthwaite, op. cit., pp. 98, 99.

45 On June 30, 1911 the New York state legislature ..., Minutes of the N.Y.S. Factory Investigating Commission, vol. 2, p. 3. see Schneiderman and Goldthwaite, op. cit., regarding the Factory Investigating Commission report recommending a fifty-four-hour week, p. 102.

47 It seemed strange ... Freidel, The Apprenticeship, p. 121, including footnote.

Historical scholars searched Franklin Roosevelt's prolific correspondence ... Freidel, The Apprenticeship, pp. 117-22. Roseberry, Capitol Story, pp. 119-23, gives an account of the fire in the assembly library at 2:15 A.M., March 29, 1911, which hampered the New York State Legislature's debate.

Yet decades later ... FDR Press Conference no. 201, vol. 5, May 3, 1935, pp. 263-64, FDRL.

48 At the preliminary hearings ... Fire Department Chief Edward F. Croker in Minutes of the N.Y.S. Factory Investigating Commission, Preliminary Report, vol. 2, pp. 14-18.

Both Senator Robert F. Wagner ... First Report of the Factory Investigating Commission, vol. 1, (Albany: Argus Co.) p. 22, lists her among its "with appreciation credits"; her testimony under Elkus, Nov. 14, 1911, vol. 2, pp. 310-11, 318, 333.

Carola Woerishoffer, a graduate ... Carola Woerishoffer had gone to the homes of the girls in the Triangle Factory fire one by one. Smikhovitch, Neighborhood, p. 162.

For her efforts ... Second Report of the Factory Investigating Commission, 1913, vol. 2, (Albany: The Argus Co.) includes her letter of recommendations as secretary, dated Nov. 29, 1912.

"Avoid snap courses ..." Reprinted from the April Mount Holyoke Alumnae Quarterly; Lynch, op. cit.

50 "Better take it as it is ..." Genevieve Parkhurst, op. cit.

Sen. Tim Sullivan did so ... Felt, Hostages of Fortune, p. 88.

In the meantime ... Freidel's interpretations of "The Winner," op. cit., p. 122. Barron's National Financial Weekly recorded this in an interview, "The Woman and the Hour: Frances Perkins," Oct. 1, 1934.

Frances was upset ... TRIK, pp. 13-14.

51 "It's all right, me gal ..." TRIK, p. 14.

She could mimic ethnic ... Various interviews.

"We knew from our own experience ..." TRIK, p. 25.

52 In 1912 the common drinking cup ... Survey, Oct. 12, 1912, p. 54, and horses, pp. 56-57.

"... It was a parade of brains ..." Shore, op. cit., p. 181.

The suffragettes wanted ... Linn, op. cit., p. 437.

The progressive campaign of 1912 ... Simkovitch, Neighborhood, p. 176.

... saw a great deal of Paul C. Wilson ... Steinberg, Mrs. R., p. 77, refers to FP as Mayor Mitchell's secretary just before the Triangle Fire in 1911. In early summer ... TRIK, p. 15.

His wife, Eleanor, had joined ... Freidel, op. cit., p. 69.

"Frances Perkins was among those ..." Tugwell, The Democratic Roosevelt, p. 61.

53 For example, Frances belonged ... FP, "One Sixth of the Nation," edited Cornell lecture, no date, p. 16.

"That cordial, interlocking group ..." FP, "My Job," p. 774.

For some time, modern art ... Corinne Lowe, "Madam Secretary," Pictorial Review, June 1933, p. 3.

... Steiglitz's "291" ... Barbara Rose, American Art Since 1900 (London: Thomas and Hudson, 1967), pp. 46-51, 70, 76. Mentioned by Shorer, op. cit., p. 181.

54 She instituted a suit ... "The Woman and the Hour: Frances Perkins," Barron's National Financial Weekly, Oct. 1, 1934; Parkhurst, op. cit.

She wrote an article ... FP, "The Fire Bills," Feb. 22, 1913, p. 732.

... an article by Paul C. Wilson ... Survey, March 22, 1913, p. 857.

Mitchel's natural talents ... Sherwood, Roosevelt and Hopkins, pp. 23, 25.

Although Robert Moses, Paul Wilson's associate, ... Josephson and Josephson, op. cit., p. 181.

One of their mutual friends ... Alice Barrows manuscript, University of Maine, through Dr. Raymond A. Mohl, Florida Atlantic University.

55 No one spoke ... Various interviews. Cal Tinney, op. cit., records her painstaking efforts to cope with Wilson's excellent bridge; Frances Parkinson Keyes, "Triumvirate: Three great Women of the Labor Department," Delineator, Sept. 1933, p. 41.

John Franklin Carter ... Carter, op. cit., p. 179

"She prowled through the factory towns ..." Lewis, Ann Vickers, p. 262.

Lillian Wald, in a kind understatement ... Mary Ross, "Portrait of a Modern Woman," Survey Graphic, Feb. 1933, p. 114.

"She would never again be thirty ..." Lewis, op. cit., p. 264.

56 "I brought back memories ..." FP, "Unemployment Insurance: An American Plan to Protect Workers and Avoid the Dole," Survey Graphic, Nov. 1, 1931, p. 117-18, 173.

Thereafter one item ... That FP retained her maiden name appears in almost every article.

Frances provided one other ... Letter to the alumnae secretary, May 22, 1914, MHC. Another letter to the Mount Holyoke Alumnae Quarterly dated Nov. 24, 1922, reflected her impatience with the trite question of combining marriage with a career. She felt possibilities were "as infinite as the variations of personality."

57 "Having reached the age of thirty-three ..." Josephson and Josephson, op. cit., p. 181.

Henry Bruere, a University of Chicago professor ... Sherwood, op. cit., pp. 23-25.

58 According to one close family friend ... Alice Barrows manuscript, p. 158.

Frances became dependent ... Their letters suggest that she looked to him as a sounding board for her ideas, FDRL.

As an investigator ... TRIK, p. 22; Cornell lectures.

One of the commissioners ... Lowe, op. cit., p. 4.

During 1914, out-of-court settlements ... Felt, op. cit., p. 87.

"It meant REVOLUTION ..." Bealle, Fugitives from a Brain Gang, pp. 79-80; see also Babson, op. cit., p. 109.

59 If these were Frances Perkins's words ... Letter written by Paul Wilson to Robert Bruere, March 3, 1948, in FDRL.

Mary Heaton Vorse remembered ... Vorse, Time and the Town, pp. 100-101. Floyd Ward Johnstone, letter of Feb. 1, 1929, Connecticut College.

Alice Barrows, excited ... Alice Barrows manuscript, p. 158.

Later that year, Lillian D. Wald ... Wald, op. cit., pp. 246-47. The committee report gathered dust from 1917 until 1933 when FP among others, incorporated its recommendations into the Bureau of Labor Statistics and legislation, according to Wald.

The great mass meetings ... Vorse, Time and the Town, p. 62.

60 In 1915 Frances was ... 1902 class letter, 1915, p. 59, MHL.

On one occasion they held an auction ... Interview with Maurice Neufeld.

And she was "keeping up ..." Lowe, op. cit., p. 42.

Isadora Duncan epitomized modern ... 1902 class letter, 1915, p. 60, MHL.

61 Like many New Yorkers ... Caylor memoir, NYPL.

In 1916 Frances became pregnant ... Mount Holyoke Alumnae Quarterly clipping, April 1917, MHL.

New neighbors, George Caylor ... Caylor memoir, NYPL.

"Frances Perkins has for some time ..." Mount Holyoke clipping, July 1917, MHL.

She accepted the position of executive director ... on Jan. 25, 1927, Clara Taylor Warne wrote of being impressed with FP's "efficient work" with the Maternity Center Association that led to her writing of "A plan for Maternity Care." FPF in Connecticut College.

62 Years later, Paul Wilson wrote ... Letter from New London, New Hampshire, c. 1947. FDRL.

Many people conjectured ... Various interviews.

"His own sympathetic and friendly personality ..." Letter from FP to Brubacker, FDRL.

Frances Perkins liked to remember...1902 class letter, 1915, p. 59, MHL.

63 "A Worcester girl ..." Unidentified clipping in MHL. Six years later Annie Matthews would be elected for the second time as registrar of New York County, at $12,000 a year earning the highest salary of any woman in public office up to that time; Breckinridge, *Women in the Twentieth Century*, p. 335.

But she feared ... "One Sixth of the Nation," p. 15.

The newly-elected governor ... Josephson and Josephson, op. cit., p. 214; FP, "My Recollections of Florence Kelley," p. 19.

64 Objections to the appointment ... "Commissioner Perkins," *Survey*, March 1, 1919, p. 803.

"The appointment of Miss Perkins ..." *New York Times*, Jan. 15, 1919; *Mount Holyoke Alumnae News*, April, 1919; *Springfield Republican*, Jan. 16, 1919; MHL.

The opposition dealt ... Bellush, *Franklin D. Roosevelt as Governor of New York*, p. 30.

"No politics whatever ..." Josephson and Josephson, op. cit., pp. 215-16; *Mount Holyoke Alumnae News* clipping, April 1919; *New York Times*, Jan. 15, 1919.

65 ... reformers would be more "reasonable." ...*TRIK*, p. 26

"That, and that alone ..." "Miss Perkins at Holyoke Backs Johnson Indirectly," *Springfield Republican*, Oct. 9, 1936.

66 Frances knew Harlem-born Mrs. Moskowitz ... Josephson and Josephson, op. cit., pp. 192, 196-97; description from Stiles, *The Man Behind Roosevelt*, pp. 107-108. Also her obituary, *Survey*, Feb. 1933, p. 75.

Governor Smith cautiously ... Warner and Hawthorne, *The Happy Warrior*, pp. 109-10.

67 The dynamic, idealistic attorney ... Memo of 1919, FDRL.

"The insurance company people ..." *TRIK*, pp. 91-92.

"The company officials ..." Warner and Hawthorne, op. cit., p. 109; Josephson and Josephson, op. cit., pp. 226-27, 230.

68 Wellesley-educated Mary W. Dewson ... Descriptions in Chambers, op. cit., p. 254; Goldmark, op. cit., pp. 136-37; Stiles, op. cit., p. 129.

"I conferred with her ..." FP letter to MWD biographer dated March 9, 1961, SL. At age eighty, FP felt the name Mary preferable to "Molly, a childish nick name used by only a few people," according to her handwritten postscript.

Adolph Berle, characterized as ... Description in Leuchtenburg, *Franklin D. Roosevelt and the New Deal*, p. 33.

He made a special point ... Telephone interview, Nov. 12, 1969.

Professor Shotwell described the genesis ... Shotwell, *The Origins of the International Labor Organization*, vol. 1, pp. xviv, xxi, xxii, 7.

69 But in 1919 when the ILO ... Hamilton, op. cit., p. 254.

"The International Labor Office ..." FP speech dated April, 1924, Mount Holyoke Alumnae Office.

70 Because of her interest ... Clipping of July, 1921, Mount Holyoke Alumnae Office.

71 Frances Perkins, representing the National Consumers League ... Southampton Colony tea in her honor, *Mount Holyoke Alumnae News*, Oct. 1922.

"I never heard a sentence that didn't pass! ..." Author's notes, FP's Syracuse speech, Feb. 12, 1960.

72 The Russell Sage Foundation ... FP, *People at Work*, p. 87.

"I saw men lined up ..." FP, *People at Work*, p. 89.

In 1924, like many others ... In MHL material from 1923; also notes membership in the Cosmopolitan Club and Women's City Club, and birth year of 1882.

She planned to spend August ... FP letter to MWD dated July 29, 1924, MWD papers, FDRL.

73 Of "Gilly," whom she hoped ... 1902 class letter, 1924, MHL.

In the state department of labor ... Grace Overmyer, "Poor Man's Justice," *Survey*, Sept. 1934, p. 280.

74 In 1926 Governor Al Smith ... Jane Dixon, "Industrial Board Head Knows Working Women," unidentified clipping, Feb. 2, 1926, Mount Holyoke alumnae file. Position paid $8,000 a year. Dixon article includes laundry code.

Frances kept in touch with Lillian Wald ... After Susanna spent a day in 1931 with Lillian Wald, FP wrote her that Susanna wanted to work at Henry Street when she got older. On March 10, 1931, she wrote Wald, "I am more touched by your telegram to my daughter than by almost anything else I have received," Wald papers, NYPL.

75 Henry Street Settlement for Tuesday dinners ... Simkhovitch, *Here Is God's Plenty*, p. 143.

In November, 1926, Frances wrote to Lillian Wald ... Wald papers, NYPL.

Often on her trips ... Josephson and Josephson, op. cit., pp. 342-44.

"I'm like the young man ..." Dixon, "Industrial Board Head Knows Working Women."

An editor invited Frances ... FP, "Industrial Relations," in Doris E. Fleischman, *An Outline of Careers for Women: A Practical Guide to Achievement* (Garden City, N.Y.: Doubleday, Doran & Co., 1934), pp. 221-29.

76 At Mount Holyoke's ninetieth ... Clipping dated July, 1927, Mount Holyoke alumnae file.

"To watch her at work ..." *Manchester Guardian*, Jan. 1928, Mount Holyoke alumnae file.

77 Governor Smith ordered ... Schneider and Deutsch, *The History of Public Welfare in New York State, 1867-1940*, p. 293.

The State Industrial Survey Commission ... "Miss Commissioner Perkins," *Survey*, Jan. 15, 1929, p. 478.

Frances, recruited to campaign ... *TRIK*, p. 46.

Touring the South ... Josephson and Josephson, op. cit., p. 388.

But then, in her beloved New York City ... *Survey*, Sept. 1933, p. 315.

78 ... vividly remembered the phone calls to FDR ... Although she stated emphatically, "I was in the room at the Hotel Syracuse the night the call was put through. I remember vividly the conversation that took place," *TRIK*, p. 41. No other writer records her interest in FDR as what actually was the Hotel Seneca in Rochester. The 1930 Democratic convention took place in Syracuse; see Warner and Hawthorne, op. cit., p. 248, among others.

"Your nomination and acceptance ..." From 1928 campaign correspondence, N.Y.C., FP to FDR, dated Oct. 11, 1928, FDRL.

In the course of her work ... FP, "My Job," p. 773.

One, George F. Johnson ... George F. Johnson papers, Archives, Syracuse University Library, letter from FP to FDR, April 1, 1930.

That December she also tucked ... Simkhovitch, *Here Is God's Plenty*, pp. 224-25.

79 "It began in 1928 ..." ER and Lorena A. Hickok, *Ladies of Courage*, p. 187; MWD, op. cit., pp. 7-8. *New York Journal American*, Dec. 27, 1928, noted that she was the first woman to hold such an important position in the state, at a $12,000 salary; clipping in New York *News* Library.

"Molly said ..." Furman, *Washington By-Line*, p. 228.

"Frances Perkins, whose position until then ..." Tugwell, op. cit., p. 173; briefly in Burns, *Roosevelt: The Lion and the Fox*, p. 117.

80 Roosevelt noted for the record ... Freidel, *Franklin D. Roosevelt: The Triumph*, p. 19; Elliott Roosevelt, *F.D.R.: His Personal Letters, 1928-1945*, vol. 2, letter for the record, April 6, 1938, p. 772. Schneiderman believed, "No one objected to her sex," *All for One*, p. 201.

Al Smith's rejection ... George S. Van Schaick, N.Y. Superintendent of Insurance, recorded her appointment as one of Smith's "grievances against FDR," unpublished memoirs, p. 27, Columbia University Library. FP's record of Al Smith's boast on appointing her,

Frances Perkins did not number ... Moses, *A Tribute to Governor Smith*, p. 40, 47.

She was actually better acquainted ... Tugwell describes FP as one of ER's contemporaries – "one of those rather like her" – and maintains ER's education in welfare matters to FP; Tugwell, op. cit., p. 61, and n. 3, p. 173. ER's "education" is discussed in Freidel; *The Apprenticeship*, p. 69.

Franklin Roosevelt invited Frances ... *TRIK*, pp. 54, 57. Other Hyde Park visits, p. 62.

81 "As a representative of her sex ..." "Miss Commissioner Perkins," *Survey*, Jan. 15, 1929, p. 478 (particularly regarding Knapp). For the story of Mrs. Florence E.S. Knapp, see Gruber, *Women in American Politics*, pp. 184-85; John Gordon Ross, "Ladies in Politics: The Gentle Experiment," *Forum*, vol. 96, no. 5, Nov. 1936, p. 211.

"The long trail is ended ..." The Industrial Commissioner file in Connecticut College contains the countless congratulatory letters FP received on her appointment. On Jan. 30, 1929, FP wrote a glowing letter to Florence Kelley regretting her absence from the swearing-in ceremonies – "all done hastily," Connecticut College Library.

That intrepid group, the League of Women Voters ... Letter dated Dec. 27, 1928 – Industrial Commissioner file, Connecticut College Library. Regarding league activities, see Florence E. Allen, "Participation of Women in Government," *Annals*, American Academy of Political and Social Science, vol. 251, May 1947, pp. 94-103.

Frances's twelve-year-old daugher ... This took place in the state labor department's offices at 124 East 28th Street. FP's phone number suggests another era: LEXington 0900; Jan. 15, 1929.

Shortly thereafter nearly 1,000 ... FP, "My Job," pp. 773-75. Also Lowe, op. cit., p. 4.

84 ... "by and large they stand aloof ..." MWD, op. cit., p. 90.

"I cannot tell you how much that luncheon ..." Letter from FP to MWD, Dewson files, FDRL.

Frances Perkins headed the largest ... *New York Times*, May 15, 1965.

85 Oftentimes these small factories ... FP, "Helping Industry to Help Itself," *Harper's*, Oct. 1930, pp. 628, 629. Also FP, *People at Work*, p. 226.

86 The industrial commissioner realized ... Felt, op. cit., p. 179.

"So long as government's only role ..." FP, "Helping Industry to Help Itself," pp. 624-25; FP, *People at Work*, p. 277.

She sent to the newspapers ... New York *News*, Aug. 1929, with photo.

In April Roosevelt set into motion ... Bernstein, *The Lean Years*, pp. 241-42.

87 Sinclair Lewis wrote ... Shorer, op. cit., p. 519 ff.

Frances restricted her social life ... Lowe, op. cit., pp. 4, 42.

88 "A stock market crash ..." FP, *People at Work*, p. 99. The entire April 1929 issue of *Survey* was devoted to the depression. See Douglas, *Controlling Depressions*; in 1932 output per man-hour increased 21 percent over 1929, yet wages declined 23 percent. Inadequate purchasing power was clearly responsible, pp. 65-67.

A census during the first week of November ... Schneider and Deutsch, op. cit., p. 293.

Frances read the *New York Times* ... *New York Times*, Jan. 21, 1930; Lindley, op. cit., p. 66. On Hoover's optimism see Bird, *The Invisible Scar*, p. 71

89 She called for Eugene Patton ... *TRIK*, p. 96.

She called in reporters ... *Mount Holyoke Alumnae News*, Nov. 1932, quoted from *Springfield Republican*, Sept. 25, 1932.

"Whoever supplied the President ..." "Disputes Hoover on Employment," *New York Times*, Jan. 23, 1930. Ethelbut Stewart's statistical assessment of the depression appears in *Survey*, Oct. 15, 1931, p. 207.

In Washington, D.C. ... *Congressional Record* – Senate, Jan. 23, 1933, vol. 72, part 2, 71st Congress-2nd session, p. 2179.

"Bully for you! ..." *TRIK*, pp. 92-97.

She was, however, reminded ... Linn, op. cit., p. 412; *New York Times*, April 9, 1935.

90 U.S. Senator Robert Wagner ... Huthmacher, *Senator Robert F. Wagner and the Rise of Urban Liberalism*, p. 59. FP's letters in *Congressional Record*, Jan. 31, 1930, 71st Cong., 2nd Session, vol. 72, part 3, p. 2762.

Local licensing bureaus ... FP, "State Regulation of Private Employment Agencies," in *Fee Charging Job Agencies in New York State Need State Supervision* (New York: American Association for Labor Legislation, 1930), p. 5.

She pleaded with manufacturers ... "Disputes Hoover on Employment," *New York Times*, Jan. 23, 1930. She also urged a shorter workweek (six-hour day or five-day week), New York *News*, Nov. 11, 1931.

91 During 1929 and 1930 ... Felt, op. cit., p. 179; FP, *People at Work*, pp. 274-76. FP applauded companies striving to stabilize employment in "Frances Perkins on Unemployment," *Woman's Journal*, Nov. 1930, pp. 8-10, 41, 42.

In July Frances sent him a note ... Dated July 15, 1930, Bellush, op. cit., p. 162; Fusfeld, *The Economic Thought of F.D.R. and the Origins of the New Deal*, p. 161. On the governor's conference on unemployment insurance, see Bernstein, op. cit., pp. 492-93.

"Frances Perkins wants us to have ..." MWD, op. cit., vol. 1, p. 12.

92 Frances Perkins spoke at a major conference ... Gruber, op. cit., pp. 142, 288, and Furman, op. cit., pp. 73, 75, 81.

The women's movement languished ... Sanders, *The Lady and the Vote*, pp. 139-42. On Harding's 1920 promise of a woman in the cabinet, Gruber, op. cit., p. 288.

"A Secretary of Labor must be something ..." Charles W. Ervin, "What's Happening in the World," *Advance*, July 25, 1930, p. 8.

By virtue of sheer size ... Ewan Claque, Oral History Collection, p. 121, Butler Library, Columbia University.

The Old Age Pension Law ... Bellush, op. cit., p. 186.

93 "Unemployment is a sympton ..." FP, "Unemployment Insurance," p. 173.

"The argument ..." Ibid., p. 119.

94 The venerable Jane Addams ... Linn, op. cit., p. 386.

95 She hastily evaluated her coworkers ... Letter from FP to MWD dated June 23, 1931, in Dewson papers; also in MWD, op. cit., p. 10. FP correspondence in Corsi files, 1943-1949, reflect her lifelong interest in the New York State Industrial Board, Archives, Syracuse University Library.

The England she visited in 1931 ... FDR received FP's report on unemployment insurance on Oct. 23, 1931, Bernstein, op. cit., p. 494; FP, *People at Work*, pp. 119-20.

96 "I went from town to town ..." FP, "Unemployment Insurance," pp. 118-19.

Many British employers ... *Survey*, Dec. 15, 1931, p. 291

97 "... In this country ..." FP, "Unemployment Insurance," p. 119.

Social Security numbers ... The story about mock Social Security identification cards appeared in newspapers many years ago and was incorporated in the author's lecture notes for Personal Finance classes at Syracuse University and Florida State University.

She was especially conscious ... "The Social Aspects of the Double Compensation Law in N.Y.," *Survey*, Oct. 15, 1931, p. 95.

98 "... we are profoundly suspicious ..." "Correspondence: What Working Women Think of Frances Perkins," *New Republic*, June 18, 1930, MHL.

99 ... a "holy hardness" about her ... Lowe, op. cit., p. 4.

She had the satisfaction ... Bellush, op. cit., p. 313.

The association filed charges ... "Window Cleaners File Charges," *Survey*, Jan. 15, 1932, pp. 430-31.

100 Next the newspapers accused her ... "Lost: Middle Age," editorial, New York *Herald Tribune*, Jan. 28, 1931, MHL.

On February seventeenth her friend ... FP numbered among the speakers at the memorial meeting held March 16, 1932, at the Friends' Meeting House, 221 East 15th St., New York; *New York Times*, March 17, 1932; Goldmark, op. cit., p. 60.

Frances wrote an article ... FP, "The Five Dollar Dress," *Survey*, May 1933, p. 208. The article developed the theme of Helen Campbell's *Prisoners of Poverty* (1887) which Bremner felt inspired the formation of consumers' leagues in the 1890s, op. cit., p. 73.

... Or what she slept in ... Sidney Skolsky, "Tintypes," New York *News* March 25, 1933.

"I had constant contact ... Alice Rogers Hager, "Miss Perkins Talks of the Tasks Ahead," *New York Times Magazine*, May 7, 1933, p. 3.

101 When she was asked to testify ... Isador Lubin, "The New Lead from Capitol Hill," *Survey*, March 1, 1932, p. 573 ff.

103 She noted that he would transpose ... *TRIK*, p. 113.

She also listened to the election returns ... FP was straightening out her bureau drawers on election day in 1932, according to the *Epworth Highroad*, Sept. 1933, p. 25.

"The election in the Fall ..." FP, *People at Work*, p. 122.

104 Roosevelt's campaign workers ... FDR dinner for MWD before Hotel Biltmore reception for campaign workers on Dec. 16, 1932, in MWD, op. cit., p. 78.

105 Only an economically advantaged ... Allen, op. cit., p. 115. Allen discusses a generalized trend toward minimizing household drudgeries and

increased activity outside of the home that in 1932 applied to a relatively small number of women.

The chairman of the National Woman's party ... The letter by Mrs. Harvey M. Wiley was published in the *New York Times*, Nov. 14, 1932. Despite extensive efforts directed at women, they wrote only 21 percent of the political letters in Roosevelt's campaign mail of 1932. In Eisenhower's presidential draft mail of 1948, 50 percent came from women. See Sussmann, *Dear FDR*, p. 107.

Mrs. Ogden Reid ... *New York Times*, Nov. 15, 1932.

106 One noted scholar ... "Lorine Pruette Nominates 'Real New Deal' Cabinet for Roosevelt," *San Francisco News*, Jan. 2, 1933. Clipping in DOLL, FPF. Dr. Pruette named Mary Beard (historian) for secretary of state, Belle Moskowitz (Gov. Al Smith's assistant) for secretary of the treasury, Florence Allen (judge) for secretary of war, Lena Madison Phillips for attorney general, Josephine Roche for secretary of commerce, Frances Perkins for secretary of labor, Dr. Alice Hamilton for secretary of public health, and Eleanor Roosevelt for secretary of education. These were topped off with Jane Addams of Hull House for vice-president.

The Democratic candidate ... Paraphrased by FP, *TRIK*, p. 166. "New Deal" was a common card-playing phrase, FP *People at Work*, p. 122. In later years FP claimed reporters picked up the "New Deal" phrase because it headlined easily, FP and J. Paul St. Sure, *Two Views of American Labor* (Los Angeles: University of California, 1965), p. 3. The "forgotten woman," Lorant, *The Glorious Burden*, p. 589.

"We women were ..." Farley, *Behind the Ballots* p. 354; Freidel, *The Triumph*, p. 319.

107 Dewson's associates prepared ... Furman, op. cit., p. 70.

Even before Roosevelt's nomination ... Ibid., pp. 229-30.

She had learned ... MWD, op. cit., p. 31.

109 Edwin E. Witte ... Witte letter dated Nov. 25, 1932, and Mary Gilson letter, Group 37, FDRL.

Although Daniel C. Roper ... Letter of Nov. 28, 1932, addressed to Emily Newell Blair of Joplin, Mo., who was working with MWD.

... a woman's place ... Chamberlain, *Sourcebook on Labor*, p. 227.

Cordell Hull, then a senator ... Hull leter to MWD, FDRL.

110 Organized labor took credit ... Fenno, *The President's Cabinet*, p. 74.

An outstanding record ... Sen. Robert Wagner is discussed editorially in *Fortune*, Jan. 1933, p. 60.

Rexford Guy Tugwell ... Tugwell, op. cit., pp. 173, 268.

"Just before the end ..." *Herald Tribune*, Dec. 12, 1932, in MWD Campaign Envelope, FDRL.

An article speculating ... *New York Times*, Nov. 20, 1932.

... 160 "favorite sons" ... *New York Times*, Nov. 13, 1932.

111 "But Mary, Franklin ..." ER and Hickok, op. cit., p. 187.

"This is a picture ..." MWD, op. cit., vol. 1, p. 90.

Just a couple of years ... Furman, op. cit., p. 70.

Roosevelt had boasted ... *TRIK*, p. 55. Freidel confirms FP's view that little bravery was required to appoint a woman with a good record and adds that ER frequently reminded him of the political value of recognizing women in making appointments, Freidel, *The Triumph*, p. 16.

She considered herself ... FP, "Eight Years as Madame Secretary," p. 77.

... and cautiously wrote ... Letter from CB to FP, Dec. 5, 1932, SL; also interviews with CB.

112 Sidney Hillman, president ... Memorandum of conversation between Sidney Hyman and FP, Washington, D.C., April 1949, FDRL.

But she made it clear ... Josephson, *Sidney Hillman*, p. 357.

113 Shortly after the election ... *New York Times*, Nov. 12, 1932.

"Dear Franklin ..." FP and FDR letters in FDR Private Correspondence 1928-1932, FDRL.

114 They both wrote ... Hofstadter, *The Age of Reform*, p. 378. Hofstadter writes that the language of the progressives during the twenties included "the plain people," "the common man," "the taxpayer," "the ultimate consumer," and "the man on the street", p. 172.

On that last evening ... Memoirs of George S. Van Schaick, p. 37, Columbia University Library.

As gossip abounded ... *New York Times*, Nov. 11 and Nov. 13, 1932. See Stiles, op. cit., p. 231; Williams, *Huey Long*, p. 637.

Roosevelt told ... Moley, *The First New Deal*, p. 73. Ruth Bryan Owen was later appointed minister to Denmark; Gruberg, op. cit., p. 144.

115 "When Molly Dewson backed her ..." ER and Hickok, op. cit., p. 189.

... he left Dewson believing ... MWD, op. cit., p. 78.

On February fifteenth Joe Caylor ... Caylor memoir, NYPL.

Elizabeth Brandeis wrote ... CBP, SL.

There are variations ... *TRIK*, pp. 150-51. Moley, op. cit., p. 94, claims that he made the introduction. For another version, see Gunther, *Roosevelt in Retrospect*, pp. 39, 133.

116 The paths of Ickes ... Linn, op. cit., pp. 219-20; Hamilton, op. cit., p. 78.

Frances Perkins followed Roosevelt ... *TRIK* p. 153-53; Moley, op. cit., p. 74; FP, "Eight Years as Madame Secretary," p. 77.

117 He anticipated her ... FP's lectures at Cornell University. She told this story frequently over the years. Regarding her nagging him, Cornell lecture, Nov. 7, 1957, p. 9.

118 ... pawing through garbage cans ... FP and St. Sure, op. cit., pp. 5,6.

Inauguration Day ... *Time*, March 6, 1933, p. 12.

Into the Cabinet Room ... *Time*, March 6, 1933, p. 12. Oveta Culp Hobby, the only other woman to serve in the cabinet up until 1970 also held the lowest-ranking cabinet position as secretary of the newly established Department of Health, Education, and Welfare from 1953 to 1955.

Some were fearful ... Ray Tucker, "Fearless Frances," *Colliers*, July 28, 1934, p. 16.

Eleanor Roosevelt denied ... ER and Hickok, op. cit., p. 277; Steinberg, op. cit., p. 223. Steinberg numbers among those who discount ER's disclaimers regarding her influence on FDR's final decision. He believes that Roosevelt considered creating a Department of Public Welfare and Education with FP as its head. Carter, op. cit., p. 215, attributes both FP's earlier appointment and FP's presence in the cabinet to ER's persuasion. Carter adds that Felix Frankfurter, a friend of Roosevelt's since the Wilson administration, drummed up a lot of support for FP's appointment, "which Roosevelt welcomed as he had decided to appoint her in any case," p. 320. Another researcher, Mrs. George Smith, received a letter from FP in March, 1961, stating that "many of the letters were stimulted by Miss Dewson at the President elect's request", letter to the author from Mrs. Robert Shanton, Assistant to the Director, Schlesinger Library.

"No matter how much ..." MWD, op. cit., p. 79.

119 Actually, Roosevelt determined ... Tugwell, op. cit., p. 269; Fenno, op. cit., p. 74.

Roosevelt showed a predilection ... Busch, *What Manner of Man?*, pp. 28, 33, 38-39, 171, 187; Biddle, *In Brief Authority*, p. 74.

Survey, the social workers' publication ... Editorial, "Madame Frances Perkins," *Survey*, March 1933, p. 110.

Newspapers, reporting the reaction ... "Assail Woodin and Miss Perkins," *New York Times*, Feb. 26, 1933.

120 Personally affronted ... Misc. Group 15, FDRL; *New York Times*, March 2, 1933; New York *News*, March 2, 1933; and FP Cornell lectures. Green's "boycott" of FP recorded in unpublished memoirs of John P. Frey, labor union official, Columbia University Library, p. 623.

Green, however, hardly represented ... Robert F. Howe, "Trade Unionism in the United States," in Bakke and Kerr, *Union, Management and the Public.*

Having retained her ... Nevins, op. cit., p. 157.

121 "Few women in high office ... Editorial, *New York Times*, March 2, 1933.

Frances Perkins's first mass press interview ... "Miss Perkins Cool under Green's Fire," *New York Times*, March 3, 1933.

122 "What right has . . ." Editorial, *New York Times*, March 4, 1933. Regarding technological exasperation, Roy Tucker, op. cit., pp. 16, 35.

125 "She had been incongruously given ..." Schlesinger, op. cit., pp. 299-300. The secretary of labor is stereotyped as "the roughneck kind of male with hell on his tongue and hair on his chest" by Ray Tucker, op. cit., p. 16.

"Up to 1933 ..." Carter, op. cit., p. 174.

Frances not only learned the full history ... see Harold D. Smith (Bureau of the Budget) diary, FDRL; FP speech, August 31, 1936, 300th Anniversary, Scituate, Mass., FDRL; Cornell lectures.

Early in 1868 ... Lombardi, *Labor's Voice in the Cabinet*, pp. 17-20, 26, 27, 60, 71.

126 During the Southwest Railway strikes ... Breen, *The United States Conciliation Service*, p. 4.

In 1898 bills urging ... Leed, *Government and Labor in the United States*, p. 290.

The year 1906 . . . Lombardi, op. cit., p. 62.

In 1910 the Democrats . . . Fenno, op. cit., p. 219 ff.

127 On March 4, 1913 . . . Smith, *History of the Cabinet of the United States of America*, pp. 501-503; Wehle, *Hidden Threads of History*, p. 42.

On March 5, 1921, President Warren Harding . . . Fenno, op. cit., pp. 74, 219; Smith, op. cit., p. 504.

In 1928 President-elect Herbert Hoover . . . Babson, *Washington and the Depression*, pp. 92, 102-103; Hoover, *The Memoirs of Herbert Hoover*, vol. 2, pp. 215-21.

A professed "Republican . . ." Babson, *Washington and the Depression*, p. 102.

On that first Monday . . . Truman Felt, *Dayton Daily News*, March 29, 1953.

128 . . . red roses sent by the Mount Holyoke Class . . . *Mount Holyoke Alumnae News*, May 1933.

The doors in the long hall . . . Interviews with Clara Beyer.

"Call me Madame." . . . Correctly spelled with or without the final *e*. The *e* indicates marital status. An article identified as the *Boston Eve. Trans.*, March 1, 1933, in MHL, indicated the propriety of calling FP "madame secretary." The second woman to hold a cabinet position, Oveta Culp Hobby, used "Mrs. Secretary," Gruberg, op. cit., p. 144.

"Miss Jay" . . . Described during interviews with Department of Labor personnel; also interviews with Clara Beyer and Maurice Neufeld. FP's poor instinct for publicity cited in ER and Hickok, op. cit., pp. 189-90; also interview with John Leslie, Information Office, Department of Labor; *TRIK*, p. 221.

"Is FP a good executive?" . . . Cal Tinney, op. cit.

. . . a Mr. Dudley Pendleton wrote . . . Letter from Frances Jurkowitz to Frieda Miller dated July 28, 1933, FDRL; also National Archives. Frieda Miller later became head of the Women's Bureau in the Department of Labor, DoL 00252, National Archives.

129 Frances relied heavily . . . Interview with CB. Mary LaDame became assistant director of the U.S. Employment Service; announcement to National League of Women Voters, June 15, 1933. Item 00184, National Archives.

Many department heads wondered . . . Ewan Claque, Oral History Collection, p. 176.

One was by closing off . . . Clara Beyer interview.

Secretary Perkins's *Survey Graphic* article . . . "Gossip: Of People and Things," *Survey*, May 1933, p. 208, referred to *Survey Graphic* article of February, 1933.

". . . if an inquiry comes . . ." AFL *Proceedings*, 1933, p. 228, courtesy AFL-CIO, Washington, D.C.

130 "She expects a great deal . . . Lord, op. cit., p. 20.

A few months later . . . *Time*, June 19, 1933, p. 40.

She was busy at her desk . . . . *Public Ledger*, clipping in MHL. "Labor Secretary Uses Chair Made for Correct Posture," *Washington Evening Star*, Sept. 29, 1933.

131 Rather impolitically . . . For general description of cabinet members' social life see Smith, *The Good New Days*, p. 31 ff. In Babson, *Washington and the Revolutionists*, she is quoted as saying that "in times like these . . . social life for a secretary of labor would not be very extensive," p. 111.

The Bureau of Immigration and Naturalization . . . Swisher, *American National Government*, p. 362.

On Tuesday, March seventh . . . Report from Peter F. Snyder to FP, March 9, 1933, in Immigration Folder, Connecticut College.

132 "Mr. Walter Pollak . . ." Lord, op. cit., p. 22; Carter, op. cit., pp. 176-77.

. . . . "more a matter of historical accident . . ." Letter from FP to the president, May 25, 1934, p. 1, FDRL.

133 In June she had the president . . . Three-page letter from FP to Lewis W. Douglas, June 14, 1934, reviews the entire situation and urges his support for the consolidation that would give legal sanction to what was already a fact. See Immigration Folder, AWC Perkins VII, Connecticut College. Also Louis Adamic, "Aliens and Alien-Baters," *Harpers Magazine*, vol. 173, Nov. 1936, pp. 563-66.

Also she sought to have MacCormack's . . . FP letter to the president, May 25, 1934, pp. 2-3, Connecticut College.

To the social workers' publication . . . *Survey*, April 1934, p. 115.

Humanitarian considerations . . . MacCormack letter to Isador Lubin, Aug. 23, 1933; MacCormack letter of Aug. 4, 1933, Immigration Folder, Connecticut College. See FDR Press Conference No. 501, Nov. 18, 1939, pp. 239-40, FDRL.

. . . "real hardship cases . . ." FDR memo to FP, July 11, 1936; FP response, July 16, 1936, FDRL. FDR quote on immigration, *TRIK* p. 13. FDR's later reversal, Biddle, *In Brief Authority*, pp. 106-107.

134 . . . "a truly helpful institution . . ." D.W. MacCormack letter of Nov. 11, 1933, to branch and division heads, Immigration Folder, Connecticut College.

One from a counsellor-at-law . . . William J. Moran letter of Sept. 27, 1933; Immigration Folder, Connecticut College.

"Examined critically . . ." *The Anvil and the Plow*, Fiftieth Anniversary Publication (Washington, D.C.: U.S. Department of Labor, 1913-1963), pp. 71-72. On cabinet role, see Notes for Secretary of Labor's Address at Meeting of All Employees, Oct. 4, 1939, SL.

135 "The record must begin with 1933 . . ." FP, Report to the President on Ten Years' Achievements in Labor and Social Improvement," Dec. 31, 1943, p. 2, FDRL.

136 "It would mean putting . . ." FP, "Ten Years' Achievements," pp. 4-5.

On March fourteenth, he sent . . . FDR memo to George H. Dern, March 14, 1933, FDRL. At her first press conference . . . Furman, op. cit., p. At her first press conference . . . Furman, op. cit., p. 162.

William Green of the AFl . . . Babson, *Washington and the Revolutionists*, p. 109; Carter, op. cit., p. 164. FP's concerns for wage depression were recorded in Raymond Moley's diary, March 14, 1933; Moley, op. cit., pp. 267-69.

138 On March twenty-third, Frances testified . . . *Time*, April 3, 1933.

On April 5th . . . Secretary of Labor, *Twenty-first Annual Report*, U.S. Department of Labor, fiscal year ended June 30, 1933 (Washington, D.C.: Government Printing Office, 1934), CCC Files, FDRL.

In June, 1933, for the first time . . . Joint statement by ER and FP dated June 1, 1933, FDRL; Black, *Eleanor Roosevelt*, p. 162.

Although around 200,000 . . . Black, op. cit., p. 210.

Of the thirty dollars a month . . . FP, "Ten Years' Achievements," pp. 6-7.

The conference of labor leaders . . . FP's report to the AFL convention that fall attributed the ideas to the labor committee, AFL *Proceedings*, pp. 223-24; Secretary of Labor, *Twenty-first Annual Report*, pp. 5-6; also interview with Clara Beyer.

140 "The suggestions from labor . . ." Unpublished transcript of lecture, University of Illinois, 1953, pp. 162-63: Murray Edelman, "New Deal Sensitivity to Labor Interests," in Derber & Young, *Labor and the New Deal*, Schlesinger, op. cit., p. 301, cites FP's social-worker propensity to do things for labor as opposed to enabling labor to do for itself.

During Hoover's administration, Senator Hugo L. Black . . . *TRIK*, p. 198; *New York Times*, April 20, 1933. Black Bill through NIRA, Goldman, *Rendezvous With Destiny*, pp. 339-40; Lindley, op. cit., p. 154.

For political reasons . . . Hawley, *The New Deal and the Problem of Monopoly*, p. 22; FP's views, Schlesinger, op. cit., pp. 95, 97.

On April 25, 1933 . . . *New York Times*, April 26 and 28, 1933.

Among the spectators . . . *TRIK* p. 195; Black op. cit., pp. 130-31.

141 Within days of her testimony . . . *New York Times*, April 19, 1933; *Literary Digest*, April 29, 1933, pp. 5-6, FDRL; Official File 15, U.S. Department of Labor; Lindley, op. cit., p. 155.

On the positive side . . . FP, "Ten Years' Achievements," pp. 16-18.

A major function . . . *TRIK*, pp. 183-87; Also Wyzanski tribute.

142 . . . "a systematic, honorable method . . ." Secretary of Labor, *Twenty-first Annual Report*, pp. 1-3.

"John L. Lewis' . . ." Memorandum of conversation between Sidney Hyman and Frances Perkins, Washington, D.C., April 1949, FDRL. In a conversation with the author, FP noted that today's unions rely on excellent economists, and union leaders are better educated.

143 ". . . I have said . . ." Carlisle Bargeron, "A Person Named Perkins," *Commentator*, undated clipping, MHL.

144 "First, those wanting government . . ." Furman, op. cit., pp. 163-65.

Rather sensitive impressions . . . Margaret G. Bondfield, "Revolution in the U.S.A.," *Survey Graphic*, Vol. 22, No. 10, Oct. 1933, pp. 491-93.

145 "One error was . . ." Civil Service Commission folder; Cornell lectures; FP, "Eight Years as Madame Secretary."

Ike Hoover, the chief usher . . . New York *Times-Herald*, June 27, 1945. Parallels ER's handshaking technique described in Black, op. cit., p. 100. Regarding social obligations, ER, *This I Remember*, p. 94

146 . . . senators who wanted to speak . . . Ewan Claque, Oral History Collection, p. 176. For biting commentary, Helen R. Whitely, "Madame La Secretary Perkins," *American Mercury*, Dec. 1937, p. 422; also Gruberg, op. cit., n. 104, p. 289.

The labor union men . . . Labor union men rather liked demonstrating their good manners, according to interviews with Boris Shishkin and others. Robert Moses felt that their attitude toward FP "is a good deal like that of habitues of a water-front saloon toward a visiting slummer – grim, polite and unimpressed." *Current Biography*, 1940, p. 643.

. . . "the prefunctory side of social life . . ." Black, op. cit., p. 101.

The first of many . . . 1902 class letter, May 1933, MHL.

"A Senator called the President . . ." MWD, op. cit., vol. 1, p. 80.

147 In June, Goucher College . . . *Mount Holyoke Alumnae News*, Nov. 1933.

"Because having achieved . . ." *Capital Times*, June 19, 1933, in Division of Archives, University of Wisconsin.

For this particular function . . . Correspondence, June 3, 1933, in Division of Archives, University of Wisconsin.

That August . . . FP, "An Interstate Authority for Unemployment Insurance," *Survey*, Aug. 1933, pp. 275-76.

148 . . . the family's dog, Balto . . . *New York Times*, March 8, 1933.

In Washington, D.C., she shared . . . Interview with Averell Harriman, Jan. 16, 1970.

149 Mary Rumsey apparently knew everybody . . . Persia Campbell, *Consumer Representation in the New Deal*, pp. 38-39, who headed the New York State Consumer Council under Governor Averell Harriman, described Mary Rumsey as "a picturesque figure with great driving force." Boris Shishkin, Oral History, p. 591, Columbia University Library, noted the problem of being a woman administrator: "In those days it was – as in the case of Miss Perkins – a handicap." See also Schlesinger, op. cit., p. 130.

NRA's General Johnson . . . FP described the Consumers' Advisory Committee as a "last-minute thought" of her own, *TRIK*, p. 206. Hawley, op. cit., p. 76, recorded that with the aid of "Henry Wallace and FP, Mrs. Rumsey persuaded Johnson to acquiesce in the establishment of a Bureau of Economic Education headed by Paul Douglas of the University of Chicago and responsible for a limited experiment in the organization of county consumer councils." These did not prove to be effective pressure groups.

150 In the fall of 1933 . . . AFL *Proceedings*, 1933, pp. 222-30, includes some of her delightful anecdotes.

153 Elizabeth Brandeis scribbled . . . Letter of March 12, 1933 and CB response, SL.

154 "Amidst panic and confusion . . ." Text of Wyzanski tribute, April 1965, p. 3., MHL.

On one occasion, Mary recommended Ethel M. Smith . . . MWD letter to FP, April 28, 1933, AWC VII, Connecticut College.

155 ". . . Miss Perkins did not have to show . . ." MWD, op. cit., p. 83.

. . . not like Thomas Jefferson . . . MWD letter to FP, April 28, 1933, AWC VII, Connecticut College, p. 2, handwritten postscript.

James Farley, an impressively big man . . . Views on patronage, Farley, *Jim Farley's Story*, p. 5.

Yet his admiration . . . Interview with James Farley; also his *Behind the Ballots*.

On July 14, 1933, Frances sent a telegram . . . Caylor memoir, NYPL, Appointments while traveling were not uncommon, e.g., John Carmody, NLRB administrator records his N.Y.C. taxi appointment with FP, unpublished memoirs, p. 363, Columbia University Library.

157 When Edward McGrady . . . Description, Bernstein, op. cit., pp. 16-17.

158 With her usual candor . . . Carter, op. cit., p. 64, appointment letter of Aug. 18, 1933, from FP to FDR, FDRL.

. . . she accepted McGrady's resignation . . . Letter to FDR dated Aug. 26, 1937, FDRL. Negative review of relationship appears in Henry Ehrlich, "The Unpopular Mme. Perkins," *Boston Herald*, March 6, 1938, MHL.

To illustrate Frances's dawdling . . . MWD, op. cit., pp. 85-86. FDRL.

Frances appointed Altmeyer . . . Appointment letter from FP, May 26, 1934, DoL item 340526, National Archives.

159 "I hear John Lewis is miffed . . ." FDR memo to FP, Aug. 5, 1937, Labor Dept. Folder, PSF, FDRL.

W. Frank Persons was named . . . Various interviews. One atypical FP memo annotated in DoL shows her exasperation with Persons: "From now on, clear all appointments, promotions, etc., with me before acting – or else." Item 9340204 DoL #525; also 9340621 regarding N.R.S.

. . ." a great majority of the cases . . ." Secretary of Labor, *Twenty-first Annual Report*, p. 11.

160 At his first meeting with her . . . Isador Lubin, "The New Lead from Capitol Hill," *Survey*, March 1, 1932, p. 573 ff.

In December, 1933 . . . Authority to collect cost-of-living data, material dated Dec. 21, 1933, FDRL.

. . . stood by the secretary of labor's side . . . Marguerite Young, "Frances Perkins: Liberal Politician," *American Mercury*, Aug. 1934, p. 398.

In an interview . . . Information that follows from interview with Isador Lubin, July 1, 1970.

162 In March 1934 . . . Interview with Lawrence Oxley, Jan. 15 and 16, 1970, Washington, D.C.

163 The matter of industrial strikes . . . FP, *People at Work*, pp. 142, 159-61.

. . . "If only they would take us for granted" . . . AFL *Proceedings*, 1933, p. 227.

165 "THOUSANDS OF PEOPLE STRIKING . . ." And FP wire of Oct. 9, 1933, to Gov. James Rolph, Jr., FDRL.

167 . . . abhored the union leader's view . . . Memorandum of conversation between Sidney Hyman and FP, Washington, D.C., April 1949, FDRL. Bernstein, op. cit., p. 27, wrote that FP "had little confidence in the union movement as an instrument of social advancement." Her views changed along with the substantive development of the union movement, as her Cornell lectures clearly indicate.

That same month in Homestead . . . *TRIK* pp. 218-21; countless newspaper articles; Schlesinger, op. cit., p. 143; Committee of Education and Labor, "Violations of Free Speech and the Rights of Labor," Senate Report No. 151 (Washington, D.C.: Government Printing Office, 1941).

The president of the company . . . Letter from Charlton Ogburn, attorney, N.Y.C., Nov. 12, 1934, General Correspondence 1934, FDRL.

168 . . . a procedure known as the Reading formula . . . Witney, *Government and Collective Bargaining*, pp. 200-23.

Brooks, *As Steel Goes*, pp. 63-67.

"McGrady and Ma Perkins . . ." "Ma Perkins" was used derisively on the Hill, e.g., by Sen. Kenneth S. Wherry in a debate, April 29, 1943, with Gov. M.M. Neely; Stromer, *The Making of a Political Leader*, p. 35. Also interview with Professor J. Woodrow Sayre.

In the saloon, pool parlor . . . Interviews with members of Carpenters and Joiners of America; also reminiscences of Erling J. Holmen of the Dockbuilders Union.

. . . "the Government only gives A.F. of L. hearings . . ." Samples collected by W.A. Sabin, March 9, 1934, FDRL.

". . . I wish particularly . . ." John Dewey's letter for the president, dated April 26, 1934, General Correspondence 1934, FDRL.

According to Rexford Tugwell . . . Schlesinger, op. cit., pp. 390-92.

170 . . . she cabled him . . . FP cable and FDR's response, July 16, 1934, FDRL.

"Long distance calls, nervous, rushing . . ." *New York Times Magazine*, Aug. 5, 1934, pp. 3, 10.

171 On August fifteenth, FP drafted . . . Dated August 15, 1934; same praise for McGrady's work with Toledo Auto, 1936, FDRL.

. . . deportation of Harry Bridges . . . On May 23, 1934, Hoff of the Immigration Service reported lack of proof of Communist affiliation, only that Bridges was "chief agitator in strikes," 934 05 03, DoL notation, National Archives.

"We are all anxious . . ." FP to the Honorable Colonel Marvin H. McIntyre, June 8, 1934, FDRL.

The Department's "virtual monopoly . . ." Edelman credits this "informational advantage" with the measure of success in the codes' wage and hour provisions, Edelman, op. cit., pp. 167-68.

"Apparently the determination . . ." Clara Beyer's letter to Grace Abbott, June 23, 1934, SL. On May 18, 1935, FP wrote an emphatic memo to the president . . . "and I want to underscore the necessity of insisting upon the Board being in the Department of Labor."

172 "There had evidently been . . . Biddle, *In Brief Authority*, pp. 12-14.

. . ." on the alert to salvage . . ." Cornell lectures; John O'Donnell, "Capital Stuff," *New York News*, Sept. 5, 1935. FP was optimistic about business support for legislation based on the NRA. Price clauses in the codes actually hit at price-cutting by small business, Hawley, op. cit., p. 83.

"The labor protectives . . ." FP, "Ten Years' Achievements," p. 28; pp. 9-12 review high points of the first years in office, FDRL.

173 On February 21, 1935 . . . One interpretation: Senator Robert Wagner "would not oppose the Secretary's plan if she were going to be Secretary of Labor forever," Rauch, *The History of the New Deal, 1933-1938*, p. "The New Deal was already proliferating . . ." Biddle, *In Brief Authority*, p. 44. Shishkin claims FP won a Pyrrhic victory in that the executive order establishing the NLRB had written in the lower left-hand corner, "Approval recommended, FP, Secretary of Labor," Oral History, p. 628.

. . . AFL President William Green apologized . . . Philip Murray, President, CIO, also wrote a letter dated Dec. 20, 1941, to the president requesting that the Employment Service be under the jurisdiction of the Department of Labor, Labor Dept., May 1941-1945, FDRL.

"Labor is a bit sentimental . . ." NLRB Senate Hearings, pp. 52-55, 233-34; Bernstein, op. cit., p. 105.

Commissioners from the Conciliation Service . . . Kaltenborn, *Government Adjustment of Labor Disputes*, p. 25.

"The House Labor Committee . . ." In Department of Labor Library.

174 "The President of the United States . . ." John O'Donnell and Doris Fleeson, "Capital Stuff," New York *News*, July 6, 1935.

". . . well-informed writers as Dorothy Thompson . . ." Breen, op. cit., p. 73, footnote from William Leiserson's "What Can We Do About Strikes," *Survey Graphic*, March 1937, p. 21.

The NLRB had an erratic career . . . FDR discussed rationale, Press Conference No. 340, Jan. 29, 1937, p. 115 (124), FDRL.

175 "One of the best things . . ." AFL *Proceedings*, 54th AFL conference, 1934, p. 335 ff. Green's praise was genuine; John P. Frey documented Green's admiration for FP two months after her appointment in his unpublished memoirs, p. 623.

176 According to Francis Biddle . . . Biddle, *In Brief Authority*, p. 11.

"More pay, more comfort . . ." Babson, *Washington and the Revolutionists*, p. 108.

177 At least "That Woman!" . . . Letter to Marvin H. McIntyre, assistant secretary to the president, from Turner W. Battle, dated Sept. 13, 1934, FDRL.

. . ."has a shining new official car . . ." Peter Carter article in *Washington Herald* quoted in *Mount Holyoke Alumnae News*, May 1935.

"Gentlemen, did you know . . ." Interview with CB.

. . . she told *New York Times* reporter Alice Rogers Hager . . . Alice Rogers Hager, op. cit., pp. 3, 17.

178 In 1934 she awarded a red ribbon . . . MWD, op. cit., pp. 86-87; also interviews with CB.

According to Clara Beyer . . . Letter from CB to Elizabeth Brandeis Raushenbush, Aug. 12, 1955, SL.

"Maybe you think that the boys . . ." Schneiderman and Goldthwaite, op. cit., pp. 201-202.

At the October, 1935, convention . . . "Labor Laws and Their Administration," *Proceedings* of the 21st Convention of the International Association of Governmental Labor Officials, Asheville, N.C., Oct. 1935 (Washington, D.C.; Government Printing Office, 1936), p. 44. Memo from CB to FP, Oct. 16, 1935, cites singular success of this conference, and reflects the ageless petty concerns when a bureau chief hasn't been included in conference planning, SL. In answer to a criticism from Wyzanski, Beyer makes the important point that care is essential "to avoid over-organization so that it looks as if we come prepared to control every committee decision."

179 At the 1935 AFL conference . . . AFL *Proceedings*, 1935, pp. 209-17.

181 "She has flouted . . ." And Johnson's vocabulary, Ray Tucker, op. cit., pp. 16, 35. She also told a senator . . . Countless newspaper stories; also Lindley, op. cit., p. 289.

"Your questions don't make sense . . ." Cal Tinney, op. cit.

182 "I am a missionary at heart" . . . E.g., March 10, 1934, with cover letter by Mrs. Robert Bruere, PPF, FDRL.

"Women Want to Know . . ." "Women want to Know about the N.R.A.," written between June 14 and November 7, 1933, 19 pp., FDRL. Statements on leisure are also based on this article.

183 . . . her book *People at Work* . . . FP, *People at Work*.

. . . "236 reviews . . ." Letter from Mrs. Robert W Bruere dated June 27, 1934, FDRL. Alicia Patterson, in a New York *News* book review of March 27, 1934, called it "an honest and optimistic report," but objected to the "high-sounding phrases."

Lewis Gannet could only complain . . . Lewis Gannet, New York *Herald Tribune*, May 24, 1934, p. 19.

In the *Saturday Review of Literature* . . . Suzanne LaFollette, "Office and Authorship," *Saturday Review of Literature*, June 23, 1934, MHL.

. . . "Something more than welfare . . . " *The Nation*, June 20, 1934.

184 A popular mock-definition . . . *Survey*, Oct. 15, 1931, p. 108.

. . . "merely a social worker . . ." John L. Lewis's standard label for FP, Josephson, p, cit., p. 402.

But in the same year . . . Babson, *Washington and the Revolutionists*, pp. 81-118.

FP served on the President's Emergency Committee on Housing . . . FDRL; the Home Owners' Loan Act, Jan. 1934, *Annual Report*, p. 14; Eccles, *Beckoning Frontiers*, p. 146.

185 In June 1933 . . . FP, "Our Crime against Children," *Parents' Magazine*, June 1933, p. 13.

For a quarter of a century . . . FP repeated Sara N. Cleghorn's poem in her Syracuse speech Feb. 12, 1960.

186 In 1916 social workers . . . See FP, "Secretary Perkins Pleads for Child Labor Amendment," *New York Times*, Jan. 28, 1934, for comprehensive review; FP letter to editor, *New York Times*, June 20, 1933; Snowman, *America since 1920*, p. 49.

"May Susie Wash the Dishes?" . . . See Felt, op. cit., n. 27 for sample editorial by R.J. Plimpton, 1924-25. The N.Y. Child Labor Committee distributed editorials to counter these arguments, FDRL.

The president of the Carnegie Foundation . . . Quote attributed to Henry S. Pritchett, Ray Tucker, op. cit., p. 16.

. . . whether to the Wellesley College Institute . . . July 8, 1933, FDRL.

. . . or to the Na tional Business and Professional Women's . . . "Miss Perkins Asks Child Labor Ban," *New York Times*, Feb. 27, 1937. FP gave a similar message at the twenty-fifth anniversary dinner of the Children's Bureau, *New York Times*, April 9, 1937.

187 The Children's Bureau study . . . File memo of telephone call to Fitzgerald of the Labor Department advising that the report was not to be publicized or released by the department, signed S.T.E., FDRL.

The head of the Children's Bureau . . . Abbott, *From Relief to Social Security*, pp. 178, 181.

Frances immediately called . . . Her ambitions for the Children's Bureau work with crippled children appear in her letter to FDR, Dec. 13, 1935, FDRL.

She personally agonized over bill H.R. 3673 . . . Passed by the House, April 25, 1934, and the Senate, May 10, 1934, Immigration Folder, Connecticut College.

"The fact that I'm a woman . . ." FP, "Eight Years as Madame Secretary."

188 "I consider myself a good feminist . . ." *Survey*, August 1934.

"I asked Miss Perkins . . ." Alice Rogers Hager, op cit.; in abbreviated form, e.g., Tinney, op. cit.; Carter, op. cit., p. 175; Schlesinger, op. cit., p. 300.

Accolade to DoL . . . Hamilton, op. cit., p. 417

189 . . . "social feminists as a group . . ." O'Neill, *Everyone Was Brave*, pp. x, 142-43.

. . . Conservative social feminists . . . See Carl N. Degler, "Charlotte Perkins Gilman on the Theory and Practice of Feminism," *American Quarterly*, Spring 1956, Vol. 3, No. 1, pp. 21-39.

190 When *Survey* magazine asked . . . FP, "Do Women in Industry Need Special Protection?" *Survey*, Feb. 15, 1926, p. 529. Rejoinder by Elizabeth Faulkner Baker, "We Don't Know – ." The discussion that follows is based on these articles.

192 Professor Baker claimed . . . Conclusion regarding "women's sharp need" by Professor E.F. Baker appears in "The Legal Protection of Women in Industry," in Beard, op. cit., p. 441.

"On a number of occasions . . ." Schneiderman and Goldthwaite, op. cit., pp. 126, 173.

"He may have failed to see . . ." ER quote from Anderson to Battle, Nov. 11, 1933, FDRL.

Most of the act . . . "Married women's clause" repealed in 1937; also Hollander, *Quest for Excellence*, p. 235. FP had written earlier to the U.S. attorney general on this law requiring dismissal of "married women regardless of superior performance," June 14, 1933; Item bet. 00177 and 00184, National Archives. Popular opinion still held that women should stay at home, e.g. James Jemail, "The Enquiring Fotographer," New York *News*, July 26, 1937, p. 204.

193 Actually, household employees . . . "Out of the Kitchen," *Survey*, Sept. 1934, p. 290.

"Women need household help . . ." Informal conversation with Dr. Gwen Bymers, Jan., 1970. At a Cornell University College of Home Economics Institute FP claimed that in the early 1920s she had caused commotion by announcing that working wives could not afford to earn less than $4,000 a year (substantially higher than the national median salary) because of the need to pay a cook-housekeeper, a nurse for the children, and the waste in the use of food, supplies, equipment, and fuel. Also Syracuse *Herald-Journal*, April 3, 1962.

Women in political positions were supposedly . . . Ross, op. cit., p. 211; also O'Neill, op. cit.

194 "Suffragists never really thought . . ." Eudora Ramsay Richardson,

"Women's Rise to Power: A Denial That Women Are Politically Ineffective," *Forum*, Jan. 1937, p. 30; also Eunice Fuller Barnard, "Madame Arrives in Politics," *North American Review*, Nov. 1928, p. 553.

When the American Association of University Women . . . FP, "Women in Public Administration," pp. 11, 14.

195 "We must think of this responsibility . . ." FP, "Women in Public Administration," p. 16. Following the above she added, "It was Plato who said that creation is the victory of persuasion, not the victory of force." SL.

"It is fatal for a woman . . ." Woolf, *A Room of One's Own*, p. 181.

"Where women perform in all respects . . ." FP letter to Gen. Hugh S. Johnson dated Nov. 15, 1933, FDRL. John P. Frey, trade union official, recorded FP's private view of Johnson as "a man that could make plenty of trouble," unpublished memoirs, p. 556.

Eleanor Roosevelt shared Frances's indignation . . . Black, op. cit., p. 183.

196 Frances enjoyed a number of advantages . . . Repeated during interviews by virtually all who knew her.

One came from Judge Lila M. Neuenfelt . . . Letter from FP dated July 27, 1935, FDRL. On the Lucy Stone League stand on name retention, Breckinridge, op. cit., p. 123; also *Boston Evening Trans.*, March 1933, clipping in MHL. FP also wrote on the subject to Nancy Mae Anderson, d'Aline, Idaho, July 12, 1933; DoL item 00228, National Archives. The general doctrine appeared in *Smith* v. *U.S. Casualty Co.*, 197 N.Y. 420 (90 N.E. 747); *Roberts v. Mosier*, 35 Oklahoma 691 (132 Pacific Reporter 678); *Lane v. Duchac*, 73 Wisconsin 646 (41 N.W. Reporter 962); *Stokes v. State*, 46 Texas 357 (81 Southwestern Reporter, p. 1213).

198 He believed "no woman on earth . . ." Anderson, *Woman at Work* p. 151.

"When Frances Perkins came in . . ." Ibid., pp. 183, 184.

(Vice-president Nance Garner . . ." Bascom N. Timmons, "Garner's Story," Part I, *Colliers*, Feb. 21, 1948, p. 49.

199 Frances Perkins unthinkingly . . . FP repeated women's predilection for "service work where the factor of monetary profits is not the objective," in her speech to the D.C. Business and Professional Women's Club, July 16, 1937; reprinted, Appendix to the *Congressional Record*, July 29, 1937, 75th Cong., 1st Sess., p. 1909.

"I can well understand . . ." Anderson, op. cit. R.N. Baldwin corroborates, "She was . . . a little fearful, I think, of her position as the only woman member of the cabinet and therefore a bit cautious and self-conscious," unpublished memoirs, p. 215, Columbia University Library.

200 Mary Anderson's files contain . . . Women's Bureau file in FDRL. Regarding appropriations, on July 8, 1937, FP wrote Mark Van Kleeck to dispel the "false report" that she no longer regarded the Women's Bureau as important. She noted the difficulty in getting appropriations, and that men were eager to make the same gains as women such as the shorter workweek, etc., but that women-employing industries still had special problems, FDRL.

The University of California at Berkeley . . . Linn, op. cit., p. 412; also clippings from University of California, Los Angeles, files.

201 On November ninth . . . Founder's Day address and trustee correspondence in MHL and Mount Holyoke alumnae files.

203 On June 19, 1934 . . . OF, FDRL.

"Civilization cannot progress . . ." *Survey*, June 1933, p. 209. FP credited the impetus for the social security program to the Townsend Plan; foreword by FP, Witte, *The Development of the Social Security Act*, p. vi.

The president reflected . . . FP invited Sir William Beveridge to meet with administrators, economists, and labor leaders on unemployment relief; Oct. 20, 1933, Item 00357, National Archives.

"Don't forget this, will you? . . ." FP memorandum to FDR dated April 17, 1934, FDRL; also Cornell lecture, Nov. 7, 1957, p. 15.

204 Early in June, 1934 . . . Brown, *The Genesis of Social Security in America*, pp. 1-3.

So little money . . . Macmahon, Millett, and Ogden, *The Administration of Federal Work Relief*, discusses FERA contribution of partly interlocked personnel through Dec. 1934. FP's trepidations about having Social Security recommended to the next Congress appear in "Security Next," *Survey*, Sept. 1934, p. 288; also "Miss Perkins Asks Social Insurance," *New York Times*, Aug. 14, 1934, p. 3.

The forenoon of November fifteenth . . . Brown, op. cit., pp. 10-16. As governor, FDR strongly supported old age assistance, Greer, *What Roosevelt Thought*, p. 11; Schneider & Deutsch, op. cit., pp. 348-49.

205 "I provided one bottle . . . Cornell lecture, Nov. 12, 1957, p. 34.

"Chronological Summary of Activities of the Committee of Economic Security and Development in Social Security Legislation," AWC Perkins II, cv. 1a, Connecticut College. See also detailed article under FP's by-line,

"Basic Idea Behind Social Security Program," *New York Times*, Jan. 27, 1935; referred to in debate on how to fund Social Security, "How to Make Job Insurance a Failure," editorial, New York *News*, Feb. 10, 1935.

206 Her almost daily memoranda . . . E.G., "Miss Perkins asks Social Insurance," *New York Times*, Aug. 14, 1934; Memorandum to Colonel McIntyre, "Present State of the Economic Security Bill," March 15, 1935 FDRL.

207 . . . New York Board of Trade . . . "Trade Board Move Irks Miss Perkins,' *New York Times*, Dec. 13, 1934.

On January 26, 1935 . . . Letter in PPF, FDRL.

208 It seemed that representatives of the American Bankers Association . . . FDR Press Conference No. 201, May 3, 1935, vol. 5, p. 266.

The label "communist" . . . "Woman Accuses Miss Perkins of 'Soviet' Drive," *New York Daily Tribune*, April 8, 1935, clipping in Misc. File, FDRL. Phillips, *From the Crash to the Blitz, 1929-1939*, p. 289, places this at a congressional hearing.

209 "Secretary of Labor Frances Perkins, on Saturday . . ." "Ideals for All," *Wall Street Journal*, Dec. 16, 1935, SL.

Actually many social workers . . . Klein, *From Philanthropy to Social Welfare*, p. 151. See also FP "Social Security: The Foundation," *New York Times*, Aug. 18, 1935.

Jane Addams of Hull House . . . Letter to FDR dated March 8, 1935, FDRL.

The matter of where . . . Strong statement by FP in memo to the president, Feb. 25, 1935, with special reference to the Children's Bureau, followed by memo of May 15, 1935 with draft to the Department of the Interior telling them to discontinue recommending that the Children's Bureau go into the Office of Education, FDRL.

211 . . . "giving the relationship . . ." FP memo to FDR, March 19, 1935, with Thermofax copy of her proposed organization chart, FDRL.

On August 14, 1935, the president approved . . . "Almost six months to a day from the submission of the Committee's report to the President," HR 7260 Social Security, FDRL.

She was also to be honored . . . Social Security number 000-00-0001 went to Ida Fuller of Ludlow, Vt., the first beneficiary of retirement benefits starting Jan. 30, 1940, and ending 35 years later with her death at age 100. W. Jaynes Macfarlan, "Social Security Signed 25 Years Ago Today by FDR," Syracuse *Herald American*, Aug. 14, 1960; obituaries, *Time*, Feb. 10, 1975.

212 On August twenty-seventh, the Committee . . . Because Social Security was not part of the Department of Labor, FP wrote a memo to FDR dated Aug. 15, 1935, asking him to tell both the Social Security Board and the Labor Board to keep closely in touch with the secretary of labor so that "she may systematically report to you at the Cabinet Meeting about their progress," PSF, FDRL.

"The passage of this act . . ." Labor Day 1935 address, FDRL. She always regretted that health insurance had not been included. In the spring of 1963 as Regents Lecturer at UCLA she parenthetically stated, "We would have had health insurance, too, if we had been able to get it, but we couldn't get our information together quickly enough to get that part ready to present in the winter of 1935, so we let it go a year and by that time it was too late: the medical profession had found its voice and was not going to let it pass." FP and St. Sure, op. cit., p. 10.

"How nice of you dear F.D. . . ." Handwritten letter, Aug. 17, 1938, FDRL.

"It represented the thinking . . ." Cornell lectures. In an interview following her lectures at Princeton University, she is quoted as stating, "Social Security was the greatest thing I did for my country," adding, "President Roosevelt told me it really was my bill," Syracuse *Herald-Journal*, Oct. 26, 1961.

213 Frances showed the effect . . . MWD, op. cit., pp. 83-84, FDRL.

"Her sweet-tempered calm . . ." "Boston Girl First Woman Cabinet Member?," *Boston Post*, Jan. 5, 1933, Mount Holyoke alumnae files.

214 . . . Frances Perkins set up a Division of Labor Standards . . . See "Extension of Remarks of Hon. Robert F. Wagner of N.Y. in the Senate of the U.S.," June 15, 1937; Appendix to the *Congressional Record*, 75th Cong., 1st Sess., vol. 81, Pt. 10, pp. 1483-85.

. . . Dr. Hamilton received a wire . . . During an interview Clara Beyer said that the story as it appears in Hamilton, op. cit., pp. 391-94, confuses some of the facts. Clara Beyer played a significant role in bringing safe working conditions to the rayon industry.

215 . . . Works Progress Administration research on depression-youth . . . FP, "Ten Years' Achievements," pp. 31-32.

. . . "hungry, ragged . . ." Cornell Lecture, Recording Session No. 1, "Labor Union History & Administration," Feb. 6, 1957, pp. 26-27.

216 On June 12, 1934 . . . FP memo to CB; also Oct. 6, 1937; FDRL.

Dedication ceremonies . . . FP memo to FDR regarding dedication of the Labor Building, Feb. 14, 1935, FDRL.

Frances had wanted cork flooring . . . Truman Felt, Dayton *Daily News*, March 29, 1953; also DoL annotation 9340406, National Archives.

217 However, periodic checks on the private elevator . . . Interview with James Dodson, Washington, D.C., Jan. 15, 1970.

Somewhat more often she lunched . . . Various interviews.

She discovered to her horror . . . FP, "One Sixth of a Nation," p. 23. She believed "a large part of race prejudice is the poverty problem." interview with Lawrence Oxley. The Problem of unemployed blacks during WWII was covered in FP's lecture, "Labor Union History and Administration," Tape No. 11, April 24, 1957.

. . . warm support of Eleanor Roosevelt . . . Interview with Lawrence Oxley. For ER's close relationship with Mary McLeod Bethune, see Lash, *Eleanor Roosevelt*, pp. 81, 171.

218 She credited herself . . . FP and Henry Wallace worked with Mary Rumsey to bring about the Bureau of Economic Education and the county consumer councils; see Hawley, op. cit., p. 76. In a draft prepared for a presidential letter to Matthew Woll of the Union Label Trades Dept., AFL, Washington, D.C., FP wrote, "I have long been convinced that the consumer wields a great power which, if consciously used to support fair labor standards, would be of great benefit to workers and to those employers who cooperate in the maintenance of such standards. I trust that the Union Label Exhibition and the work of the Women's Auxiliaries will help to make the public aware of the tremendous influence it can exercise through wisely directed buying power . . ." Dated May 9, 1938, PPF 3189, FDRL.

A Department of Labor history . . . U.S. Department of Labor, *The Anvil and the Plow*, 1913-1963, p. 96.

"More than two-thirds . . ." Edited draft of untitled speech, 1936, p. 13, SL; Snowman, op. cit., p. 44; editorial, New York *News*, Nov. 15, 1933.

219 The United States joined . . . FP, "Ten Years' Achievements," pp. 21-27.

"I have always been very grateful . . ." FP letter to CB, SL.

"The top person gets the credit . . ." Telephone interview with Adolph Berle, New York City, Nov. 12, 1969.

"Without Frances Perkins, the U.S. membership . . ." Interview with C.W. Jenks, Principal Deputy Director-General, Aug. 1969, Geneva, Switzerland; Hamilton, op. cit., p. 339.

220 . . . the British economist John Maynard Keynes . . . *TRIK*, pp. 225-26. Many articles refer to her hands, which she used gracefully, and accented with bracelets.

Around this time C.W. Jenks, . . . Interview with C.W. Jenks.

"It is from the exchange . . ." Draft of suggested message to Congress signed by FP, SL.

Grace Abbott, as one . . . Anderson, op. cit., p. 213; Anderson's role in ILO, pp. 202-204.

221 . . ."contemptible trickery and gross fraud . . ." New York *News*, Dec. 26, 1934 clipping with handwritten letter to FDR suggesting that FP "may be of English extraction" and ILO membership "a stroke of English diplomacy," FDRL. Tinkham was discussed by C.W. Jenks with author.

"She has therefore gone out . . ." Furman, op. cit., p. 241.

222 Frances wrote a mutual friend . . . FP letter of July 18, 1936 to Howard Brubacker, FDRL. FP and FDR telegrams dated July 16 and 17, 1936, FDR, June 25, 1938, FDRL.

Here she was honored . . . New York *News*, July 30, 1936.

In the previous session of Congress . . . Report advising FDR of appropriations problem, May 27, 1935, FDRL.

223 "Her stature was rated high . . ." Clarence K. Streit, "Geneva's Acclaim," *New York Times*, Aug. 16, 1936.

In 1938 in the light . . . FP speech, International Labour Conference, 24th Session, 1938, pp. 195-98, ILO Library, Geneva, Switzerland.

First she stopped off briefly . . . Letter from Ambassador William C. Bullitt, American Embassy, Paris, France, to DFR, June 25, 1938, FDRL.

President Roosevelt had recruited Frances . . . John G. Winant had been president of the National Consumers League; MWD, op. cit., p. 16. Regarding political debt, Bellush, *He Walked Alone*, pp. 133-40. First regional conference in Havana under Winant's directorship was discussed in FP address to ILO Conference, April 15, 1943; excerpt in FP, "Ten Years' Achievements," p. 23.

Before resigning his position with the ILO . . . As Ambassador to England, Kingdon, *As FDR Said*, pp. 140-41, 143. Review of plans for wartime conference discussed with Jeff Rens in FP letter to Clara Beyer, Feb. 12, 1957, SL.

. . . And Frances Perkins's name . . . Rumors on FP's presidency in letter to FDR, dated Sept. 25, 1941, signed A.A.B., Jr., Assistant Secretary, Department of State; PSF State Department, FDRL.

224 At the meeting . . . Proposal by Assheton, British Empire delegate, International Labour Conference, 1941, New York and Washington, D.C., pp. 6, 7; FP acceptance speech, pp. 7-12; ILO Library, Geneva, Switzerland.

227 "Has not the fact . . ." Genevieve Forbes Herrick, "Madame Secretary Perkins Lauds American Gallantry," *Springfield Republican*, Feb. 10, 1935. Laski repeats this thought, *The American Presidency*, p. 79.

Hull, for one, wrote . . . Hull, op. cit., p. 210. Daniel Roper concurred that "her greatest and most beneficial accomplishments never found outlet in the public press," op. cit., pp. 294-95. Farley agreed: "She took many a blow for him (FDR) and served him loyally and faithfully at all times," *Jim Farley's Story*, pp. 115, 328.

As a practical person . . . Derber and Young, op. cit., p. 174.

228 Generally, Frances shared a warm feeling . . . In an interview at Princeton, N.J., FP reportedly said that cabinet members treated her "like a sister," Syracuse *Herald-Journal*, Oct. 26, 1961. On presidential greeting, Nelson, *Arsenal of Democracy*, p. 14; the exception, Dec. 7, 1941, *TRIK*, p. 379. On story-telling after cabinet meetings officially ended, Carter, op. cit., p. 205. The cabinet met Tuesdays and Fridays, eventually just Fridays; Hull, op. cit., p. 204; *TRIK*, p. 153.

Jurisdictional squabbles . . . Biddle, *In Brief Authority*, p. 187 regarding dirty linen; Gunther, op. cit., p. 133; Wann, *The President as Chief Administrator*, p. 49.

"But Miss Perkins loved . . ." Biddle, *In Brief Authority*, p. 15; High, *Roosevelt – and Then?*, pp. 183-84. A contradictory view is given by Crosby, *Essay on Roosevelt's Second Inaugural Address*, p. 44.

"I can't stop Harold . . ." Interview with James Farley. Farley told MWD: "Frances instructed them (the cabinet) too much, " p. 49, MWD, op. cit., FDRL.

229 European biographer Emil Ludwig . . . Ludwig, *Roosevelt*, p. 314. Various interviews.

Frances thought of him as . . . Cornell lecture identified as "Perkins's (sic) lecture," undated, transcribed, p. 22; lecture, Feb. 6, 1957, p. 4.

According to his recollections . . . Bascom N. Timmons, "Garner's Story," Part II, *Colliers*, Feb. 28, 1948, p. 22. Her own views on the questionable legality of the sit-down strike appear in the *New York Times*, May 27, 1937, in a published letter to Congressman John McCormack. Roper thought he was the only cabinet member to speak against sit-downs, op. cit., p. 295. Farley felt she could see the wrong of sit-downs, but "she was also familiar with wrongs on the other side," interview with author.

230 "As usual, only the President . . ." Schlesinger, op. cit., pp. 299, 300, 519. Only brain truster Raymond Moley presents contradiction: ". . . Roosevelt in his personal contacts with Mrs. Perkins (sic) was fairly abrupt and not always attentive to her somewhat lengthy discourses on social philosophy," op. cit., p. 239. See also Fenno, op. cit., p. 138. Ickes numbered among those who complained of her talking, and although "Horrible Harold" warred periodically with his colleagues in the cabinet, FP is cited as the only exception. Bargeron, *Confusion on the Potomac*, pp. 194-95; Bealle gives the harshest report, op. cit., p. 81; Farley, *Jim Farley's Story*, p. 54.

"You know, you discuss it . . ." Cornell lecture, Nov. 7, 1957. Wann, op. cit., reports on an interview with FP in 1953.

Assistant Secretary to the President, Marvin McIntire . . . McIntire, *White House Physician*, pp. 68-69; Gunther, *Roosevelt in Retrospect*, p. 40; *TRIK*, p. 323-24.

So Frances was quite surprised . . . Ray Tucker, op. cit., p. 16.

231 Roosevelt's son names her . . . James Roosevelt and Sidney Shalett, *Affectionately, F.D.R.*, p. 53.

At the *Washington Post's* author luncheon . . . FP, "Between the Lines of The Roosevelt I Knew." *Washington Post*, March 2, 1947, in CSCL. Rationale for *TRIK* in FP letter to Charley Ross, secretary to President Harry S. Truman, Dec. 9, 1946, HSTL.

232 . . . that Roosevelt lacked direction . . . FDR's statistics were "good guesses," including his "one-third of the nation is ill housed, ill clothed and ill fed," FP, "One Sixth of the Nation," p. 6. MWD and ER felt FP did not give FDR "much credit for knowing where he was going," letter from Fred W. Shipman, Director of FDR Library to MWD, Feb. 27, 1947, MWD file, FDRL. See also Fusfeld, op. cit., p. 4.

"What we need to do . . ." Cornell lecture, Dec. 16, 1957, p. 58.

"I have thought for some time . . ." FP memorandum dated March 12, 1935, to FDR, FDRL.

A master politician . . . Burns, op. cit., p. ix.

234 . . . executive assistants should be chosen . . . FDR Press Conference No.

336, Jan. 11, 1937, pp. 44, 52; Tugwell, op. cit., p. 354; rationale in Hobbs, *Behind the President*, p. 83.

"I'd like to see all . . ." Roper, op. cit., p. 268.

Frances criticized his approach . . . Cornell lectures and interviews. See Wann, op. cit., pp. 83, 98.

Actually Roosevelt's most overt action . . . E.g., FDR's editing of letter of regrets regarding AFL convention drafted by FP, dated Sept. 30, 1937, FDRL.

235 Rather, he asked his wife . . . ER memo to MWD, original in MWD letterbook marked Social Security, quoted in MWD, op. cit., vol. 1, p. 197. In a letter to the author, Herman Kahn, director of the Franklin D. Roosevelt Library, states that matters such as this are always "approached in a gingerly fashion," Sept. 19, 1960. The Smith diary states that FP "did not know, of course that the President had asked us not to discuss the moving of the Employment Service with her," FDRL.

"In retrospect, one wonders . . ." *TRIK*, p. 385.

Roosevelt at times went directly . . . Wann, op. cit., p. 69.

Roosevelt's wife, Eleanor, also did a bit . . . Tugwell, op. cit., p. 527.

Eleanor Roosevelt took umbrage . . . Furman, op. cit., p. 165; Stiles, op. cit., p. 249; Black (then of United Press), op. cit., *Roosevelt*, p. 93.

236 "You girls have got to realize . . ." Elliott Roosevelt, op. cit., p. 998. "I'm glad the 'boys,' as we always have called them, liked it," FP to CB, Oct. 22, 1959, SL.

"Mrs. Perkins was remarkable . . ." Lash, op. cit., p. 167.

These decided that Frances Perkins was a Jewess . . . New York *Herald Tribune*, April 5, 1936; Carlisle Bargeron, "A Person Named Perkins," *Commentator*, undated clipping, MHL. For review of xenophobes, Louis Adamic, "Aliens and Alien-Baiters," *Harpers Magazine*, vol. 173, Nov. 1936, pp. 561-72.

. . . a genealogist from Boston . . . MWD, op. cit., p. 88.

237 Finally Frances wrote a public letter . . . FP letter to Mrs. W. MacMillan, Essex House, New York, April 1, 1936, FDRL. This letter states her birth date as April 10, 1882; *New York Times*, April 5, 1936.

In 1960 when a group of Cornell . . . Interview with Professor Woodrow Sayre. She confessed her age to the Josephsons, *Al Smith*, p. 104.

238 "One of the most interesting phenomena . . ." John Kenneth Galbraith, "The Landlord of the Public Estate," *Reporter*, Oct. 31, 1957, p. 45.

. . . "the knees of our rugged individualists . . ." Kingdon, op. cit., pp. 210-11.

"Criticism, unless constructive . . ." McIntire, *White House Physician*, pp. 77-78.

". . . the wife of someone . . ." George Wolfskill and John A. Hudson, *All But the People* (London: The Macmillan Co., 1969), pp. 50-51, 271-72; Encyclopedia Britannica Library Research.

Author Morris Bealle wrote . . . Bealle, op. cit., p. 79. The Bureau of Standards label for her black dresses appears frequently.

"One may guess from her anterooms . . ." Ludwig, op. cit., p. 315. James Dodson during an interview with the author said the staff did not feel uneasy about having a lady as boss, Jan. 15, 1970.

"Why should people strike . . ." Cornell tape, Dec. 16, 1957, p. 3. Leuchtenberg, op. cit., p. 108.

240 . . . the lowest third of all American families . . . Schlesinger, *The New Deal in Action*, p. 29.

Frances remembered that Samuel Gompers used to say . . . Cornell lecture, Dec. 16, 1957, p. 29.

Frances met with steelworkers . . . *TRIK*, pp. 218-20; the story appears in articles and her Cornell lectures; also Senate Report No. 151, "Violations of Free Speech and the Rights of Labor," Committee of Education and Labor, 1941; Vorse, *Labor's New Millions*, p. 46; Schlesinger, *The Coming of the New Deal*, p. 143.

241 "We attempted to heal the breach . . ." Cornell lecture, tape No. 11, April 24, 1957, pp. 17-18, 23. On open break in unions, Nov. 9, 1935, see Creel, *Rebel at Large*, p. 299. New York City Mayor Fiorello LaGuardia wrote a detailed analysis and recommendations on the rift and strikes to FDR, June 10, 1938, FDRL. Galenson, *The CIO Challenge to the AFL*, p. 47 ff.

242 The sit-down strike in the auto industry . . . *TRIK*, pp. 319-27. Logic, objectivity, and human concern characterize Sidney Fine's *Sit-Down*, pp. 254-55. See also Beasley, *Knudson*, pp. 170-71; Vorse, *Labor's New Millions*, pp. 73-79; Alinsky, *John L. Lewis*, pp. 114, 125; Sulzberger, *Sit Down with John L. Lewis*, pp. 74-75.

"I have been all day in conference . . ." FP memo to FDR dated Jan. 19, 1937, PSF, FDRL.

243 ". . . An episode like this . . ." Galenson, op. cit., p. 139. In her personal

view, the sit-down strike was "full of hazards" to trade union development and should be abandoned, "Sit-Down Perilous, Miss Perkins says," *New York Times*, July 4, 1937. See also Lunt, *The High Ministry of Government*, pp. 171-80.

4, 1937. See also Lunt, *The High Ministry of Government*, pp. 171-80.

On January twenty-seventh, the secretary . . . *New York Times*, Jan. 28, 1937.

"This morning, when I woke up . . ." FDR Press Conference No. 340, Jan. 29, 1937, FDRL.

245 The response to Frances's request . . . Fine, op cit., pp. 257-59, 333. FP's memo on FDR conversation with principals in strike, Feb. 5, 1937, in PSF, FDRL.

"I hope some day . . ." FDR letter to Edward A. LeRoy, Union Club, Park Ave. & 69th St., New York, Feb. 2, 1937, in PPF, FDRL.

Many more requests came . . . On the "two-fisted male" see especially FDR Official File — Misc. Labor Department, May 1941-1945, FDRL. Bernarr Macfadden's front-page story, "A Nation-Wide Demand for the Resignation of Madam Perkins," *Liberty*, Oct. 22, 1938, was clipped and mailed to the president, frequently with ugly comments. The American Legion printed up a list of charges and a resolution urging FP's removal, and quantities of these were mailed to the White House. A rare laudatory article by Owen L. Scott, "FP Held Satisfactory Labor Secretary," appeared in the *Springfield Republican*, Feb. 7, 1937, MHL.

"Mme. Perkins, we believe . . ." New York *News*, Dec. 2, 1937. On July 3, 1937, the *News* said FP echoed the president's sentiments: "A plague on both your houses," and noted that both parties prefer "a good, bloody, long-drawn-out fight better than they like a quiet, bloodless and no doubt tedious round-table discussion of points in dispute."

246 "Well may FDR Boast . . ." *Congressional Record*, June 15, 1937, 75th Congress, First Session, Vol. 81, part 2, pp. 5736-5737.

"Secretary Perkins' suggestion . . ." and "I never made any such . . ." "Miss Perkins Denies Making Any Proposal to Have Steel Chiefs Held for Signing," *New York Times*, June 27, 1937.

248 President Roosevelt had decided . . . Leed, *Government and Labor in the United States*, p. 146. FP's statement on the Fair Labor Standards Bill before the Joint Hearing of the Senate Committee on Education and Labor and HR Committee on Labor, June 4, 1937 in Appendix to the *Congressional Record*, vol. 81, pt. 10, p. 1483.

The AFL and CIO opposed . . . Patterson, *Congressional Conservatism and the New Deal*, p. 150; Southerners feared the loss of competitive advantage, p. 152.

249 According to Dr. Jonathan Grossman . . . Grossman, *The Department of Labor*, p. 198; also interview with author. Some positive effects appear in FP, "Minimum-Wage Standards Must Be Preserved," Labor Information Bulletin, vol. III, no. 7, July 1936 (Washington, D.C.: Bureau of Labor Statistics), pp. 1, 2. Her analysis of wartime effects appear in the Secretary of Labor, Thirtieth *Annual Report*, 1942, p. 151.

Periodically Frances received . . . Memo from FDR to secretary of labor, marked confidential, Aug. 29, 1935, and from FDR at Hyde Park, Sept. 18, 1935, in Misc., FDRL. Detailed memo from FP to the president on West Coast labor situation, Sept. 21, 1937, FDRL.

To avoid a tie-up . . . Letter from Harry Bridges to the author, Aug. 5, 1969.

The tense situation caused the president . . . FDR Press Conference No. 322, Sept. 25, 1936, pp. 122-23, FDRL.

250 During this time . . . Telephone interview with Judge Charles E. Wyzanski, Boston.

By January, 1938, the Harry Bridges case . . . For a full review, Ogden, *The Dies Committee*, pp. 69-111; also *TRIK*, pp. 315-19. Biddle's *The Fear of Freedom* presents his views as attorney general.

". . . ." that neither through fear nor cowardice . . ." Secretary of Labor, Twenty-Seventh *Annual Report*, Fiscal Year Ended June 30, 1939, pp. 12-13, 213-221.

Solicitor Wyzanski tried to persuade . . . Telephone interview with Judge Charles E. Wyzanski.

251 "Secretary of Labor Perkins . . . New York *News*, April 24, 1939.

John P. Frey, a metal trades . . . Frey, unpublished memoirs, pp. 509, 699-700.

James Farley openly declared . . . Derber and Young, op. cit., p. 164. In an interview with the author, Farley had vivid recollection of the matter.

On June 6, 1938, Representative Martin Dies . . . "Perkins Won't Evict Bridges: Chides Dies," New York *News*, Aug. 31, 1938. Ogden, op. cit., pp. 64-65; Dies, *Martin Dies' Story*, pp. 106-107. On Oct. 29, 1938, Martin Dies wrote a twenty-four page letter to Robert H. Jackson, solicitor general, Department of Justice, on FP's withholding of evidence, misrepresentation to committee, DoL 04320, National Archives.

252 "Slowly but surely . . ." John O'Donnell and Doris Fleeson, "Bridges' Deportation Likely Cause Celebre," New York *News*, Feb. 14, 1938.

Francis Biddle, who became involved . . . Biddle, *The Fear of Freedom*, pp. 79, 114-17. Origins of D.C. "red rider" amendment, Ogden, op. cit., p. 39.

. . . Father Charles E. Coughlin . . . Father Coughlin said of FP's three-cornered hats: "one corner for communism, one for socialism and one for Americanism," "Coughlin Declares Rome Report a Lie," *New York Times*, Sept. 7, 1936.

Action against Frances Perkins . . . *Congressional Record*, 76th Cong., 1st Session, vol. 84, pt. 1, pp. 703-11; New York *News*, Jan. 25, 1939.

253 "Mr. Speaker, on my own . . ." Secretary of Labor, Twenty-Seventh *Annual Report*, pp. 220-21; the entire text appears in *New York Times*, Feb. 9, 1939, p. 14; also front-page story, "Miss Perkins Tells Committee Bridges Gets No Favoritism."

254 Then as now, the general public . . . "Impeachment: Its History," *Civil Liberties*, Jan. 1974, pp. 6-7.

The highest-ranking elected official . . . Stan Isaacs, "History Ignores William Sulzer," *Pensacola News-Journal*, July 28, 1974.

. . . William W. Belknap . . . George Rothwell Brown, "Political Parade," *Washington Times*, Jan. 24, 1939. See Grossman, op. cit., p. 23, on the impeachment of Assistant Secretary of Labor Louis Post under Wilson, also on failure to deport immigrants.

. . . January 24, 1939, an eager press corp . . . FDR Press Conference No. 520, FDRL.

255 ". . . first, to state . . ." "Statement of Secretary of Labor Perkins before the House Judiciary Committee," Feb. 8, 1939, SL. Entire text in *New York Times*, Feb. 9, 1939.

256 On March ninth Clara Beyer . . . CB to MWD, March 9, 1939, SL.

Not read into the *Record* . . . Report No. 311 to accompany H. Res. 67, p. 10.

Mary Dewson wrote . . . MWD, op. cit., p. 82.

257 "Don't talk foolish." . . . Biddle, *The Fear of Freedom*, p. 297. FP tried to resign a number of times; another FDR reaction in *TRIK*, p. 136.

"We know not only that our liberties . . ." FP, "The ILO as an Agency of Democracy," Philadelphia, pp. 4-7, SL.

Hardly two days after . . . NBC radio address on immigration laws, March 29, 1939, FDRL.

. . . incensed Representative John A. Martin . . . *Congressional Record*, April 3, 1939, 76th Congress, First Session, pp. 3-7 in MHL.

259 Sophonisba P. Breckenridge . . . Letter to FDR dated May 9, 1939, FDRL.

On April 27, 1939 Clara Beyer wrote . . . SL. See also Polenberg, *Reorganizing Roosevelt's Government*, p. 90. The unpublished memoirs of Harold D. Smith, Columbia University Library, reveals her true hurt over the Employment Service shift, which she saw as " . . . a slap at her and she wondered how many more such slaps she would be justified in taking."

In 1940 when the House voted . . . Leed, op. cit., pp. 176-78.

Harry Bridges busied himself . . . Biddle, *The Fear of Freedom*, p. 299.

In 1947, the stocky, choleric J. Parnell Thomas . . ." Encyclopaedia Britannica Library Research Service; M. Lehman, "White Knight or False Prophet," *New York Times Magazine*, Aug. 1, 1948, p. 11 ff. Dies, op. cit., p. 84, presents an "everyone-does-it" defense of Thomas.

260 She answered simply . . . Various interviews. Cynthia Lowry, "A Backward Glance by Miss Perkins," AP story datelined July 6, 1957, clipping in FDRL.

263 Public opinion polls ranked unemployment . . . Bailey, *The Man in the Street*, p. 119.

"Why doesn't some government department . . ." NBC Blue Network, April 20, 1939, FDRL. Dispute on unemployment figures with Sen. Arthur H. Vandenberg, New York *News*, April 20, 1937; Morgenthau had urged a census of the unemployed but FP questioned its value, Blum, *From the Morgenthau Diaries*, p. 243.

265 ". . . we no longer look at life . . ." FP's speech to editors of college papers, June 6, 1939, PPF, FDRL.

"And it won't be a woman either!" *TRIK*, p. 117.

"Oh, I have been reading that . . ." FDR Press Conference No. 655, June 25, 1940. See also *New York Times* front-page story,"Miss Perkins Quits Cabinet – Views Her Job As Finished," Nov. 25, 1940. Repeat perfor-

mance, Press Conference No. 734, April 11, 1941. FDRL.

New York City's Mayor Fiorello LaGuardia . . . 1941 postal card campaign in Official File – DoL, FDRL. See also New York *News* editorial on "persistent rumours," Nov. 28, 1940. LaGuardia purportedly insisted "on the War Department or nothing"; W.F. Holloway, April 10, 1941, OF DoL, FDRL.

"Just another story . . ." FDR Press Conference No. 734, April 11, 1941, p. 244, FDRL.

"Many people have thought . . ." Letter to FP, June 12, 1941, FPP, FDRL.

"This labor situation is a disgrace . . ." Letter from Arthur J. Smith, Toledo, Ohio, April 1, 1941. Ouster demands were renewed with the Allis-Chalmers strike, OF, FDRL. On FDR's exasperation with perpetual labor problems, Elliott Roosevelt, op. cit., pp. 1462-63.

"She is lacking . . ." April 29, 1941, OF, FDRL. In a letter to the author, dated Aug. 12, 1969, Dirksen would not reevaluate his appraisal of FP.

266 . . . and the president tried to put them . . . Memo on strikes, May 1, 1941, FDRL.

Writers covering the forties . . ." The Bypassed Lady," editorial, *Boston Herald*, Jan. 3, 1944, FDRL. See also Bargeron, *Confusion on the Potomac*, pp. 111-12.

"She was at her best . . ." ER and Hickok, op. cit., pp. 193-94.

268 With her daughter married . . . Various interviews, Cornell University.

On Sunday, December seventh . . . *TRIK*, p. 378; Biddle, *In Brief Authority*, p. 206.

On a note pad . . . FDRL. On FP's resistance to the National Mediation Board, forerunner of the War Labor Board, see Johnson, *1600 Pennsylvania Avenue*, p. 149.

269 . . . efforts of the National Safety Council . . . Memo from FP to the president, July 25, 1941; answered affirmatively by M.H. McIntyre, Aug. 19, 1941; see also letter of July 10, 1941 on Federal Interdepartmental Safety Council; FDRL.

". . . In addition to the loss . . ." "To establish Safe and Healthful Working Conditions in Industry," Hearings before a Subcommittee on the Committee on Labor, HR 2800, 78th Cong., 1st Sess., Dec. 31, 1943.

"Those days," she remembered . . . FP, "Eight Years as Madame Secretary," p. 78; *Fortune* story told to Katherine Hammill, carbon copy in folder 998-WRC - Connecticut College. The Department of Labor's view on strikes appears in a letter over FP's signature to Harold D. Smith, Bureau of the Budget, June 18, 1943, FDRL.

A Harvard Law School professor . . . Cornell lecture, tape no. 10, April 17, 1957, transcribed, pp. 14, 15, 21-23. Also Clara Beyer memo dated May 28, 1943, DoL Library.

270 "There were elements . . ." Cornell lecture, April 17, 1957, p. 15.

In one plant in three weeks' time . . . Address before the Canadian-American Women's Committee on International Relations, Montreal, Canada, April 15, 1943, SL. FP also used "Rosie the riveter" phrase in Syracuse speech Feb. 12, 1960.

. . . examined production output curves . . . Secretary of Labor, Thirtieth *Annual Report*, 1942, p. 52-53.

To combat her own fatigue . . . Various interviews.

. . . Except when photographers caught her . . . "Hard hat" photos in newspapers nationwide, April 25, 1940.

271 "They stopped me . . ." FP Cornell lecture, "Labor Union History and Administration," April 24, 1957, tape no. 11, pp. 13-14.

Frances herself boasted . . . Interview with Professor Woodrow Sayre.

She opposed the War Manpower Commission . . . Cornell lecture, tape no. 10, April 17, 1957, pp. 7-9.

272 "At his direction I sat in . . . *TRIK*, p. 360.

. . ." they want assurance . . ." The Full Employment Act passed in 1946 was prepared in the last year of Roosevelt's administration, according to FP & St. Sure, op. cit., p. 15; radio address at Town Hall, Jan. 19, 1943, FDRL; "New Perkins Social Security Plan Raises Payroll Levy to 10 P.C.," *Journal of Commerce*, Jan. 20, 1943, SL; FP memorandum, Feb. 12, 1943, PSF, DoL; Elliott Roosevelt, op. cit., pp. 1401-1402.

Frances also assured the president . . . FP's "Ten Years' Achievements" pp. 53-54; also VF Biog.-Perkins, DoL; FP memo to FDR, March 31, 1945, DoL.

In April, 1944, Philadelphia . . . "Verbatim Report of the Proceedings," 26th Session, pp. 1-2, 22-26, 257, ILO, Geneva, Switzerland.

Elizabeth Johnstone of the ILO staff . . . Interview with the author, Geneva, Switzerland.

One of Frances's last reports . . . Peacetime problems as FDR-FP concern, "Ten Years' Achievements," pp. 53-54. Similar ideas presented in "Social

Security Extension Plea by Labor Sec'y," Jan. 18, 1943, *Back Bay Merchants' Paper*, and "New Perkins Social Security Plan Raises Pay Roll Levy to 10 P.C.," *Journal of Commerce*, Jan.20, 1943, SL.

274 . . . thought she was lonely. . . . Maurice F. Neufeld's eulogy for her requiem mass, May 18, 1965, refers to FP's gallantry "in the grip of enduring tragedy and years of loneliness." Also Mary Dublin Keyserling interview, April 20, 1970, Syracuse, N.Y.

Sometimes she joined . . . Rosenman, op. cit., pp. 343-44.

" . . . we'd have a woman president ." . . . Hassett, *Off the Record with F.D.R.*, p. 238. Thomas, *Franklin Delano Roosevelt*, p. 162; Kingdon, op. cit., p. 57; ER, op. cit., p. 249.

At a state dinner for Stanislaw Mikolajczyk . . . ER and Anna Roosevelt Boettiger (Halstead) were the only other women present. Thomason and Perkins flanked the president; Hassett, op. cit., 248-49.

A few weeks later the cabinet members . . . Ibid., p. 260.

On July 10, 1944 . . . Elliott Roosevelt, op. cit., p. 1519.

276 In October, 1944 . . . Josephson and Josephson, op. cit., p. 471.

His assurances that he would name . . . Various clippings in FDRL. Also see undated letter from Felix Frankfurter enclosing article from Louisville *Courier-Journal*, Jan. 1, 1945, Misc. file, FDRL.

Her five-page documentary . . . FP to FDR dated Dec. 1, 1944, 5 pages long, in PSF, FDRL; Washington *Daily News*, Jan. 19, 1945.

Three days before the inauguration . . . New York *News*, Jan. 19, 1945.

". . . there were three of us . . ." Press Conference No. 990, Jan. 19, 1945, p. 44, FDRL.

Frances Perkins recorded what . . . *TRIK*, p. 393.

On January 22, 1945 . . . Elliott Roosevelt, op. cit., p. 1569; *New York Times*, Jan. 23, 1945. Rose Schneiderman wrote on Jan. 23, 1945 thanking FP for retaining FP in post; Misc. file, FDRL. ER and Hickok, op. cit., wrote that FP could not refuse "a weary, preoccupied President," p. 194.

277 . . . the war would end by May . . . *TRIK*, p. 74.

. . . weeping soundlessly . . . Asbell, *When F.D.R. Died*, p. 104 and photo; Biddle, *In Brief Authority*, p. 360.

Although Truman told a confidante . . . Harold D. Smith, unpublished memoirs, vol. 1, p. 28 ff. Smith's conference with HST took place on April 26, 1945, FDRL.

"Miss Perkins was among the first . . ." A concise, one-page letter of resignation "to take place at the President's convenience," dated May 21, 1945, HSTL. Truman, *Memoirs*, p. 325; also p. 96. HST's acceptance, dated May 23, 1945, particularly notes the reflection of her social philosophy in the Fair Labor Standards Act, the National Labor Relations Act and the Social Security Act.

Frances led the moving . . . V-E Day service, May 8, 1945; address in FPP, SL. She read the *Te Deum* by St. Ambrose, Psalm 100, the *Jubilate Deo*, and concluded with everyone saying the Lord's Prayer.

On May twenty-third . . . Telegram drafted by Hassett in PPF 1668, HSTL; also her acknowledgment dated June 30, 1945.

278 During her last weeks . . . June 29, 1945, material and note to Schwellenback regarding organization of Labor Department, PPF 15, HSTL; also Box 165, National Archives.

Daniel W. Tracy, the assistant . . . Washington *Times-Herald*, June 27, 1945, Vertical File, DoL Library.

"I salute you . . ." Truman's telegram from San Francisco, June 26, 1945, PPF 1668, HSTL.

. . . "wozzy in the head" . . . *Herald Tribune*, March 30, 1940; Benjamin Stolberg, op. cit.

. . . his wife was her greatest admirer . . . Interview with Isador Lubin, July 1, 1970.

The *New York Times* editorialized . . . Quoted in the *Journal of the American Association of University Women*, Fall 1945, p. 41; reprinted by Mount Holyoke Alumnae Office, Feb. 1946.

279 "I'm going into private life . . ." Washington *News*, Sept. 13, 1946, CSC.

. . . she penned a letter . . . Handwritten to HST from FP, New Castle, Maine, Aug. 16, 1945, PPF 1668, HSTL. His response of Aug. 20, 1945, indicated that he had plans for her to work for him again.

One from Grace Abbott's sister . . . Letters received through Dec. 1945, OF 670-A, HSTL. Women in World Affairs letter acknowledged Oct. 26, 1946, PPF 1668, HSTL.

"This is a tough baby . . ." Hassett's memo dated Feb. 14, 1946, refers to FP's statement as old, "but the best and most recent thing we have," OF 120-A, HSTL. David K. Niles, administrative assistant to HST, wrote that the "Equal Rights thing is dynamite whichever way you place it," Feb. 18, 1946. FP, "Comments to the Judiciary Committee of the House of Representatives, July 1944," mimeo, DoLL; ER's statement of opposition

to the ERA, June 1, 1946, 120-A, HSTL. FP refused to donate funds to the National Woman's party in a sharply worded letter of criticism dated July 10, 1944, SL.

280 . . . to attend the ILO conference . . . FP letter to HST from Paris, Nov. 14, .1945, PPF 1668, HSTL. International Labour Conference, Twenty-seventh Session, 1945, Paris, p. 137, ILO Library, Geneva, Switzerland.

. . . an unexpected gift from President Truman . . . Acknowledged by FP on Dec. 29, 1945, FPF 1668, HSTL.

"I had a dreadful time . . ." *Washington Post*, March 2, 1947, CSC Library. Library.

Frances's husband, Paul . . . Letter from Paul Wilson to Howard Brubacker, May 31, 1946. On Jan. 5, 1947, he wrote of the book that he believed it was "filled with good solid information and sound judgments." He urged Frances to work with a collaborator on a movie of FDR's life (letter to Brubacker, Feb. 2, 1947), FDRL.

281 Taubman called her . . . Telephone interview, Jan. 1970.

283 Woodrow Wilson had been the first . . . Gruberg, op. cit., p. 136.

The morning of September twelfth . . . "P" General Correspondence 32 (1945-1946), HSTL.

While some viewed . . . *Washington Star*, April 12, 1953; "Perkins Appointment Boosts Women's Role in Government," *Christian Science Monitor*, Sept. 14, 1946.

. . . Which took less than one minute . . . *Washington Star*, Jan. 21, 1947, CSC Library and Personal 2 (1947), HSTL.

As a commissioner . . . *Washington Post*, Jan. 25, 1948, CSCL.

284 "The personnelists who packed . . . "Miss Perkins Pokes Fun at CSC Rules," in the *Federal Diary*, clipping in CSCL.

Newspapers quickly sensed a controversy . . . Joseph Young, "Miss Perkins Opposes Flemming on Issue of Personal Freedom for U.S. Employees," *Washington Star*, Nov. 14, 1946.

Frances next attacked . . . Natalie Davis Springer, "FP is no Jargonee," unidentified clipping; Jeanne Rogers, " 'Governmental' Writing Hit by Miss Perkins in Talk," *Washington Star*, Jan. 27, 1949; Genevieve Reynolds, "Vets aren't 'Ousting' Women from Jobs, says Miss Perkins," *Washington Post*, Feb. 24, 1947, CSCL.

285 During the Korean conflict . . . Glendy Culligan, "Stenographers in Demand for Civil Service Army," *Washington Post*, Nov. 8, 1941.

"Even the simple task . . . FP, "U.S. & Us," Washington *Times-Herald*, Aug. 20, 1951.

"It is a source of pride . . ." "Civil Service Held Tax Bureau Need," *New York Times*, Oct. 27, 1951.

286 "So long as we are part . . ." U.S. CSC Addresses, vol. 2, League of Women Voters, CSCL.

"No program of social assistance . . . *New York Times*, Nov. 15, 1950.

The Society for Personnel Administration . . . U.S. CSC Addresses, vol. 2, May 2, 1952, CSCL.

The American Personnel and Guidance Association . . . Ibid., March 31, 1953, CSCL.

"Political science is not to be confused . . . Ibid., is not to be confused . . . Ibid., Roosevelt College, Chicago, Illinois, Oct. 19, 1950, CSCL.

287 They should know as much . . . Ibid., March 31, 1953, CSCL.

In March of 1952 . . . *Washington Star*, March 4, 1952; New York *News*, March 5, 1952.

At the end of May . . . Mount Holyoke alumnae letter, June 7-8, 1948, MHL.

288 "I didn't hear one biting remark . . ." Mount Holyoke alumnae letter, May 30-June 2, 1952, p. 6, MHL.

Paul Wilson died . . . *Washington Star*, Jan. 1, 1953. President Truman's letter of condolence dated Jan. 1, 1953, refers to Paul Wilson's "real contribution to good government in New York," PPF 1668, HSTL.

Her last day in office . . . *Washington Star*, April 12, 1953; CSCL. "FP, The First Woman in Cabinet, Is Dead," *New York Times*, May 15,1965; Encyclopaedia Britannica Library Research Service.

Jerry Klutz . . . *The Federal Diary*, undated, CSCL.

. . . she could not fathom the rift . . . Various interviews. Also speech at American Historical Association, *New York Times*, Dec. 30, 1960. Blasted in Moses, op. cit., p. 39.

"Great demand for a lecture . . ." FP to MWD, March 15, 1955. Although friends MWD and Polly Porter lived in Maine, she did not consider retiring there. "*Me*. I'm strictly a city girl & know I am better off where the white lights blaze & the motors honk & where I can drop in at the Club for a gossip of an afternoon." Letter misdated April 15, 1948, probably written 1958 (her grandson is three years old), FDRL.

She would have liked . . . Reba Morse wrote MWD, Dec. 29, 1954, that FP came to New York to rerent her apartment, but had no luck selling the Washington, D.C., house, FDRL.

290 "It was something too . . ." At age seventy-seven, FP gave reporter Cynthia Lowry the humble view that she was unimpressed with her career. "What you might say," she said with a smile, "is that I happened to be a woman born in my own time." This obscure statement was intended to hide the fact that her career amazed and delighted her.

In 1955 she wrote Mary . . . FP to MWD, Sept. 19 and Nov. 15, 1955, FDRL.

She would live at Teluride House . . . Various interviews, Cornell University, Ithaca, N.Y. She had many visitors while there. C.W. Jenks of the ILO recalled that on his visit in 1958 she insisted he take her sleeping pills for the train ride back to New York City.

. . . she felt "just like a bride" . . . Interview with Dr. Maurice Neufeld, Nov. 1969.

"It is possible . . ." FP and St. Sure, op. cit., p. 7; also Cornell lectures.

291 "I have always liked the Salvation Army . . ." and "And, of course, you remember . . ." "Frances Perkins," Industrial and Labor Relations Report, New York State School of Industrial Relations, Cornell University, vol. 2, no. 2, p. 3.

Some thirty years before . . ." Lowe, op. cit., pp. 41-42.

292 Walking along the ice-covered paths . . . Interview with Dr. Maurice Neufeld.

No one knew . . . Letter to the author from Margaret Janeway, M.D., Feb. 12, 1970.

"Students no longer . . ." Interview with Dr. Alice Cook, Dec. 1969.

"I endured a lot . . ." FP letter to CB, Oct. 22, 1959, SL.

In December, 1960 . . . Regarding Peterson, FP note to CB, Dec. 15, 1960, FDRL.

. . . to adress the International Association of Government Labor Officials . . . Four months prior to the meeting of Sept. 9-12, 1959, she wrote to CB, FDRL.

293 "Be not afraid . . ." Informal conversation with Dr. Arch Troelstrup.

In 1957 the faculty . . . Interview with Professor Woodrow Sayre. In April, 1962, when the author congratulated FP on what was presumed to be her eightieth birthday, Miss Perkins responded glowingly, "Why, thank you very much. How very nice of you . . ."

. . . the "Living History" dinner . . . "Research Institute Recommendations," Weekly Business Report & Forecast reprint, May 14, 1960. Later that year she enjoyed a reunion with the pioneers of the Social Security Act at the twenty-fifth anniversary in HEW auditorium, New York Times, Aug. 16, 1960.

"I received a note . . ." Mount Holyoke alumnae file.

294 . . . Frances informed her secretary . . . Interview with Evelynn Richards.

In November, 1962, James Farley drove her . . . Interview with the author. He was also FP's visitor at Telluride House.

The thirtieth anniversary . . . Christian Science Monitor, March 6, 1963.

But the dashing young president . . . Dorothy McCardle, op. cit.

In citing the "extraordinary record" . . . Transcript of Proceedings at Fiftieth Anniversary Banquet Dinner, Sheraton Park Hotel, Washington, D.C., March 4, 1933.

. . ."the poor people's department." . . . Fenno claims this reflected her social welfare view of the department, op. cit., p. 219.

295 . . . Esther Peterson declared . . . Washington Post, Nov. 19, 1964; New York Times, May 15, 1965.

Frances caught a cold . . . Phone conversation with Dr. Margaret Janeway, June 1970.

When Dean Bernice Wright . . . Dean Wright was a principal supporter of this biography. The author ordered a smaller robe than FP specified.

On May 14, 1965 . . . Letter from Margaret Janeway, M.D., Feb. 12, 1970, and phone conversation with author, June 1970, New York Times, May 15, 1965, CSCL.

"It is not something . . ." "Thinking in Terms of the Other Man," an interview with FP, in Nall, op. cit., p. 140.

"What is my duty? . . ." FP's Syracuse speech, Feb. 12, 1960.

A solemn requiem mass . . . New York Times, May 16, 18, 1965. President Johnson was represented by Secretary of Labor W. Willard Wirtz.

. . . a handsome old English drop-leaf coffee table . . . Interview with John Leslie, director, Office of Information, Department of Labor. It was moved to the new Department of Labor building where it again resides in the office of the secretary of labor according to Dr. Jonathan Grossman.

"Ten years after I'm gone . . ." Interview with James Dodson, Jan. 15, 1970.

Bibliography

Abbott, Grace. *From Relief to Social Security: The Development of the New Public Welfare Services and Their Administration.* Chicago: University of Chicago Press, 1941.

Adamic, Louis. *Dinner at the White House.* New York: Harper & Bros., 1946.

Addams, Jane. *Twenty Years at Hull House.* 1911. Reprint. New York: Signet Classics, 1960.

Alinsky, Saul. *John L. Lewis: An Unauthorized Biography.* New York: G.P. Putnam's Sons, 1949.

Allen, Frederick Lewis. *Since Yesterday: The Nineteen-Thirties in America.* New York: Bantam Books, 1940.

Alsop, Joseph, and Kintner, Robert. *Men around the President.* New York: Doubleday, Doran & Co., 1939.

Anderson, Mary. *Woman at Work.* As told to Mary N. Winslow. Minneapolis: University of Minnesota Press, 1951.

Asbell, Bernard. *When F.D.R. Died.* New York: Holt, Rinehart & Winston, 1961.

Babson, Roger W. *Washington and the Depression.* New York: Harper & Bros., 1932.

_____. *Washington and the Revolutionists: A Characterization of Recovery Policies and of the People Who Are Giving Them Effect.* New York: Harper & Bros., 1934.

Bailey, Thomas A. *The Man in the Street: The Impact of American Public Opinion on Foreign Policy.* Gloucester, Mass.: Peter Smith, 1964.

Bakke, E. Wight, and Kerr, Clark, eds. *Union, Management and the Public.* New York: Harcourt, Brace & Co., 1949.

Bargeron, Carlisle. *Confusion on the Potomac: The Alarming Chaos and Feuds of Washington.* New York: Wilfred Funk, 1941.

Bealle, Morris A. *Fugitives from a Brain Gang.* Washington, D.C.: Columbia Publishing Co., 1940.

_____. *Washington Squirrel Cage.* Washington, D.C.: Columbia Publishing Co., 1944.

Beard, Charles A. *President Roosevelt and the Coming of the War, 1941: A Study in Appearances and Realities.* New Haven: Yale University Press, 1948.

Beard, Mary R., ed. *America through Women's Eyes.* New York: Macmillan Co., 1933.

Beasley, Norman. *Knudsen: A Biography.* New York: McGraw-Hill Book Co., 1947. 1947.

Becker, Joseph M. *Shared Government in Employment Security.* New York: Columbia University Press, 1959.

Bellush, Bernard. *Franklin D. Roosevelt as Governor of New York.* New York: Columbia University Press, 1955.

_____. *He Walked Alone: A Biography of John Gilbert Winant.* The Hague: Mouton & Co., 1968.

Berle, Adolf A. *The Three Faces of Power.* New York: Harcourt, Brace & World, 1967.

Bernstein, Irving. *The Lean Years: A History of the American Worker, 1920-1933.* Boston: Houghton Mifflin Co., 1960.

_____. *The New Deal Collective Bargaining Policy.* Berkeley: University of California Press, 1950.

Biddle, Francis. *The Fear of Freedom.* Garden City, N.Y.: Doubleday & Co., 1952.

_____. *In Brief Authority.* Garden City, N.Y.: Doubleday & Co., 1962.

Bird, Caroline. *The Invisible Scar.* New York: David McKay Co., 1966.

Black, Ruby. *Eleanor Roosevelt: A Biography.* New York: Duell, Sloan & Pearce, 1940.

Blum, John Morton. *From the Morgenthau Diaries: Years of Crisis.* Boston: Houghton Mifflin Co., 1959.

Braeman, John; Bremner, Robert H.; and Walters, Everett, eds. *Change and Continuity in Twentieth-Century America.* Columbus, Ohio: Ohio State University Press, 1964.

Breckinridge, Sophonisba P. *Women in the Twentieth Century: A Study of Their Political, Social and Economic Activities.* New York: McGraw-Hill Book Co., 1933.

Breen, Vincent I. *The United States Conciliation Service.* Washington, D.C.: Catholic University of America Press, 1943.

_____. *From the Depths: The Discovery of Poverty in the United States.* New York: New York University Press, 1956.

Brogan, Denis W. *The Era of Franklin D. Roosevelt: A Chronicle of the New Deal and Global War.* New Haven: Yale University Press, 1951.

Brooks, R.R.R. *As Steel Goes . . . .* New Haven: Yale University Press, 1940.

Brown, J. Douglas. *The Genesis of Social Security in America.* Princeton: Industrial Relations Section, Princeton University, 1969.

Burns, James MacGregor. *Roosevelt: The Lion and the Fox.* New York: Harcourt, Brace & Co., 1956.

Busch, Noel F. *What Manner of Man?* New York: Harper & Bros., 1944.

Campbell, Persia. *Consumer Representation in the New Deal.* New York: Columbia Press, 1940.

Carter, J. Franklin [Unofficial Observer]. *The New Dealers.* New York: Simon & Schuster, 1934.

Cavan, Ruth Shonle, and Ranck, Katherine Howland. *The Family and the Depression: A Study of One Hundred Chicago Families.* Chicago: University of Chicago Press, 1938.

Chamberlain, John. *Farewell to Reform: The Rise, Life .and Decay of the Progressive Mind in America.* Chicago: Quadrangle Books, 1932.

Chamberlain, Neil W. *Sourcebook on Labor.* New York: McGraw-Hill Book Co., 1958.

Chambers, Clarke A. *Seedtime of Reform: American Social Service and Social Action, 1918-1933.* Minneapolis: University of Minnesota Press, 1963.

Childs, Marquis W. *I Write from Washington.* New York: Harper & Bros., 1942.

Churchill, Allen. *The Roosevelts: American Aristocrats*. New York: Harper & Row, 1965.

Cochran, Thomas C. *The Great Depression and World War II: 1929-1945*. Glenview, Ill.: Scott, Foresman & Co., 1968.

Conkin, Paul K. *FDR and the Origins of the Welfare State*. New York: Thomas Y. Crowell Co., 1967.

Creel, George. *Rebel at Large*. New York: G.P. Putnam's Sons, 1947.

Crosby, Percy. *Essay on Roosevelt's Second Inaugural Address*. McLean, Va.: Freedom Press, 1937.

Cussler, Margaret. *The Woman Executive*. New York: Harcourt, Brace & Co., 1958.

Daniels, Johnathan. *The Man of Independence*. Philadelphia: J.B. Lippincott, 1950.

_____. *They Will Be Heard: America's Crusading Newspaper Editors*. New York: McGraw-Hill Book Co., 1965.

_____. *Washington Quadrille: The Dance beside the Documents*. Garden City, N.Y.: Doubleday & Co., 1968.

Derber, Milton, and Young, Edwin, eds. *Labor and the New Deal*. Madison: University of Wisconsin Press, 1957.

Dies, Martin. *Martin Dies' Story*. New York: Bookmailer, 1963.

Douglas, Paul H. *Controlling Depressions*. New York: W.W. Norton & Co., 1935.

Dulles, Foster Rhea. *Labor in America: A History*. New York: Thomas Y. Crowell Co., 1949.

Eccles, Marriner S. *Beckoning Frontiers: Public and Personal Recollections*. New York: Alfred A. Knopf, 1951.

Enzler, Clarence J. *Some Social Aspects of the Depression (1930-1935)*. Washington, D.C.: Catholic University of America Press, 1939.

Farley, James A. *Behind the Ballots: The Personal History of a Politician*. New York: Harcourt, Brace & Co., 1938.

_____. *Jim Farley's Story: The Roosevelt Years*. New York: McGraw-Hill Book Co., 1948.

Fay, Bernard. *Roosevelt and His America*. Boston: Little, Brown & Co., 1933.

Felt, Jeremy P. *Hostages of Fortune: Child Labor Reform in New York State*. Syracuse, N.Y.: Syracuse University Press, 1965.

Fenno, Richard F., Jr. *The President's Cabinet: An Analysis in the Period from Wilson to Eisenhower*. Cambridge: Harvard University Press, 1959.

Fine, Sidney. *The Automobile under the Blue Eagle: Labor, Management, and the Automobile Manufacturing Code*. Ann Arbor: University of Michigan Press, 1963.

_____. *Laissez Faire and the General-Welfare State: A Study of Conflict in American Thought, 1865-1901*. Ann Arbor: University of Michigan Press, 1956.

_____. *Sit-Down: The General Motors Strike of 1936-1937*. Ann Arbor: University of Michigan Press, 1969.

Flynn, John T. *Country Squire in the White House*. New York: Doubleday, Doran & Co., 1940.

_____. *The Roosevelt Myth*. New York: Devin-Adair Co., 1948.

Frankfurter, Felix. *Felix Frankfurter Reminisces*. Recorded in talks with Dr. Harlan B. Phillips. New York: Reynal and Co., 1960.

Freidel, Frank. *Franklin D. Roosevelt: The Apprenticeship.* Boston: Little, Brown & Co., 1952.

_____. *Franklin D. Roosevelt: The Ordeal.* Boston: Little, Brown & Co., 1954.

_____. *Franklin D. Roosevelt: The Triumph.* Boston: Little, Brown & Co., 1956.

Fried, Albert, and Elman, Richard M., eds. *Charles Booth's London: A Portrait of the Poor at the Turn of the Century, Drawn from his "Life and Labour of the People in London."* New York: Pantheon Books, 1968.

Furman, Bess. *Washington By-Line: The Personal History of a Newspaperwoman.* New York: Alfred A. Knopf, 1949.

Fusfeld, Daniel R. *The Economic Thought of F.D.R. and the Origins of the New Deal.* New York: Columbia University Press, 1956.

Gabriel, Ralph Henry. *The Course of American Democratic Thought: An Intellectual History Since 1815.* New York: Ronald Press Company, 1940.

Galenson, Walter. *The CIO Challenge to the AFL: A History of the American Labor Movement, 1935-1941.* Cambridge: Harvard University Press, 1960.

Gilman, Charlotte Perkins. *The Living of Charlotte Perkins Gilman: An Autobiography.* New York: D. Appleton-Century Co., 1935.

Gilman, Charlotte Perkins Stetson. *Women and Economics: A Study of the Economic Relation between Men and Women as a Factor in Social Evolution.* Boston: Small, Maynard & Co., 1900.

Goldman, Eric F. *Rendezvous with Destiny: A History of Modern American Reform.* New York: Alfred A. Knopf, 1953.

Goldmark, Josephine. *Impatient Crusader: Florence Kelley's Life Story.* Urbana: University of Illinois Press, 1953.

Gompers, Samuel. *Seventy Years of Life and Labor: An Autobiography.* New York: E.P. Dutton & Co., 1957.

Greer, Thomas H. *What Roosevelt Thought: The Social and Political Ideas of Franklin D. Roosevelt.* East Lansing: Michigan State University Press, 1958.

Grossman, Jonathan P. *The Department of Labor.* New York: Praeger Publishers, 1973.

Gruberg, Martin. *Women in American Politics: An Assessment and Sourcebook.* Oshkosh, Wisc.: Academia Press, 1968.

Gunther, John R. *Roosevelt in Retrospect: A Profile in History.* New York: Harper & Bros., 1950.

Hacker, Louis M. *American Problems of Today.* New York: F.S. Crofts & Co., 1938.

Hall, Fred S. *Forty Years, 1902-1942: The Work of the New York Child Labor Committee.* Brattleboro, Vt.: E.L. Hildreth & Co., n.d.

Hamilton, Alice. *Exploring the Dangerous Trades: The Autobiography of Alice Hamilton, M.D.* Boston: Little, Brown & Co., 1943.

Hardman, J.B.S. *Sidney Hillman: Labor Statesman.* USA: Lerman Printing Co., 1948.

Hartz, Louis. *The Liberal Tradition in America: Interpretation of American Political Thought since the Revolution.* New York: Harcourt, Brace & Co., 1955.

Hassett, William D. *Off the Record with F.D.R., 1942-1945.* New Brunswick, N.J.: Rutgers University Press, 1958.

Hatch, Alden. *Franklin D. Roosevelt: An Informal Biography.* New York: Henry

Holt & Co., 1947.

Hawley, Ellis W. *The New Deal and the Problem of Monopoly: A Study in Economic Ambivalence*. Princeton: Princeton University Press, 1966.

Henry, Laurin L. *Presidential Transitions*. Washington, D.C.: Brookings Institution, 1960.

Hill, C.P. *Franklin Roosevelt*. London: Oxford University Press, 1966.

Hobbs, Edward Henry. *Behind the President: A Study of Executive Office Agencies*. Washington, D.C.: Public Affairs Press, 1954.

Hofstadter, Richard. *The Age of Reform: From Bryan to F.D.R.* New York: Alfred A. Knopf, 1955.

Hollander, Herbert. *Quest for Excellence*. Washington, D.C.: Current Publications, 1968.

Hoover, Herbert. *The Memoirs of Herbert Hoover: The Great Depression, 1929-1941*. New York: Macmillan Co., 1952.

Hoover, Irwin Hood (Ike). *Forty-Two Years in the White House*. Boston: Houghton Mifflin Co., 1934.

Hull, Cordell. *The Memoirs of Cordell Hull*, vol. 1. New York: Macmillan Co., 1948.

Hurd, Charles. *When the New Deal Was Young and Gay*. New York: Hawthorn Books, 1965.

Huthmacher, J. Joseph. *Senator Robert F. Wagner and the Rise of Urban Liberalism*. New York: Atheneum, 1968.

Ickes, Harold L. *The Autobiography of a Curmudgeon*. New York: Reynal & Hitchcock, 1943.

Irwin, Inez Haynes. *Angels and Amazons: A Hundred Years of American Woman*. New York: Doubleday, Doran & Co., 1933.

Johnson, Walter. *1600 Pennsylvania Avenue: President and the People, 1929-1959*. Boston: Little, Brown & Co., 1960.

Jones, Jesse M. *Fifty Billion Dollars: My Thirteen Years with the RFC (1932-1945)*. New York: Macmillan Co., 1951.

Josephson, Matthew. *Sidney Hillman: Statesman of Labor*. Garden City, N.Y.: Doubleday & Co., 1952.

Josephson, Matthew, and Josephson, Hannah. *Al Smith: Hero of the Cities*. Boston: Houghton Mifflin Co., 1969.

Kaltenborn, Howard S. *Government Adjustment of Labor Disputes*. Chicago: Foundation Press, 1943.

Karl, Barry Dean. *Executive Reorganization and Reform in the New Deal*. Cambridge: Harvard University Press, 1963.

Keller, Morton, ed. *The New Deal: What Was It?* New York: Holt, Rinehart & Winston, 1963.

Kingdon, Frank. *As FDR Said: A Treasury of His Speeches, Conversations and Writings*. New York: Duell, Sloan & Pearce, 1950.

Klein, Philip. *From Philanthropy to Social Welfare: An American Cultural Perspective*. San Francisco: Jossey-Bass, 1968.

Lash, Joseph P. *Eleanor Roosevelt: A Friend's Memoir*. Garden City, N.Y.: Doubleday & Co., 1964.

Laski, Harold J. *The American Presidency: An Interpretation*. New York: Harper &

Bros., 1940.

Lawson, Don. *Frances Perkins: First Lady of the Cabinet.* New York: Abelard-Schuman, 1966.

Learned, Henry Barrett. *The President's Cabinet.* New Haven: Yale University Press, 1912.

Leed, John H. *Government and Labor in the United States.* New York: Rinehart & Co., 1952.

Lens, Sidney. *Left, Right and Center: Conflicting Forces in American Labor.* Hinsdale, Ill.: Henry Regnery Co., 1949.

Leuchtenburg, William E. *Franklin D. Roosevelt and the New Deal: 1932-1940.* New York: Harper & Row, 1963.

_____, ed. *The New Deal: A Documentary History.* Columbia: University of South Carolina Press, 1968.

Lewis, Sinclair. *Ann Vickers.* Garden City, N.Y.: Doubleday, Doran & Co., 1933.

Lindley, Ernest K. *The Roosevelt Revolution.* New York: Viking Press, 1933.

Linn, James Weber. *Jane Addams.* New York: D. Appleton-Century Co., 1935.

Lippmann, Walter. *An Inquiry into the Principles of the Good Society.* Boston: Little, Brown & Co., 1937.

Lombardi, John. *Labor's Voice in the Cabinet.* New York: Columbia University Press, 1942.

Lorant, Stefan. *The Glorious Burden: The American Presidency.* New York: Harper & Row, 1968.

Ludwig, Emil. *Roosevelt: A Study in Fortune and Power.* Toronto: Macmillan Co., 1937.

Lunt, Richard D. *The High Ministry of Government: The Political Career of Frank Murphy.* Detroit: Wayne State University Press, 1965.

McCoy, Donald R. *Angry Voices: Left-of-Center Politics in the New Deal Era.* Lawrence: University of Kansas Press, 1958.

McIntire, Ross T. *White House Physician.* New York: G.P. Putnam's Sons, 1946.

Mackenzie, Compton. *Mr. Roosevelt.* New York: E.P. Dutton & Co., 1944.

Macmahon, Arthur W.; Millett, John D.; and Ogden, Gladys. *The Administration of Federal Work Relief.* Chicago: Public Administration Service, 1941.

Major, John. *The New Deal.* London: Longmans, Green and Co., 1968.

Meyers, Robert C.V. *Theodore Roosevelt.* Philadelphia: P.W. Ziegler & Co., 1902.

Minutes of the New York State Factory Investigating Commission, New York Preliminary Report, vol. 2. Transmitted to the Legislature March 1, 1912. Albany: Argus Co., 1912.

Moley, Raymond. *The First New Deal.* New York: Harcourt, Brace & World, 1966.

Moses, Robert. *Public Works: A Dangerous Trade.* New York: McGraw-Hill Book Co., 1970.

_____. *A Tribute to Governor Smith.* New York: Simon & Schuster, 1962.

Myers, Elisabeth P. *Madam Secretary: Frances Perkins.* New York: Julian Messner, 1972.

Nall, T. Otto. *Youth's Work in the New World.* New York: Association Press, 1936.

Nelson, Donald M. *Arsenal of Democracy: The Story of American War Production.* New York: Harcourt, Brace & Co., 1946.

Nesbitt, Henrietta. *White House Diary.* Garden City, N.Y.: Doubleday & Co., 1948.

Nevins, Allan. *Herbert H. Lehman and His Era.* New York: Charles Scribner's Sons, 1963.
Newcomer, Mabel. *A Century of Higher Education for American Women.* New York: Harper & Bros., 1959.
Nutt, Charles. *History of Worcester and Its People.* 4 vols. New York: Lewis Historical Publishing Co., 1919.
Ogden, August Raymond. *The Dies Committee: A Study of the Special House Committee for the Investigation of Un-American Activities, 1938-1944.* Washington, D.C.: Catholic University Press, 1945.
O'Neill, William L. *Everyone Was Brave: The Rise and Fall of Feminism in America.* Chicago: Quadrangle Books, 1969.
Patten, Simon Nelson. *The New Basis of Civilization.* New York: Macmillan Co., 1913.
_____. *The Theory of Dynamic Economics.* University of Pennsylvania Political Economy and Public Law Series, vol. 3, no. 2, chapter 7.
Patterson, James T. *Congressional Conservatism and the New Deal: The Growth of the Conservative Coalition in Congress, 1933-1939.* Lexington: University of Kentucky Press, 1967.
Perkins, Dexter. *The New Age of Franklin Roosevelt, 1932-1945.* Chicago: University of Chicago Press, 1957.
Pessota, Rose. *Bread upon the Waters.* New York: Dodd, Mead & Co., 1944.
Phillips, Cabell. *From the Crash to the Blitz, 1929-1939.* London: Macmillan & Co., 1969.
Polenberg, Richard. *Reorganizing Roosevelt's Government: The Controversy over Executive Reorganization, 1936-1939.* Cambridge: Harvard University Press, 1966.
Rattner, Faye. *Reform in America: Jacksonian Democracy, Progressivism, and the New Deal.* Chicago: Scott, Foresman & Co., 1964.
Rauch, Basil. *The History of the New Deal, 1933-1938.* New York: Creative Age Press, 1944.
Richberg, Donald R. *Labor Union Monopoly: A Clear and Present Danger.* Chicago: Henry Regnery Co., 1957.
Riis, Jacob A. *The Children of the Poor.* New York: Charles Scribner's Sons, 1898.
Robinson, Edgar Eugene. *The Roosevelt Leadership, 1933-1945.* Philadelphia: J.B. Lippincott Co., 1955.
Rollins, Alfred B., Jr. *Roosevelt and Howe.* New York: Alfred A. Knopf, 1962.
Roosevelt, Eleanor. *This I Remember.* New York: Harper & Bros., 1949.
Roosevelt, Eleanor, and Hickok, Lorena A. *Ladies of Courage.* New York: G.P. Putnam's Sons, 1954.
Roosevelt, Elliott. *As He Saw It.* New York: Duell, Sloan & Pearce, 1946.
_____., ed. *FDR: His Personal Letters, 1928-1945,* vol. 2. Assisted by Joseph P. Lash. New York: Duell, Sloan and Pearce, 1950.
Roosevelt, James and Shalett, Sidney. *Affectionately, F.D.R.: A Son's Story of a Lonely Man.* New York: Harcourt, Brace & Co., 1959.
Roosevelt, Nicholas. *A Front Row Seat.* Norman: University of Oklahoma Press, 1953.
Roper, Daniel C. *Fifty Years of Public Life.* In collaboration with Frank H.

Lovette. Durham: Duke University Press, 1941.

Roper, Elmo. *You and Your Leaders.* New York: William Morrow & Co., 1957.

Roseberry, Cecil R. *Capitol Story.* New York: State of New York, 1964.

Rosenman, Samuel I. *Working with Roosevelt.* New York: Harper & Bros., 1952.

Sanders, Marion K. *The Lady and the Vote.* Boston: Houghton Mifflin Co., 1956.

Schlesinger, Arthur M., Jr. *The Ages of Roosevelt: The Politics of Upheaval.* Boston: Houghton Mifflin Co., 1960.

_____. *The American as Reformer.* Cambridge: Harvard University Press, 1950.

_____. *The Coming of the New Deal.* Boston: Houghton Mifflin Co., 1959.

Schlesinger, Arthur Meier. *The New Deal in Action, 1933-1937.* New York: Macmillan Co., 1938.

Schneider, David M., and Deutsch, Albert. *The History of Public Welfare in New York State, 1867-1940.* Chicago: University of Chicago Press, 1941.

Schneiderman, Rose, and Goldthwaite, Lucy. *All For One.* New York: Paul S. Eriksson, 1967.

Schulman, Sammy. *"Where's Sammy?"* New York: Random House, 1943.

Shannon, David A. *The Great Depression.* Englewood Cliffs, N.J.: Prentice-Hall, 1960.

Sherwood, Robert E. *Roosevelt and Hopkins: An Intimate History.* New York: Harper & Bros., 1948.

Shorer, Mark. *Sinclair Lewis: An American Life.* New York: McGraw-Hill Book Co., 1961.

Shotwell, James T., ed. *The Origins of the International Labor Organization.* New York: Columbia University Press, 1934.

Simkhovitch, Mary Kingsbury. *Here Is God's Plenty.* New York: Harper & Bros., 1949.

_____. *Neighborhood: My Story of Greenwich House.* New York: W.W. Norton & Co., 1938.

Sinclair, Andrew. *The Better Half: The Emancipation of the American Woman.* New York: Harper & Row, 1965.

Sloan, Alfred P., Jr. *My Years with General Motors.* Garden City, N.Y.: Doubleday & Co., 1964.

Smith, Ira T., and Morris, Joe Alex. *"Dear Mr. President . . .": The Story of Fifty Years in the White House Mail Room.* New York: Julian Messner, 1949.

Smith, Merriman. *The Good New Days: A Not Entirely Reverent Study of Native Habits and Customs in Modern Washington.* Indianapolis: Bobbs-Merrill Co., 1962.

Smith, William Henry. *History of the Cabinet of the United States of America.* Baltimore: Industrial Printing Co., 1925.

Snowman, Daniel. *America since 1920.* New York: Harper & Row, 1968.

Soule, George. *Sidney Hillman: Labor Statesman.* New York: Macmillan Co., 1939.

Stein, Leon. *The Triangle Fire.* Philadelphia: J.B. Lippincott Co., 1962.

Steinberg, Alfred. *Mrs. R: The Life of Eleanor Roosevelt.* New York: G.P. Putnam's Sons, 1958.

Sternsher, Bernard. *Rexford Tugwell and the New Deal.* New Brunswick, N.J.: Rutgers University Press, 1964.

Stiles, Lela. *The Man Behind Roosevelt: The Story of Louis McHenry Howe.* New

York: World Publishing Co., 1954.

Stolberg, Benjamin, and Vinton, Warren Jay. *The Economic Consequences of the New Deal.* New York: Harcourt, Brace & Co., 1935.

Stromer, Marvin E. *The Making of a Political Leader: Kenneth S. Wherry and the United States Senate.* Lincoln: University of Nebraska Press, 1969.

Sulzberger, C.L. *Sit Down with John L. Lewis.* New York: Random House, 1938.

Sussmann, Leila A. *Dear FDR: A Study of Political Letter-Writing.* Totowa, N.J.: Bedminister Press, 1963.

Swisher, Carl Brent. *American National Government.* Cambridge, Mass.: Riverside Press, 1951.

Thomas, Henry. *Franklin Delano Roosevelt.* New York: G.P. Putnam's Sons, 1962.

Timmons, Bascom N. *Garner of Texas: A Personal History.* New York: Harper & Bros., 1948.

Truman, Harry S. *Memoirs: Year of Decisions.* Garden City, N.Y.: Doubleday & Co., 1955.

Tugwell, Rexford Guy. *The Democratic Roosevelt: A Biography of Franklin D. Roosevelt.* Garden City, N.Y.: Doubleday & Co., 1957.

_____. *FDR: Architect of an Era.* New York: Macmillan Co., 1967.

Tully, Grace. *F.D.R., My Boss.* New York: Charles Scribner's Sons, 1949.

U.S. National Commission on Law Observance and Enforcement. *Report on the Enforcement of the Deportation Laws of the United States.* Washington, D.C.: U.S. Government Printing Office, 1931.

Venkataramani, M.S., ed. *The Sunny Side of FDR.* Athens, Ohio: Ohio University Press, 1973.

Vorse, Mary Heaton. *A Footnote to Folly: Reminiscences of Mary Heaton Vorse.* New York: Farrar & Rinehart, 1935.

_____. *Labor's New Millions.* New York: Modern Age Books, 1938.

_____. *Time and the Town: A Provincetown Chronicle.* New York: Dial Press, 1942.

Wald, Lillian. *Windows on Henry Street.* Boston: Little, Brown & Co., 1934.

Wann, A.J. *The President as Chief Administrator: A Study of Franklin D. Roosevelt.* Washington, D.C.: Public Affairs Press, 1968.

Ware, Caroline F. *Greenwich Village, 1920-1930: A Comment on American Civilization in the Post-War Years.* Boston: Houghton Mifflin Co., 1935.

Warfel, Harry R.; Gabriel, Ralph H.; and Williams, Stanley T., eds. *The American Mind: Selections from the Literature of the United States*, vol. 1. New York: American Book Company, 1937. (Reprints FP's chapter on government and cooperation from *People at Work*, pp. 1256-59.)

Warner, Emily Smith, and Daniel, Hawthorne. *The Happy Warrior: A Biography of My Father, Alfred E. Smith.* Garden City, N.Y.: Doubleday & Co., 1956.

Wehle, Louis B. *Hidden Threads of History.* New York: Macmillan Co., 1953.

Williams, T. Harry. *Huey Long.* New York: Alfred A. Knopf, 1969.

Witney, Fred. *Government and Collective Bargaining.* Chicago: J.B. Lippincott Co., 1951.

Witte, Edwin E. *The Development of the Social Security Act.* Madison: University of Wisconsin Press, 1962.

Woolf, Virginia. *A Room of One's Own.* New York: Harcourt, Brace & Co., 1929.

Index